MALEBRANCHE

ARGUMENTS OF THE PHILOSOPHERS

The purpose of this series is to provide a contemporary assessment and history of the entire course of philosophical thought. Each book contains a detailed, critical introduction to the work of a philosopher or school of major influence and significance.

Also available in the series:

AQUINAS
Eleonore Stump

* DESCARTES
Margaret D. Wilson

* HEGEL
M.J. Inwood

* HUME
Barry Stroud

KANT
Ralph C.S. Walker

KIERKEGAARD
Alastair Hannay

* LOCKE
Michael Ayers

* KARL MARX
Allen Wood

* MERLEAU-PONTY
Stephen Priest

* NIETZSCHE
Richard Schacht

PLATO
Justin Gosling

* PLOTINUS
Lloyd P. Gerson

* ROUSSEAU
Timothy O'Hagan

* THE PRESOCRATIC
PHILOSOPHERS
Jonathan Barnes

* SANTAYANA
Timothy L.S. Sprigge

* THE SCEPTICS
R.J. Hankinson

* WITTGENSTEIN, 2nd edition
Robert Fogelin

* also available in paperback

MALEBRANCHE

Andrew Pyle

Routledge
Taylor & Francis Group

LONDON AND NEW YORK

First published 2003
by Routledge
11 New Fetter Lane, London EC4P 4EE

Simultaneously published in the USA and Canada
by Routledge
29 West 35th Street, New York, NY 10001

Routledge is an imprint of the Taylor & Francis Group

© 2003 Andrew Pyle

Typeset in Garamond by
HWA Text and Data Management, Tunbridge Wells
Printed and bound in Great Britain by
Biddles Ltd, Guildford and King's Lynn

British Library Cataloguing in Publication Data
A catalogue record for this book is available from the
British Library

Library of Congress Cataloging in Publication Data
Pyle, Andrew.
Malebranche / Andrew Pyle.
p. cm. – (The arguments of the philosophers)
Includes bibliographical references and index.
1. Malebranche, Nicolas, 1638–1715. I. Title. II. Series.
B1897 .P95   2002
194–dc21   2002032459

ISBN 0–415–28911–4

In memory of David Hirschmann (1939–97), teacher, colleague and friend, lover of the good things of life – French civilisation, slow food, red wine, bridge, and the rationalist philosophy of the seventeenth century.

My one regret regarding this book is that he will never read it, although it owes so much to him in so many ways.

CONTENTS

CONTENTS

ABBREVIATIONS
AND EDITIONS

Works by Malebranche

I have worked entirely with the *Oeuvres Complètes de Malebranche*, ed. André Robinet, 20 Volumes, Paris, Vrin, 1958–78. References are given to OCM, by volume and page. Individual works by Malebranche are referred to by means of the following abbreviations.

R.V.   *Recherche de la Vérité, ou l'on traite de la nature de l'esprit de l'homme et de l'usage qu'il en doit faire pour éviter l'erreur dans les sciences* (1674). OCM Volumes 1 and 2.

Ecl.   *Éclaircissements sur la Recherche de la Vérité* (1678). *OCM* Vol. 3.

C.C.   *Conversations Chrétiennes* (1677). *OCM* Vol. 4.

T.N.G.   *Traité de la Nature et de la Grâce* (1680). *OCM* Vol. 5.

C.A.   *Correspondance avec M. Arnauld* (1684–87). *OCM* Vols 6–9.

M.C.   *Méditations Chrétiennes et Métaphysiques* (1683). *OCM* Vol. 10.

T.M.   *Traité de Morale* (1684). *OCM* Vol. 11.

E.M.   *Entretiens sur la Métaphysique et sur la Religion* (1688). *OCM* Vol. 12.

E. Mort.   *Entretiens sur la Mort* (1696). *OCM* Vol. 13.

T.A.D.   *Traité de l'Amour de Dieu* (1698). *OCM* Vol. 14.

Lamy.   *Trois Lettres au Père Lamy* (1698). *OCM* Vol. 14.

Chin.   *Entretien d'un Philosophe Chrétien et d'un Philosophe Chinois* (1707). *OCM* Vol. 15.

Pre.Ph.   *Réflexions sur la Prémotion Physique* (1715). *OCM* Vol. 16.

Rep Régis.   *Réponse a M. Régis* (1693). *OCM* Vol. 17–1.

Def. la Ville   *Défense de l'Auteur de la Recherche de la Vérité contre l'Accusation de Mons. de la Ville* (1682). *OCM* Vol. 17–1.

Math.   *Mathematica. OCM* Vol. 17–2.

Corr.   *Correspondance et Actes. OCM* Vols 18 and 19.

English translations

For the *Search after Truth* and the *Dialogues on Metaphysics and Religion* I have made use of the existing English translations, both of which have recently appeared in the Cambridge Texts in the History of Philosophy. Thanks are due to Professor Lennon for permission to use his English translation of the *Search*, and to Cambridge University Press and Professors Jolley and Scott for permission to use their English translation of the *Dialogues*.

For the *Treatise on Nature and Grace* I have sometimes been able to use the recent translation by Patrick Riley. Since his translation is of the short first edition of 1680, I have been obliged to use the *Oeuvres Complètes* for material added to later editions.

Nicolas Malebranche, *The Search After Truth*, translated and edited by Thomas Lennon and Paul Olscamp. Plus *Elucidations of the Search after Truth*, translated and edited by Thomas Lennon, Cambridge University Press, 1997.

Nicolas Malebranche, *Dialogues on Metaphysics and on Religion*, translated by David Scott and edited by Nicholas Jolley, Cambridge University Press, 1997.

Nicolas Malebranche, *Treatise on Nature and Grace*, translated with an introduction and notes by Patrick Riley, Oxford, Clarendon, 1992.

These translations will be referred to as LO, JS, and R respectively. References to the *Recherche,* the *Entretiens* and, where appropriate, the *Traité* will be to both the *OCM* version and the English translation (e.g. *OCM* III 163, LO 633). Translations of all other works by Malebranche are my own.

Works of Descartes

AT = *Oeuvres de Descartes*, Charles Adam and Paul Tannery, eds, 12 Volumes (Paris, Cerf, 1897–1910).

CSM(K) = *The Philosophical Writings of Descartes*, translated and edited by John Cottingham, Robert Stoothoff, Dugald Murdoch, and (for Vol. 3) Anthony Kenny, 3 Volumes (Cambridge University Press, 1985–91).

References to the works of Descartes will be given both to the original French or Latin, and to the English translation where available (e.g. AT IX 37, CSM II 31).

PREFACE

This book has been more than a decade in the writing. The idea for it came to me during my two years teaching at the University of Ghana at Legon, from 1986 to 1988. The university's Balme Library was not well stocked with modern books and journals but contained, by way of compensation, many treasures from the past. In an idle moment during the long vacation I picked up Malebranche's *Recherche de la Vérité*, partly to improve my French, partly for its intrinsic interest. I have been wrestling with Malebranche's philosophy ever since. It is not, I hasten to add, that I share many of his opinions; my own philosophical views could scarcely be further removed from his. But I have no doubt at all that he is a major philosopher, frequently misrepresented and – at least until recently – quite unjustly neglected in the English-speaking world. In the past few years, largely through the efforts of Steven Nadler, Malebranche has enjoyed a small but significant revival among anglophone historians of philosophy.

Since my return to Bristol I have finished my study of the twenty volumes of Robinet's great *Oeuvres Complètes de Malebranche*, together with a fair selection of the secondary literature in French and English. I have also written articles on various aspects of Malebranche's philosophy for a number of different occasions and audiences, and these articles have been pressed into service as draft chapters for this book. Apologies are owed to readers for the occasional small repetition that may have escaped the revision process. Draft versions of chapters three and eight were presented to meetings of the British Society for the History of Philosophy, and drafts of chapters four and nine to Tom Sorell's study group for Seventeenth Century Philosophy. I am grateful to Tom Sorell, John Cottingham, Stuart Brown, Pauline Phemister, Susan James, Sarah Hutton, John Rogers, Ian Tipton, Peter Alexander, Martin Stone and others both for their encouragement and for their objections. Draft versions of chapters six and seven were presented to meetings of the Australian History and Philosophy of Science community at the universities of Sydney and Melbourne in June and July of 1997. I am grateful to Alan Chalmers, Stephen Gaukroger and Keith Hutchison, among others, for helpful questions and criticisms.

A major debt of thanks is also owed to my department here in Bristol. A succession of heads of department – Michael Welbourne, David Hirschmann, Chris Bertram and Keith Graham – have provided support and encouragement combined with only the gentlest of pressure. Thanks too to the Research Committee for the period of study leave that has enabled me to complete this book. After seeing off our TQA inspection in March 2001 it was a pleasure to return to the library and the purer joys of research, and to be able to work more or less uninterrupted until October. Most of my colleagues, past and present, have discussed draft chapters at our departmental staff seminars. The influence of these discussions on the final book is too diffuse to document in detail, but no less real for that. So although this project may have been conceived under the tropical sun of Africa, it grew to maturity in the milder climate of the West Country.

Thanks are also due to the two anonymous referees chosen by Routledge, both for their praise and for their criticisms. Their praise reassured me that the work would have some value; their criticisms helped me to clarify some key points and eliminate a handful of small but significant errors. These readers will find that their detailed criticisms have been met by a mixed strategy of concession, clarification, and rebuttal. Suggestions for more fundamental re-structuring of the work have been quietly resisted. Once a book has taken its final shape in the mind of its author, it is much easier to address objections to points of detail than to rethink the form of the whole.

1

INTRODUCTION

Life and works

Nicolas Malebranche was born and died in the same year as Louis XIV (1638–1715), and thus belongs firmly to the *siècle des lumières* celebrated in Voltaire's history.[1] Born in Paris, he was the youngest of the many children of Nicolas Malebranche senior, a counsellor of the king and a senior official in the department of taxation.[2] Nicolas junior was a feeble child, and was not expected to live long; as a man, he remained frail and sickly, as if made for the secluded life of an ascetic and an intellectual. The obvious profession for a bright but feeble-bodied child was the Church. From 1654 to 1656 Malebranche studied philosophy at the Collège de la Marché in Paris, then in 1656 he started his theology at the Sorbonne (*OCM* XVIII 13). According to his first biographer, André, the theology he was taught failed to impress him on two counts. In philosophy, where reason alone should be sovereign, he was fobbed off with the mere authority of Aristotle; in theology, where authority alone should rule, he was offered human (and usually bad) reasoning (*OCM* XVIII 16).

Although originally destined for the secular priesthood, the young Malebranche withdrew into the congregation of the Oratory in 1660, giving up his share of the family property. The Oratorian Order had been founded by Pierre Bérulle in 1611. Its members had no official duties, but were expected to devote their lives to prayer, fasting and works of charity. Dogmatic and mystical theology was permitted, but independent philosophical thinking was associated with the sin of pride, and was officially discouraged: Malebranche's writings would earn him the bitter hostility of his superiors. As a student, he plodded diligently through vast tomes of Church history, and even began the study of Hebrew, before he found his true vocation. In 1664, the year of his ordination, he encountered Descartes' *Traité de l'Homme* (*OCM* XVIII

16). For the young Malebranche, as for so many others, Descartes' ideas had the force of a revelation. Here, he felt, was the true philosophy, firmly based on clear and distinct ideas, and providing demonstrative arguments with all the rigour of mathematical proofs. For the next few years, he devoured the works of Descartes and his disciples, developing a distinctive philosophical position in which a Cartesian, i.e. mechanistic, natural philosophy is incorporated into a spiritualistic metaphysics derived largely from Augustine.[3] As André puts it, 'The sublime metaphysics of Saint Augustine seemed entirely made for the physics of Mr Descartes, and the physics of Mr Descartes for the metaphysics of Saint Augustine' (*OCM* XVIII 51). This modified Cartesianism was to be put into the service of Christian theology. As Gueroult points out, a pagan or a Turk could be a Cartesian: there is nothing specifically Christian about Descartes' metaphysics and epistemology.[4] Malebranche deliberately set out, by contrast, to create a Christian philosophy. His explicitly stated aim was to do for Descartes what Augustine had done for Plato, or Aquinas for Aristotle, i.e. to use the philosophy to provide new explanations for the unchanging dogmas of the faith. This is not merely, of course, a concession to the philosophical fashions of the age. Malebranche thought that, with certain modifications which we shall note, Cartesianism was the true philosophy, so the true philosophy supports – as of course it should – the true religion.[5]

The fruits of Malebranche's assimilation of Descartes appeared in the *Recherche de la Vérité*, published anonymously in 1674.[6] The *Recherche* is a long and rambling work, ostensibly devoted to the causes of human error, although frequently digressing into substantive matters of mathematics, physics, metaphysics, ethics and theology. It deals at length with our various faculties – sense, imagination, the passions, and reason – and with the various ways in which they can lead us astray. Drawing heavily on Descartes' *Fourth Meditation*, Malebranche announces two rules for the guidance of the mind that desires to free itself from such errors and arrive at the truth. Once our minds have been properly purged of vulgar errors, Malebranche claims, two great truths will become manifest, opening clear paths into the subjects of metaphysics and epistemology. In metaphysics, we will see clearly that only God can be a true cause, and that what we commonly call 'natural' or 'second' causes are mere *occasions* for God to act in accordance with His own self-imposed rules. In epistemology, we will find that human knowledge is only possible by means of the 'Vision in God', i.e. if ideas are archetypes in the Creator's mind, not merely modifications or 'modes' of our own souls. These twin theses of occasionalism and the Vision in God constitute the heart of Malebranche's philosophy. In his later works he would refine these doctrines, provide further explanations of them, and defend them against objections; he would never abandon them.[7]

The *Recherche* was, from the first, the subject of heated controversy. The sceptic Simon Foucher took issue with Malebranche's epistemology, and objected strongly to the mixture of religion and philosophy that is such a striking feature of the book.[8] The Jesuits, still wedded to scholastic Aristotelianism, sought to portray Malebranche's Cartesian exposition of Christian doctrine as dangerously heretical.[9] Initially at least, the Jansenists' response was favourable: Arnauld spoke warmly of the *Recherche*, and clearly hoped that its author could be drawn into a Cartesian/Augustinian/Jansenist camp, in opposition to the Aristotelian/Thomist/Jesuit one. The publication in 1678 of the *Éclaircissements* to the *Recherche* put an end to this hope. In *Éclaircissement* XV (*OCM* III 220–1, LO 666–7), Malebranche argued that an all-perfect being must, by its very nature, act by means of general laws. Since the proof of this proposition is *a priori*, it is perfectly general in its application. In the *Traité de la Nature et de la Grâce* (1680), Malebranche's most controversial work, the application of this thesis to the theological domain of grace is spelt out. The distribution of grace, we are told, is effected by a general law by means of which the (human) soul of Jesus Christ is established as an occasional cause. God, says Malebranche, wills that all men be saved. But He distributes grace to sinners in accordance with the above rule. This means that many men do not receive enough grace to accomplish their salvation, and so are damned. Why does God act in such a way? Because He owes it to Himself to act in a manner that is worthy of His attributes – in this case, His wisdom. As in the realm of nature, so in that of grace, God acts as a general cause rather than a particular cause.

The *Traité* was, in effect, a declaration of war against the Jansenists. At the heart of their theology was the doctrine of 'efficacious grace', i.e. the belief that God's gift of grace always effects the conversion of the soul of the sinner and thus leads to salvation. This requires that God distribute grace by particular volitions, never giving any of the chosen elect less than he or she needs. On Malebranche's theory, such unfortunate events are common: just as some fields receive too little rain for the crops to grow, so some souls receive too little grace to effect conversion and reconciliation with God. From Arnauld's point of view, Malebranche tacitly denies God's omnipotence: he says that God wills that all men be saved, but that this end is not achieved. From Malebranche's point of view, Arnauld effectively denies God's universal benevolence, and falls into a position akin to Calvinism. If God acts by particular volitions, and some men are damned, it is because God didn't give them enough grace, so could not have willed their salvation.

After the publication of the *Traité*, Arnauld published a series of attacks on the philosophy of Malebranche; his attacks and Malebranche's replies occupy no less than four volumes of the *Oeuvres Complètes* (*OCM* VI–IX). Arnauld attacked Malebranche's philosophy on two separate fronts. In his *Vraies et Fausses Idées*[10] he rejects the Vision in God and defends what he takes to be the orthodox Cartesian view that our ideas are modes (acts) of our own souls, not archetypes in the divine intellect. But why does Arnauld choose to attack Malebranche's theology by way of his epistemology? The reason is clear.[11] The doctrine of the Vision in God allows the human mind to participate, at least to some extent, in the divine intellect, and thus to grasp, at least in some cases, God's reasons for acting.[12] This rationalisation of theology is anathema to Arnauld. For him, whatever God does is right simply because God does it – there are no standards of right and wrong independent of the divine will. In essence, we have here another episode in the endless struggle between the rival voluntarist and intellectualist traditions in Christian theology.[13] Arnauld sees Malebranche's intellectualism as lying behind and supporting his theology, and so launches his first salvo directly against the Vision in God. He goes on, of course, in his subsequent series of letters, to attack the theology of the *Traité* directly, launching a vigorous polemical exchange with Malebranche that lasted until Arnauld's death in 1694.

Malebranche's other major philosophical work, the *Entretiens sur la Métaphysique*, was published in 1688. These dialogues are, without question, Malebranche's mature philosophical masterpiece. The *Recherche* is a young man's book – ambitious in its scope, rambling in its structure, full of digressions, and not always clear in the presentation of its central ideas. It was also subject to substantial revisions, resulting in a stratified text in which inconsistent opinions from different periods are sometimes visible in startling juxtaposition.[14] The *Entretiens* are, by contrast, a model of lucid exposition, with Malebranche's spokesman Theodore guiding his young pupil Ariste (and thus also the reader) through his central doctrines, addressing difficulties and objections as they arise. If a modern reader has time to read only one work of Malebranche, it should be the *Entretiens* rather than the *Recherche*.

These works, the *Recherche de la Vérité* and its *Éclaircissements*, the *Traité de la Nature et de la Grâce*, the *Correspondance avec Arnauld* and the *Entretiens sur la Métaphysique*, constitute the philosophical core of Malebranche's work, and will provide the bulk of the material for this study. On occasions we may dip into our author's lesser works, such as the *Conversations Chrétiennes*, the *Méditations Chrétiennes*, the *Traité de l'Amour de Dieu*, the *Prémotion Physique*, and the *Traité de Morale*, but we shall do so only where they cast light on the central texts.

Descartes and Augustine

The most cursory and superficial reading of Malebranche's works will suffice to discover the main influences shaping his philosophy. As he himself explains in a letter to Arnauld, there are only two earlier philosophers who exerted a major formative influence on his thought: Augustine and Descartes (*OCM* VIII 998). He never acknowledges any debt to the scholastics, although this may not be entirely fair on his part.[15] It is important not to think of Augustine and Descartes as the spokesmen, respectively, of faith and reason. For Malebranche, both are voices of reason; where they part company is in their very different conceptions of reason itself.[16] Descartes thinks of reason as a natural (albeit doubtless God-given) power of the human soul; Augustine stresses the essential dependence of our minds on the 'light' of divine illumination. On this point Malebranche sides with Augustine: all our knowledge is some form or other of revelation.

The assimilation of Cartesian and Augustinian philosophy was quite common in the seventeenth century, usually in opposition to the Aristotelianism of the scholastics. Scholastic Aristotelianism is denounced by Malebranche as both bad philosophy and bad theology. It is bad philosophy because it possesses no clear and distinct ideas, and thus falls into vulgar errors regarding causality and the relation between mind and body. It is bad theology because the admission of natural causes risks a slide into pagan naturalism, and the failure to distinguish clearly between mind and body threatens the Christian doctrine of the immortality of the soul. The precarious reconciliation of Aristotelianism and Christianity effected by Thomas Aquinas was never very robust: the tensions which had been present in Thomism from the beginning threatened, by the seventeenth century, to tear scholasticism apart. The time had come, according to Malebranche, to replace scholastic Aristotelianism with a new Christian philosophy derived from Descartes and Augustine.

Malebranche adopts from Descartes, first and foremost, the famous method – this is clear from the two opening chapters of Book One of the *Recherche* (*OCM* I 39–57, LO 1–11). In Malebranche's version of the method of doubt, however, the radical scepticism of Descartes' *First Meditation* disappears without trace. Malebranche never entertains the slightest doubt of the veridical nature of his clear and distinct ideas. If I have a clear and distinct idea of X that represents it as having feature F, I know that X is F, and know that I know that X is F, with no room for further doubt. Doubt remains appropriate until clear and distinct ideas are grasped; after that, it simply evaporates. Errors arise, for Malebranche as for Descartes, by precipitate acts of judgement, assenting to or dissenting from propositions before we are in a proper position to do so.[17] The account of error contained in the *Recherche* is a sort of extended commentary on Descartes' *Fourth Meditation*: error is always our own fault, since it results from an abuse of our liberty. Where matters are obscure, we should suspend judgement and attend more closely, seeking further illumination. Attention itself is, for Malebranche, a sort of prayer, and such prayers are always answered, provided we are sincere and persistent, and the matter itself is one that lies, in principle, within the compass of our understandings.

Malebranche also endorses Descartes' strict metaphysical dualism. Indeed, Malebranche was a more rigorous and thoroughgoing dualist than Descartes himself. In his correspondence with the Princess Elizabeth,[18] Descartes invites readers to take the notion of a mind–body union seriously, and suggests that a certain range of psychological powers (sensation, imagination, memory) are powers of the mind–body union rather than of the separate incorporeal soul.[19] Malebranche will have none of this. In Book Two of the *Recherche* he tells us clearly that the notion of a substantial union of mind and body is unintelligible. All that the notion of 'union' can mean here is that God has established regular and lawlike correlations between states of the brain, on the one hand, and states of the immaterial soul on the other (*OCM* I 215, LO 101–2). But all the modes of the soul are, in their own nature, independent of the body – a disembodied soul could enjoy the same phenomenology as an embodied one.[20]

Malebranche's other great debt to Descartes is to his mechanistic natural philosophy. Throughout his career Malebranche would make modifications to Cartesian mechanism (regarding, for example, the laws of motion), but he never dreamed of abandoning the vision that inspired the whole programme. The basic idea is brilliantly simple, and is set out with striking lucidity in Book Six of the *Recherche* (*OCM* II 321–45, LO 453–66). Starting with the clear and distinct idea of matter as essentially just three-dimensional extension, one can derive all its possible modes (shapes, motions and arrangements of parts). Ideally, one would then go on to derive the laws of succession of these modes, i.e. the laws of motion. (Malebranche would eventually concede that this could not be done *a priori*.) The 'substantial forms' and 'real qualities' of the scholastics are dismissed as unintelligible verbiage. As for the (supposed) souls of animals, they too are eliminated: Malebranche is one of the firmest advocates of the notorious Cartesian doctrine of the *bête-machine*.[21] Natural philosophy shows, he argues, that a beast–machine is possible, i.e. that a sufficiently complex machine could perform all the actions of animals; metaphysics and theology provide positive reasons for thinking the doctrine is true. A just God, for example, could not permit innocent suffering; but the beasts are innocent, so they do not suffer.

Malebranche's debts to Augustine are equally profound. At the heart of Augustine's philosophy lies the simple thought that nothing of value can be created or sustained without the direct involvement of God. This 'theocentrism' or 'supernaturalism'[22] has striking implications in fields as diverse as ethics, natural philosophy and epistemology. In ethics, the Augustinian emphasises the dependence of our virtues on God's gift of grace and the impossibility of our developing any genuine virtues without this divine aid. (The picture painted by the Stoics of their sage reeks of pride and folly.) In natural philosophy, the exquisitely contrived forms of plants and animals testify not only to transcendent divine design but also to immanent divine guidance in the form of 'seminal reasons' dispersed by the Creator throughout His creation. Likewise in epistemology we err if we think we can obtain any knowledge by our own powers. Just as the eye needs light to see, so the mind requires ideas in order to know. Malebranche takes both the analogy and the moral from Augustine.[23] As the sun is to the eye, so is God to the human mind, he explains in Book Six of the *Recherche* (*OCM* II 244–8, LO 408–10). There is, he writes to Arnauld, no such thing as natural knowledge (*OCM* VI 144). We commonly contrast 'natural' with 'revealed' knowledge, but the distinction we should be drawing is between two different types of revelation. This 'illuminationist' epistemology is Augustine's main legacy to Malebranche. Human knowledge, Malebranche will argue, is only possible at all if our ideas are God's ideas, i.e. if we have epistemic access to the archetypes God uses in His ongoing creation of our world.

This is one of a number of topics on which Malebranche uses Augustine to correct Descartes (*OCM* XVIII 51). Descartes generally writes as if he thinks of ideas as merely modes of our own souls – this is certainly how Arnauld, like most second-generation Cartesians, reads him. But if this were the case, Malebranche argues, there would be no justification for inferring 'X is F' from 'My idea of X represents it as F', and hence no escape from veil-of-ideas scepticism (*OCM* IX 915). But God's Idea of X is the archetype in accordance with which X was created, so it is logically impossible for it to misrepresent X. If my ideas are God's ideas, objective knowledge is secured. Only this 'Vision in God', counterintuitive and visionary as it may seem, blocks scepticism by licensing inferences from the properties of things-as-represented by their ideas to the properties of the things themselves (*OCM* XII 7–26, JS 3–18).

On two other issues of crucial importance Malebranche also parts company with Descartes. He accepts neither Descartes' voluntarism about necessary truths nor his rejection of final causes in natural philosophy. Descartes tells us that God could have made it the case that 2 + 2 = 5, although of course we cannot conceive how this could be.[24] Given Malebranche's Augustinian conception of ideas, he must dismiss this Cartesian thesis as absurd: for 2 + 2 to make 5 would require a change in the eternal and immutable intellect of God Himself, which is nonsense. God's mere will, Malebranche argues in *Éclaircissement* X (*OCM* III 127–61, LO 612–32) does not of itself constitute Order; rather, it is subject to an Order which exists eternally in the divine intellect.

As for final causes, Descartes explicitly rejects them in his *Principles of Philosophy*, on the ground that we are completely ignorant of God's designs and purposes.[25] But such false modesty, replies Malebranche, has dangerous consequences for morality and religion. If we are completely ignorant of God's purposes, we must abandon the traditional argument to design. A plenum of nauseous excrement, or a single atom in an endless void, would prove God's wisdom as well as our rich, diverse, and harmonious cosmos. Final causes, Malebranche insists in the correspondence with Arnauld, are useless in physics but essential in theology (*OCM* VIII 674). If we really believed ourselves ignorant of God's purposes in creation, we could find no evidence in nature for His wisdom or benevolence.[26]

Yet another important departure from Descartes concerns our knowledge of our own souls. When I reflect on my own thoughts and feelings, says Malebranche in *Éclaircissement XI* (*OCM* III 163–71, LO 633–8), I become aware of myself as a thinking and feeling being. When I think about matter, I grasp its essence by means of my clear and distinct idea of extension. I can show, by means of a negative argument *a priori*, that thinking and feeling cannot be modes of any material thing. But I still lack a clear and distinct idea of the soul. Doubtless there is such an archetype of the human soul, a model or blueprint rendering intelligible the substance and its diverse modes, but this idea exists only in the mind of God and has not been revealed to humans. I have therefore only a confused and obscure knowledge of the modes of my own soul: I have no rational insight into its essence. There is no rational psychology, no science of the soul in the strict sense (i.e. a body of demonstrated knowledge) which stands to the soul as geometry does to matter.[27]

Malebranche's modifications of Augustine's philosophy are less radical. Here he sees himself as simply bringing Augustine up to date with developments in natural philosophy in general, and with the mechanical philosophy in particular. This point is made in the preface of the *Recherche* (*OCM* I 20, LO xxxix–xl) and in *Éclaircissement* XV (*OCM* III 235–6, LO 676). Augustine, for example, accepted that colours, tastes, smells, etc. were properties of bodies, but a short tutorial on the mechanical philosophy and on the subjectivity of such sensible qualities would have been sufficient to make him change his mind. And Augustine never doubted the common belief in animal souls, but this may simply indicate a failure on his part to reflect deeply enough to rid himself of a vulgar prejudice. The Cartesian thesis of the *bête-machine* should have appealed to him on metaphysical and theological grounds, had he ever become aware of it. Nothing essential to Augustine's central philosophical concerns, Malebranche insists, is inconsistent with a mechanistic natural philosophy.

Faith and reason

For Malebranche, as for Augustine, all knowledge is revelation. Revealed knowledge, however, is of two distinct kinds. Our clear ideas are revelations of God's ideas, which are the models or archetypes employed in creation. Rational knowledge (in mathematics, metaphysics and ethics) is therefore a kind of natural revelation, available to all men who are willing to reflect and to meditate. By contrast, there is the revelation of God's Word in scripture, as interpreted over the centuries by the authorities of the Church. Since these two kinds of knowledge stem from the same source, the divine *logos*, they cannot contradict one another. Any apparent contradictions between human reason (philosophy) and Christian faith (dogmatic theology) must be illusory, the products of misunderstanding. In the *Traité de la Nature et de la Grâce*, for example, Malebranche warns his readers against interpreting Saint Paul as a Calvinist (*OCM* V 63). To suppose that God has predestined the great majority of mankind to eternal damnation would be to make scripture contradict reason, which tells us clearly that a perfectly wise and benevolent being could have no such sinister design.

But if faith and reason cannot contradict one another, two distinct possibilities remain. They may give rise to entirely independent disciplines of philosophy and theology, each with its own separate domain. Or they may provide one another with mutual support and illumination, giving rise to a coherent body of philosophical theology. Descartes had taken the former view. In the *Meditations* he attempted, of course, to prove the existence of God and the real distinction of mind and body, but he regarded these as philosophical theses, supported by philosophical arguments. As for dogmatic theology (the Trinity, the Incarnation, the Eucharist, Heaven and Hell) Descartes refused – at least in his published works – to meddle with such sensitive matters.[28] For this consistent and sustained separation of philosophy and theology he was praised by Arnauld,[29] who carefully divided his own objections to the *Meditations* into 'philosophical' and 'theological'. But this vision of two independent disciplines with distinct and clearly demarcated domains was alien to Malebranche. When Arnauld, following his usual practice, divided his objections to the *Traité* into 'philosophical' and 'theological' points, Malebranche protested against being thus cut in two. 'One must not say that I act sometimes as a philosopher and sometimes as a theologian: for I always speak, or claim to speak, as a rational theologian' (*OCM* VIII 632).

The first significant critic of the *Recherche*, the sceptic Simon Foucher, accused Malebranche of confusing matters of faith with matters of reason. Our author, says Foucher in his critique, first takes care to distinguish the mysteries of faith from the clear ideas of reason, and then mixes them up again! To discuss the fall and the incarnation in a work of philosophy is, in Foucher's eyes, a serious error: such matters should be left for sermons.[30] A similar objection would later be made by Fontenelle against Malebranche's *Traité de Morale*.[31] In an appendix added to later editions of the *Recherche*, Malebranche replied to Foucher's objection (*OCM* II 493). To combine, he explains, is not to confound. To speak of God, for example, according to our idea of an absolutely perfect being belongs to philosophy, which can prove what dogmatic theology must assume, i.e. that God is not a deceiver. And, as we shall see, there may be many aspects of the world of our experience that philosophy can only discover, but theology can explain. The crucial point is that philosophy does not rely upon theology for its premises. In the whole of the *Recherche*, Malebranche insists, Foucher 'will not find that I suppose any article of faith as a principle ...' (*OCM* II 495).

What Malebranche is seeking to do is to re-establish the harmony between reason and faith which he saw breaking down around him. Scholastic Aristotelianism, in his view, had failed. For all the subtleties of the Jesuits, the naturalism of Aristotle's philosophy could never be assimilated into a Christian world view. What was needed was a new and genuinely Christian philosophy.[32] In this new philosophy, there will be a subtle interdependence of reason and faith, more or less along the following lines.

Reason supporting the foundations of faith

Christianity presupposes the existence of a veridical God: dogmatic theology would be impossible without the assumption that the Word of the Lord, as contained in scripture, is true. But, says Malebranche in Book Six of the *Recherche* (*OCM* II 372, LO 482) and again in the *Conversations Chrétiennes* (*OCM* IV 14), the dogmatic theologian cannot prove this assumption. If proof is demanded, it must come from the philosopher. Likewise, the Christian doctrine of the afterlife requires the assumption that conscious experience does not end with bodily death. The Cartesian philosopher, unlike his Aristotelian colleague, can support the doctrine of the afterlife by demonstrating the real distinction of mind and body. This proof of the real distinction, says Malebranche in a letter of 1693, does not amount to a demonstration of immortality, but does establish a powerful presupposition in its favour.

> Since the passage from nothingness to being is incomprehensible to the human mind, the immortality of the soul has been sufficiently demonstrated to philosophers when one has proved that the soul is a substance distinct from the body, for by nature it is only the modes of beings that perish
>
> (*OCM* XIX 605).

In seeking to show, by philosophical argument, the existence of a veridical God and an immortal soul, Malebranche was not being adventurous or innovative: such proofs were required of Catholic philosophers by the Council of Trent.[33] In attempting to use Cartesian philosophy to explain Christian theology, however, Malebranche would be venturing into much more perilous territory.

Reason explaining the mysteries of faith.

It has always been permitted, Malebranche insists in the *Traité* (*OCM* V 7–8), and again in his replies to Arnauld (*OCM* VIII 632), to use philosophy to explain the mysteries of the Christian religion. This is not a matter of seeking to impose new dogmas: innovation in theology is always a mark of error. One may nevertheless offer new accounts or explanations of such dogmas as the Trinity, the Incarnation and the Eucharist. This has always been the practice of the Church: as Augustine was to Plato, or Aquinas to Aristotle, so Malebranche proposes to be to Descartes. It is necessary, he says, 'to make philosophy serve theology' (*OCM* VIII 643). In this way, he hopes, we can 'silence the unbelievers, and … place reason on the side of religion' (*OCM* VII 592).

In proposing new accounts of the Christian mysteries, Malebranche's aim is not merely to explain but also to justify the ways of God to man. Only thus, he argues, will we 'faire taire les impies'. Pierre Bayle, for example, in his famous article *Manichaeism* from the *Dictionnaire*, had argued that the disorders and evils of our world are better accounted for by the Manichaean doctrine of two opposed deities, one good and the other evil, than by the orthodox Christian belief in a single wise, omnipotent and benevolent God.[34] Malebranche seeks to answer Bayle (and the *libertins* in general) by his account of the creation, the fall and the incarnation. Unfortunately, his attempts to defend particular Christian dogmas by philosophical argument are by far the weakest part of his entire *oeuvre*. And once one admits the competence of reason in this domain, one runs the risk of arriving at manifestly heretical conclusions.[35] A just God, the freethinkers began to argue, would not (could not) act in the unjust and arbitrary manner described by Christian dogma.

Faith explaining the difficulties of reason

In examining both the external world and the workings of the human mind, we encounter what seem to be manifest design flaws. The world contains deserted wastes, natural disasters, plagues and famines – on the face of it, there seems no reason to believe that it was created for us by a wise, powerful and benevolent God. Even our minds show traces of bad design. How often do we deliberate carefully about what to do next, form a considered judgement 'X is better than Y', and then proceed to choose Y rather than X? Our choices should be determined by our reflective judgements of value, yet all too often this is not the case in practice. In Book Seven of the *Nicomachean Ethics* Aristotle described this phenomenon, and gave it the name of *akrasia* (weakness of will, lack of self-control), but to describe is not to explain, and the existence of *akrasia* remained an anomaly for the rationalistic ethical theories of the Greeks.

Here, says Malebranche, philosophy stumbles over puzzling limits to its comprehension. Knowing that the natural world is the creation of an all-perfect Being, we can't understand why it should be so manifestly flawed. And knowing that our reflective and considered value judgements should determine our choices, we are at a loss to explain why they so often fail to do so. Here faith comes to the aid of reason, and theology illuminates philosophy. According to the Christian doctrine of the fall, both the natural world and the human soul are mere 'ruins', imperfect remains of a perfect prior creation.[36] The moral is drawn by Malebranche in the second *Éclaircissement* of the *Traité* (*OCM* V 182). The Christian philosopher, he there claims, can shed light on problems that would forever vex the mere natural philosopher. In the fourth dialogue of the *Entretiens,* Ariste asks his teacher Theodore how it can be that, contrary to all the principles of Order, the superior being (the human soul) often finds itself subordinated to and dependent on the inferior (the human body), and thus distracted from its true good (union with God). Theodore replies as follows: 'Yes, no doubt, there is some mystery there. My dear Aristes, how philosophers are indebted to religion, for only religion can extricate them from the predicament in which they find themselves!' (*OCM* XII 101, JS 63).

If natural philosophy and psychology fall into hopeless perplexities and insoluble problems which only faith – in this case, the Christian doctrine of the fall – can resolve, then we have the makings of a powerful inference to best explanation for the truth of the religious dogmas. Critics like Foucher, who accused Malebranche of subordinating philosophy to theology, have missed the point here. We don't need any reliance on faith to see that the natural world and the human soul are both badly flawed creatures; this is evident from observation and a little reflection. Likewise, we don't need to rely on faith to prove the existence of an all-perfect God. But then we find ourselves, as mere philosophers, wondering how these two truths can be compatible. We need recourse to faith, Malebranche thinks, if we are to explain how a perfect Creator could make an imperfect universe. Malebranche is not basing his philosophy on theology in the objectionable sense that he derives philosophical conclusions from theological premises. Rather, the facts to be explained are already known, independent of Christian dogma, and the argument takes the unobjectionable form of an inference to best explanation of those facts. If Malebranche is right, natural philosophers and psychologists will find themselves drawn into Christianity in the attempt to complete their own projects.

Difficulties

The Cartesian method of doubt, Malebranche warns his readers early in the *Recherche*, does not extend to matters of faith. In philosophy, it is wrong to assent to any proposition without proof; merely plausible reasons are never good enough. In theology, however, the opposite is the case: here it is the demand for evidence that is a dangerous source of heresies and errors. 'In a word, to be among the Faithful, it is necessary to believe blindly; but to be a philosopher, it is necessary to see with evidence ...' (*OCM* I 62, LO 14). In Book Four, Malebranche contrasts those who believe blindly whatever they are told with those who demand evidence in all things (*OCM* II 33–8, LO 278–82). The former people are just stupid, feeble intellects; the latter tend to become heretics or freethinkers. To be a good Christian is to accept the articles of faith in the absence of proof. But this submission to the authority of the Church on points of dogma does not extend to philosophical explanations of dogma. We must believe, for example, that the body of Christ is present in the wafer; we need not accept incomprehensible scholastic accounts of how this takes place. The dogma is from God, and must be accepted; to subject it to doubt would be un-Christian. The scholastic explanation of the dogma, however, is merely human; to doubt it is permissible and may even be required of us. In the *Méditations Chrétiennes*, this point is put in the mouth of the Word of God itself. 'Know therefore', we are told, 'that evidence and faith can never deceive: but do not take plausibility for evidence, nor the opinion of some doctors for faith' (*OCM* X 29).

We have, according to Malebranche, one infallible guide, the divine word or *logos*, which speaks to us in two ways: by the inner light of reason and by the external light of revelation. But how does he deal with the sceptical problem of the criterion?[37] Do we always know, from introspection, when a proposition is rationally self-evident? Or are we sometimes deceived into confusing mere plausibility with genuine self-evidence? And do we always know, with regard to supposed revelations, which books are genuine repositories of the Word of God, and how to interpret them?[38]

In answer to the first of these two sceptical questions, Malebranche has quite a lot to say. In the *Méditations Chrétiennes*, for example, he boldly puts his own metaphysics and epistemology into the mouth of the Word, but does so with the following warning in the preface. The Word, he says, is universal reason itself, and thus the source of all truth. I interrogate it, and try to record its answers faithfully. But 'I have a great fear of not rendering its responses as I have received them; and even of not always distinguishing them from my prejudices, or from those obscure and confused sentiments inspired by the senses, the imagination, and the passions' (*OCM* X 7). The same problem emerges in *Éclaircissement XIII* of the *Recherche*, which discusses the need for spiritual directors (*OCM* III 181–95, LO 644–52). When faced with a difficult decision, says Malebranche, one should withdraw into solitude and meditate: it is better to trust the inner light than any human guide. But we don't always know whether we have effectively stilled our passions, and thus sometimes mistakenly think something evident when in fact it is not so. For this reason, spiritual directors may still on occasion be of use to us.

In the *Traité de Morale*, the worrying implications of this admission are explicitly spelled out. Sometimes, Malebranche admits, it is hard to be certain that one is listening to the Word, because 'the secret promptings of the passions are of the same nature as this inner sentiment. For when one acts against opinion and custom, one often feels inner reproaches very like those of reason and Order' (*OCM* XI 68). But if conscience can torment us for a mere violation of some arbitrary social custom, mistaken for an edict of Order itself, Malebranche has failed to resolve the epistemological problem posed by the sceptics. They demanded a criterion of truth; Malebranche, it now appears, has failed to provide one. If we rely on introspection and phenomenology alone, we may fall into error, yet nothing better is on offer. What is delivered by the inner light is self-evident and infallibly true. But not everything that seems self-evident to introspection is the genuine deliverance of the inner light.[39]

In applying the problem of the criterion to revealed knowledge, Malebranche shows himself at his most dogmatic and conservative. The question is raised in *Entretien* XIII, but Malebranche's spokesman Theodore, in launching a bitter attack on Protestantism, does little but parrot Catholic commonplaces. The universal Church is, he insists, 'the blessed storehouse of tradition' (*OCM* XII 324, JS 257). It is 'perpetual through all time and universal in all places' (*OCM* XII 326–7, JS 259). But to identify the doctrine of 'the universal Church' with that of late seventeenth-century Roman Catholicism is simply question-begging. Many Protestants claimed that their doctrines were those of the early Church, and that the theology of latter-day Roman Catholicism was little more than a mass of corruption. Malebranche never seriously addresses this problem.

The dogmas of the Church include some that are explicitly labelled and taught as 'mysteries'. Such doctrines, Malebranche insists, must be accepted as matters of faith even in the absence of clear ideas. In Book Three of the *Recherche* he denounces those theologians who seek to rid Christianity of its mysteries (*OCM* I 390–6, LO 203–6). The Socianians cannot understand the Trinity and the Incarnation, and are thus led to deny that God could become man; the Calvinists cannot understand how the body of Jesus Christ could be present in the communion wafer, and thus deny that it is (literally) present at all; some philosophers cannot reconcile God's omniscience with human liberty, and end up denying free will. Even orthodox theologians sometimes fall into such errors. Here, for a moment, Malebranche sounds positively anti-rationalistic:

> It might be said ... that the objections raised against the main articles of our faith, especially against the mystery of the Trinity, are so strong that they cannot be given solutions that are clear and convincing and that do not in any way shock our feeble reason, for these mysteries are indeed incomprehensible.
>
> (*OCM* I 395, LO 206)

This passage is, however, uncharacteristic of Malebranche's considered views. Elsewhere, and especially in his later works,[40] he attacks anti-rationalism in theology. In the *Traité de Morale*, for example, he denounces the claim that blind obedience is the principal virtue of Christians. Such an attitude, he warns, only flatters the pride of ecclesiastical superiors and justifies the sloth of inferiors; it is unworthy of the true Christian (*OCM* XI 36). We must, he advises, accept the dogmas of the faith without doubts or reservations, but we are always permitted to seek further enlightenment regarding them. Given that the true philosophy of nature (Cartesianism) tells us that the essence of matter is extension, for example, we may legitimately enquire how this is compatible with the Christian dogma of the Eucharist. In an unpublished letter, Descartes had broached this sensitive subject, only to drop it when it threatened to lead him into dangerously controversial theological territory.[41] Malebranche was prepared to go further, developing, in the context of a vigorous polemical exchange with the Jesuit Louis le Valois, a properly Cartesian account of the real presence (*OCM* XVII–1 445ff). The details need not concern us here: the crucial point is that the search for intelligibility in theology is not forbidden *a priori*. What is prohibited is the inference from failure to falsehood, i.e. from 'We can't make sense of p' to 'It cannot be true Christian doctrine that p'.

But is the very search for clear and distinct ideas implicitly anti-Christian, in the spirit if not in the letter? Is the intellectual independence of the Cartesian philosopher already subversive of religion? Many Christians of the period thought so, and would have endorsed Bossuet's public attack on Malebranche's theology as excessively rationalistic:

I see, not only with regard to this point about nature and grace, but also with regard to many other very important articles of religion, a great conflict brewing against the Church under the name of the Cartesian philosophy.[42]

Malebranche, it should be clear, is walking a fine line, trying to remain within the Catholic Church while developing an epistemology of religion that is closer to the Quaker theory of the 'inner light'. Problems arise when we try to explain a Catholic dogma but fail miserably in the attempt or (as so often with Malebranche himself) fall into blatant excesses of special pleading. To maintain orthodoxy, we must never permit the inference from 'I can't understand how p could be true' to 'p cannot be true'. An obvious example would be the inference from 'I can't understand why a just God should care whether someone sprinkles water on a baby's head' to 'a just God wouldn't care about something as trivial and morally insignificant'. Malebranche himself will have nothing to do with such reasoning. But when the gulf between our moral and metaphysical understanding on the one hand, and the dogmas of religion on the other, is filled by only feeble reasoning and manifest special pleading, doubts will become pressing. Bad explanations of how p could be true may backfire and cast doubt on the proposition itself. The reader may find himself thinking 'p could be true only if q were true, but q is incredible'. Instead of asking how a wise and just God could permit the eternal damnation of most men for a sin committed by a remote ancestor, one may find oneself concluding that this simply could not be the case at all. Since reason, for Malebranche, is universal, the reason of the Christian is no different from that of a pagan or even an atheist.[43] By his attempts to rationalise Christian doctrines, Malebranche is prepared to meet unbelievers and sceptics on their own ground. As Paul Hazard says, Malebranche's valiant attempts to show the reasonableness of the Christian religion may have served, in the end, only to undermine it.[44] The conservative Bossuet may have been right after all.

2

TENSIONS IN CARTESIAN
METAPHYSICS

Richard Watson's *Downfall of Cartesianism*

In his 1966 book *The Downfall of Cartesianism*,[1] and in a succession of later books and articles,[2] Richard Watson has painted a wonderfully vivid portrait of the trials and tribulations of the rationalist metaphysics of the seventeenth century. Although his central claim was scarcely original – he ascribes it himself to the seventeenth-century sceptic Simon Foucher, whose critique of Cartesianism he largely follows – the brilliant lucidity of his exegesis and the light his approach throws on major aspects of post-Cartesian metaphysics combine to make the book a seminal work in late twentieth-century history of philosophy.

Watson's central claim was that Cartesian metaphysics collapsed because it failed to meet its own standards or norms of intelligibility. The Cartesians, he claimed, were committed to two key principles, which he labelled the Causal Likeness Principle (CLP) and the Epistemological Likeness Principle (ELP). According to CLP, all causal relations are subject to the principle that the effect must resemble the cause, so that the causal relation is a sort of transformation of the patient into the form or likeness of the agent. The begetting of a horse by a horse, or the heating of a cold body by a hotter one might serve as examples of such a process. According to ELP, an idea in the mind of a knower must represent its object by way of resemblance, i.e. by sharing certain properties with it. The obvious analogy would be with the way in which a picture can represent its object.

Cartesian metaphysics, according to Watson, was committed to these principles by its very rationalism, by the quest for intelligibility that lies at its heart. They belonged to the 'hard core' of the research programme, and were therefore non-negotiable. But Cartesian metaphysics was also committed to a variety of claims about what substances exist and how they interact, and these claims seem flatly incompatible with CLP and

ELP. Descartes' strict dualism of mind and body provides the most obvious and familiar source of such problems. If the impact of a stream of corpuscles on my retina can cause a visual sensation in my immaterial mind, what becomes of CLP? How can there be resemblance between cause and effect in such a case? Likewise for the role of the will in voluntary bodily motions: where is the resemblance between the volition in my mind and the motion of my legs? As for ELP, a corporeal image imprinted on the brain might resemble a physical object, but Descartes consistently denied that his ideas were corporeal images. They are, he says, not images, but 'like' images in the way they represent objects. This is scarcely enlightening. A non-extended thing can't represent an extended thing by way of resemblance.

Watson's book has proved a wonderful source of insight for students, young and old, of seventeenth-century metaphysics. Once the student has grasped CLP and ELP, and seen how the Cartesians were *both* committed to them *and* to metaphysical theses that violate them, the big picture is suddenly illuminated. Given this understanding of the tensions that drove late seventeenth-century metaphysics, we could better understand both the transformations of Cartesianism effected by Spinoza, Malebranche and Leibniz, and the eventual collapse of traditional metaphysics in the face of sceptical attacks.

Although I am, as should be obvious, a great admirer of Watson's work, I don't think he got it exactly right. In particular, I think his emphasis on resemblance is over-played. The rationalist metaphysician is, by the nature of his project, committed to certain *a priori* principles of intelligibility governing the causal and epistemological relations. He is, let us say, committed to causal and epistemological *intelligibility* principles, CIP and EIP. But resemblance, although it may be the most obvious, is not the only way in which intelligibility can be secured. The idea of a circle, for example, need not itself be a circle. A circle can be made known to the mind by way of an image (resemblance), or by way of its mathematical formula ($a^2 + b^2 = r^2$), or by way of a mechanical rule of construction. We shall see the relevance of this when we come to discuss Malebranche on *étendue intelligible* or 'intelligible extension'.

The best way to understand seventeenth-century rationalist meta-physics, I suggest, is to see it as firmly committed to principles of causal and epistemological intelligibility, CIP and EIP, and then engaging in fierce controversy over how CIP and EIP are to be interpreted. Does intelligibility require resemblance, in which case my CIP and EIP would be indistinguishable from Watson's CLP and ELP? Or might causal and epistemological intelligibility be secured by relations other than resemblance? We have already seen how EIP might be satisfied without resemblance. Does the same hold for CIP? Descartes suggests in *Meditation Three* that the cause must be adequate to produce the effect, i.e. that it must have enough 'reality' or 'perfection' to do the job. If it did not, then some or all of the reality or perfection of the effect would have been produced *ex nihilo*, which is impossible. But this causal adequacy principle (CAP) is perfectly consistent, he thinks, with causal interaction between mind and body, i.e. without resemblance. And CAP also allows 'eminent' causality, where the cause of an effect with property F is not actually F, but possesses the reality or perfection of F in some higher form.

What I propose, then, is that we replace Watson's CLP and ELP with my CIP and EIP. For the moment these can be stated in somewhat vague terms, since a central object of controversy among second-generation Cartesians is precisely how these principles should be stated, what they require and what they exclude.

CIP: For a genuine causal relation to hold between cause C and effect E, there must be some *intelligible connection* between C and E. This notion is usually glossed in terms of what could in principle be discerned by rational insight or *nous* by a sufficiently enlightened mind. Such a mind, we are told, could 'see' the effect in the cause, and thus perceive *a priori* that the effect would result from the cause. The most obvious but not necessarily the only way in which CIP could be met is by some sort of 'containment' of the effect 'in' the cause.

EIP: For a mind M to know the properties of an object O by way of its idea I, the idea must be 'present' to the mind, and the presence of I to M must render intelligible to M (some of) the properties of O. The Aristotelians would say that the form of the object, without its matter, must be present in the knowing mind. The Cartesians reject the Aristotelian terminology, but must find some adequate replacement that preserves the same basic thought. Once again, the most obvious – though not, perhaps, the only – explanation would be in terms of literal resemblance, which would assimilate ideas to images.

Why is it important to distinguish my CIP and EIP from Watson's CLP and ELP? The answer will become clear in subsequent chapters where we discuss Malebranche's views about causality (occasionalism) and about ideas (the Vision in God). Malebranche's work lies at the heart of the Cartesian metaphysics discussed in Watson's book, which focuses on the period from 1673 to 1712. But Malebranche, in seeking to defend rational principles of intelligibility, is led to deny both of Watson's resemblance principles, at least as they would naively be understood. If causal and epistemological intelligibility can only be secured by resemblance then Malebranche's position is flatly self-contradictory. Charity thus requires us to regard Cartesian metaphysicians as committed to the somewhat looser and more open-ended principles I have spelled out. We can then see whether there is a consistent position that affirms CIP and EIP, but denies CLP and ELP. If we assume from the start that rationalist metaphysicians are absolutely committed to resemblance principles, it is too easy to convict them of inconsistency.

Our strategy in this chapter is as follows. We shall look briefly at Descartes' views on the nature of ideas (the second section), then spend some time on the accounts of ideas in later Cartesians such as La Forge, Arnauld and Régis (the third section). After that, we shall turn our attention to Descartes' views about causation (the fourth section) and the nature and extent of his concessions to occasionalism. The final section (the fifth section) discusses the views of later Cartesians such as La Forge and Cordemoy on causation, tracing the emergence of occasionalist themes and arguments. The chapter provides essential background for our reading of Malebranche. Without a proper grounding in the intellectual context provided by Descartes and by second generation Cartesian metaphysics, the writings of Malebranche would be almost incomprehensible.

Descartes on ideas

Descartes has a great deal to say about ideas, but still leaves many questions unanswered. What exactly are Cartesian ideas, how do they arise, and how do they serve their function in the cognition of objects? His readers must search through scattered remarks in his published works and his correspondence, seeking as ever the most plausible and coherent overall interpretation of his views. The following four quite different kinds of things are labelled 'ideas', at various places in the Cartesian corpus:

1 Corporeal images in the brain.
2 Direct or immediate objects of thought or perception.
3 Mental acts or operations.
4 Mental dispositions.

The first supposed sense of 'idea', as a corporeal image traced on the brain, can be set aside. Descartes does use 'idea' in this sense in early works such as the *Regulae* (AT X 414 and 441, CSM I, 43 and 56–7), and the *Treatise on Man* (AT XI 174–7, CSM I, 105–6), but he never uses the term in this sense in the *Meditations*, and explicitly distinguishes ideas from corporeal images in a number of the *Replies*. In the *Second Replies*, for example, he writes as follows:

> I do not myself think that the idea is of the same kind as the images of material things which are pictured in the imagination; I maintain it is simply that which we perceive with the intellect, when the intellect apprehends, or judges, or reasons.
>
> (AT IX 109, CSM II 99)

There are corporeal images in the imagination, but they must be sharply distinguished from ideas proper:

> Thus it is not only the images depicted in the imagination which I call 'ideas'. Indeed, in so far as these images are in the corporeal imagination, that is, are depicted in some part of the brain, I do not call them 'ideas' at all; I call them ideas only in so far as they give form to the mind itself, when it is directed towards that part of the brain.
>
> (AT IX 124, CSM II 113)

In the *Third Replies*, he accuses his critic (Hobbes) of confusing ideas with images in his criticisms of the *Third Meditation*:

> Here my critic wants the term 'idea' to be taken to refer simply to the images of material things which are depicted in the corporeal imagination; and if this is granted, it is easy for him to prove that there can be no proper idea of an angel or of God. But I made it quite clear in several places throughout the book, and in this passage in particular, that I am taking the word 'idea' to refer to whatever is immediately perceived by the mind.
>
> (AT IX 141, CSM II 127)

In a letter to Mersenne of July 1641, the same point is reiterated:

> For by 'idea' I do not just mean the images depicted in the imagination; indeed, in so far as these images are in the corporeal imagination, I do not use that term for them at all.
>
> (AT III 392–3, CSMK III 185)

In his post-*Meditations* writings, Descartes takes pains to draw a sharp distinction between corporeal images traced on the brain, and ideas in the strict sense, which lie on the mental side of the mind–body divide. Mental functions such as imagination and memory may depend on corporeal images,[3] but the idea should never be identified with the image. Unfortunately, Descartes continues to say that ideas are 'like' (*comme*) images, which is unhelpful. An image can represent a body by resemblance; an idea, it seems, cannot do so in any straightforward sense.

Having set aside ideas in sense 1 (corporeal images), we can go on to set aside – as irrelevant to our current concerns – ideas in sense 4 (dispositions). In the 1641 letter to Hyperaspistes and in his *Comments on a Certain Broadsheet* (written against some theses of his wayward erstwhile disciple Regius) Descartes seeks to spell out his conception of innate ideas, and thus to prevent possible misunderstandings of innatism. I have no doubt, Descartes writes to Hyperaspistes, that the soul of the human infant concerns itself with the demands of the body rather than with lofty metaphysical subjects:

> None the less, it has in itself the ideas of God, of itself and of all such truths as are called self-evident, in the same way as adult human beings have these ideas when they are not attending to them; for it does not acquire these ideas later on, as it grows older. I have no doubt that if it were released from the prison of the body, it would find them within itself.
>
> (AT III 424, CSMK III 190)

The fact that some men – and even perhaps whole peoples – never think explicitly about God does not refute the Cartesian claim that the idea of God is innate:

> I do not doubt that everyone has within himself an implicit idea of God, that is to say, an aptitude to perceive it explicitly; but I am not surprised that not everyone is aware that he has it or notices that he has it.
>
> (AT III 430, CSMK III 194)

In the *Comments on a Certain Broadsheet*, Descartes is concerned not only to defend innatism, but also to explain what the innatist is and is not committed to. He dismisses out of hand the crudest interpretation of innate ideas: 'I have never written or taken the view that the mind requires innate ideas which are something distinct from its own faculty of thinking' (AT VIII 357, CSM I 303). To say that a given idea is innate is to say that the mind has the power to form it from its own resources, without requiring instruction from without. Ideas may thus be said to be innate in the sense that

> … we say that generosity is 'innate' in certain families, or that certain diseases such as gout or stones are innate in others: it is not so much that the babies of such families suffer from these diseases in their mother's womb, but simply that they are born with a certain 'faculty' or tendency to contract them.
>
> (AT VIII 358, CSM I, 303–4)

If ideas in the dispositional sense (4) are merely capacities or tendencies to have ideas in some more robust sense (2 or 3), then we can regard them as being called 'ideas' only in some secondary or parasitic sense. Let us set them aside, and concentrate our attention on the central sense or senses of 'idea' in Descartes.

There is no doubt whatsoever that Descartes often – indeed, standardly – uses 'idea' in sense (3), to stand for mental acts or operations, which are modes or modifications of the immaterial substance of the soul. All ideas, he tells us in *Meditation Three*, are 'modes of thought' (*modi cogitandi*). As such, they differ from one another not in their 'formal' or intrinsic reality but in their 'objective' (representational) reality (AT IX 31, CSM II 27). The same point is reiterated at *Principles*, 1, 17:

> When we reflect further on the ideas that we have within us, we see that some of them, in so far as they are merely modes of thinking, do not differ much from one another; but in so far as one idea represents one thing and another represents another, they differ widely.
>
> (AT IX 32, CSM I 198)

There is no doubt that this use of 'idea' for mental act or operation is fundamental for Descartes. In his well-known and helpful article, Vere Chappell refers to such mental acts as ideas(m), or ideas taken 'in the material sense'.[4] But an idea can always be thought of in two different ways, or under two different aspects. We can think of it either in terms of its intrinsic features, as an act or operation of thinking substance, or we can think of it in terms of its role in cognition, i.e. in terms of its representative content. If we think of ideas in this latter sense, we may find ourselves positing what Chappell calls ideas(o), ideas taken 'in the objective sense'. Ideas in this sense are differentiated by their contents, which allow one person to entertain the same idea (in this sense) on several different occasions, or for two or more people to have the same idea. It is ideas(o) that Descartes is gesturing towards when, in the *Second Replies*, he defines 'idea' as the form of a thought:

> II. Idea. I understand this term to mean the form of any given thought, immediate perception of which makes me aware of the thought. Hence, whenever I express something in words, and understand what I am saying, this very fact makes it certain that there is within me an idea of what is signified by the words in question.
>
> (AT IX 124, CSM II 113)

We thus need to talk of ideas(o) if we assume that thoughts can be shared and communicated. We may also need to posit ideas(o) as immediate objects of perception, if we are to make sense of non-veridical perceptions. Descartes does speak in a number of places, e.g. in the *First Replies*, of ideas as immediate objects of perception. But are Chappell's ideas(o) a distinct set of entities, intermediaries between the mind and the world of bodies? This traditional interpretation of Descartes has been coming under increasing fire in recent years.[5] Chappell suggests that an idea(m) and its idea(o) differ only by what Descartes would call a 'distinction of reason', i.e. they are the same thing conceived in two different ways, and could not exist separately.[6] If this is correct, we will need to distinguish between two different interpretations of ideas as mental objects:

> (2a) Ideas = mental objects really distinct from ideas(3), capable of serving as the immediate objects of perception, and thus as intermediaries between the perceiving soul and external objects.
> (2b) Ideas = mental objects not really distinct from ideas(3), but rather the objective contents of ideas(3). We may still talk of ideas in this sense as 'immediate objects' of perception, but this only means that in any perception the mind has a direct grasp of the content of its thought.

As we shall see, the second generation Cartesians, led by Arnauld,[7] interpreted Descartes as committed to ideas(3), acts of the soul, and ideas(2b), the contents of ideas(3), but denied that Descartes' theory

25

had any need for ideas as distinct intermediate objects (2a). An idea, Arnauld will explain, can always be seen under two different aspects or in two different relations: *qua* mode of the soul it modifies it can be called 'perception'; *qua* (purported) representation of some external object it can be called 'idea'. But one should not infer from this duality of aspects or relations a real duality of things. Arnauld takes this view to be faithful to Descartes, and we have seen no reason to doubt him. Insofar as Descartes had a clear conception of the nature of ideas, it may well have been this 'double aspect' theory subsequently articulated by Arnauld.

Before leaving Descartes, we must ask his views on the source of our ideas, since this issue would become one of fundamental importance for the later Cartesians and for Malebranche in particular. In the *Third Meditation* Descartes divided ideas into three categories: innate, adventitious (sensory) and artificial. The idea of God is innate (stamped on the human soul at its creation, like the craftsman's trademark on his work); the idea of a dog is adventitious (derived from sense experience); the idea of a centaur is artificial (made up by the Greek poets). The reader might be permitted to think that our sensory ideas are directly caused by the physical stimuli affecting our sense organs. In the *Comments on a Certain Broadsheet*, however, Descartes rejects any such concession to empiricism. In an important sense, he now insists, all our ideas are innate:

> ... if we bear well in mind the scope of our senses and what it is exactly that reaches our faculty of thinking by way of them, we must admit that in no case are the ideas of things presented to us by the senses just as we form them in our thinking. So much so that there is nothing in our ideas which is not innate to the mind or to the faculty of thinking.
>
> (AT VIII 358, CSM I 304)

Our minds form the ideas of colours, tastes, smells, etc. on the *occasion* (Descartes' word) of certain corporeal motions in our sense organs and the sensory centres of our brains, although there is no *resemblance* between those motions and the resulting idea. The lack of any resemblance between our sensations of, e.g. heat and colour and any properties of external objects is of course a cornerstone of Descartes' mechanistic account of sense perception, explicitly emphasised in *Le Monde* and the *Dioptrique*. Why, asks Descartes at the start of *Le Monde*, 'should nature not also have established some sign which would make us have the sensation of light, even if the sign contained nothing in itself which is similar to this sensation?' (AT XI 4, CSM I 81). There may be picture-like images imprinted on the brain, he writes in the *Dioptrique*, but 'we must not think that it is by means of this resemblance that the picture causes our sensory perception of these objects – as if there were yet other eyes within our brain with which we could perceive it' (AT VI 130, CSM I 167). The sensation of red does not resemble the spin of the corpuscles of the second element; the sensation of heat does not resemble the agitation of the corpuscles of a hot body. Should we then take these sensations as non-intentional, devoid of any representative content? Or should we think of them as confused perceptions[8] ? Malebranche will take the former view, Arnauld and most of the later Cartesians will take the latter.

Strictly speaking, Descartes concludes, none of our ideas may be said to be drawn from, or copied from, the impressions made by external objects on our sense organs. Even where there is resemblance between the brain trace and some properties of the external object (in respect of size, shape and arrangement of parts), the brain trace or image can't itself get into the mind. The body, it seems, can prod or prompt the mind; it can't inform or instruct it. But if our sensory ideas are not drawn from objects, how do they come about? Three possible accounts come to mind:

a   Sensory ideas are produced by the mind itself, on the occasion of a physical stimulus.
b   Sensory ideas are directly and individually produced by God, on the occasion of a physical stimulus.
c   All the sensory ideas a given human mind will ever need are placed in it by God in advance, in its creation. The role of the physical stimulus, on this account, is merely to evoke something already present.

Descartes' language in the *Comments* strongly suggests theory (a). God, according to this theory, has created the human mind with a certain range of active powers, prominent among which is the power to produce its own sensory ideas on the occasion of the physical stimulation of the sense organs of its body. But this theory ascribes an astonishing range of powers to the mind, none of which it is aware of possessing or exercising. As Malebranche would later insist, my sensations may be 'en moi' but they also take place 'sans moi' and even 'malgré moi', i.e. against my will. This might lead us to reject theory (a) in favour of (b) or (c). In his eliminative argument for the Vision in God Malebranche will explicitly reject all three of the above theories.

Later Cartesian accounts of ideas

Among the disciples of Descartes, a rough consensus gradually emerged about the nature of ideas. The fundamental sense of 'idea', it appears, is idea(m), ideas taken in the material sense as acts or operations of the soul, and therefore as modes of spiritual substance. In this sense, there is no distinction between ideas and perceptions. If we need on occasion to speak of ideas as immediate objects of thought or perception, and thus to posit ideas(o), we should be on our guard not to think of these as having any really distinct existence. In having a thought or a perception we are immediately aware of its content, and can thus speak of this content as the object of the thought or the perception. This allows us to make sense of cases where there is nothing to think of (Descartes' malicious demon) or to perceive (the alcoholic's pink rats).

Louis de la Forge expresses this view clearly in his *Traité de L'Esprit de L'Homme*. Ideas, he says, can be considered in two ways, either in themselves or in their representative role.

> When considered in themselves, they can be defined as 'the forms, modes or ways of thinking of the mind by the immediate perception of which we perceive the thing which they represent to us and are certain that we have such a thought'.[9] I call them 'modes' or 'ways' of thinking because I cannot conceive of any of them without a substance which thinks, although I can very easily conceive of this substance without any one of them in particular. Thus they are not distinct from the substance of the mind, nor are they distinct from each other except as different modes of the substance to which they belong.[10]

La Forge also quotes a lengthy passage from Descartes' *Comments on a Certain Broadsheet*, and endorses Descartes' claim about the origin of our ideas.[11] Material things, La Forge notes, can only transmit motions to the sense organs of our bodies; these motions cannot reach the spiritual soul:

> ... these corporeal species could only be modes or accidents of some body which have these two properties: first, they are incapable of leaving their subject to go into another one; and secondly, even if they could leave, they could be received only into an extended subject. It follows clearly from this that they could not be received into our mind. Therefore since all our kinds of knowledge are acts which do not leave the inside of

the soul, it is impossible for corporeal species to be the form by the immediate perception of which we have such or such thoughts.[12]

What La Forge calls 'corporeal species' are patterns of activity in our brains and nervous systems. Such patterns, he tells us, are not in general iconic, and should not be thought of as little images imprinted on the brain. But even if they were images, it would make no difference, because all that these 'species' can impart is motion, and motion cannot be imparted to the immaterial substance of the soul. The role of these 'species' is simply to prompt the soul's own faculty of forming ideas. If asked about the causes of our ideas, La Forge explains, we need to distinguish the 'primary and effective' cause from the 'remote and occasional' one. A body can only ever be the remote and occasional cause of an idea, something which 'by the union of mind and body, causes our faculty to think and determines it to produce the ideas of which the faculty of thinking itself is the principal and effective cause'.[13]

All our ideas thus originate from the mind as primary and effective cause; some – those labelled 'adventitious' by Descartes – also require the remote and occasional cause of a physical stimulus. This account, says La Forge, allows us to answer the famous question whether our ideas are innate or acquired:

I reply that they are both. They are innate in the mind not only because the mind never received them from the senses but also because it is created with the faculty of thinking and of forming ideas and is the principal and proximate cause of them, in the same way in which one says that gout and stones are innate in certain families if those born into them carry dispositions towards those illnesses. But ideas are acquired and are not innate if by this word 'innate' is meant that they are in the substance of the soul as in a reservoir, in the way one arranges pictures in a gallery to look at them when one wishes. For there is none of them in particular which needs to be actually present in our mind which, since it is a substance which thinks, cannot have anything actually present without being aware of it. That is why they are contained in the mind only in potency and not in act, in approximately the way in which shapes are contained in a piece of wax. There is this difference, however, that in the wax this potency is merely passive, whereas in the case of the mind it is also active.[14]

But this last difference, merely noted in passing by La Forge, is of fundamental importance. A piece of wax has the passive power of plasticity, of allowing itself to be shaped by external pressures. To explain the shape it has taken on, one cites the external forces that most recently acted on it and imparted a particular form. Such a passive power seems easily comprehensible. But the mind's capacity to form ideas is not passive but active. Without being informed by the impressions on the senses, and without any resemblance to merely corporeal (and hence 'remote') causes, the mind must impart form to itself, producing its ideas in a manner that has a reliable one-to-one correspondence with those remote corporeal causes. Of this mysterious productive process we have no conception whatsoever.

We also find it hard to understand how the modes of a purely immaterial substance can represent bodies. La Forge is aware of the difficulty:

> I realize that I will not avoid being asked, in this context, how it is possible for spiritual things such as the ideas or forms of our thoughts to make us think about the body and its properties with which they have no similarity or resemblance. That is not without difficulty. However you should not doubt what I have just said, especially if you keep two things in mind. First, since the mind is a thing which thinks, its nature is necessarily such that it can represent everything to itself by its own thoughts. Secondly, our mind is like a part of the divine mind. Now this infinite mind which knows everything in itself would not be able to know bodies if it were impossible for its thought (which is completely spiritual) to represent bodies to itself.[15]

This passage takes us right into the heart of the controversy between Malebranche and Arnauld, which we shall discuss in Chapter Four. Of the two considerations adduced by La Forge, the first leads to Arnauld, the second to Malebranche. Arnauld says that the human mind thinks, i.e. that its modes are representations, because that is its nature. It is simply a brute fact, incapable of further explanation, that God has created such beings. Malebranche says that we can think only because we participate in the divine mind through the Vision in God. But we are getting ahead of our story.

Part One of the Port Royal Logic, the celebrated *Art de Penser* of Arnauld and Nicole, deals with conception, the first action or operation of the mind, and hence with the nature of ideas. The term 'idea', says Arnauld in Chapter One, is so clear and so simple that it cannot be explained in terms of other words.[16] There is a need, however, to distinguish clearly between ideas and the corporeal images formed in the imagination. The idea of a figure of 1,000 sides is clearly distinct from the idea of a figure of 10,000 sides, though it would be easy to confuse the corresponding images.[17] We have a perfectly clear idea of our own thoughts, though we form no image of thought. Affirmation and negation are clearly distinct mental operations, although the image (a round earth) might be exactly the same for the opposite judgements 'The earth is round' and 'The earth is not round'. Arnauld's conclusion is plain:

> When therefore we speak of ideas, we do not call by that name the images which are painted in the imagination, but everything which is in our mind when we can say truly that we conceive a thing, in whatever manner we conceive it.[18]

Ideas, he continues, are the bearers of the meanings of words, so whenever we understand a word such as 'God' or 'soul', it follows that we have a corresponding idea, even if we find ourselves unable to represent such things in the imagination. But where do our ideas come from? The empiricist position, most recently championed by Gassendi, holds that all our ideas are derived from the senses. Arnauld starts by denying that empiricism can account for such ideas as those of thinking and existence. By what sense, he asks, do we derive these ideas? Are they bright or dark, blue or red, treble or bass, hot or cold, bitter or sweet? From what sensible images, and by what processes of recombination, could such ideas have been formed? If the empiricist can come up with no remotely credible answers to such questions, then, argues Arnauld,

> ... it must be admitted that the ideas of being and of thought do not in the least derive their origin from the senses, but our soul has in itself the faculty of forming them, although it often happens that it is excited to do so by something which strikes the senses ...[19]

It is therefore false, Arnauld concludes, that all our ideas come from the senses. Indeed, one should go further, and deny that any of our ideas owes its origin to the senses:

> ... it could be said, on the contrary, that no idea which is in our minds derives its origin from the senses, except by occasion, in

31

that the movements which take place in the brain, which is all that the senses can produce, give the occasion to the soul to form for itself various ideas which it would not form for itself without that, although almost always these ideas have no resemblance to what takes place in the senses and in the brain, and there are furthermore a very great number of ideas which, having no relation to any corporeal image cannot, without an evident absurdity, be referred to our senses.[20]

The *Art de Penser* does not discuss in any detail the precise ontological status of ideas. Arnauld's views on the subject are, however, perfectly clear from his other works. He regards ideas as acts or operations of the soul, equivalent to perceptions. In V*raies et Fausses Idées*, this is made perfectly explicit: 'I also take the idea of an object and the perception of an object to be the same thing'.[21] Although there is no real distinction between idea and perception, there is a difference of aspect. When we speak of it as a perception, we are thinking of its formal or intrinsic reality as a mode of the soul; when we speak of it as an idea we are thinking of its intentionality, its representational content:

I have said that I take *the perception* and *the idea* to be the same thing. Nevertheless it must be noted that this thing, although only one, has two relations: one to the soul which it modifies, the other to the thing perceived insofar as it is objectively in the soul; and that the word *perception* indicates more directly the first relation and the word *idea* the second.[22]

If we ask Arnauld to explain how it can be that the modes of the human soul have such representational content, he will answer that it is their nature to do so, i.e. that that is simply how God created the human soul. Intentionality is accepted as the mark of the mental, and is regarded as irreducible, not susceptible to further explanation. This null theory of intentionality, treating it as a brute fact about the mind, was something that Malebranche, as we shall see, could not accept. To say that the modes of our soul represent external objects because it is their nature to do so is, he insists, to explain nothing at all.

Another spokesman for this Cartesian orthodoxy was Pierre Sylvain Régis, whose *Cours entier de Philosophie* or *Système général selon les principes de M. Descartes* appeared in three volumes in 1690. Régis explicitly identifies ideas with perceptions, which are simply modes of the soul. By the terms 'idea' and 'perception', he writes, 'I do not understand anything besides the modes of thinking which I know by themselves; but which represent to me things which are external to myself'.[23] Régis criticised Malebranche on a number of points in three letters dealing with the Moon Illusion, the nature of ideas, and the pleasures of the senses.[24] Malebranche's *Réponse a M. Régis* was included in later editions of the *Recherche*. The second part of the reply, dealing with the nature of ideas (OCM XVII–1 279–310) reveals clearly that Régis followed closely the account of ideas we have found in Arnauld. When asked by Malebranche whether the idea of infinity can itself be finite, Régis replies by invoking Descartes' distinction between 'formal' (intrinsic) and 'objective' (representational) reality. *Qua* mode of a finite spiritual substance, i.e. considered in its intrinsic nature or formal reality, the idea of infinity (or of God) is finite; *qua* representation, i.e. considered in its 'objective' reality, it is infinite (OCM XVII–1 285).[25] A similar stratagem copes with the generality of ideas. Each idea, *qua* mode of a particular soul, is itself a particular, but *qua* representation it can be general in its signification (OCM XVII–1 302). On Régis' view, according to Malebranche, the soul is itself a *monde intelligible*, i.e. it can know all things merely by considering its own perfections (OCM XVII–1 291). As we shall see in the next chapter, Malebranche's argument for the Vision in God includes a sustained attack on this notion of the soul as a *monde intelligible* in its own right, a theory attacked by Malebranche on both philosophical and theological grounds.

Descartes on causation

Descartes' considered views about second causes and natural powers continue to perplex commentators and to provide plenty of material for lively scholarly debate.[26] At first sight, it would seem that he is committed to the full range of natural causal powers recognised by common sense. Four such powers will be central to our discussion. They are the power of a moving body (1) to set another body in motion, or (2) to cause sensations in a mind; and the power of a mind (3) to move its own body by an act of will, and (4) to excite ideas in its own substance. But there are three central themes in Cartesian metaphysics that seem to tell against the acceptance of natural causes and to impel Descartes towards occasionalism.

In the first place, there is the strict substance–mode metaphysic. Substances are capable (DV) of independent existence; modes are only conceivable as modifications of substances. So if motion is a mode of the moving body, it becomes impossible to conceive how it could be transferred from one body to another. In a letter to Henry More of 1649, Descartes distinguishes bare motion from motive force, and suggests that the moving force of a body in motion may not be in the body itself but in God, the ultimate cause of all bodily motions. 'The transfer which I call "motion" is no less something existent than shape is: it is a mode in a body. The power causing motion may be the power of God himself preserving the same amount of transfer in matter as He put in it in the first moment of creation' (AT V 403–4, CSMK III 381). So motion, which is a mode of the moving body, cannot be transferred; and motive force or power is not truly in the moving body at all.[27] The problem is even worse for the action of minds on bodies. If I can't understand how one body can push another, how will I be able understand how a volition (a mode of an unextended spiritual substance) can be the cause of the motion of an arm or a leg (a mode of extended corporeal substance)?

When the substance–mode metaphysic is married to a rationalist conception of the causal relation, the problems become still more acute. But what thesis or theses of causal intelligibility is Descartes committed to? In the *Third Meditation* he is careful only to commit himself to a fairly weak thesis of causal adequacy. This causal adequacy principle (CAP) states only that the complete efficient cause of a given thing must contain at least as much reality or perfection as the thing it produces (AT IX 32, CSM II 28). If not, something would be coming from nothing. This principle, he insists, in response to the objections of Gassendi, is perfectly consistent with mind–body interaction. When asked how the soul can move the body if it is in no way itself material, and how it can receive the forms of corporeal objects, Descartes responds brusquely that the question betrays a fundamental misunderstanding:

> ... the whole problem contained in such questions arises simply from a supposition that is false and cannot in any way be proved, namely that, if the soul and body are two substances whose nature is different, this prevents them from being able to act on each other.
>
> (AT IX 213, CSM II 275)

This defence will hold if cause and effect are permitted to be equally real or perfect, and if the modes of finite minds and of bodies are supposed to be equal in their degree of perfection. Some recent commentators have taken Descartes at his word here and dismissed the supposed 'scandal' of mind–body interaction as a pseudo-problem.[28] The difficulty with such a view is that Descartes appears to commit himself to stronger theses of causal intelligibility than CAP.[29] At a number of places, he seems committed to the claim that the cause–effect relation is perspicuous in the sense that a sufficiently enlightened mind could 'see' (i.e. rationally intuit) the effect in the cause. This suggests causal containment or pre-existence rather than mere causal adequacy. In the *Second Replies*, for example, we read that 'Whatever reality or perfection there is in a thing is present either formally or eminently in its first and adequate cause' (AT IX 128, CSM II 116). There is nothing in the effect 'which was not previously present in the cause, either in a similar or in a higher form' (AT IX 106, CSM II 97). In the 1648 *Conversation with Burman* he tells his young interlocutor that 'It is a common axiom and a true one that the effect is like the cause' (AT V 156, CSMK III 339–40). This principle, he adds by way of qualification, applies only to the total cause, the 'cause of being itself'. 'Anything produced by this cause must necessarily be like it'. Even in the *Third Meditation*, as Radner has shown, one of the arguments turns on a causal containment principle rather than on the weaker principle of causal adequacy.[30]

There is therefore substantial evidence to suggest that Descartes endorsed a much stronger principle of causal intelligibility than CAP. Explicit or implicit at various points in his writings we can find a principle of causal containment or pre-existence to the effect that the effect pre-exists in the cause. Such a principle clearly rules out mind–body interaction. If modes cannot be conceived except as modifications of particular substances, then we can construct an even stronger argument for the conclusion that no mode can be communicated from any substance to another. This would rule out not just mind–body interaction but also body–body or mind–mind interactions.[31] Maybe, as Leibniz was to suggest, the only intelligible causal relations are those between the modes of a single substance, unfolding in accordance with the formula that expresses its complete notion. The 'windowless monads' of the *Monadology* may represent the only metaphysical system consistent with the thorough working out of the implications of the substance–mode metaphysic.

The third metaphysical theme drawing Descartes away from the naïve belief in natural powers and towards occasionalism is his belief that God's conservation of His creatures is indistinguishable from their continuous (re)creation. In both the *Meditations* (AT IX 39, CSM II 33) and the *Principles* (AT IX 34, CSM I 200) Descartes writes that the existence of a creature at any given moment is logically independent of its existence at the previous moment. It follows that God must continually re-create each and every one of His creatures, none of which could exist for more than a moment without His sustaining action. The distinction between preservation and creation is only a conceptual distinction, not a real one. In itself, the thesis of continuous creation was a perfectly orthodox piece of scholastic theology, found in Aquinas and many others. Now Aquinas and the majority of the schoolmen were firm believers in the reality of second causes. But in Malebranche, as we shall see, continuous creation is taken to imply the non-existence of any natural powers and to provide a rigorous proof of occasionalism. Two questions spring to mind. What has changed in the interpretation of continuous creation between Aquinas and Malebranche? And where does Descartes stand?

To turn continuous creation from a commonplace of scholastic theology into a radical argument for occasionalism, additional theses are needed. Let us first state the most basic claim – the dependence of all created substances (material and immaterial alike) on God's sustaining activity – as CC(S).

CC(S) Every created substance (mind or body) depends for its continued existence on God's sustaining action.

What of the modes of created substances, e.g. the motions of bodies and the thoughts and volitions of finite minds? Are these also within the scope of continuous creation? The transformation of the doctrine between Aquinas and Malebranche turns on the following pair of theses, CC(AM) and CC(DM) which express, respectively, the continuous creation of *all* modes and of *determinate* modes.

CC(AM) Every mode of every created substance S is as it is because of God's re-creation of S, i.e. God re-creates not just S but all the modes of S.

CC(DM) Every creature is re-created with a perfectly determinate set of modes.

If God re-creates not just the substance but its modes, and if this re-creation must maintain in existence a complete and perfectly determinate set of modes, then continuous creation entails occasionalism. The historical evidence suggests that this transformation of the doctrine of continuous creation occurred after Descartes, and that he would have been able to reconcile the weak version of continuous creation CC(S) with a belief in the reality of natural powers.[32]

If we re-examine Descartes' views on the four types of causal relation outlined earlier, we find a mixed picture. When he sets out the rules of collision in the *Principles*, he writes cheerfully of the 'force of motion' and the 'force of rest', and begins to develop and articulate these notions into a worked-out system of dynamics.[33] But when challenged about this 'force of motion', he is prepared to retreat in the direction of occasionalism. As he writes to Henry More, this 'force' may simply be God's power, re-creating bodies in such a way as to preserve the quantity of motion impressed on them in their creation.[34] So the 'force of motion' of a moving body may need to be read in a sort of 'as if' sense. This might be interpreted as pure occasionalism, but it need not be. Descartes could be endorsing CC(S) but denying CC(DM), accepting that God's re-creation is responsible for the continued existence of bodies, and for the conservation of the grand total of motion in the physical universe, but not for all the determinate motions of particular bodies.

When it comes to the supposed power of bodies to cause sensations in minds, Descartes' considered opinions are even harder to pin down. In the *Comments on a Certain Broadsheet*, as we have already seen, he suggests a sense in which all our ideas may be called innate. The mind, he suggests, has the power to produce ideas on the mere occasion of certain events in the sense organs and the brain. This theory, labelled 'occasional causation' by Nadler, is quite distinct from pure occasionalism in two important respects.[35] In the first place, the true cause of our ideas is said to be the mind itself, not God. In the second place, the body is not deprived, on this theory, of all causal power. Even if the brain-state is not the primary or direct cause of the idea, it retains a prompting or triggering role. The mind has a sort of divinely pre-programmed innate repertoire, responding to physical stimuli arriving in coded form by producing representations, sometimes clear and distinct, sometimes confused, of the external world. So physical stimulus 17 elicits the idea of red and physical stimulus 18 elicits the idea of blue, without there being any perspicuous reason why this should be so. The physical stimulus is not the total cause, but still plays an essential role. Take this causal role away, and Descartes' proof of the external world in the *Sixth Meditation* would collapse, leaving us with no defences against idealism.[36]

As regards the powers of finite minds, either to move their own bodies by acts of will, or to excite ideas or volitions in themselves, Descartes never seems to have entertained any doubts. 'The freedom of the will is self-evident', he tells us bluntly in the *Principles* (AT IX 41, CSM I 205–6). Supposing him to apply continuous creation in this domain, he must have supposed that God re-creates all the substances of finite spirits, and re-creates each with some thoughts or other, perhaps with a fixed 'quantity of thought' characteristic of each mind, but not with fully determinate thoughts and volitions. He writes confidently in the *Conversation with Burman* that we know our own liberty on the basis of introspection (AT V 159, CSMK III 342), and never seems to doubt that this is an awareness of real causal powers, both over the voluntary motions of our bodies and over (many of) our thoughts.

What should we conclude from this brief foray into Descartes' views about causation? We seem almost to be engaged in an exercise in Hegelian dialectics. Thesis: Descartes accepts from common sense all four types of causal power: body–body, body–mind, mind–body, and mind–mind. Antithesis: Descartes endorses metaphysical theses (causal rationalism, continuous creation) that are strictly incompatible with naïve views about the existence of such causal powers. Synthesis: Descartes' commitments to causal rationalism and to continuous creation are *not* of such a kind as to rule out acceptance of natural causal powers. Although God does continuously re-create each created substance, whether mind or body, He does not re-create it with a fully determinate set of modes. This in turn means that the explanation of any given mode of a particular mind or body can't just be of the form 'God willed it so', but must refer to some secondary cause or natural agent. As for causal relations, it looks as if Descartes has to admit, as *bona fide* cases of 'equivocal' (but still genuine) causation, the power of a mind to move a body and of a body to prompt a mind to think.[37] His considered view seems to be that the causal containment principle holds only for the *total* cause, which would allow us to continue to admit non-resembling causes.[38] In giving everyday causal explanations, we hardly ever cite the total cause, generally citing only one salient causal factor among many, selected no doubt for pragmatic reasons.

In his 1987 article on this topic, Dan Garber argued that Descartes conceived continuous creation as modally indeterminate, thus allowing some causal powers to both minds and bodies.[39] In his 1993 discussion of the same issue, he changes his mind and concludes that Descartes denies causal powers to bodies but allows them to finite minds.[40] This would make him a sort of semi-occasionalist. The authority of such a scholar should not be lightly dismissed. His later view also has the advantage that it fits a hierarchic conception of created substances, with the higher (mind) able to act on the lower (body) but not *vice versa*. I still incline, however, to the rival view of Scott[41] and Nadler[42] that Descartes is not an occasionalist at all, but holds views that allow him to reconcile a weak version of continuous creation with the reality of natural powers in minds and bodies alike. For a Cartesian, minds are more obviously loci of power, since each of us is immediately aware of such powers in introspection, but it does not follow that bodies are altogether devoid of power. Bodies may contribute to the determination of the motions of other bodies, and may play a modest causal role in triggering the mind to produce ideas. The scholastic theory of divine concourse will be invoked to explain how the First Cause and a variety of second causes co-operate to produce any given effect.[43]

This section has discussed some of the recent scholarship on Descartes' views about causation. It has provided grounds for thinking that Descartes was not as muddled about the subject as he is sometimes portrayed, and for resisting attempts to represent him as at least half way to occasionalism. My purposes, however, were relatively modest ones. I was not seeking to provide a perfectly consistent account of all Descartes' utterances about causation. It may be that no such reading is possible. My main aim was to set up the tensions in Cartesian metaphysics that would trouble disciples such as La Forge and Cordemoy, whose writings would in turn set the stage for Malebranche.

Later Cartesian accounts of causation

It is a commonplace in the history of philosophy that the second generation of Cartesians tended to embrace occasionalism. In the previous section we discussed some of the factors in Descartes' metaphysics that were responsible for this transformation of Cartesianism.[44] In this section we shall discuss the views of two of the most important of the intermediate figures between Descartes and Malebranche, Louis de la Forge (1632–66) and Gerard Cordemoy (1626–84). We focus on these two second-generation Cartesians at the expense of others[45] because of their influence on Malebranche – known in one case, inferred with overwhelming probability in the other. Malebranche refers his readers in Book One of the *Recherche* to Cordemoy's *Six Discours sur la Distinction et l'Union du Corps et de l'Âme*, and expresses general approval of Cordemoy's arguments for substance dualism (*OCM* I 123, LO 49). As for La Forge, we know that he contributed illustrations and critical comments to Clerselier's famous edition of Descartes' *L'Homme*, which made such an impression on the young Malebranche.[46] We also know that a copy of La Forge's own *Traité de L'Esprit de l'Homme* was found in Malebranche's library. Some degree of influence of La Forge on Malebranche seems beyond reasonable doubt.[47]

Chapter 16 of La Forge's *Treatise* discusses mind–body interaction. Given substance dualism, says La Forge, it is natural to worry about how mind and body can interact, and to suppose that it raises special difficulties that do not arise for interactions between bodies. But this thought, however natural, is mistaken:

> I think most people would not believe me if I said that it is no more difficult to conceive how the human mind, without being extended, can move the body and how the body without being a spiritual thing can act on the mind, than to conceive how a body has the power to move itself and to communicate its motion to another body. Yet there is nothing more true.[48]

The natural error was vividly expressed by Lucretius, who taught that a body could be moved only by being touched, i.e. by the contact of another moving body. Lucretius assumed that this is the only intelligible manner of causal operation, but in this, La Forge insists, he was simply mistaken. To clarify our ideas we need to draw a distinction between motion itself, as it is in the moving body, and motive force or power. Considered in itself, motion is a mere mode of the moving body, its transfer from the vicinity of one body to that of others.[49] It is nonsense to suppose that such a mode could be transferred from one body to another. The motive force or power of the moving body is, however, something quite distinct from this, and cannot be assumed to be a mode of the moving body at all. Every moving body, says La Forge, 'must be pushed by something which is not itself a body and which is completely distinct from it'.[50] How do we know that this motive force is not a property of any body? All we need to do is to consult our clear and distinct idea of material substance (three-dimensional extension) to see that the idea involves no such motive power.

Bodies are moved, La Forge continues, by being successively re-created, in different places, by God. A body exists at place A because God creates it at A rather than at B. But, he continues,

> ... not only can it not change its condition by its own power: I also claim that there is no creature, spiritual or corporeal, which can cause change in it or in any of its parts, in the second moment of their creation, if the Creator does not do so himself. Since it was He who produced this part of matter in place A, for example, not only must He continue to produce it if He wishes it to continue to exist but also, since He cannot create it everywhere or nowhere, he must put it in place B himself if He wishes it to be there. For if He put it anywhere else there is no force capable of removing it from that location.[51]

Even God cannot create a body without creating it somewhere. This looks like an explicit statement of the principle I earlier labelled CC(DM), continuous creation plus modal determinacy, at least for bodies. But this version of continuous creation, as Nadler reminds us, seems to establish too much.[52] If developed in its full generality – i.e. applied to finite spirits as well as to bodies – it implies the complete non-existence of causal powers in the natural world. Malebranche would enthusiastically embrace that doctrine and seek ways of making its paradoxes more digestible; earlier Cartesians like La Forge would pull back from the brink.

Although God is 'the first, universal, and total cause' of all the motions we observe in our cosmos, La Forge explains, 'I also recognise bodies and minds as particular causes of these same motions …'.[53] God has, for example, created human beings, establishing the union of mind and body:

> … it is easy to see that He who willed to join them in this way had to resolve at the same time to give to the mind the thoughts which we observe it acquiring on the occasion of motions of its body, and to determine the motions of its body in the way they should be in order to be subject to the mind's will.[54]

This is unclear. Has God given the mind and body powers to act on one another in certain ways, or has He merely decided to intervene Himself? And is there any difference between body–mind and mind–body causation? It is worthy of note that La Forge uses the term 'occasion' for the first of these relations but not for the second. Maybe the mind has a genuine causal power over the body but not vice versa? La Forge's considered view is never sufficiently articulated. He does however explicitly reject at least the language of full-blooded occasionalism:

> However you should not say that it is God who does everything and that the body and mind do not really act on each other. For if the body had not had such a movement, the mind would never have had such a thought, and if the mind had not had such a thought the body might also never have had such a movement.[55]

So La Forge rejects pure occasionalism, on the basis of a counterfactual thought-experiment. Unfortunately, the occasionalist could cheerfully endorse the test and its results. If the second cause (occasion) had not been present, God would not have willed the effect, so it would not have taken place. So this test will not serve to distinguish believers in genuine natural powers from occasionalists.

The soul has no power, La Forge thinks, to create or destroy motion, the total quantity of which is conserved by God. It can, however, redirect it, i.e. alter the direction of the currents of animal spirits in the pineal gland and the nerves.[56] But this suggests that God's re-creation of the physical universe is less than fully determinate, i.e. that He recreates each and every material substance, and re-creates the total 'quantity of motion', but leaves the determination of the modes of motion (which particles are moving in which directions and with which speeds) to second causes. So we have an unresolved tension between the strong interpretation of continuous creation as fully modally determinate (which La Forge seems to endorse) and his explanation of the human mind's control over its own body. A similar problem will arise for the modes of finite minds, i.e. their thoughts and volitions. Once again, it seems, continuous re-creation must be less than fully modally determinate if the mind is to retain any genuine powers over its own thoughts and volitions. The active, self-determining power of the will is simply evident to consciousness, La Forge tells us (echoing Descartes); it is not something that can be rendered doubtful.[57] But if the will is an 'active principle' by which the mind 'chooses from itself and by itself and determines itself'[58] then it surely follows that God, in sustaining the immaterial substance of each human mind, is not Himself the direct cause of each and every one of its modes. There is no evidence that any Cartesian before Malebranche embraced that radical opinion.

When asked how mind and body can interact, given their completely different natures, La Forge has recourse to the scholastic distinction between univocal causes (where cause resembles effect) and equivocal causes (where this does not hold):

> It is obvious that the mind cannot act on the body as a univocal cause by forcing it to produce some thought and that the body likewise does not act on the mind by communicating some motion to it, because the mind cannot be moved nor can the body think. It must therefore be as an equivocal cause that the mind, by its thoughts, forces the body to move and that the body, by moving, provides an occasion for the mind to produce some thought. However it does not follow that the body is not the cause of the thoughts which arise in the mind on its occasion, nor that the latter is not equally the cause of the movements

which occur in the body as a result of its thoughts, just because they are only equivocal causes. For God is no less the creator of all things, and workmen are no less the authors of their workmanship, despite the fact that they are all merely the equivocal causes of these effects.[59]

Merely citing a familiar scholastic distinction, however, is not much help. If we want to know how spiritual modes and material modes can interact without any resemblance, it is not much help to be told that there is a familiar scholastic concept, 'equivocal cause' for such puzzling causal relations. Neither is the reference to God's power helpful, since God was supposed to 'contain' all the perfections of His creation either 'formally' or 'eminently', i.e. in some higher form. La Forge, it seems, faces a choice between admitting the existence of utterly occult and unintelligible causal powers (i.e. abandoning causal rationalism) or retreating to occasionalism.

Cordemoy's *Six Discours sur la Distinction et L'Union du Corps et de L'Âme* (1666) takes us significantly closer to pure occasionalism. Cordemoy's natural philosophy is fundamentally Cartesian, with the significant difference that he attempts to reconcile Descartes' matter–theory with a version of atomism. After introducing his atoms in the first discourse, he proceeds in discourses two and three to set out a more or less orthodox mechanical philosophy of nature, with the local motion of subtle matter as the main cause ('considering bodies alone') of the phenomena.[60] The explicit qualification is of course meant to prepare readers for the occasionalism of Discourse Four.

Discourse Four is entitled 'On the First Cause of Movement', and begins with a proof that matter is not self-moving, and must therefore be set in motion by a non-material first mover. But the same cause (God) is needed to maintain bodies in motion as was required to set them in motion in the first place.[61] It is this proposition, Cordemoy admits, which we find hardest to believe, however rigorously it has been demonstrated. We tend to assume that once a body has been set in motion it will continue in motion, and even that it possesses, by virtue of its motion, the power to move other bodies. But this is mere prejudice:

When we say, for example, that the body B has driven the body C from its place; if we examine closely what we know for certain in this, we will see clearly that B was in motion, that it struck C, which was at rest; and that after this encounter, the first ceasing to be in motion, the second began to move. But when we think

43

that B gives movement to C, that is in truth only a prejudice, which stems from the fact that we only see, in this case, the two bodies; and that we are accustomed to attribute all the effects that are known to us to the things which we perceive, without taking care to note that often those things are incapable of producing such effects, and without considering that there could be a thousand causes which, however imperceptible they may be, could produce sensible effects.[62]

We can conceive of a body in motion without conceiving of any such motive power, Cordemoy continues. Indeed, we cannot conceive how such a power, assuming it to be (*per impossibile*) a mode of the moving body, could be transferred from one body to another. Given that the first mover of all bodies is a spirit, the only intelligible account of how motion is conserved and transferred from one body to another is occasionalism. The collisions between bodies thus provide occasions for a spirit (God) to re-allocate motions to bodies in accordance with some fixed set of rules. When we say that B has moved C we are therefore guilty, strictly speaking, of a misunderstanding, 'citing the occasion in place of the cause'.[63]

What about our own bodily motions? A significant proportion of them are labelled 'voluntary' because they occur in accordance with our acts of will. Is the will the true cause of such voluntary motions? 'No', replies Cordemoy: to assume that would be to repeat the same error of confusing occasion with cause. Experience teaches that such motions often follow acts of will, not that our acts of will are their true causes. Strictly speaking, the volitions of finite spirits (human souls, angels, demons) are no more true causes of the motions of bodies than are collisions with other bodies. The deficiency of power of the human soul is simply a result of its finitude and dependency; only the will of God can be a true cause. The motions of all bodies are therefore both created and sustained by God's power. He can, of course, give the direction of affairs to a subordinate, i.e. to an angel, but all that this means is that He can choose to direct His power in accordance with the angel's will, not that the angel would become a true cause in its own right.[64]

In Discourse Five, Cordemoy goes on to apply this occasionalism to the mind–body union. What it means to say that a particular mind has been 'united' to a particular body is just that systematic relations have been established by God between the thoughts of one and the movements of the other. In creating human beings, God establishes these psychophysical laws, which He never breaks. Given such an account of the causal relation, it is no harder to conceive the action of spirits on bodies, or bodies on spirits, than that of bodies on bodies.[65] If we try to model mind–body causation on body–body causation, we find ourselves asking stupid questions such as how an incorporeal thing can exert a push, but such questions reveal only our own misconceptions. Everything acts according to its nature: spirits think and will; bodies move. Experience teaches that bodies move when struck by other bodies, and that our own arms and legs usually move at will, but the former type of causal action is no more intelligible than the latter. The only intelligible account of causation is occasionalism, and this copes equally easily with mind–body and body–mind causation as with body–body causation.

If one read only the *Six Discours*, one might conclude that Cordemoy was indeed a complete and thoroughgoing occasionalist. It should be noted, however, that nowhere in the work does he discuss mind–mind causation, i.e. the power of the human mind to control (for the most part) its own thoughts. Nor does he explicitly link the doctrine of continuous creation with the thesis of complete modal determinacy, which would provide a clear demonstration that God is the direct cause of all my thoughts, feelings, and volitions. The *Six Discours* are not, however, our only source of evidence. In the second part of his *Traité de Métaphysique* Cordemoy addresses, with tantalising brevity, the question of human freedom.[66] God, he explains, is the creator of everything real in our actions, without taking away our liberty. But does this make sense? One might suppose that God re-creates my soul at t2 with modes dependent on its modes at t1. But this seems to generate a regress, and still to leave no room for freedom. Perhaps God's re-creation of the soul involves an element of modal indeterminacy? Such a theory could in principle allow space for human freedom. But was that in fact Cordemoy's opinion?

God, explains Cordemoy, incessantly propels each and every soul towards the good – this is the proper object of desire. But several alternative courses of action may appear to us as good. In such circumstances, we may experience indecision, and decide to suspend judgement. This suspension of judgement is an action on our part, as is the eventual decision to do X rather than Y. That decision could not of course be effective without God's executive power, but the action remains ours rather than God's. Two identical men, faced with the same pair of conflicting motives, might make different choices.

In the light of such remarks, one might seek to save freedom by having God merely re-create souls with a desire for the good in general, i.e. with a sort of indeterminate yearning that becomes determinate only as a result of our choices. Cordemoy's illustration, however, suggests a very different account. He supposes two equally hungry men – let us call them Smith and Jones – who have the opportunity to take some food, and a moral reason (unspecified) for refraining. God impels Smith, by way of his appetite, to take the food and eat it, and impels Jones, by way of his conscience, to refrain. We are meant to suppose that both men experience both of these conflicting motives. This suggests that God doesn't just create each soul with an indeterminate yearning for the good, but also creates it with a determinate set of motives. But if both men have both motives, what factor or factors determine which motive prevails? Does God give us conflicting desires without fixing their relative strengths? Or does our freedom reside merely in our power of suspending judgement? Do we, as it were, have an on–off switch within our control, so that we can prevent any given desire spilling over into precipitate action? Given vacillating motives, and such an on–off switch, one could account for the possibility of at least a measure of genuine freedom.

Cordemoy never answers these questions. His attempt to sketch a sort of reconciling project, showing how God's sustaining activity might be compatible with human freedom, remains too short and too vague to dispel our doubts and answer our queries. The questions he raises, however, are exactly those that would trouble Malebranche. When we come to Chapter Nine, we shall see Malebranche grappling – at much greater length and in much greater depth, if not, ultimately, with more success – with just this family of issues linking metaphysics, theology and morals. If we are to follow the argument from continuous creation to pure occasionalism, do we not inevitably find ourselves denying human freedom and making a nonsense of moral responsibility? Have we not provided every intelligent and well-informed sinner with the ultimate excuse: 'it's a fair cop, but God is to blame?'

3

THE VISION IN GOD

The argument for ideas

Malebranche's most fundamental argument for ideas turns on his oft-repeated maxim, *voir rien, ce n'est point voir*. To see nothing is not to see at all.[1] This axiom can be found in the *Recherche* (*OCM* II 99, LO 320), is repeated in the first of the *Entretiens* (*OCM* XII 35, JS 8), and re-appears in the late *Entretien d'un Philosophe Chrétien et d'un Philosophe Chinois* (*OCM* XV 5). Malebranche assumes that any perception must have an object, i.e. that the proper analysis of perception is relational.[2] But if perception always requires a really existing direct object, what are we to say about non-veridical sensory experiences? We could of course deny them the status of perceptions, but that would fly in the face of introspection. As far as phenomenology is concerned, dreams and hallucinations are indistinguishable from normal cases of sense perception. If we want to defend the *voir rien* principle and the relational analysis of perception that goes with it, we will find ourselves obliged to introduce ideas as intermediate objects, at least for cases of non-veridical perception.

Everything we see clearly, directly and immediately, says Malebranche in Book Four of the *Recherche*, necessarily exists:

> I say what we immediately see, attest to, or conceive; for to speak strictly, the objects we immediately see are very different from those we see externally, or rather from those we think we see or look at; for in one sense it is true that we do not see these latter, since we can see, or rather believe we see, external objects that are not there, notwithstanding the fact that nothingness is not perceptible. But there is a contradiction in saying that we can immediately see what does not exist, for this is to say that at the same time we see and do not see, since to see nothing is not to see.
>
> (*OCM* II 99, LO 320)

Since ideas are the objects of direct or immediate perception, they cannot be other than they appear. There is no reality–appearance distinction for ideas. They can therefore serve as bearers of phenomenal properties for non-veridical experiences. At a number of places, Malebranche trots out standard versions of the argument from illusion, taking such arguments to provide a definitive refutation of direct or 'naïve' realism about perception (*OCM* IV 73, *OCM* IX 945, *OCM* XV 5).

To avoid contradiction, says Malebranche, we must carefully distinguish the direct and immediate objects of all perception (ideas) from the indirect and mediate objects of most sense perception (bodies). The *voir rien* principle applies to the former but not to the latter. Every perception has its direct and immediate object (an idea); most sensory perceptions also have an indirect and mediate object (a body). We do not perceive bodies immediately and in themselves, we learn in the third of the *Conversations Chrétiennes*, because we often see bodies that do not exist at all (*OCM* IV 61–2).

A direct realist might respond at this point by adopting either of two different strategies. He could say that the direct object of, e.g. visual perception is usually a body but sometimes an idea. Or he could say that perception always takes a body (or at least an external object of some kind)[3] as its direct object, and that some of the mental events we take to be perceptions are simply not perceptions at all.[4] Neither of these responses would have impressed Malebranche. The Cartesian assumption of the transparency of the mental rules out the latter strategy. On Cartesian principles, I know with certainty when I am having a perception, and what I am (directly, immediately) perceiving. The possibility of error only arises when I infer from the idea that is directly present to my mind something about the external object that I naturally take to be its cause. As for the former strategy, Malebranche just seems to assume that all the objects of direct or immediate experience are of the same kind.[5] So if some are ideas, all must be ideas.

As for the possibility that bodies could be objects of immediate experience, Malebranche thinks it can be ruled out by a simple metaphysical argument. It isn't just that we need to posit ideas to provide direct objects for dreams and hallucinations; every case of perception takes an idea as its direct object. The most famous (or infamous) argument for this thesis is the 'walking soul' of the *Recherche*. Everyone must agree, Malebranche tells his readers, 'that we do not perceive objects external to us by themselves'.

We see the sun, the stars, and an infinity of objects external to us; and it is not likely that the soul should leave the body to stroll about the heavens, as it were, in order to behold all these objects. Thus, it does not see them by themselves, and our mind's immediate object when it sees the sun, for example, is not the sun, but something that is intimately joined to our soul, and this is what I call an *idea*. Thus, by the word *idea*, I mean here nothing other than the immediate object, or the object closest to the mind, when it perceives something, i.e. that which affects and modifies the mind with the perception it has of an object.

(OCM I 413–14, LO 217)

This much-derided passage[6] makes it look as if mere spatial distance were what counted, but that cannot be Malebranche's serious point. Nothing, after all, could be closer to me (spatially) than my own neurons, but I have even less awareness of these than of the sun and stars. In his reply to Arnauld's objection, Malebranche describes the walking soul argument as 'a sort of joke' (*OCM* VI 95–6). The distance between my mind and the sun is not so much spatial as ontological and – more precisely – causal (*OCM* VI 212).[7] The notion of 'presence', likewise, shifts from a literal (spatial) sense to a metaphorical (cognitive) one. The reason why the sun can't be present to my mind is not *where* it is but *what* it is. Causation requires, on Cartesian principles, some intelligible relation between cause and effect, either resemblance or some analogue of resemblance.[8] As we saw in Chapter Two, Cartesians such as La Forge and Cordemoy had already drawn the inference that bodies cannot, strictly speaking, act on our minds at all. The same moral could have been derived from Augustine, whose principles involve a natural hierarchy in which the higher (soul) can act on the lower (body) but not *vice versa*. The direct and unmediated perception of the sun by my soul would, Malebranche sees, violate both sets of principles. It would be a case of causation without intelligible connection, and it would involve a transgression of the ontological hierarchy.

When I see the sun, Malebranche concludes, the direct and immediate object of my perception is an idea. Whatever ideas may turn out to be, they must be the sort of things that can act on the human soul. This, as we shall see, will provide Malebranche with one of his key premises in his argument for the Vision in God. But what are these ideas? They are, Theodore explains in the first *Entretien*, often overlooked by unreflective men. Ideas remain, however, real beings with an existence and properties of their own. Suppose, says Theodore to his disciple Ariste, that God were to annihilate all material things except our two bodies.

> Let us further suppose that God impresses on our brains all the same traces, or rather that He presents to our minds all the same ideas we have now. On this supposition, Aristes, in which world would we spend the day? Would it not be in an intelligible world? Now, take note, it is in that world that we exist and live, although the bodies we animate live and walk in another. It is that world which we contemplate, admire, and sense. But the world which we look at or consider in turning our head in all directions, is simply matter, which is invisible in itself and has none of those beauties we admire and sense in looking at it.
>
> (*OCM* XII 38, JS 10–11)

In this passage, as elsewhere, Malebranche flirts with idealism by suggesting that bodies as such are actually invisible. When challenged on this point by Arnauld,[9] however, he beats a tactical retreat. It does not follow from my principles, he explains, that we never see bodies, only that we do not see them '*en eux-mêmes*' (*OCM* VI 101, *OCM* IX 959). We do see bodies, it now seems, but only indirectly, by means of the direct perception of their ideas. This indirect or representative realism has been the standard reading of Malebranche, from contemporaries such as Arnauld and Locke down to most of the modern commentators.[10] In the final section of this chapter we shall discuss the radical reinterpretation that has been urged by one of the finest of modern scholars. Steven Nadler now thinks (revising his own earlier view)[11] that Malebranche's account of perception is a form of direct realism.[12] Nadler's challenge, I shall argue, requires us to clarify the sort of indirect or representative realism we ascribe to Malebranche, but does not force us to re-interpret him as a direct realist.

The eliminative argument for the Vision in God

What is the ontological status of ideas? Cartesians like La Forge, Arnauld and Régis say that they are 'modes' or modifications of the substance of the soul, and add that they are, by their very nature, representations of (possible) external objects. It is here that Malebranche makes his most radical innovation in the fabric of Cartesian metaphysics. The ideas by which I perceive cannot, he contends, be modes of my own soul; rather, they must be archetypes of bodies in the all-seeing mind of God. The problem of intentionality, like the problem of causality, demands a supernatural solution.[13]

Malebranche's argument for the Vision in God occupies chapters 1–6 of Part Two of Book Three of the *Recherche* (*OCM* I 413–47, LO 217–35), and is repeated, in all essentials, in the first of the *Méditations Chrétiennes* (*OCM* X 11–18). The form of his argument is somewhat surprising, at least at first sight. It is an eliminative argument, first listing the various hypotheses that might be thought to explain how the mind knows external objects, then seeking to eliminate all but the Vision in God. Of course this argument will only work, as Malebranche admits in his reply to the criticisms of Régis, if the list is exhaustive and the refutations definitive (*OCM* XVII–1 290–1).[14] For the sake of logical completeness, we ought to list one further assumption, i.e. that the mind has knowledge of external objects at all. Without that assumption, the conclusion could only be disjunctive; either the Vision in God or scepticism.[15]

Malebranche is confident that his list is complete:[16]

> We assert the absolute necessity, then, of the following: either (a) the ideas we have of bodies and of all other objects we do not perceive by themselves come from these bodies or objects; or (b) our soul has the power of producing these ideas; or (c) God has produced them in us while creating the soul or produces them every time we think about a given object; or (d) the soul has in itself all the perfections it sees in bodies; or else (e) the soul is joined to a completely perfect being that contains all intelligible perfections, or all the ideas of created things.
>
> (*OCM* I 417, LO 219)

He sounds less confident, however, regarding the rigour of his eliminative proof of (e), which is his own hypothesis of the Vision in God:

> Perhaps we can resolve the question with some clarity though we do not pretend to give demonstrations that will seem incontrovertible to everyone; rather, we merely give proofs that will seem very persuasive to those who consider them carefully, for one would appear presumptuous were one to speak otherwise.
>
> (*OCM* I 417, LO 219)

Let us examine Malebranche's list of hypotheses, and then glance briefly at his refutations of the rivals to the Vision in God. Here is the list:

H1   External objects cause ideas in our minds by emitting their images or likenesses through the intervening medium. This is the Aristotelian theory of *species*.

H2   The soul creates its own ideas on the occasion of impressions being made on the sense organs by external objects. This is the *production* theory.

H3a   God produced all the ideas a soul will ever need and placed them 'in' the soul at the moment of its creation. This is the *storehouse* theory of the soul.

H3b   God produces in each soul just the ideas it needs on the occasions of particular patterns of stimulation of its sense organs. This is the *occasionalist* theory.

H4   The soul contains within itself all the perfections of other creatures, and can therefore know them 'in' itself. This is the *monde intelligible* theory.

H5   We see all things in God.

What is the source of this list? According to Connell, it is derived from scholastic accounts of angelic cognition, almost certainly by way of Suarez's treatise *De Angelis*.[17] The suggestion is not as far-fetched and implausible as it may seem. Although Malebranche is consistently scathing in his criticism of scholastic philosophy, hardly ever referring positively to scholastic sources, he would certainly have been familiar with mainstream authors such as Aquinas and Suarez. It is also clear that what Malebranche found objectionable in scholastic philosophy was its Aristotelian hylomorphism and its empiricism, and in particular its endorsement of the conception of the human soul as the form of the body. As a strict Cartesian dualist he could reject Aristotelian accounts of man and still draw on scholastic accounts of angels (purely immaterial substances) and angelic knowledge (completely independent of senses and sense organs) applying such accounts directly to the human soul and its cognitive powers. But even if Connell is right and the list was originally derived from Suarez, there can be no doubt that Malebranche thought it applicable to the second-generation Cartesian theories of La Forge, Arnauld, Cordemoy and Régis.

Why might Malebranche think this division exhaustive? Is there some principled basis for it? The most plausible answer I know of comes from Connell[18] and Nadler.[19] H1–H4 can be divided, says Nadler, on the following basis. H1 and H2 are (roughly) empiricist doctrines; H3 and H4 are innatist, or at least non-empiricist. (Hypothesis 3b, the occasionalist theory, can scarcely be called a form of innatism, but it is clearly non-empiricist.) In H1 and H3 the mind is passive in receiving ideas; in H2 and H4 it is active. We therefore have the following division:

H1   Empiricist and passive. External objects simply impress their image or likeness on the mind, which is like wax passively receiving an impression. This is how Malebranche understands the Aristotelian species theory.

H2   Empiricist and active. The sense-impression is still necessary, but now serves as only the occasion for the mind to exert its native power and create for itself a corresponding idea.

H3a   Innatist and passive. The mind is just a vast storehouse, stocked from its very creation by God with all the ideas it will ever require.

H3b   Neither empiricist nor innatist, and passive. Ideas are neither derived from experience nor innate, but merely created by God as and when occasion demands.

H4   Innatist and active. The mind is itself an 'intelligible world' and as such is able to discover, by searching its own nature, the properties of external things.

Malebranche's refutation of the species theory (*OCM* I 418–21, LO 220–1) is noteworthy only for its crude caricature of the theory under attack.[20] He consistently confuses the Aristotelian theory with the Epicurean, construing 'species' as little material pictures emanating in all directions from the visible body and eventually striking our eyes.[21] Malebranche rehearses a familiar battery of objections to this theory, mostly based on physical optics (perspective, interpenetration of rays, microscopes, wasting away of visible objects), but no Aristotelian would regard the critique as a fair one. Is Malebranche simply guilty of an elementary misunderstanding? Perhaps not. What he might say is that if one reasons only from clear ideas one must reject Aristotelian 'forms' and 'qualities', and accept that the physical world is purely mechanistic. On this basis he may feel entitled to state the species theory in a form that is at least intelligible, even if this intelligibility comes at the cost of easy refutation.[22] In any event, H1 is dismissed without getting a fair and sympathetic hearing.

What about H2, the production theory (*OCM* I 422–8, LO 222–5)? On this hypothesis, the external object makes an impression on the sense organs, which impression serves as the occasion for the mind to create an idea. Man thus shares in the work of creation. This theory is certainly in the offing in Descartes' critique of Regius, and in La Forge's commentary, and is ascribed by Malebranche to certain 'Cartesian gentlemen'.[23] This account, Malebranche retorts, elevates human powers too far. Ideas are real, spiritual beings, intrinsically nobler than bodies, so this view ascribes to the human soul the power to create something better than God's creation. To suggest that the mind creates the idea from the material impression is no help at all – it is unintelligible how the latter could serve as raw material for the former.

In any case, Malebranche continues, even if the soul could create its ideas, it would (like a painter) require prior familiarity with its object in order to produce a representation of it. A painter can't depict an animal he has never seen; nor could the soul create an idea without an exemplar – i.e. without a prior idea. If one already possesses the idea, one doesn't need to re-create it; if one doesn't, one cannot create it *ex nihilo* for lack of a model. This theory thus ascribes to the human soul a miraculous power to create, and even to create with wisdom and order, yet without knowing what it is doing.

As for H3a, the infinite storehouse theory of mind, it is hard to find anyone who actually held this theory.[24] We have seen in Chapter Two that it was explicitly rejected by Descartes and La Forge as a mis-understanding of innatism. The hypothesis doesn't occupy Malebranche for long (*OCM* I 429–32, LO 226–7). There are, he says, any number of types of geometrical figure, and infinite variety within each kind. There is an infinity of triangles, of quadrilaterals, of ellipses, and so on. We can think of any of these figures at will. Does it then follow that our minds must actually possess, prior to doing any geometry, ideas of them all? Is it reasonable to suppose that God, who always acts by the simplest means, should have furnished us with such a super-infinite stock of innate ideas? And if we did possess such a super-infinite stock, how would we ever find the things we needed in the infinite storehouse?

Hypothesis H3b, the occasionalist theory, has sometimes been attributed to Cordemoy.[25] It is briefly mentioned at the end of the chapter refuting the storehouse theory, as if it were merely a variant of that theory. But in fact it is a quite distinct hypothesis, and doesn't involve God trying to cram an infinity of ideas into each and every human soul in its creation. So most of the arguments against the storehouse theory don't work against the occasionalist theory. Malebranche sees the difficulty, and provides a new argument. The occasionalist theory, he tells us, is incompatible with our power to think of things at will.

> Furthermore, we must at all times actually have in us the ideas
> of all things, since we can at all times will to think about anything
> – which we could not do unless an infinite number of ideas

were present to the mind; for after all, one cannot will to think about objects of which one has no idea. Furthermore, it is clear that the idea, or immediate object of our mind, when we think about limitless space, or a circle in general, or indeterminate being, is nothing created. For no created reality can be either infinite or even general, as is what we perceive in these cases. But all this will be seen more clearly in what follows.

(*OCM* I 432, LO 227)

At first sight, Malebranche's criticism of the occasionalist theory looks inconsistent with his attack on the storehouse theory. He seems to be telling us, first, that the mind cannot have an infinite stock of ideas, and then, only a page later, that it must have an infinite stock of ideas. What he means, of course, is that the mind doesn't have all these ideas actually present as part of its own resources, but that it must have access to an infinite stock of ideas if it is to be capable of intellectual activity. As he himself says, this will become clear once the Vision in God has been explained.

What of H4, the theory that the mind contains within itself, 'eminently' (i.e. in a higher form) all the perfections of creatures, and is therefore a *monde intelligible* in its own right? This hypothesis, according to Malebranche, is the view of Arnauld[26] and Régis (*OCM* XVII–1 291).[27] Malebranche's response takes us from metaphysics into theology (*OCM* I 433–6, LO 228–9). It is certain, he says, that the soul does see some things 'in itself', but this is true only of sensations such as pain and such supposed qualities as hot and cold, colours, tastes, etc. These are perceived by the soul in itself, without ideas, but are known in this direct way precisely because they are mere modes of the soul's own substance, representing nothing at all beyond themselves. The claim made by some scholastics (and endorsed by Régis) that the human soul is itself a *monde intelligible* is dismissed by Malebranche as rash and presumptuous, a human attempt to usurp the privileges of God. All His creatures are indeed comprehended 'in' God: His intellect grasps each essence and perceives its possible instantiation; His will selects for actual existence some optimum subset of possible creatures. God therefore does know His creatures 'in Himself', i.e. He knows their essences in His intellect and their existence through His will. We, however, cannot claim to know either the essences or the real existence of things in a parallel manner.[28]

Having dismissed the rival theories as lacking any plausibility, Malebranche can go on to set out his positive view, the Vision in God. God, you will remember, re-creates all His creatures continuously, and does so in full awareness of what He is doing. It follows that there is something 'in' God that represents each creature. We also know that there is a peculiarly intimate union between the divine mind and human minds.

> Given these two things, the mind surely can see what in God represents created beings, since what in God represents created beings is very spiritual, intelligible, and present to the mind. Thus, the mind can see God's works in Him, provided that God wills to reveal to it what in Him represents them.
>
> (*OCM* I 437, LO 230)

God's wisdom, says Malebranche, is manifest in the production of great effects by the simplest means. Since God can make a created mind see X simply by revealing to it His idea of X, He doesn't have to pack an infinity of innate ideas into each and every created finite mind, as the storehouse theory H3a requires. Nor does He have to intervene in an *ad hoc* manner, as required by hypothesis H3b. His ideas are always at our disposal, so long as we ask the right questions in the right manner.

Just as occasionalism emphasises the causal dependence of all creatures on the divine will, so the Vision in God emphasises our absolute cognitive dependence on the divine intellect. Just as I have no real causal powers of my own, but can only invoke His aid to move my own body, so I have no real cognitive powers of my own, but must invoke His aid in order to understand anything at all. In the final analysis, all knowledge is revelation, and attention to a problem (e.g. in mathematics) is just a form of prayer. Illumination always comes from without.

Thus far Malebranche's argument for the Vision in God has scarcely been overpowering. He has dismissed rival accounts of ideas as lacking in plausibility, and has ascribed to his own theory a couple of theological advantages, emphasising the wisdom of God (achieving the greatest ends by the simplest means) and our cognitive dependence on Him. Does he have any positive philosophical grounds for his theory?

The strongest philosophical reason for accepting the Vision in God is, we are told, the following. When I want to think of an object I must, as it were, cast my mind's eye over all objects – they must all be 'present' to me at once if I am to find what I am looking for. But this infinite capacity would not be possible except via the 'union' of my mind with the all-encompassing mind of God:

> It is certain, and everyone knows this from experience, that when we want to think about some particular thing, we first glance

over all beings and then apply ourselves to the consideration of the object we wish to think about. Now, it is indubitable that we could desire to see a particular object only if we had already seen it, though in a general and confused fashion. As a result of this, given that we can desire to see all things, now one, now another, it is certain that all beings are present to our mind; and it seems that all beings can be present to our mind only because God, i.e. He who includes all things in the simplicity of His being, is present to it.

(*OCM* I 440–1, LO 232)

We could present this as a transcendental argument in the Kantian manner. We all have a certain infinite capacity to think of whatever we choose. How is this capacity possible? Only, says Malebranche, by means of the Vision in God. Therefore the Vision in God is true. This is valid, but everything turns on the second premise, for which Malebranche provides no additional support.

The Vision in God is also invoked by Malebranche to explain how the mind can possess general ideas, and how it can possess the idea of infinity in particular. Once again, we can see Malebranche as providing a quasi-Kantian argument from the existence of a science like pure mathematics to the Vision in God as its necessary condition.[29] The argument is plainly Augustinian in its ancestry.[30] But for Augustine the Vision in God is a theory of pure intellection only, an account of how we can know the eternal truths. Malebranche wants to extend the doctrine to the knowledge we possess, through sense perception, of changeable and corruptible things. God creates such things, so it follows that He must have knowledge of them. This knowledge need not, of course, resemble our sensory awareness. When I see a body like the sun, my perception consists of *idée pure* (a circular figure) and *sentiment* (yellow). God causes the *sentiment* in my soul but doesn't share it; God discloses the *idée pure* which is 'in' Him as its archetype. What I see is the idea (the circle), but I find myself spontaneously 'projecting' the yellow (which is just a sensation) onto the object. I therefore see the object yellow-ly, as it were.[31]

The argument from properties

Malebranche never abandoned the eliminative argument for the Vision in God. It is repeated in successive editions of the *Recherche*, reproduced in the *Méditations Chrétiennes* (1683), and explicitly defended in the

Réponse à M. Régis (1693). He may vacillate regarding whether the eliminative argument provides a conclusive proof or merely a plausible argument, but he never retracts or qualifies his commitment to its validity. In his later writings, however, the eliminative argument for the Vision in God is supplemented (and, increasingly, supplanted) by a further argument which we can label the 'argument from properties'[32] .

The target of the argument from properties is the account of ideas common to the mainstream second-generation Cartesians (La Forge, Arnauld, Régis). As we saw in Chapter Two, the emerging consensus among these Cartesians was that ideas should be identified with perceptions. Such mental acts are modifications or 'modes' of the substance of the soul. These modes are essentially representative; they are, by their very nature, representations of actual and possible objects. On this theory, intentionality is the mark of the mental, and is regarded as simply a brute and irreducible fact about the mental, not something susceptible to further explanation. In creating minds, God has created substances whose modes are representations – there is nothing more to say. Malebranche, not surprisingly, identifies this position with his H4, the *monde intelligible* of the eliminative argument. One way to regard the argument from properties is therefore as an *ad hominem* continuation of the eliminative argument. If it is agreed that the earlier hypotheses H1–H3 are untenable, then only H4 (the *monde intelligible*) and H5 (the Vision in God) are left standing. A refutation of H4 would then provide a proof – subject to the usual provisos of eliminative arguments in general – of H5.

Malebranche's argument against the identification of ideas with modes of the soul is quite straightforward in form. If one wants to prove that $X \neq Y$, one must prove that X has some property that Y lacks, or *vice versa*. So if we list the properties of ideas, then the properties of modes of the soul, and find that the properties of ideas are quite distinct from and incompatible with the properties of modes of the soul, we have the desired proof of a real distinction.

This argument can be found clearly spelled out in Book Four, Chapter Eleven, of the *Recherche*, in *Éclaircissement* X, and in the first of the *Entretiens sur la Métaphysique*. There are, says Malebranche, a number of ways of proving that ideas are distinct from perceptions:

> For it is clear that the soul's modes are changeable but ideas are immutable; that its modes are particular, but ideas are universal and general to all intelligences; that its modes are contingent, but ideas are eternal and necessary; that its modes are obscure and shadowy, but ideas are very clear and luminous (i.e. its modes are

only obscurely, though vividly, felt, but ideas are clearly known as the foundation of all the sciences); that these ideas are indeed efficacious because they act in the mind, they enlighten it and make it happy or unhappy, which is evident by the pain that the idea of the hand causes in those who have had an arm cut off.

(*OCM* II 103, LO 322–3)

The argument re-appears in a somewhat different guise in *Éclaircissement* X, where Malebranche is arguing for the existence of a universal reason shared by all minds:

I am certain that the ideas of things are immutable, and that eternal laws and truths are necessary – it is impossible that they should not be as they are. Now, I see nothing in me of a necessary or immutable nature – I am able not to be, or not to be such as I am; there might be minds unlike me, yet I am certain that there can be no mind that sees truths and laws different from those I see – for every mind necessarily sees that twice two is four, and that one's friend is to be valued more than one's dog. It must be concluded, then, that the reason consulted by all minds is an immutable and necessary Reason.

(*OCM* III 130, LO 613–14)

In the first of the *Entretiens*, Ariste has difficulty grasping the reality of the realm of ideas, and suggests that the contents of the intelligible world simply lapse back into nothingness when one is not actually thinking of them. If this were true, Theodore retorts, ideas would indeed be '*peu de chose*':

True, Aristes. If you gave being to your ideas, if an idea requires but the blink of an eye to annihilate it, it is indeed a slight thing. However, if they are eternal, immutable, necessary, in a word, divine – I mean the intelligible extension from which they are formed – surely they will be more considerable than that matter which is inefficacious and absolutely invisible by itself.

(*OCM* XII 40, JS 12)

Our perceptions are modes of our souls, and are contingent, fleeting, changeable things, readily altered or even annihilated. Ideas are eternal, immutable, and necessarily existent. They are also, in an important sense, 'infinite',[33] whereas modes of our souls are finite particulars. If relations of ideas like 2 + 2 = 4 are necessary and eternal truths, the constituent ideas themselves must be eternal and necessary. But if so, they cannot be identified with our perceptions.

When challenged by Arnauld on this point, Malebranche invokes the Christian Platonism of Augustine.[34] According to Augustine, we are told, ideas are eternal, immutable, necessarily existent and common to all spirits – i.e. wholly distinct from the modes of human souls. Ideas, for Augustine, are:

> … certain stable and immutable first models or archetypes of all things, which have not been created, and which in consequence are eternal and remain always the same in the eternal Wisdom which contains them.
>
> (*OCM* IX 915)

The preface of the 1696 edition of the *Entretiens* involves another sustained attempt to invoke the authority of Augustine.[35] Since the Vision in God appears paradoxical to many readers, writes Malebranche, I thought it best to remind readers of Augustine's notion of ideas as the eternal and immutable archetypes of all creatures (*OCM* XII 10–11). God needs no model external to Himself to create the universe, and knows the universe He has created simply by His immediate familiarity with His own perfections, in which creatures participate. For Augustine, then, ideas (archetypes in the mind of God) are quite distinct from perceptions (modes of our souls). I admit, says Malebranche, that Augustine's version of the Vision in God only applies to our knowledge of eternal and necessary truths (arithmetic, geometry, morality), but if he had been aware of seventeenth-century advances in natural philosophy he would have extended his theory and arrived at my conclusions (*OCM* XII 17–18).

If ideas are divine archetypes, then by having access to ideas we can gain knowledge of things. Certain types of sceptical objection can be laid to rest once and for all. It is, after all, logically impossible that a creature should fail to conform to God's idea of it, which is the model or archetype after which it was (and is) created.[36] On this Platonist theory, an idea is not a copy of a thing, capable of greater or lesser fidelity to the original; on the contrary, the thing is a copy of its idea, and cannot (because of continuous creation) depart from the original. This epistemological advantage of the Vision in God would be emphasised by Malebranche in his polemical exchanges with Arnauld.

The contrast Malebranche emphasises is between ideas on the one hand and all the modes of the soul on the other. The most obvious and striking modes of the soul are of course sensations, but there are also pure perceptions, inclinations and habits. Pure perceptions are the modifications our souls undergo when we become aware of ideas. Malebranche notes their existence, as he must, but has little to say about them because, as he says, they don't deeply affect the soul, and have no characteristic phenomenology.[37] When I am deep in thought about the properties of the circle or the requirements of justice it is the idea that occupies my consciousness; my own act of awareness is as it were transparent. But all modes of the soul (sensations, pure perceptions, inclinations, and habits) are contingent (as modes of a contingent substance, they could hardly be otherwise), changeable, and capable of ceasing to be. As such they all fall equally within the scope of Malebranche's argument.

The contrast between ideas and sensations is therefore, for Malebranche, no more than a corollary of his general distinction between ideas on the one hand and all modes of the soul on the other. The idea-sensation antithesis is, nevertheless, central to Malebranche's account of the soul and self-knowledge. On the Cartesian theory, our soul contains ideas of sizes, shapes and motions, which are 'clear and distinct', and ideas of colours, sounds, tastes, smells, etc, which are confused. It is natural, on such a theory, to think of all these ideas as representations, and to think of their clarity and distinctness as admitting degrees. A modern reader might think of photographs taken in better or worse light, from close up or far away, in good or bad focus. Malebranche will have none of this. He insists on a sharp contrast between sensations, which are modes of our souls and represent nothing beyond themselves, and ideas, which are 'in' God and represent objects.[38] His rejection of the *monde intelligible* hypothesis H4 thus carries with it an absolute denial of the thesis that intentionality is the mark of the mental.[39] All I can tell when I have a sensation such as hot or cold, red or blue is that my soul is capable of being modified in such a way. When I think of a triangle, a square or a circle, by contrast, I gain knowledge of the real properties of material creatures, actual or possible. But I gain this knowledge by way of the idea itself (the archetype in the divine intellect), not by way of the mode of my soul which is my pure perception of that idea.

Intelligible extension

Malebranche's theory is clearly a Christian version of Platonism, identifying ideas with archetypes in the divine intellect. This would suggest that God's ideas are universals: that His mind contains the ideas or forms of Cat, Dog,

Horse and Cow, but not ideas of each individual cat or dog, horse or cow. But the theory of creation pulls in the opposite direction. It is individual cats and dogs, horses and cows that God created in the beginning and continues to sustain in being. Since He must know what He is doing, He must have ideas of each and every individual creature. This objection was urged by Arnauld,[40] and has been endorsed by Gueroult.[41]

But if God has ideas of each and every individual creature, and it is these ideas which are the immediate objects of our experience, all manner of bizarre and counterintuitive conclusions follow. Since, on this view, every creature has its idea, the intelligible world becomes as complex, confused and changeable as the material world. The moon illusion provides a good illustration of this point. As I watch the moon sail across the heavens, I see it as larger at the horizon than when directly overhead. The direct or immediate object of my experience (the idea) is the bearer of these phenomenal properties. So the idea, we would have to infer, is itself changeable. But astronomy teaches us that the moon does not in fact change in size. So if God has an idea of the moon it seems that it must both stay the same size (to serve as the model or archetype of an unchanging object) and vary in size (to serve as the direct object of our experience). A contradiction threatens to open up in the Malebranchian theory of ideas. Similar objections can be raised for any number of cases of perceptual illusion and perceptual relativity.

This objection is raised and addressed in *Éclaircissement* X of the *Recherche* (*OCM* III 151–5, LO 626–8), which marks a significant modification in Malebranche's account of ideas. Although nothing 'in' God is actually figured or mobile, He must be able to understand figured and mobile things 'in' Himself:

> But to clarify this matter, it must be realized that God contains in Himself an ideal or intelligible infinite extension; for since He has created it, God knows extension, and He can know it only in Himself.
>
> (*OCM* III 151–2, LO 626)

For the entire material creation, a single idea or archetype, *étendue intelligible*, is sufficient. Since God created the entire material universe *ex nihilo*, and understood what He was doing, He must have had a model or archetype in His mind, and this is intelligible extension. The point is repeated in the controversy with Arnauld (*OCM* VI 117) and in the second *Entretien* (*OCM* XII 51, JS 21). Given this single idea of intelligible extension, God sees all possible material creatures as modes or modifications of extension. That is, He sees how extension must be modified to produce sun and moon, trees and flowers, cats and dogs. The infinite intellect of God thus contains all possible material creatures, and all possible material universes, simply by having the idea of intelligible extension. The actualisation of some subset of all these possible creatures depends of course on the will of God, which brings about an optimal expression of the divine attributes.[42]

Malebranche goes on, in *Éclaircissement* X, to explain what happens when we see particular bodies, and how we can observe change and motion when the intelligible realm is eternal and immutable. We see a given body, he explains,

> ... when its idea, i.e. when some figure composed of intelligible and general extension, becomes sensible and particular through color or some other sensible perception by which its idea affects the soul and that the soul ascribes to it, for the soul almost always projects its sensation on an idea that strikes it in lively fashion. Therefore, there need be in God no sensible bodies or real figures in intelligible extension in order for us to see them in God or in order for God to see them in Himself. It is enough that His substance, insofar as it can be participated in by the corporeal creature, should be able to be perceived in different ways.
>
> (*OCM* III 152, LO 626)

For me to see the full moon, all that is required is to perceive a circular portion of intelligible extension silver-ly, i.e. for that sensation of colour (actually a mode of the soul) to be 'projected' onto a suitable part of *étendue intelligible*. When the moon is at the horizon human viewers will perceive a greater portion of intelligible extension silver-ly than when it is overhead. A similar account will handle our perception of motion:

> Likewise, if, as it were, a figure of intelligible extension made sensible by color should be taken successively from different parts of this intelligible extension, or if a figure of intelligible extension could be perceived as turning on its center or as gradually approaching another, we would perceive motion in an intelligible or sensible figure without there being any actual motion in intelligible extension.
>
> *OCM* III 152, LO 627)

Intelligible extension is like a blank canvas or cinema screen onto which different sensations are projected. For me to see a cricket ball is just to see a circular portion of intelligible extension red-ly. To see the cricket ball flying across my visual field is just for me to see successive circular portions of intelligible extension red-ly. Motion can thus be represented 'in' intelligible extension without literally being present there. Since all the parts of intelligible extension are perfectly homogeneous, 'they may all represent any body whatsoever'. Once we understand this, says Malebranche, we will see that:

> It should not be imagined that the intelligible world is related to the sensible, material world in such a way that there is an intelligible sun, for example, or an intelligible horse or tree intended to represent to us the sun or a horse or a tree, or that everyone who sees the sun necessarily sees this hypothetical intelligible sun.
>
> (*OCM* III 153, LO 627)

Arnauld thought that Malebranche had simply abandoned his earlier theory of particular ideas and replaced it with the completely different and incompatible theory of intelligible extension.[43] This accusation is echoed by some of the commentators.[44] Malebranche replies that the theory of intelligible extension is a clarification of his earlier position, not a rejection of it. This opinion too has found support among the commentators.[45] What matters, however, is not Malebranche's alleged change of mind but how the new theory is meant to work. Intelligible extension, although it doesn't actually contain within itself all material creatures, contains them virtually, in the sense that it contains the means of engendering or constructing them.[46] But, as a number of the commentators note, particular ideas don't drop out of the story.[47] Malebranche continues to speak, for example, of the ideal arm of the amputee (e.g. at *OCM* XIX 910), or of my ideal hand affecting my soul with ideas of both warmth and colour (*OCM* XVII–1 287–8). So Malebranche's theory involves both *étendue intelligible* (the archetype or blueprint of all possible bodies) and ideas of the particular bodies which are the objects of our experience. Is this consistent?

Malebranche, it should be clear, needs both the single 'infinite' idea of *étendue intelligible*, and the many 'finite' ideas of particular created things. The former is timelessly present in the divine intellect; the latter exist – with appropriate temporal qualifiers – in the divine will. Since the divine will is not blind, God must, as Arnauld insisted, have ideas of particulars.

The idea of *étendue intelligible* is a precondition of all ideas of bodies, but it could never serve as a substitute for them. When we do geometry, we consult intelligible extension alone, conceiving of triangles, squares and circles merely as possible modes of extension.[48] In our experience of bodies, by contrast, intelligible extension is necessary but not sufficient: we also need ideas of particulars, impressed on our souls through a sort of natural revelation of the divine will.

What we see when we see a body is intelligible extension, 'painted' red or green or blue by the projection of a mode of our own souls. As Theodore explains in the third of the *Conversations Chrétiennes*, 'It is evident that to see a body is nothing else but to be modified with different sensations of colour by diverse parts of intelligible extension' (*OCM* IV 75).

As Malebranche explains to Régis, we visually distinguish and differentiate bodies by their colours. To make such judgements requires that 'the idea of extension, according to its different parts, modifies my soul, here with one colour and there with another' (*OCM* XVII–1 281).

It would be easy to cite any number of passages in which Malebranche speaks of the *parts* of intelligible extension, and uses the notion to explain, for example, our capacity to distinguish and differentiate objects, our susceptibility to perceptual illusions, and our perception of motion. The most natural reading of such passages is to think of *étendue intelligible* as a blank canvas, or, if you prefer, a featureless block of marble awaiting the sculptor's chisel.[49] But Malebranche firmly and explicitly denies that intelligible extension itself consists of spatial parts, i.e. that it is itself literally extended. In the first of the *Three Letters* to Arnauld he insists that the 'intelligible places' where the soul sees colours are not real places. The greater parts do not occupy more space than the smaller, because they do not occupy space at all (*OCM* VI 211–12). In the fourth of the *Entretiens* Theodore takes some pains to distinguish material spaces from intelligible spaces. The spaces we see, he maintains, 'are simply intelligible spaces which fill no place (*OCM* XII 95, JS 58).' 'I never', Malebranche writes in response to Arnauld, 'thought that the idea of length, breadth and depth was itself long and broad and deep' (*OCM* VI 242).[50]

We appear by now to have arrived at a hopeless tangle. Malebranche frequently employs the blank canvas analogy, and speaks freely of parts or portions of intelligible extension. This is not a mere lapse or aberration on his part, but an essential aspect of his explanatory theory, his attempt to extend the Vision in God to our ordinary sensory perceptions of bodies. But when challenged by Arnauld he insists that he never dreamed that intelligible extension itself consists of spatial parts. Intelligible extension is the idea of matter, the archetype God consults in His ongoing creation of matter. It must therefore contain, for Malebranche, all the perfections of matter, albeit in an 'eminent' or higher form. Its parts, he insists in reply to his critics, are intelligible parts and not spatial parts.[51]

The problem is, of course, that at the conceptual level the idea of extension does not consist of parts at all. There is not the least reason to suspect that the concept of extension is subject to further analysis, and every reason to regard it as a primitive. Malebranche, it appears, has been guilty of an illegitimate slide from ideatum to idea. It belongs to the concept of extension that any instance of extension will consist of parts. It does not follow that the concept consists of 'intelligible' parts, or that these stand in some sort of isomorphism with the spatial parts of the body.[52] Malebranche's critics sense that he is floundering at this point, and move in like sharks for the kill. Foucher thinks that resemblance is a necessary condition for representation, and hence that the theory of ideas requires something like the blank canvas theory, with spatial relations represented by spatial relations.[53] Arnauld thinks that Malebranche has identified intelligible extension with God's immensity, and thus made God literally extended.[54] Locke finds it inconceivable that something spiritual (and hence unextended) should represent an extended thing[55] . And Malebranche's last critic, De Mairan, suggests that Malebranche's theory slides into Spinozism (*OCM* XIX 861). If *étendue intelligible* is infinite and eternal and necessarily existent, De Mairan asks, and is the archetype of matter, why isn't matter infinite and eternal and necessary?

There is no way to save Malebranche's theory as it stands. The reason is simple. He requires intelligible extension to play two distinct and incompatible roles. On the one hand, it is the logical concept of extension, which is not the sort of thing that could intelligibly be said to be extended. If it consisted of parts at all, they would be conceptual parts (as 'animal' is a part of 'bear' and 'male' is a part of 'bachelor'), but there is no reason to suppose it consists of parts in this sense. Possession of this concept is a necessary but not a sufficient condition for certain types of perceptual experience. On the other hand, intelligible extension plays a role akin to the Kantian notion of space as the pure form of outer intuition, i.e. as an *a priori* particular and not a concept at all. It is particulars, Kant reminded us, that divide into parts, and Malebranche's blank canvas analogy positively lends itself to interpretation as an *a priori* particular. Lacking Kant's doctrine of space, and his associated distinction between pure and schematised concepts, Malebranche could not help but fall into confusion.[56]

Efficacious ideas

Malebranche's attempts to explain how the divine archetypes can act on our minds lead, according to Martial Gueroult, not to a clear solution but to a 'labyrinth'.[57] How, for example, does *étendue intelligible* produce our perceptions of bodies? We can represent the action as that of the idea as such, as distinct from the substance of God and of the other archetypes. On this account, the effect is conceivable, but not the manner of the causal action. Or we can say that God Himself is the cause. Here the causal action is intelligible, but not the effect – it is after all intelligible extension that we see, not the substance of God Himself. Malebranche wants to maintain both that God and God alone acts on my soul when I perceive, but also that the Vision in God is not a Vision of God. Can these two theses be reconciled?

According to Robinet, Malebranche came increasingly to stress the first of Gueroult's two models at the expense of the second. This theory of efficacious ideas, we are told, is Malebranche's preferred model from 1695.[58] Ideas are characterised not just as eternal, immutable and necessarily existent, but as efficacious, i.e. as possessing precisely the power of acting on our souls that is denied to bodies. To see a body, Malebranche writes in his *Réponse à M. Régis*, written in 1693 and included in the 1700 and 1712 editions of the *Recherche*, is:

> ... to have present to the mind the idea of extension which touches it or modifies it with different colours: for one does not see them [bodies] directly or immediately in themselves.
>
> (*OCM* XVII–1 282)

When I speak of extension, he continues, I mean intelligible extension, the archetype of matter: 'For it is clear that material extension cannot act efficaciously and directly in our minds. It is absolutely invisible of itself' (*OCM* XVII–1 283).

In a letter to De Mairan from the last year of Malebranche's life, the causal agency of ideas is still more clearly highlighted:

> It is the idea of the hand that affects with pain the soul of the amputee: the *ideatum*, that is to say the hand, no longer exists, it has been eaten by worms. It is the idea of a spectre which frightens a madman, its *ideatum* does not exist at all.
>
> (*OCM* XIX 910)

But the theory of efficacious ideas only raises further questions. How, Jolley asks, can an abstract object like an idea have causal powers?[59] And what, Nadler asks, is the ontological status of these ideas?[60] Are they substances or modes? How do they relate to the substance of God?

In his refutation of the 'production' theory, Malebranche was wary about specifying the precise ontological status of ideas. They are, he insists, 'real beings', and real beings of a 'spiritual' nature, superior to bodies and beyond our power to create (*OCM* I 423, LO 222). If my critic objects that an idea is not a substance, he writes, I would agree – but it is still a 'spiritual thing', and a spiritual thing can neither be created by the human soul *ex nihilo* nor made from a material thing (an impression on the sense organs).

In the first of the *Three Letters* to Arnauld, the status of intelligible extension is explicitly addressed. Notwithstanding the axioms of the philosophers, we are told, it is neither a mode nor a substance (*OCM* VI 245). This is a puzzling remark. Other philosophers of the seventeenth century (e.g. Gassendi and Locke) challenged the metaphysics of substance and mode, but Malebranche is generally faithful in his allegiance to it.[61] So why does he appear to depart from it in this case? Ideas, Malebranche thinks, cannot be modes of God because God's substance is not susceptible to modification (*OCM* III 149, LO 625).[62] And we cannot simply identify ideas with the substance of God, for a number of reasons. To see an idea is not to see God. And to see one idea (e.g. *étendue intelligible*) is not to see another (e.g. the archetype of the human soul). But if A is identical to B and B is identical to C, A is identical to C. But if Malebranche has reasons not to identify ideas with the substance of God, he also has pressing reasons forcing him to make that identification. Ideas act on the soul. But only God can act on the soul. So ideas cannot be really distinct from God.[63]

Malebranche's final attempt to extricate himself from this apparent contradiction is to say that ideas can be identified with the substance of God, but with an all-important qualification. God's ideas, he tells us in the preface to the *Entretiens*, are 'nothing more than the essence of God, insofar as creatures can imitate it or participate in it' (*OCM* XII 12).[64] Intelligible extension, for example, is 'the substance of God as representative of body' (*OCM* XII 184, JS 136–7). Every creature must participate, more or less, in one or more of the divine perfections – it is not just man who was created in the image of God (*OCM* IV 64). In creating the human soul, as in the creation of matter, God needs only to look to His own perfections to find intelligible archetypes. The point is expressed most clearly – with a rare reference to Aquinas – in Chapter Eleven of Book Four of the *Recherche*:

> God knows the nature of the soul clearly because He finds in Himself a clear and representative idea of it. God, as Saint Thomas says, knows His substance or His essence perfectly, and as a result He discovers all the ways in which created things can participate in His substance. Hence His substance is truly representative of the soul, because it contains its eternal model or archetype. For God can only draw His knowledge from Himself.
>
> (*OCM* II 97–8, LO 319)

Arnauld thinks that Malebranche's theory entails the impossible conclusion that we do indeed see God, i.e. that the Vision *in* God collapses into a Vision *of* God.[65] If what we perceive is an intelligible world of ideas, and these ideas are not really distinct from God, then surely we are seeing God? Malebranche had already done his best to address this problem in his replies to objections in *Éclaircissement* X of the *Recherche*. The fourth objection quotes Saint John to the effect that no one has seen God. Malebranche replies that:

> I answer that seeing His creatures in Him is not really seeing God. Seeing the essences of creatures in His substance is not seeing His essence, just as merely seeing the objects it represents is not seeing a mirror. Seeing the essence of God, not in its absolute being, but in relation to creatures or insofar as it is representative of them, is not seeing the essence of God.
>
> (*OCM* III 155, LO 628)

So ideas are God, but only insofar as His essence is participable or imperfectly imitable by creatures (*OCM* III 149, LO 625). The point is repeated in the *Réponse à M. Régis* (*OCM* XVII–1 293). If forced to say whether ideas are substances or modes, we must say they belong to the category of substance, since God is a substance and they are not really distinct from God.[66] He could not exist without His perfections, nor without perfect knowledge (a) of those perfections and (b) of the capacity of creatures to participate in them. So He could not exist without the ideas of creatures. But the ideas could not exist without Him. So there is no real distinction between God and his ideas. Gueroult's two models, contrasting God's action with efficacious ideas, are just two different ways of saying the same thing. In the final analysis, he has hit on a distinction without a difference.

How much sense can we make of this doctrine? The continual references to participation sound Platonic, and bring back thoughts of Plato's forms. But this in turn only revives age-old worries about self-predication. The form of F, Plato thought, was 'the F itself'; other things are more or less F by participation in the form. But Malebranche explicitly denies self-predication – at least in the case of intelligible extension.[67] The form or idea of extension is not itself extended, not something that could intelligibly be said to be long or broad or deep. So how can it be the form, model, or archetype of extension? How can God, as it were, look to the model and say to Himself 'I'll create something *like* that'? What can 'like' mean in such a context? Malebranche says that the ideas of things 'resemble them in some manner', but then denies the obvious interpretation of resemblance.[68] He will of course say that extension is present in God not formally but eminently, i.e. in a higher form. He can insist on the orthodoxy of his position, and quote Aquinas. God is Himself unextended, but He creates extended things. But God must know (i.e. understand) what He is doing in creation. So there must be *something* in God that represents extension to Him. The premises of this argument are impeccably orthodox; the inference seems valid. But the conclusion is only a thin, almost skeletal existential claim, of no explanatory power. We seem to have arrived at the limits of our comprehension.

In the case of intelligible extension, we might begin to develop – albeit speculatively – a reply along the following lines. In the infinite intellect of God there are no figures, only equations. While human minds naturally turn to geometry, God prefers algebra and analysis. In creating circular bodies, He looks to the formula $a^2 + b^2 = r^2$, not to any literally extended model. But the mathematical formula does 'resemble' the geometrical figure in the crucial sense that it contains what is intelligible about the latter. So Malebranche can defend what I called an Epistemological Intelligibility Principle (EIP) while rejecting Watson's Epistemological Likeness Principle (ELP). Unfortunately, this only gets us so far. In creating the bodies of the solar system, God looks to the formula of the sphere and not to a three-dimensional model or set of blueprints. But He must still say to Himself, 'The system will consist of nine of these (approximate) spheres in elliptical orbits about a larger central sphere'. The formula for the sphere can be present in the divine intellect without extension, but could the plans of the whole solar system be just a more complex set of mathematical equations? Even if this were possible, such a vast and complex formula would provide only the blueprint for a possible material creation. The actual creation of concrete particulars is a matter for God's will rather than His intellect, and this will – if it is not to be blind – seems to require ideas of particulars.

Nadler's Malebranche

In *Malebranche and Ideas*, Steven Nadler has challenged the traditional view of Malebranche as an indirect realist, an advocate of a representative theory of perception.[69] Malebranche's ideas, Nadler claims, are not the sense data of the empiricists; rather, they are logical concepts. To have an idea of X is not to have a little picture of X before the mind's eye; it is to comprehend the essential properties of X, and thus to see what properties X must possess and what properties X cannot possess. The negative part of this case is clearly correct. Whatever Malebranche's ideas are, they cannot be sense data. Any merely sensible image present to the mind's eye would just be a mental particular, not a source of insight into necessary and universal truths. But Nadler's positive claim – that ideas are logical concepts, or sets of necessary and sufficient conditions – involves, to my mind, just too much special pleading and selective reading of the texts.[70] Could all the commentators, from Arnauld and Locke down to Nadler himself in his earlier book, have been so mistaken for so long? And how is Nadler going to explain away all those passages[71] in which Malebranche does represent ideas as direct or immediate objects of quasi-visual perception? There are just too many places in which Malebranche speaks of ideal arms and legs, an ideal sun and moon – i.e. ideal particulars – as immediate objects of perception.

On Nadler's reading, Malebranche's theory of ideas is primarily an account of pure intellection, and the relation between idea, mind and object is a cognitive one – to have an idea of X is to know the properties of X.[72] For pure intellection, the Nadler interpretation seems to work well. But to apply his interpretation to Malebranche's account of sense perception, Nadler finds himself having to torture the text. Malebranche says, for example, that we do not see bodies 'immediately' and 'in themseves'; rather, we see them by the mediation of ideas. What this means, says Nadler, is that sense perception involves judgement, and judgement requires concepts, i.e. that we couldn't see shapes unless we had the concept of extension and of its possible modifications. Nadler's Malebranche is thus a sort of precursor of Kant, reminding his readers that perceptions without concepts are blind.

Now I have no quarrels with the truth of all this. Perception does involve judgement; judgement does require concepts. Nor is it a thought that would have been alien to a Cartesian – indeed, it is precisely what Descartes was trying to show in the famous example of the wax in the second *Meditation*. But this insistence on the central role of concepts in sense perception cannot be all that Malebranche had in mind. In the first place, Malebranche's denial that we see bodies 'immediately' and 'in themselves' is clearly meant to be contrastive. Bodies are not, but ideas are, the objects of such immediate awareness. And logical concepts just aren't the right sort of things to serve this role. If we are to have an account of perception that can do justice to the phenomena, there is no getting away from an ideal realm consisting of sensible particulars.

To extend the theory of ideas from the intellect to the senses Malebranche needs some Kantian apparatus that he simply does not possess. He needs space as a 'form of intuition', an *a priori* particular that is simply 'given' to the perceiving mind rather than grasped through concepts. And he needs the Kantian notions of schemata and schematized concepts. On this view, seeing a triangle in the mind's eye is not just a matter of possessing a concept, but of exhibiting it to intuition by a process of construction.[73] The logical concept still serves a role (e.g. guaranteeing universality) but it is schematised concepts that I will be employing all the time in my perceptual judgements. I don't claim, of course, that Malebranche had all this Kantian apparatus (although there are important constructivist strands in seventeenth-century mathematics), merely that I don't see how his theory can work without it.

To account for the role of the understanding in visual perception, we will need, it seems, a threefold distinction between ideas(l) or logical concepts, ideas(s) or schematised concepts, and ideas(v) or visible particulars, which are schematised concepts made manifest to sight by means of colour. Without ideas(s) there could be no ideas(v); I cannot see the sun as a yellow circle in the sky without the capacity to imagine a circle. Without ideas(l) there can be no ideas(s); I cannot mark out a circle in my mind's eye unless I possess the pure concept of extension, *étendue intelligible*. Malebranche, of course, nowhere makes these distinctions, but his theory cannot work without them.

In conclusion, we can learn much from Nadler, and endorse many of his insights, without accepting his central contention that Malebranche is a direct realist about sense perception. He is right to deny that Malebranche's ideas are like the sense data of the empiricists. If Malebranche comes close to any form of idealism, it is Kantian rather than Berkeleyan. He is right to emphasise that Malebranche's theory of ideas is primarily an account of the intellect, and only secondarily applied to sense perception. This puts Malebranche squarely in a tradition stemming from Plato via Augustine. And he is right to stress the role of the understanding, and hence of concepts, in the processes of discrimination, recognition and anticipation that are integral to sense perception. But Nadler cannot be right to deny that, for Malebranche, the direct or immediate object of perception is an intelligible world of intelligible particulars, the existence of which is logically independent of the material world of material particulars.[74] The texts simply will not bear such an interpretation.

4

THE DISPUTE WITH ARNAULD OVER THE NATURE OF IDEAS

Malebranche's early relations with the Port Royal group were amicable, with Arnauld in particular responding favourably to the *Recherche* on its first appearance in 1674.[1] Arnauld clearly hoped to draw the promising young philosopher into a Cartesian–Augustinian–Jansenist alliance against the Aristotelian–Thomist–Jesuit traditions of the schools.[2] In the light of Malebranche's later works, this might seem to have been a forlorn hope. But the views of the early Malebranche, as Robinet has shown,[3] were close to Jansenism in a number of important respects. At this stage, Malebranche still accepted the omnipotent but inscrutable '*Dieu caché*' of the Jansenists, and was correspondingly wary about the incursion of philosophical rationalism into theology.

The publication in 1678 of the *Éclaircissements* to the *Recherche* marked a radical change in the situation, and precipitated the final and definitive rupture between Malebranche and the Jansenists. In *Éclaircissement* VIII Malebranche launched an outright attack on the voluntarism of the Jansenists, arguing that such a position 'overthrows everything', science, religion and morality alike (*OCM* III 84, LO 586). A God worthy of the name must rule by Wisdom, not by mere omnipotent Will. His volitions must be in accordance with an Order that is in principle accessible to all minds.[4] It follows, says Malebranche in *Éclaircissement* XV, that God's actions in the domain of grace, as in that of nature, must be in accordance with *volontés générales* rather than *volontés particulières*. There are simple and universal laws of grace as there are laws of nature (*OCM* III 221, LO 666–7).

It was this claim that scandalised Arnauld, and led – by way of an acrimonious meeting between the two men in 1679 – to the publication in 1680 of Malebranche's *Traité de la Nature et de la Grâce*. For Arnauld, Christianity requires us to believe in a God who cares for particular human beings, and who distributes grace to individual men and women by means of *volontés particulières*. We say, of course, that God is wise and just, but we should not presume that there are independent and universally binding norms of conduct binding God's will as well as ours. Whatever God wills is wise and just precisely because He wills it.

So why, given that his primary disagreement with Malebranche was over the theological topic of grace, did Arnauld choose to begin his attack in 1683 with the *Vraies et Fausses Idées*? At first sight, the metaphysical issue of the nature of ideas seems far removed from the theological controversy about grace. Malebranche, indeed, accused Arnauld of perversely changing the subject in choosing to attack the most abstract and difficult part of his entire system, rather than engaging directly with the *Traité* (*OCM* VI, 18). In fact, however, Arnauld is not merely being perverse or wilful – the two subjects are more closely related than one might at first suppose. But we must return to this subject later.

Arnauld's *Vraies et Fausses Idées*

Arnauld's objective in writing *Vraies et Fausses Idées* (VFI) can be simply stated. We shall demonstrate, he claims, that

> … what the author of the book THE SEARCH FOR TRUTH says about the subject [ideas] is based on nothing more than false prejudices, and that nothing is more groundless than his claim that WE SEE ALL THINGS IN GOD.[5]

Arnauld sets out to refute the Vision in God by discrediting Malebranche's conception of ideas as *êtres représentatifs*. If there are such ideas, with properties of their own, existing independently of our perceptions, then questions can be asked regarding the ontological status of these ideas, and the Vision in God will come into play as one hypothesis among others. But if our ideas simply are our perceptions, i.e. modes of human souls, their humble ontological status is already settled, and the Vision in God can be dismissed as an unnecessary answer to an ill-conceived question.

The fundamental assumptions of VFI can be stated very briefly. Most basic of all are the metaphysics and epistemology of Descartes: Arnauld is at some pains to present himself as the true Cartesian and Malebranche as the dangerous innovator.[6] Next comes the appeal to the evidence of introspection: Arnauld shares with Descartes the principle that the mind has certain knowledge through introspection of all of its states and operations.[7] Finally there is a version of Ockham's razor: God will not perform by complex and roundabout means what He can perform by simple and direct ones.[8] Since Malebranche explicitly makes use of the same principles, Arnauld feels himself entitled to assume Malebranche's assent to all these premises.

What, asks Arnauld, are our perceptions *for*? The answer is obvious: their primary function is to enable us to know the existence and properties of the bodies surrounding us. But if this can be achieved by simple means, he asks, what need is there of complex ones? The simplest means of all is for God to give each soul the power or faculty of forming ideas on the occasion of certain physical events in its associated brain. These ideas are our perceptions of external objects. There is therefore no need of Malebranche's ideas, representative entities distinct from perceptions:

> God did not will to create our soul and to put it into a body surrounded by countless other bodies, without also willing that it be capable of knowing bodies, and consequently without also willing that bodies be conceived by our soul.[9]

But all of God's volitions are efficacious, so He has created our souls with just this capacity. Now God does not accomplish by complex and roundabout means what can be brought about by simple and direct means. So there is no need to posit an intermediate realm of ideas; it is simpler to suppose that the mind knows bodies directly than that it only knows them indirectly by means of representations.

Although my mental acts are modifications or modes of my soul, they are also *essentially representative* of objects. The soul, says Arnauld, is by its nature a thinking substance. The soul thinks because that it is essence: there is nothing more to say. But thought is always thought *of* something or other:

> So, since there can be no thought or knowledge without an object known, I can no more ask what is the reason why I think of something than why I think, since it is impossible to think without thinking of something. But I can very well ask why I think of one thing rather than another.[10]

In other words, intentionality is simply built into our mental states: a particular modification of the soul is essentially a perception-of-F. Such an account of the mind, Arnauld contends, has two great virtues to recommend it. It is the simplest account that does justice to the phenomena. And it is in conformity with the authentic testimony of introspection, which tells me that my perceptions are perceptions of things, not perceptions of *êtres représentatifs* distinct from and independent of my mind. If, says Arnauld, Malebranche had reflected on the contents of his own mind when perceiving a cube, 'I am sure that he could not have seen there anything other than the perception of the cube, or the cube objectively present to the mind'.[11]

Arnauld thus has an 'act' theory of ideas and a direct realist account of perception. We must still, however, take account of one small quirk of terminology that has misled some of the commentators. Arnauld does speak in VFI of the idea as the immediate object of perception and of the external body as (normally) the mediate object.[12] Although he takes some pains to explain what he means by this, the damage had been done, and some critics inferred (erroneously) that he meant by those terms more or less what others had meant by them. What Arnauld means is just that every mental act involves a 'virtual reflection' on itself, as well as being directed onto its proper intentional object. The mental act of perceiving the sun is not itself the object perceived, although of course it may become the object of a distinct act of introspective reflection.[13] So although it is trivially true that I can't see the sun without having an idea of the sun (because the idea is the seeing), it doesn't follow that the idea is the only thing that is directly or immediately perceived in the usual sense of those words.

Although Arnauld identifies ideas with perceptions, he admits a sort of dual aspect theory. The same things can be conceived and spoken of in two different ways. In some contexts it will be appropriate to speak of perceptions (when the emphasis is on their ontological status as modes of the soul); in other contexts, we should speak of ideas (when the emphasis is on their representative role). This is made perfectly explicit in VFI:

> I have said that I take the perception and the idea to be the same thing. Nevertheless it must be noted that this thing, although only one, has two relations: one to the soul which it modifies, the other to the thing perceived in so far as it is objectively in the soul; and that the word *perception* indicates more directly the first relation and the word *idea* the second.[14]

Given the superiority of Arnauld's direct realism on the two crucial counts of (a) simplicity and (b) conformity with the testimony of introspection, we must ask why Malebranche felt obliged to introduce his representative ideas as intermediates between the mind and its objects.

Arnauld suggests that Malebranche was led astray by a misleading analogy with physical optics. He is assuming, Arnauld suggests, that the object of perception must be present to the mind in some literal sense, if not itself then by some likeness or proxy. But this is a mere prejudice. All the optical talk about images has led Malebranche (and others) astray.[15] In the first place, when I look at my face in a mirror, it is *my face* that I see, not some distinct entity called an image. Even if one admits that an image in some literal sense, i.e. a miniature picture of the object, plays an essential role in the causal story of how vision occurs, this story (concerning the production of retinal images) lies wholly on the physical sense of the mind–body divide. There can be no resemblance across that divide. To attempt to explain the mind's perceptions in terms of little pictures is to put the cart before the horse, to reverse the proper order of explanation. A picture does not wear its meaning on its sleeve: the intentionality of pictures (and for that matter of spoken and written language) is a secondary affair, dependent on the primary and original intentionality of the mind's own perceptions. Unless our mental states had this original and intrinsic intentionality, no picture, and no written or spoken word, would mean anything at all.

Malebranche's ideal theory, Arnauld contends, is completely self-defeating. He has set out to explain *how* our minds perceive external objects. In other words, he has started with the common sense presumption that we do perceive tables and chairs, trees and houses, and raised the question of how this can be the case. But his *explanans* is inconsistent with the original *explanandum*. The proper conclusion to derive from Malebranche's theory is that we do not perceive trees and houses at all, but only variously coloured portions of the intelligible extension that is in God.[16] One might expect Arnauld to press charges of scepticism against Malebranche at this point, but in fact scepticism about the external world plays a very small role in the whole debate. Presumably, Arnauld is aware that his own direct realism merely shifts the point of the sceptic's attack. Granted, the sceptic can argue, that the direct object of a normal veridical act of perception is an independently existing body, how then do I know which if any of my perceptual states are thus veridical? If none of them are, then perhaps there is no external world at all, and I actually see no objects at all, all the objects I seem to see being merely intentional objects, having only 'objective being' in the Cartesian sense. In answer to such scepticism, Arnauld will merely refer his readers to the familiar argument of Descartes' *Meditation Six*: if this were the case, God would be a deceiver, which is impossible.[17]

As for Malebranche's use of the argument from illusion in support of his ideal theory, this is easy for Arnauld to meet.[18] Given the scholastic notion of 'objective being', Arnauld can readily reply that one and the same object (e.g. the sun in Descartes' famous example[19]), can exist objectively in different minds (or in the same mind at different times) with different properties, and that an object with no intrinsic or 'formal' reality at all (e.g. a green dragon) could nevertheless have objective reality, i.e. be an object of immediate perception. There need be no actual (i.e. non-intentional) bearer of merely apparent properties. The direct object of perceptual experience, Arnauld will say, is normally an independently existing external object, but on rare occasions there are perceptual states that have as their content representations of merely possible objects.

For Arnauld, it is perfectly proper to say that the soul thinks because that is its nature. What this means is simply that it has this power or faculty because that is how God chose to create it. This is where explanation stops. To ask how perception is possible is like asking how matter can be divisible:

> Since it is the nature of the mind to perceive objects, some necessarily, so to speak, and others contingently, it is ridiculous to ask whence it arises that our mind perceives objects.[20]

Intentionality is indeed, as Brentano would later claim, 'the mark of the mental', a primitive and irreducible feature of mentality. For Arnauld, all mental states (including bodily sensations, perceptions of secondary qualities, and even pleasures) are intentional, i.e. are more or less clear and distinct perceptions. All attempts to explain intentionality – e.g. by positing impressions and ideas that are images or resemblances of objects – turn out to presuppose it. If one cannot perceive things, how will it help to have pictures of things? And if one can perceive things, what use are pictures of things?

Malebranche's *Réponse*

Malebranche's reply to the *Vraies et Fausses Idées* is a great disappointment. It consists largely of complaints about Arnauld's conduct, repetitions of points and arguments already made elsewhere, and accusations of misunderstanding – possibly wilful and malicious – on the part of his critic.[21] The controversy between the two men was to drag on, its philosophical quality declining, until Arnauld's eventual death in 1694.

Régis would enter the fray on Arnauld's side in defence of what I have labelled the 'mainstream' Cartesian identification of ideas with perceptions. I shall not attempt to follow all the details; it suffices for our purposes here to extract the few points of philosophical substance made by Malebranche in his replies first to Arnauld and later to Régis.

The state of the argument between Arnauld and myself, Malebranche begins, boils down to this. He believes that the modes of our souls are essentially representative; I believe that the modes of our souls are mere sensations, which represent to the soul nothing distinct from itself (*OCM* VI 50). We need no ideas (*êtres représentatifs*) to know the modes of our own souls, Malebranche explains – these are knowable in themselves, and evident to introspection. By contrast, our knowledge of external objects cannot be immediate in Arnauld's sense.

Arnauld thinks that it is ridiculous to enquire how our souls are able to perceive bodies. To those who find this incomprehensible, all Arnauld can reply is that it is the nature of mind to have this power or faculty. But, Malebranche retorts, the word 'nature' means no more in the mouth of a Cartesian than it did in the mouth of an Aristotelian (*OCM* VI 142). Talk about powers and faculties may be merely descriptive, a sort of innocuous place-holder for a real explanation, i.e. an intelligible account of how the substance in question comes to have the power or faculty. (Mechanistic accounts of gravity and magnetism would provide obvious analogies drawn from physics.) Alternatively, talk about powers and faculties may be meant as a sort of explanation in its own right; if so, such talk can only provide a pseudo-explanation that ultimately explains nothing at all. Arnauld's claim that the mind thinks because it is its nature to think is manifestly a pseudo-explanation of this latter kind.[22]

What, Malebranche asks, is the source of Arnauld's error? His problem, we are told, is that he has missed the significance of the deep metaphysical distinction between ideas and sensations (*OCM* VI 54). He should have heeded the distinction marked in the French language by the distinct terms *connaître* and *sentir*, between on the one hand knowledge of objects by way of their ideas and on the other hand mere immediate awareness of one's own sensations. One can know 'in oneself' only such sensations as heat and cold, pleasure and pain, modes entirely devoid of representational content. Arnauld, says Malebranche, gives no explanation whatsoever of how a mere mode of my soul could be a representation of something quite different from itself, something it resembles in no way at all (*OCM* VI 91).[23] As for all his apparatus of axioms and definitions, they are dismissed as merely question-begging. On Arnauld's theory, every created spirit is trapped in the domain of its own perceptions; all it really perceives are its own modes. Arnauld thus turns the soul into a *monde intelligible* in its own right,[24] thereby violating the precept of Saint Augustine, 'Do not say that you are your own light' (*OCM* VI 63). But this theory, Malebranche insists, is not just impious and un-Christian; it is strictly unintelligible. How can the particular modes of a merely finite mind represent general truths, and infinity?

The argument seems to have reached a stalemate – small wonder that no progress was being made. Malebranche is requiring, on *a priori* grounds, a very strict principle of intelligibility. For me to know something, it must in some way be assimilated to my mind, or represented by some proxy that is thus assimilated. Now bodies, mere chunks of extension, are not knowable in themselves, and are incapable of the right sort of union with the knowing mind.[25] Therefore there must be some intermediary that is (a) of such a nature that it is capable of entering into such a union with my mind, and (b) has some intelligible intrinsic intentionality – its very nature is to be an idea-of-F. Only the ideas in the divine mind meet these two joint requirements, so only the Vision in God can provide an intelligible account of the nature of mind. Arnauld would reply by simply denying the epistemological intelligibility principle (EIP) that is bearing the weight of Malebranche's argument. For Arnauld, it is a peculiar but essential feature of the mind that its states can and do represent things with which they have no resemblance, no 'rapport', no intelligible relation.

The historical situation thus seems to be as follows. The twin principles of causal and epistemological intelligibility (CIP and EIP) were inherited by Cartesian metaphysicians from their scholastic predecessors. Unfortunately, as we noted in Chapter Two, Descartes' own metaphysics and epistemology seem to violate them. Malebranche, on my interpretation, is taking the 'high priori road', insisting that we retain CIP and EIP (though he doesn't require resemblance in any naïve sense). Given CIP and EIP, he argues, only supernatural solutions will suffice: only God's action can provide genuine necessary connections; only God's ideas can provide genuine objective knowledge. Arnauld, by contrast, has less confidence in metaphysics and more respect for common sense. On his view we cannot doubt that our perceptions (the modes of our souls) are representations of objects; but equally, we cannot explain how they are, except by saying that God made them so. The crucial difference, in their metaphysics as in their theology, concerns the degree to which God's acts and volitions must be intelligible to us.

Why is Malebranche so confident that the modes of the human soul cannot be representations? He answers that every such mode is a particular, and that no mere particular can represent something universal. And the idea of extension, *étendue intelligible*, is 'infinite' (in at least two distinct senses[26]), and therefore cannot be a mode of the finite human soul (*OCM* XVII–1 283). The obvious reply is made by Régis, who took up the defence of mainstream Cartesianism against Malebranche (*OCM* XVII–1 285). Intelligible extension, says Régis, is 'objectively' infinite but may still be 'formally' (i.e. intrinsically) finite, and hence can still be a mode of a finite soul. To block Malebranche's argument, it seems, Régis need only re-emphasise the absolute distinction between formal (intrinsic) and objective (representational) reality, and deny the validity of arguments that illegitimately slide from one domain to the other.

So does Malebranche's argument depend on nothing more than a simple fallacy of self-predication? Is he simply assuming that the idea of F must itself be F? If so, there is little more to be said on the subject, and no defence to offer. But we have already seen Malebranche vigorously reject any such interpretation of *étendue intelligible*. Although it is the idea of length, breadth and depth, intelligible extension is emphatically not itself extended in three dimensions (*OCM* VI 242). But if it is not extended at all, it cannot be literally infinite in extent. When Malebranche says that *étendue intelligible* is infinite and the human soul is only finite, he cannot mean that the former is literally too big to fit into the latter. He defends only a principle of epistemological intelligibility EIP, not a principle of epistemological resemblance ERP. The idea must make the object known, and this need not involve resemblance in any crude sense.[27] A mathematical equation may represent a circle as well as a diagram.

So when Malebranche says that *étendue intelligible* is 'infinite' what he means – or at any rate, what he should mean – is that it is *objectively* infinite, i.e. infinite in its content. Our familiarity with intelligible extension makes possible a sort of unlimited power or capacity to construct, identify, and comprehend all the infinite varieties of all the infinite kinds of geometrical figures. His point is not that intelligible extension is literally too big but that its content is too rich to fit into our limited minds.[28] The point is repeated in the first of the *Méditations Chrétiennes*. Your thoughts, explains the Word, can fly through the infinity of space:

> What, do you think you are big enough to contain within yourself the immense spaces you perceive? Do you think that your being can receive modifications which represent to you the actual infinite? Do you think that you even have the capacity to contain in yourself the idea of everything you can conceive in what is called an atom; for you conceive clearly that the

smallest part of matter that you imagine, being divisible ad infinitum, potentially contains an infinity of distinct figures and relations.

(*OCM* X 16)

The first two sentences of this passage suggest the crude thought that intelligible extension is simply too big for our souls. But the reference to 'what is called an atom' quickly supplies the necessary correction, and thus wards off misunderstanding.[29] Malebranche's point is that in thinking of any portion of matter, however small, we can think of it as consisting of an infinity of parts, and as entering into an infinity of relations with other bodies. This capacity, he argues, is only possible in virtue of the Vision in God.

What is at stake? Arnauld's version of the debate

When reading Arnauld's VFI and Malebranche's *Réponse*, the attentive reader will be struck by a puzzling and somewhat disquieting thought. The protagonists in this prolonged and heated controversy appear to disagree not just about the subject under debate (the nature of ideas) but also about exactly what philosophical issues are at stake and which of these issues are of central importance. This thought must have struck Steven Nadler between the publication of *Arnauld and the Cartesian Philosophy of Ideas* (1989) and that of *Malebranche and Ideas* (1992). In that short period of three years, Nadler changed his mind not only about his interpretation of Malebranche, as we saw in our previous chapter, but also about the primary focus of his controversy with Arnauld.[30] The earlier book views the controversy more or less through Arnauld's eyes; the later book adopts Malebranche's point of view. Let us begin with Arnauld's version of the issues at stake.

For Arnauld, the debate is, first and foremost, about the role of ideas in perception. Arnauld sees himself as the champion of an act theory of ideas and of a direct realist account of our perception of external objects. He doesn't use precisely these terms, of course, but his intentions are sufficiently clear. Malebranche, he thinks, has an object theory of ideas and an indirect realist account of perception. On Malebranche's theory, says Arnauld, all we are ever directly or immediately aware of in perception is an idea, which is an object with an independent reality of its own, distinct both from the mind of the perceiver and from the external object (if any) which is the indirect or mediate object of the perception. Malebranche insists, of course, that it is still true to say that we perceive bodies, but Arnauld denies that he is entitled to say this. On Malebranche's theory, we are told, the soul is:

> … condemned, by an irrevocable sentence of this philosophy of false ideas, never to see any body through itself, present or absent, close or distant. I would even dare to remove the words *through itself*, and say absolutely that it is condemned never to see any body, as we will see in what follows.[31]

God wills that we perceive tables and chairs, trees and houses. But God's will is both efficacious and economical. To invent an intermediate realm of ideas between the mind and its objects would be at best a clumsy means of achieving God's purpose and at worst a way of actually frustrating it.[32] What I see when I look at the sun, Arnauld insists, is the material sun itself, not a mere intelligible sun in the mind of God.[33] Malebranche will say, of course, that the intelligible sun (or at least a portion of intelligible extension) is the direct or immediate object of my perception, while the material sun is its indirect or mediate object. But his language, Arnauld objects, is not consistent. Sometimes he writes that we see the ideas (in God) of things; sometimes that we see the things themselves. On his own principles, Arnauld argues, he should entirely abandon the language of realism. The immediate object of all perceptions must be, for Malebranche, something intimately united to our souls. God is capable of such union; bodies are not. On Malebranche's principles, then, God is Himself, strictly speaking, the immediate object of all our perceptions. The Vision in God collapses into a Vision of God.[34] Malebranche thus sets out to explain how we can see creatures, and ends up with a theory that entails that we see only God and not creatures.

Arnauld also depicts himself as the defender of Descartes against the dangerous innovations of Malebranche. Descartes, Arnauld insists, never thought of ideas as distinct from perceptions. His most explicit discussion can be found in the *Second Replies*, which lends some support to Arnauld's interpretation. For Descartes, ideas are modes of the soul, mental acts: an idea is 'our thought itself, insofar as it contains objectively what is formally in the object'.[35] On such a view, there is no need whatsoever to postulate a distinct realm of representative entities. When I am seeing the sun what I am aware of is *the sun itself*, insofar as it is 'objectively' present to my mind.

Malebranche would reply that this is not so much a theory of intentionality as an anti-theory, an implicit rejection of the demand for an explanation. If all we can say is that it is the nature of mental states to have representational content, and that this is so because God willed it, nothing whatsoever has been explained. Arnauld responds explicitly to this objection. It is a mark of wisdom, he suggests, to know where to stop in our search for explanations. We say that the soul thinks because it is its nature to think, or because God gave it the faculty of thought. Malebranche objects that this is non-explanatory. But, Arnauld replies, there are many contexts in which this is 'the best reply that can be given'.[36] If we ask why iron is magnetic, it is idle to posit a magnetic faculty when a superior (mechanistic) account is in principle possible. Cartesian physics eliminates talk of faculties in this sort of context. But if we ask why matter is mobile, all we can say is that that is its nature, i.e. that God has made it that way. All our physical theories presuppose this power of mobility, so no physical theory can possibly account for it. It is in this latter sense, Arnauld explains, that I say that the mind has the faculty of thought.

Any attempt to explain how thought is possible, i.e. how the modes of the soul can be representations of actual and possible objects, will be dismissed by Arnauld as (a) a presumptuous piece of hubris on our part, and (b) an error derived from mistaken and misapplied physical analogies. Malebranche is immodest in not knowing when explanation has to stop, and muddled in thinking that models borrowed from physics will cast any light on the mind. Hence his 'walking soul' argument and his confusion about the notion of presence.[37] Arnauld rejects not just any naively literal sense of resemblance (Watson's ELP), but also any principle of epistemological intelligibility (our EIP). There is nothing about the intrinsic features of the mode of my soul that represents F that particularly fits it to be the idea-of-F rather than the idea-of-G. We can make no valid inferences from objective reality (representational content) to formal reality (intrinsic features) or *vice versa*. Intentionality must simply be accepted as a primitive and irreducible feature of the mental.[38]

What is at stake? Malebranche's version of the debate

For Malebranche, the correct analysis of perception (direct versus indirect realism) is a mere distraction, far from the centre of his concerns. He continues to maintain that we do see bodies, adding only the qualification that we do not see them *en eux-mêmes* (*OCM* VI 101). But all he is seeking to do here is to fend off Arnauld's objections, to show that his version of indirect or representative realism does not collapse into

THE DISPUTE WITH ARNAULD

idealism, and that the Vision in God is not a Vision of God. What is important to Malebranche in the controversy is not the theory of perception but the very possibility of objective thought.[39]

If ideas are just modifications of our souls, Malebranche maintains, there will be no escape from the Pyrrhonian scepticism he saw gathering strength all around him.[40] On inspecting my idea of X, I can say confidently that my idea represents X as having properties FGH, so I can affirm that I perceive X as FGH. But if my idea is just my perception, this is merely a judgement about how things seem to me, not how they are in themselves. I can't infer anything about how X will appear to other finite minds, or about whether X objectively is as I perceive it. Every mind will remain trapped within its own ideas, with no escape from subjectivity.

Malebranche clearly intends his theory of the Vision in God to block two related sceptical doubts. There is the inference from the subjective to the objective: how do I know that what seems F to me is objectively F? And there is the inference from the subjective to the intersubjective: how do I know that what appears F to me will appear F to others? The sceptic will challenge both inferences, insisting that we should only judge how things appear to us, not how they are in themselves or how they appear to other observers (if other observers exist). The Vision in God answers the first question directly, but also supplies as a corollary an answer to the second. By providing a guarantee of the objectivity of thought it also ensures intersubjectivity. If X is objectively F, any observer who perceives X clearly and distinctly will perceive it as F.

Without ideas in my sense, Malebranche maintains, there is no escape from scepticism. He even attempts to enlist Arnauld's own testimony by citing the famous Port Royal Logic. In the *Art de Penser*, the following principle is established as necessary to all certainty in the sciences: whatever is contained in the clear and distinct idea of X can be truly affirmed of X (*OCM* IX 924). If, for example, our idea of matter (three dimensional extension) represents it as infinitely divisible, then matter is infinitely divisible.[41] But unless our ideas were the divine archetypes according to which things were (and are) created, there would be no reason to suppose that this principle was true. Things must conform to their divine archetypes, so the Vision in God provides knowledge of objectively necessary truths.[42] If Arnauld is right and my ideas are mere modes of my soul, the principle would not hold, and we would have no escape from scepticism:

A creature necessarily conforms to the idea of whoever created
it. I agree. But the idea that you have of it, you say, is nothing

but a modification of your soul. And this modification is certainly not the Creator's idea on the basis of which He formed this creature. It is thus in no way certain that the thing conforms to your idea, but only that you think it does. Thus, your view establishes Pyrrhonism, but mine destroys it.

(*OCM* IX 925)

If clear and distinct ideas compel assent, as Descartes has taught, then I may find myself unable to doubt that things are as my ideas represent them, but subjective certainty is no substitute for objective truth.[43]

The same point is repeated in the supplementary material appended to the *Entretien d'un Philosophe Chrétien et d'un Philosophe Chinois* (1708). To maintain that ideas are nothing distinct from perceptions, Malebranche claims, is to eliminate objective standards, and thus to establish Pyrrhonism in the sciences and libertinage in morals:

This principle is generally accepted: That one can affirm of a thing what one clearly perceives to be contained in the idea one has of it. But if the idea which one has is not distinct from the perception, or from the modification of the mind which perceives it, this principle is not certain. For assuredly God has not created things on the basis of our fleeting perceptions, but on the basis of His eternal ideas: which ideas we perceive when they touch us, and by means of them we perceive the things which are necessarily in conformity to them.

(*OCM* XV 50–1)

The first principle of the sciences, according to the Cartesians themselves, is that we may affirm of the thing whatever is contained in the clear and distinct idea of it. But that principle would not be certain unless the Vision in God were true. So the Cartesians face a stark choice: abandon all claims to certainty in the sciences, or embrace the Vision in God.

By solving the problem of the objectivity of thought, Malebranche also solves the problem of intersubjectivity. There is a single creator, and a single set of ideas that serve Him as archetypes. In geometry, there is one model or archetype, intelligible extension, equally accessible in principle to all minds capable of sufficient attention. In morals, there is one common notion of Order, equally accessible – albeit perhaps with rather more difficulty because of the need to still our passions and silence our prejudices – to all minds. Since all humans participate in a common reason, there is no ground for relativism, either in mathematics or in morality.[44] We can learn the arithmetic of the Hindus and the astronomy of the Chinese, and they can learn ours. Exactly the same must hold for the rational principles of morality. For Arnauld, by contrast, intersubjectivity could only hold *Deo volente*, as a result of a sort of divinely pre-established harmony between the contents of the perceptions of individual souls.

Malebranche's position might best be set out as a sort of transcendental argument in the Kantian manner.[45] It starts from the assumption that *objective thought* is possible, and then enquires into the preconditions for that possibility. Schematically, we might present the argument thus:

1 Objective thought is possible.
2 Objective thought is only possible if the Vision in God is true.

Therefore, the Vision in God is true.

This is clearly valid, so criticism must focus on the truth of the premises. To defend (1) Malebranche would simply point to the existing sciences of mathematics and (more controversially) morality. That $2 + 2 = 4$, and that the three angles of a triangle add up to $180°$, are necessarily and absolutely true, not true on some condition or for some minds rather than others. That God is superior to a man, and a man to his dog, are for Malebranche just as clear examples of necessary and absolute truths. No element of subjectivity enters into the content of these thoughts, nor into the considerations which establish their truth. Critics of Malebranche would be well advised to grant (1) and challenge (2). This is Jolley's strategy. He praises Malebranche for his 'resolute anti-psychologism',[46] seeing in him a precursor of the views of Frege. Malebranche might have enjoyed, for example, reading the following passage from Frege's famous article *On Sense and Meaning*:

> If every thought requires a bearer, to the contents of whose consciousness it belongs, then it would be the thought of this bearer only and there would be no science common to many, on which many could work. But I, perhaps, have my own science, namely a whole of thought whose bearer I am and another person has his ... No contradiction between the two sciences would then be possible and it would really be idle to dispute about truth, as idle, indeed almost ludicrous as it would be for two people to dispute whether a hundred mark note

were genuine, where each meant the one he himself had in his pocket and understood the word 'genuine' in his own particular sense.[47]

But, Jolley continues, it is one thing to establish the existence of an objective 'World Three' of ideas (logical concepts) and propositions, and quite another to endorse the Vision in God.[48] It is possible to endorse the first premise of Malebranche's transcendental argument but to reject the second, and thus to escape his conclusion. We simply replace the mind of God with 'World Three', the realm of objective thought. There are of course well-known objections to such an extensive ontology of abstract objects, but are these difficulties any greater than those of Malebranche's theism?

Deeper reasons

Why, we asked at the beginning of this chapter, did Arnauld write *des Vraies et Fausses Idées*? His primary concerns were theological, and his most violent disagreement with Malebranche was over the subject of grace. If Malebranche had argued from his theory of ideas to his opinions on grace, it would be easy to understand why Arnauld should choose to undermine support for the latter by refuting the former, but there is no such explicit argument in Malebranche. He in fact accused Arnauld of simply changing the subject in choosing to attack the Vision in God rather than the account of grace in the *Traité* (*OCM* VI 18). The Vision in God, he explains, is the most abstract part of my work, and has no relation at all to the arguments of the *Traité*. Rather than deal with the arguments of the *Traité* on their merits, he protests, Arnauld has resorted to personal attack and unfair caricature, portraying me as a mere dreamer and a visionary.

But this is disingenuous on Malebranche's part. There is a connection between the theory of ideas on the one hand and the account of grace on the other. Although Malebranche insists that the issues are quite distinct, the more perceptive of the commentators disagree.[49] On this point, says Alquié, we cannot follow Malebranche:

> The doctrine of ideas is indeed the foundation of the doctrine of grace, since the doctrine of grace assumes that we can know the principles of divine action. Now we can only do this through perceiving, by Reason, ideas in God.[50]

Denis Moreau helps to make the connection clearer in his admirable account of the controversy.[51] The connection, he explains, is univocity: if our ideas are God's ideas, then we can make confident judgements about God's intentions and God's reasons for acting. 'We do see, in God and as God, our ideas; we are thus well-grounded in our evaluations of what God wants and does'.[52] Since our ideas are God's ideas, it is not, *pace* Arnauld, 'rash' or 'presumptuous' to claim some rational insight into God's designs and His methods for realising those designs. In so doing, I am not boldly asserting my own human reason but humbly following universal reason, which is the reason of God Himself. As Malebranche puts it in the *Traité*,

> Were I not persuaded that all men are rational only because they are enlightened by the Eternal Wisdom, I would, without a doubt, be rash to speak about God's plans and to want to discover some of His ways in the production of His work. But because it is certain that the Eternal Word is the universal Reason of minds, and that by the light that it shines on us incessantly we can all have some communication with God, I should not be blamed for consulting this Reason, which, although consubstantial with God Himself, does not fail to answer those who know how to interrogate it with serious attention.
>
> (*OCM* V 24–5)

All knowledge of truth, Malebranche explains in Book Five of the *Recherche*, is a sort of union with God. When the mind discovers some truth, or sees things as they are in themselves, it sees things in God's ideas, not in its own modes. (God is, but the soul is not, a *monde intelligible*.) So whenever the mind knows the truth, it is to that extent united with God and can therefore be said to know and possess God:

> But not only might we say that the mind that knows the truth to a certain extent also knows God who contains the truth, we might even say that to a certain extent it knows things as God knows them. Indeed, this mind knows their true relations, which God also knows. The mind knows them in the perception of God's perfections that represent them, and God, too, knows them in this way.
>
> (*OCM* II 168, LO 364)

Malebranche thus shares in what Edward Craig has called 'the insight ideal' that is such a characteristic feature of seventeenth century rationalism.[53] Our knowledge, at its best, equals God's knowledge in its clarity and certainty though not of course in its extent. Mathematics provides, as ever, the most convincing examples of this rational insight, but it was not mathematical knowledge that proved contentious. For Malebranche, our rational insight extends not just to mathematics but to morals: through our perception of Order we are able to gain some insight into God's designs, and thus even to criticise His creation. As Ariste exclaims at the end of the ninth *Entretien*,

> Ah Theodore, how well all your principles are connected! By what you have just told me I understand further that it is in God and in an immutable nature that we see beauty, truth, justice, since we are not afraid to criticize His work, to note the defects in it, and even to conclude thereby that it is corrupt. Indeed, the immutable order, which we see partly, must be the law of God Himself, written in His substance in eternal and divine characters, since we are unafraid of judging His conduct by the knowledge we have of that law.
>
> (*OCM* XII 221, JS 169)

Arnauld thinks that it is presumptuous for men to claim sufficient knowledge of God's intentions to criticise His works. He never tires of repeating the words of Isaiah, 'My thoughts are not your thoughts', and emphasising the distance and difference between our knowledge and God's knowledge.[54] But without knowledge of God's intentions, Malebranche retorts, we can neither praise His wisdom in creation nor recognise the effects of the fall. We praise the wisdom of an artificer when we see how well his work serves his design; if we are entirely ignorant of the design, we can't assess the skill of the workman. Likewise, if we can't trust our own judgements of value, we can't see that our world is the mere ruin of a perfect creation. Order tells us, for example, that souls are superior to bodies, and that it is therefore a disorder, in a perfectly objective sense, for a man to live for his belly. But this argument relies on a conception of Order as something real and objective, binding alike on God and man. The superior must be preferred to the inferior; the inferior exists for the sake of the superior. Without such an Order, Malebranche argues, there would be no proof of morality and religion:

> For how would one prove to a libertine that nature is disordered, if there is no necessary and immutable Order? He has only to

reply boldly that God has made minds for the sake of bodies, for eating and drinking and the peaceful enjoyment of sensible objects. How will we prove to him that God will recompense good works and punish crimes, and even that justice and injustice are not phantoms that are used to strike fear into the credulous? The libertine has only to reply proudly and brutally that God's wisdom and reason are quite different from ours: that it seems just to us to recompense what are called good works, but that what appears just is not in the least so, or is not in the least so with regard to God, who is the absolute master of His creatures: finally, that His wisdom and justice, if one wants to attribute such qualities to Him, have nothing in common with our feeble thoughts.

(*OCM* VI, 23)

The rational theologian, Malebranche maintains, must seek to silence the unbelievers, '*faire taire les impies*'. The unbelievers point to all manner of evils in our world, and argue that it could not be the creation of a wise and benevolent God. Where is the wisdom, they will ask, in making an animal so deformed that it cannot survive, or helping crops to grow only to ravage them by hail? Worse still, where is the wisdom and benevolence in establishing unjust princes, letting whole nations perish, and causing heresies to flourish at the expense of true religion? (For the freethinker, of course, this latter argument would be *ad hominem*.) The theology of Arnauld, Malebranche argues, can provide no answer at all to such doubts. Arnauld's God is omnipotent but inscrutable, exercising His power by means of particular volitions. So on Arnauld's theory God does intend – for utterly mysterious reasons of His own – each monster, each hailstorm and each unjust prince. Such a theology will not, Malebranche argues, convince the doubters:

It is a question of silencing the unbelievers, and placing reason on the side of religion. It is not enough to satisfy the believers, we must put pressure on the freethinkers, and force them to keep quiet: or rather, we must convince them that God's conduct is worthy of His wisdom and His goodness, which is very easy on my principles.

(*OCM* VII 592)

Malebranche sees his philosophical theology as a weapon for use not only against the freethinkers but also against Christian heretics (Protestants,

Socinians) and adherents of other religions (Jews, Moslems, Confucians). In the *Conversations Chrétiennes*, for example, we find an explicit discussion of the Trinity and the hierarchy of persons, against the more austere monotheism of the Socinians and of Islam. Two powerful objections of a Chinese bonze are also discussed. Christianity, says the bonze, is not a universal religion, so belief in Christ cannot be necessary to salvation. As for the Christian theory of eternal damnation, it is rejected by the bonze as inconsistent with God's goodness.[55] The *Conversations* can thus be regarded, as Robinet shows, as an early contribution to the field of comparative religion.[56] And towards the end of his career Malebranche re-entered this field with his *Entretien d'un Philosophe Chrétien et d'un Philosophe Chinois* (1708). Written against the supposed 'atheism' of the Chinese (in fact, the position Malebranche ascribes to them is remarkably close to Spinozism), it also takes issue with Jesuit missionaries who were – in the eyes of many Christians – making too great concessions to Chinese 'idolatry' (e.g. ancestor worship) in order to gain large numbers of spurious converts.

When Malebranche says that reason should be placed on the side of religion, he does not mean merely that – as the Church demanded – philosophers should provide proofs of the existence of God and the (natural) immortality of the soul, and then leave the rest to the theologians. He thinks that reason can go much further than this into the Christian mysteries. In the *Conversations Chrétiennes*, for example, he argues that only the incarnation of the Word makes the creation worthy of God (*OCM* IV 132–3). It follows that all religions other than Christianity can offer no credible account of creation. God is, after all, sufficient unto Himself: it is not as if He needed anything from the world He has created. But Malebranche's attempts to extend philosophical reasoning into theology can easily backfire. Without the incarnation of the Word, says Malebranche, the world would not be worthy of God. Why not? Because there can be no relation or 'rapport' between the finite and the infinite. But if this is so, the freethinker will retort, there can be no Incarnation and no single person, Jesus Christ, with two natures, divine and human. Malebranche's supposed solution tacitly helps itself to an assumption which is – on his own principles – strictly impossible.

Similar difficulties will surface in the moral domain. If we trust our intuitions of Order, we will surely find ourselves endorsing the argument of the Chinese bonze – a just and benevolent God wouldn't condemn the vast majority of mankind to eternal torment for the crime of a remote ancestor. Only a cruel and vindictive tyrant would do that. And if belief in Christ is necessary to salvation, what is to become of all those millions who are excluded from the Christian Church by accidents of history and/or geography? Our intuitions of justice tell us clearly that it would be unfair to penalise such people, and justice is not one thing for God and another for man. Such arguments would become a prominent feature of Enlightenment deism.

The controversy between Malebranche and Arnauld thus marks a fissure within Christian theology, a fundamental parting of the ways. Malebranche demands a theology that appeals to uniform and universal norms or standards, and seeks to defend orthodox Christian dogmas in terms of those universal norms.[57] His arguments are designed to be culture-neutral, to appeal to all men whatsoever, simply in their capacity of rational beings. He can thus take on the freethinkers on their own terms, and persuade Moslem imams and Chinese bonzes of the superiority of Christianity – if the arguments work. But equally he leaves himself wide open to the counter-arguments of the freethinkers and of the spokesmen of other faiths. Arnauld, by contrast, wants only the most modest of philosophical theologies, confined perhaps to the Cartesian proofs of God and the soul. For further insights into matters of theology, we must turn to Scripture and to the authority of the Fathers. The division of philosophy from theology remains fixed and impassable. To claim that we can see the universe through God's eyes is dangerous and presumptuous folly.

For Malebranche, the introduction of philosophical rationalism into theology is not presumptuous or sacrilegious. Universal reason is itself the voice of the Word, so when we seek to 'rationalise' scripture, i.e. to make its message consistent with our metaphysical and moral intuitions, we are not taking it upon ourselves to correct God's revealed word. Rather, we know for certain that God cannot contradict Himself, so His word as revealed in scripture must be consistent with His word as manifest through reason. Apparent contradictions must be explained away, e.g. some passages in scripture may be mere concessions to the level of understanding of the vulgar.[58] Christian theology can in principle be taught from rational first principles, without reliance on the established opinions of the Fathers. This was Malebranche's strategy in the *Traité*, and was one of the features of the work that gave most offence to critics such as Bossuet and Fénélon as well as Arnauld. Malebranche denies, of course, that he is rejecting the authority of the Fathers. Truth, he will say, is truth, whatever its source, and a short work of Christian theology resting only on rational first principles is far more likely to persuade the infidels than yet another weighty tome full of interminable quotations in archaic Greek and Latin (*OCM* V 3–6).

So when Arnauld chose to launch his long campaign against Malebranche with *des Vraies et Fausses Idées,* he knew exactly what he was doing. He saw the Vision in God – correctly – as the foundation of Malebranche's philosophical theology. He also saw – equally correctly – that Malebranche's rationalism represented a potential threat to many aspects of Christian tradition. Malebranche was of course confident that reason could be co-opted onto the side of religion in the battle against the unbelievers, and that the few small concessions that might prove necessary in the interpretation of scripture would not threaten anything fundamental to Catholic orthodoxy. But such confidence was naïve. By the time of Malebranche's death in 1715, Pierre Bayle had already raised serious doubts about the harmony of reason and religion, and the deists were challenging – in the name of universal reason – orthodox Christian views of the Trinity, Providence, Miracles and the Afterlife. From Malebranche to Voltaire (via Bayle) is not as big a leap as it might appear.

5

OCCASIONALISM AND CONTINUOUS CREATION

How not to think of occasionalism

Malebranche's occasionalism is sometimes represented – often on the basis of a superficial reading of a remark in Leibniz's *New System*[1] – as if it were merely an *ad hoc* solution to Descartes' mind–body problem, with God intervening to fill the causal gaps between physical and mental events.[2] This is a gross misrepresentation, based on a failure to understand both the full generality of Malebranche's doctrine and the grounds on which it rests.[3] It is not that he, like other Cartesian dualists, faces a problem in explaining how body and mind can interact, and is obliged to drag God in to plug the explanatory gaps. Rather, he has a perfectly general account of the nature of the causal relation which entails that only God can be a true cause, and this account yields, as a straightforward corollary, his solution to the mind–body problem.

Occasionalism states that all so-called 'second' or 'natural' causes are not true causes at all, but serve merely as occasions on which the true cause (God) operates. As we saw in Chapter Two, earlier Cartesians such as Cordemoy and La Forge had articulated semi-occasionalist positions, usually denying causal powers to bodies. It is only in Malebranche, however, that we find a full-blooded occasionalism, denying all causal powers also to finite spirits.[4] Only God, for Malebranche, has the power to bring anything about. But God does not act in random or arbitrary ways: on the contrary, He exerts His power in accordance with general rules, by means of what Malebranche calls *volontés générales*. So the impact of the white billiard ball does not, strictly speaking, cause the red ball to move (the white ball has no such power); the moment of impact merely serves as the occasion for God to redistribute motions according to certain universal laws. Similar stories can be told for all other so-called natural causes. The occurrence of certain events in my nerve organs and brain do not cause a sensation, but whenever my brain is in state ϕ God produces state Ψ in my mind. Likewise, my volition to raise my arm does not cause the motor nerves to fire, but serves as the occasion for God to produce that brain-state. Finally, my mind doesn't even have any power over its own thoughts: attention is, for Malebranche, a species of prayer. I pray for illumination and, so long as my prayer is sincere, and persistent, and directed towards an appropriate object, God will reveal the required idea.

The general thesis of occasionalism is stated clearly in the *Recherche*, where Malebranche seeks to show that there is only one true cause, and that all so-called 'second' or 'natural' causes are mere occasions. Because God acts in reliable, predictable ways, in accordance with universal rules, we will come to notice that events of type C regularly precede events of type E, will call the former 'causes' and the latter 'effects', and will come to expect an E-type event when we observe a C-type event. This is, of course, essential for everyday life and for the natural sciences, but has fatal consequences for metaphysics. (See *OCM* I 171–5, LO 76–8; *OCM* II 76–84, LO 307–11.) The belief in natural causes is 'the most dangerous error of the philosophy of the ancients' (*OCM* II 309–20, LO 446–52), and the deep reason why the philosophy of Aristotle is not just un-Christian but anti-Christian. The Aristotelian acceptance of natural powers is, Malebranche argues, inseparable from pagan attitudes to nature. If one believes that the apple is the real cause of one's pleasure, and that the sun is the sustaining cause of all vegetation, it is only reasonable to love the apple and to worship the sun. To refute this 'miserable' philosophy, the contrary truths must be established, namely that 'there is only one true cause, because there is only one true God; that the nature or power of each thing is nothing but the will of God; that all natural causes are not *true* causes, but only *occasional* causes' (*OCM* II 312, LO 448).

The purpose of teaching occasionalism, in Malebranche's eyes, is therefore moral and spiritual.[5] Since humans naturally come to love whatever they regard as causes of their pleasures, Christians should be forever repeating the lessons of occasionalism, and seeking to learn them by heart. The Christian must love and fear only God, we are told in *Éclaircissement* XV of the *Recherche* (*OCM* III 211–52, LO 657–85), but this is impossible for a believer in second causes. The point is reiterated in the *Conversations Chrétiennes* (*OCM* IV 20). Whatever can cause us pleasure and pain, explains Malebranche's spokesman Theodore, is a proper object of love and fear, so belief in natural causes leads inevitably to paganism and idolatry.

Malebranche has two very different lines of argument in support of his occasionalism. There is what might be called the 'thin' argument, starting with the notion of cause as necessary connection, and arguing that only God's will meets this condition. Then there is the 'deep' argument, taking its origin from the theological doctrine of continuous creation, which we touched on briefly in our discussion of Descartes in Chapter Two. The second and third sections of this chapter focus on the thin argument; the fourth and fifth sections set out the deep argument and its implications; the final section discusses objections and replies.

The idea of necessary connection

Malebranche takes it for granted that a true cause is necessarily connected with its effect (*OCM* II 316, LO 448). What sort of necessary connection does he have in mind? Although he never spends much time on the topic, it is clear that he draws no sharp distinction between logical and metaphysical senses of necessity.[6] The test for what is metaphysically possible is what can be conceived or described without self-contradiction. So for there to be a genuine causal relation between events C and E, one must be able to 'see' (i.e. rationally intuit) that C could not occur without E, i.e. that this would involve a contradiction. But this is never the case, Malebranche argues, for so-called 'second' or 'natural' causes. It is evident, he argues in Book Six of the *Recherche*, that no body has the force required to move itself, far less to set another body in motion (*OCM* II 312–13, LO 448). Our idea of body actually excludes such powers. So only a spirit can be a cause. But there is no necessary connection between the will of a finite spirit and its effects. We cannot discern any necessary connection between my willing to raise my arm and my arm going up. Indeed, we can see clearly that there is no such necessary connection: it is perfectly conceivable that the volition can occur without the action. So it seems that no finite spirit can move a body, any more than another body can.

The search for necessary connections leads naturally into an analysis of our idea of power. (For Malebranche, as later for Hume, the ideas of power and of necessary connection are two sides of the same coin.) Previous generations of philosophers, says Malebranche, have spent enormous amounts of time and effort arguing about the powers of natural things, trying to define such terms as 'force', 'power', 'efficacy' and the like. But all such talk is, in the final analysis, unintelligible (*OCM* I 458–9, LO 242). The very notion of such a 'force', 'power', or 'efficacy', says Malebranche in *Éclaircissement* XV of the *Recherche*, is completely inconceivable. 'Whatever effort I make in order to understand it, I cannot find in me any idea representing to me what might be the force or the power they attribute to creatures' (*OCM* III 294, LO 658). The philosophers who believe in second causes are arguing without a clear idea of what they are talking about, which explains their endless controversies and confusions.[7]

Naturalistic philosophers, Malebranche explains, have been misled and seduced by their senses (*OCM* III 207–8, LO 659–60, and *OCM* III 232–3, LO 673–4). When they see plants growing after the rains, they assume that the rains have caused the vegetation, although they have no comprehension of how this could be. Averroes, for example, accuses the occasionalists of his day of having cracked brains for denying that fire burns and the sun illuminates, but his pretended 'demonstration' of these supposed causal powers amounts to nothing more than a blatant *petitio principi*. In fact, of course, occasionalists do not deny the manifest evidence of their senses. We need, Malebranche explains, to distinguish carefully between what is actually presented to the senses, and what is added by the mind of the observer, and may be the result of mere habit or prejudice, albeit a prejudice that seems to come naturally to us:

> When I see one ball strike another, my eyes tell me, or seem to tell me, that the one is truly the cause of the motion it impresses on the other, for the true cause that moves bodies does not appear to my eyes. But when I consult my reason I clearly see that since bodies cannot move themselves, and since their motor force is but the will of God that conserves them successively in different places, they cannot communicate a power they do not have and could not communicate even if it were in their possession. For the mind will never conceive that one body, a purely passive substance, can in any way whatsoever transmit to another body the power transporting it.
>
> (*OCM* III 208, LO 660)

Strictly speaking, my eyes only seem to teach me that the first ball moves the second, or that sun and rain are the causes of vegetation. We need to consult reason, not to correct sense itself, but to correct an all-too-human prejudice, a naïve tendency to confuse constant conjunction with genuine causation. In the *Méditations Chrétiennes*, this Malebranchian doctrine is voiced by no less an authority than the Word of God:

> Renounce your prejudices, my son, and never judge, with regard to natural effects, that one thing is the effect of another, because experience teaches you that it never fails to follow it. For of all false principles this is the most dangerous and the most fertile source of errors. As the action of God is always uniform and

constant, because His volitions are immutable and His laws inviolable, if you follow this false principle, although God does all, you will conclude from it that He does nothing.

(*OCM* X 59)

As Pierre Bayle puts it, human beings are 'drawn by their nature, and in some way instructed by a natural lesson, to judge that anything which is regularly connected with a certain effect, and without which that effect is not produced, is the true cause of it' (*OCM* XVII–1 591). This natural tendency, harmless and even benign both in practical everyday contexts and in the natural sciences, is the source of dangerous errors in metaphysics. The natural judgements in question must be automatic, powerful, but *resistible* – if not, our Creator would be to blame for our errors. To correct the error, one must carefully distinguish what is actually 'given' to the senses from what is automatically added in judgement, and then subject this extra element of judgement to rational scrutiny. Reason, once consulted, corrects the error, but does not eliminate its source – we remain liable to go on making the same errors again and again. Occasionalism is a lesson we will forever have to learn anew and repeat to ourselves, day after day, without any hope of it becoming second nature.

If a true cause must be necessarily connected with its effect, it is easy to show that only the will of God can be such a cause. There is a necessary connection between 'God wills that X' and 'X occurs', so long as God is conceived as omnipotent and X as logically possible (not self-contradictory). This argument appears in Book Six of the *Recherche* (*OCM* II 313, LO 448) and is repeated in Part 1 of the *Traité* (*OCM* V 27). Here Malebranche draws the further inference that, since God's will is sufficient for the willed effect to occur, He has no need of any instruments to bring about His designs – His volitions are, in and of themselves, efficacious. There would be a contradiction, explains the Word in the *Méditations Chrétiennes*, in God's willing a man's arm to move, and the arm not moving (*OCM* X 64). There is a necessary connection between the will of an omnipotent being and its effects. To deny this, explains the Christian philosopher in the *Entretien d'un Philosophe Chrétien et d'un Philosophe Chinois*, is simply to deny the existence of an omnipotent being (*OCM* XV 33).

Critics of Malebranche, from Fontenelle[8] and Hume[9] down to Church[10] and Watson,[11] have objected to the tautological and seemingly merely verbal character of this argument. I understand, writes Fontenelle in his *Doutes*, that

> ... since He [God] is all-powerful by His essence, it is impossible that He should will that a thing exist, and that that thing not exist. But do I conceive how that thing is, as soon as God wills that it exist? Not at all; on the contrary ...[12]

I must grant that the will of God is a real cause because I can see that there is a necessary connection between it and its effects, although I don't understand how it produces those effects. But can I not say exactly the same, asks Fontenelle, regarding the collision of bodies? I see that the red ball must move when struck by the white ball (because both are impenetrable) even though I cannot conceive how 'force' (whatever that may be) can be transferred from one body to another.

Hume expresses this objection with characteristic clarity and vigour. If, he writes, we say that:

> ... the idea of an infinitely perfect being is connected with that of every effect, which he wills, we really do no more than assert, that a being, whose volition is connected with every effect, is connected with every effect; which is an identical proposition, and gives us no insight into the nature of this power or connexion.[13]

We seek rational insight into the relation between cause and effect, and are fobbed off with what looks like a merely verbal proof. If I can't understand how my volitions can bring about the voluntary motions of my body, does it help to be told that the volitions of an omnipotent being are, necessarily, efficacious? If I understand 'omnipotent', I will grant the validity of the inference from 'An omnipotent being willed X to occur' to 'X occurred', but it seems to shed no light whatsoever on the nature of the causal relation.

Malebranche has a twin-track response to this fundamental objection.[14] His main line of response is his theory of continuous creation, which we shall discuss later. He also seeks, however, to meet the objection more directly. In the ninth of the *Méditations Chrétiennes* he admits frankly that we have no clear idea of power, and thus cannot conceive how God creates the world, but he denies that this invalidates his argument (*OCM*, X, 97). The point is repeated in his reply to Fontenelle. To judge that A is the cause of B, he insists, we need only to see that A could not occur without B. One need not also see why this necessary connection holds, i.e. how A brings B about (*OCM* XVII–1 580).

Particular causal relations

We must now examine how Malebranche applies the general doctrine of occasionalism to particular types of causal relation: body to body (impulse), body to mind (sensation), mind to body (voluntary motion), and mind to mind (thought). Let us deal with each in turn, starting with the apparent power of a moving body to set another body in motion.

We have already seen Malebranche's denial, in *Éclaircissement* XV of the *Recherche*, that the mind can conceive of any genuine moving force or power, transferred from one body to another in collisions. In the fifth of the *Méditations Chrétiennes*, the author admits his embarrassment regarding his incapacity to form any clear idea of this supposed power. The Word promptly replies that, if a man will but still his senses and set aside his prejudices, the truth will become apparent to him. Suppose the physical universe consisted of only one cubic foot of solid matter:

> Could this body move itself? In your idea of matter, do you discover any power? You do not reply. But supposing that this body truly had the power of moving, in which direction will it go? How fast will it move? You are still silent?
>
> (*OCM* X 47)

These rhetorical questions run together two clearly distinct arguments. First of all, there is an appeal to our clear idea of body or material substance. This idea, as Descartes taught us, contains only size and shape and the capacity for local motion – geometric and kinematic properties but no dynamic ones. But a clear idea, for Malebranche, excludes whatever it does not include. If I have a clear idea of X, I can tell *a priori*, for any property F, whether X is F or non-F. If the idea of X contains F, X is F; if it does not contain F, X is non-F. That is what it is, for Malebranche, to have a clear idea. This principle licences the inference from 'My clear idea of body doesn't represent it as possessing any dynamical properties' to 'My clear idea of body represents it as devoid of dynamical properties'.

The second strand of argument involves an application of the principle of sufficient reason. If our hypothetical body had a motive power, and was thus capable of self-motion, the power would have to produce some determinate motion, in terms of speed and direction. But no sufficient reason could be provided in such a case.

What happens, the Word continues, when a moving body strikes another body?

... what will become of it, when it encounters another of which it knows neither the solidity nor the size? It will give to it, you will say, a part of its motive force? But who has taught you this? Who has told you that the other will receive it? What portion of this force will it give to it? And how will it be able to communicate or spread this force? Do you conceive all this clearly?

(*OCM* X 48)

Your senses, the Word continues, tell you only that the resting body begins to move after being struck by the moving body; to infer from this that the moving body possessed a motive force or power, some part of which it imparted to the other, is a mere prejudice.

This argument finds its definitive statement in the seventh of the *Entretiens sur la Métaphysique*, where Malebranche's spokesman Theodore seeks to show his young pupil Ariste that it is self-contradictory to suppose that one body can act upon another (*OCM* XII 154–5, JS 110). Consult your clear idea of body, says Theodore. 'Do you not clearly see that bodies can be moved, but that they cannot move themselves?' Once again, there is an appeal to sufficient reason to reinforce the point. If this chair could begin to move, asks Theodore, how fast would it move, and in which direction? The final and conclusive proof depends on the theory of continuous creation, but the lack of any motive force or power in bodies can be established independently.

As for the supposed power of bodies to act on minds or spirits, this is even more incomprehensible. Experience can of course establish that whenever a human brain comes to be in state $\phi 1$, the mind of that human will come to be in state $\psi 1$. Precisely which part of the brain serves as the seat of the soul is of no great significance for Malebranche. He alludes vaguely to the 'principal part' of the brain, and mentions Descartes' notorious pineal gland hypothesis without endorsing it (*OCM* I 193–4, LO 89), merely as one physiological theory among others. Given a physical effect on the organs of sense and thence on the brain, the mind will come to experience a certain sensation. We must not infer, however, that the mind considers the brain-traces (it certainly has no awareness or knowledge of them), nor that the brain-traces are the real causes of our sensations. The mind can receive nothing from bodies.

In place of the supposed action of body on mind Malebranche postulates a 'mutual correspondence' between brain-states and sensations, which correspondence is sustained by the 'general laws of the union of soul and body' (*OCM* I 216, LO 102). A similar story can be told for the passions, which have as their (occasional) causes agitations of the blood and animal spirits. It is impossible, Malebranche insists, that there could be any sort of necessary connection between an agitation of the blood and/or animal spirits on the one hand, and an emotion on the other:

> For I cannot understand how certain people imagine that there is an absolutely necessary relation between the movements of the spirits and blood and the emotions of the soul. A few tiny particles of bile are rather violently stirred up in the brain – therefore, the soul must be excited by some passion, and the passion must be anger rather than love. What relation can be conceived between the idea of an enemy's faults, or a passion of contempt or hatred, on the one hand, and the corporeal movement of the blood's parts striking against certain parts of the brain on the other? How can they convince themselves that the one depends on the other, and that the union or connection of two things so remote and incompatible as mind and matter could be caused and maintained in any way other than by the continuous and all-powerful will of the Author of nature?
>
> (*OCM* II 129, LO 338–9)

When considering supposed body–body interactions, we are asked to concentrate our attention simply on the clear idea of matter to see that it doesn't contain any causal power. For the supposed effects of bodies on minds, Malebranche prefers to deploy his dualist metaphysics. Once we see that the presence of bile particles in the blood can be conceived as quite distinct from the feeling of anger, we will grant that each is capable of existence independently of the other. If so, there can be no metaphysically necessary connection between them, and the question of why they tend to co-occur must be referred to the will of God in establishing one the (occasional) cause of the other.

In the *Conversations Chrétiennes* we find a somewhat different version of the argument, turning on an explicit principle of causal containment. Fire, Theodore reminds his pupil Ariste, is just a rapid state of agitation of the minute constituent particles of a body, not itself possessed of pleasure or pain. Can fire, then, be the cause of pleasure or pain in the mind of a spirit? Ariste replies simply that he does not think so (*OCM* IV 15–16). The third participant in the conversation, the naturalistically-minded Aristarche, replies that the fire causes only the sensation of heat, and that the pleasure or pain result from the mind's perception of the beneficial or harmful effects of the fire upon the body of the subject.

This, responds Theodore, makes no sense at all. The soul is completely ignorant of the physiological changes in the body, so can't be responding to them. Nor is the soul active in sensation – if experience teaches us anything in this regard, it is that such sensations are passive. In any case, Aristarche has failed to answer the original objection: the heat (as sensed) is no more in the fire than is the pleasure or pain. The moving parts of the fire can – or at least, so it seems – impart motion to the fibres of the hand, but they cannot communicate a sensation they do not themselves possess (*OCM* IV 19).

In the seventh of the *Entretiens sur la Métaphysique,* Theodore is seeking to persuade Ariste that he is more closely united with God than with his own body. Ariste thinks that it is certain that bodies act on minds – if the thorn pricks my body, I will feel pain. Experience, he insists, leaves no room for doubt on this score. Theodore's reply is as follows:

> Nevertheless I strongly doubt it, or rather I do not believe it at all. Experience teaches me that I feel pain when a thorn pricks me. That much is certain. But let us leave it at that. For in no way does experience teach us that the thorn acts on our mind, or that it has any power. Let us believe nothing of the sort – that is my advice to you.
>
> (*OCM* XII 151, JS 107)

Theodore dismisses the idea of a 'union' between soul and body as hopelessly obscure. 'This word "union", then, explains nothing. It requires explanation itself' (*OCM* XII 153, JS 109). Experience teaches us that there are reliable correlations between mental and bodily states, but it sheds no further light. Reason tells us that mental and physical states are quite distinct, and therefore cannot be true causes of each other. Malebranche here reveals himself as a more strict and rigorous dualist than Descartes, who was prepared to take the notion of a mind–body union seriously, at least in his replies to the objections of Princess Elizabeth.[15] One of Malebranche's earliest critics, Desgabets, objects that his dualism is so strict that it leaves, effectively, no distinction between a human soul and an angel (see *OCM* XVIII 81–93). If the soul can exist and have its full range of modes (thoughts, feelings, sensations, etc.) quite independently of the body, then, says Desgabets, the disembodied state is 'natural' to it, and embodiment would be merely accidental.[16] This is in stark contrast to the more orthodox Thomist view, espoused by Desgabets, that the human soul is 'naturally' embodied, and can only exercise its full range of powers in the embodied state, whereas disembodiment is a 'violent' state possible only by supernatural power.

The question of the cause of our sensations is addressed once again in a late work, the *Entretien d'un Philosophe Chrétien et d'un Philosophe Chinois*. When I open my eyes in the countryside, says the Christian, the objects reflect light rays, which produce images when focused onto the retinas of my eyes, which images in turn give rise to agitations in my optic nerves and brain. But none of these things is a perception. That, replies the Chinese sage, is just what our philosophers deny:

> For what we call spirit or soul is, according to them, nothing but subtle organic matter. The vibrations of the fibres of the brain, joined with the movements of those little bodies or animal spirits are the same things as our perceptions, our judgements, our reasonings. In a word, they are the same thing as our various thoughts.
>
> (*OCM* XV 12)

Malebranche thus ascribes to the Chinese philosophers an identity theory of mind and body that has a striking resemblance to Spinozism. The Chinese (and Spinozist) identity theory is dismissed, however, as inconsistent with our clear ideas:

> I clearly conceive, by means of the idea of extension or of matter, that it is capable of shapes and of movements, of permanent or successive relations of distance, and nothing more; and I speak only of what I clearly conceive. I find that there is even less of a relation between the movement of little bodies, the vibration of the fibres of the brain, and our thoughts, than there is between the square and the circle, which no one ever mistakes for one another.
>
> (*OCM* XV 12)

How can a particular arrangement or motion of the fibres of the brain be a certain thought or feeling? In this argument Malebranche grants, for the sake of argument, that $\phi \rightarrow \phi$ causal relations are intelligible, but insists that, even if this were so, $\phi \rightarrow \Psi$ causal connections would still be ruled out by dualist metaphysics, which in turn rest on the principle of clear ideas. There could only, it seems, be an intelligible connection between physical cause (stimulation of the sense organs) and mental effect (sensation) if some sort of identity theory were true, but that is inconceivable.

Turning now to the supposed power of the human mind to move its own body by an act of will, Malebranche needs, once again, to reject the seeming verdict of common sense as mere unreflective prejudice. To deny that I can raise my own arm, or flex my own leg, might seem crazy, he admits. But the arguments against the assumption of any such causal power are simply unanswerable. There is no necessary connection, we are reminded in Book Six of the *Recherche*, between my will to raise my arm and my arm going up (*OCM* II 315, LO 450). The volition is a mode of a finite mind or spirit; the motion is a mode of a quite distinct material substance; so each can be conceived independently and there can be no necessary connection between them. Such a *liaison nécessaire* exists only between the Divine will and its effects. Nor can God communicate such a power to creatures, any more than He can communicate His divinity. Omnipotence is incommunicable, and only an omnipotent agent can be a true cause. The reason why this seems so obvious to Malebranche will become clearer when we discuss the metaphysics of continuous creation.

In addition to the standard argument from the lack of a necessary connection, Malebranche adds a new and quite distinct argument to refute the common-sense opinion that our volitions are the causes of our voluntary bodily motions. When I will to raise my arm, animal spirits course along the motor nerves leading from my brain to the muscles of my arm. So, says Malebranche, to move my arm, I first have to dispatch the animal spirits down the requisite channels. But even men who know nothing of anatomy can move their arms at will (*OCM* II 315, LO 449–50). Often, indeed, the mere yokel will move more dextrously than the learned physician or anatomist. A man may will to raise his arm, but only God knows how to do it. Lacking this knowledge, how can my mind be the true cause?[17]

This typically Malebranchian argument can also be found in *Éclaircissement* XV of the *Recherche*, where Malebranche replies to a series of standard arguments for the reality of second causes. When I will to move my arm, the arm will (normally) move as willed. This, says Malebranche, cannot be denied:

> But I deny that my will is the true cause of my arm's movement … for I see no relation whatever between such different things. I even see clearly that there can be no relation between the volition I have to move my arm and the agitation of the animal spirits, i.e. of certain tiny bodies whose motion and figure I do not know and which choose certain nerve canals from a million

others I do not know to cause in me the motion I desire through an infinity of movements I do not desire.

(*OCM* III 226, LO 669)

It follows, Malebranche concludes, that the 'union' of mind and body is completely unintelligible, except as a somewhat misleading way of referring to God's constant sustaining action. By establishing my volitions as (normally) occasional causes of the motions of my limbs, God has laid down certain rules for His own operations. To say that He has given me the 'force' or 'power' needed to move my limbs is to say nothing at all. An opponent might retort that this 'force' is known by introspection, through our familiarity with the sensation of *effort*. Granting that the sensation of effort often accompanies voluntary motions, Malebranche replies that (a) this sensation often merely makes us aware of our own weakness; and (b) there is still no '*rapport*' or intelligible relation between the sensation and the bodily motion. No sensation (a mode of the soul) could have the right sort of necessary connection to a bodily motion.

In the sixth of the *Méditations Chrétiennes* we can find essentially the same argument, now put in the mouth of the Word of God. To judge the powers of creatures, says the Word,

> ... it is necessary to retire into yourself and consult their ideas, and if one can find in their ideas any force or virtue, it must be attributed to them: for one must attribute to beings what one clearly conceives to be contained in the ideas which represent them, since these are the eternal models on which they have been formed

> (*OCM* X 60)

So if you wish to know whether the soul can move the body, you must seek to discover a necessary connection between a volition and a bodily movement, or rather between their respective ideas. (This raises a serious problem for Malebranche: by his own explicit admission, we have no clear idea of the soul and its modes.[18] Small wonder that we soon switch back to the argument from ignorance). To move its body itself, the soul would need detailed anatomical knowledge, yet an ignorant peasant can dance more nimbly than the most learned physician. 'Can one do, can one even will what one doesn't know how to do?' (*OCM* X 62). As for the suggestion that the sensation of effort provides some insight into a real causal power located in the will, it is again dismissed as merely a mistake: 'do you clearly see that there is some relation

108

between what you call effort, and the direction of the animal spirits in the tubes of the nerves which serve the movements that you want to produce?' (*OCM* X 64).

Since the answer to this rhetorical question has to be a clear and decided 'no', it follows that the sensation of effort is only contingently associated with the motion of the animal spirits. So there is no necessary connection between the act of will (with or without the sensation of effort) and the resulting bodily motion. The fact that such volitions are (normally) followed by appropriate bodily motions can only be put down to God's constancy and benevolence in establishing the laws governing the operations of mind and body.

Let us turn finally to the mind's supposed control over its own states, i.e. to $\Psi \rightarrow \Psi$ causal connections. That the human soul has considerable power over its own states was common ground to almost all metaphysicians before Malebranche. Yet this too is denied, as attributing to the creature too high a degree of independence of its Creator. To understand Malebranche's position, we need to distinguish the intellectual from the purely sensory domains, and to show that God is the only true cause operative in both these realms of our experience.

In the intellectual domain, as we have seen, Malebranche asserts that ideas are archetypes in the mind of God, not modes of the human soul. The act of attention, e.g. to a mathematical problem, is a sort of analogue of prayer. But there is no necessary connection between a prayer and its realisation, any more than there is for any other human act of will. As for questions of value and motivation, God causes in me both my general inclination towards the good, and my first-order love of particular offered goods. The only thing that remains up to me is my second-order act of consenting to proffered first-order goods. Whether this suffices to give Malebranche a defensible account of human freedom will be our topic in Chapter Nine.

In *Éclaircissement* XV of the *Recherche*, the passivity of the mind in the reception of ideas is supported by a familiar argument. Introspection teaches me that, when I will to think of a certain subject, the required idea comes (usually) to mind. This may need a little spelling out, to avoid obvious paradoxes. I can't will to think of Vienna, it might seem, without already thinking of Vienna. What I will, presumably, is to visualise the front of the *Karlskirche*, to remember the dates of Emperor Franz Joseph, or to call to mind the opening bars of Mozart's Fortieth Symphony. Once described in such terms, it is clear that the act of will is only contingently connected with its fulfilment. But since such volitions regularly precede the reception of ideas, prejudice leads us to conclude – quite mistakenly – that our minds have the active power to create ideas, rather than the merely passive power of receiving them.[19] This is, of course, the same old error of confounding regular succession with real causal power.

In the first of the *Méditations Chrétiennes*, the same metaphysical point is expressed in theological language, in terms of Augustine's notion of illumination. The human mind, says the Word, is not the source of its own light: it is an 'illuminated light', not an 'illuminating light' (*OCM* X 12). When one makes an effort to understand a topic then, so long as it is within our limited capacities, illumination will normally be forthcoming. But there is no necessary connection between the will and the illumination. The sense of intellectual effort, of striving to understand, is no more an indication of real causal power than in the parallel case of bodily motion.

As for sensations, experience teaches us unequivocally that our minds are passive: they occur in us, but 'sans nous et même malgré nous' (*OCM* XV 14). As Theodore puts it in the *Entretiens sur la Métaphysique*,

> … each of us certainly senses that we are not the cause of our pain when we bleed, for example, or when we burn ourselves. We feel it despite ourselves and we cannot doubt that it comes from an external cause.
>
> (*OCM* XII 93, JS 57)

If the pain of bleeding or burning is not caused by the soul itself (which introspection shows to be passive), nor by bodily damage (a point already established by previous arguments), there remains only God who possesses the necessary knowledge and power. In addition, many sensations (e.g. visual ones) involve natural judgements. Since such judgements seem to require detailed knowledge of geometry and optics, yet to come to us in an instant without any calculation on our parts, it is easy for Malebranche to show that only God could be the cause of such sensations (*OCM* XV 14). My soul isn't aware of the images on the retinas of my eyes, nor do I know enough geometry and optics to derive, from the properties of the images, inferences about the sizes, shapes and distances of the bodies around me. Nor again could I calculate with sufficient rapidity to arrive at dozens of such natural judgements in an instant. Yet all these operations must take place somehow to generate judgements that are 'en nous' but 'sans nous' and even 'malgré nous'. I need only open my eyes to find myself not just bombarded with mere sensations, but also spontaneously forming the integral natural judgements. Only God, Malebranche concludes, could be the cause of such sensations and judgements.[20]

110

Continuous creation

The doctrine of continuous creation is not an innovation by Malebranche. Indeed, in the first *Éclaircissement* of the *Recherche* he describes it as 'the general view among theologians' (*OCM* III 26, LO 551). What is new in Malebranche is his clear perception of the radical implications of this orthodox thesis of scholastic theology. Where the majority of the schoolmen had sought to explain how continuous creation could be reconciled with the ordinary belief in natural powers,[21] Malebranche thinks that all such reconciling projects are unintelligible, and that continuous creation, properly understood, entails the complete non-existence of any natural powers.

The doctrine of continuous creation provides Malebranche with his final and definitive argument for occasionalism.[22] The arguments against particular types of causal power, wrongly supposed to exist in created minds and bodies, can now be relegated to a secondary and subordinate status. Since the argument from continuous creation is perfectly general, it applies indifferently to all supposed causal relations.

Suppose, explains Malebranche in the first *Éclaircissement* to the *Recherche*, that God has created a body at point X. A creature, we are then told, moves the body from X to another point Y. But, asks Malebranche, what are we to conceive in such a case?

> A body ... exists because God wills that it exist, and He wills it to exist either here or there, for He cannot create it nowhere. And if He creates it here, is it conceivable that a creature should displace it and move it elsewhere unless God at the same time wills to create it elsewhere in order to share His power with His creature as far as it is capable of it?
>
> (*OCM* III 26, LO 551–2)

If the continued existence of any given body is nothing but its continuous re-creation by God then, given that a body cannot exist without a determinate set of modes (size, shape and relations to other bodies) it follows that for a body to move from X to Y is simply for God to create it at X, then to re-create it at Y. But if this is the correct metaphysical account of the continued existence of a body, the only possible role for a secondary agent is that of occasional cause. An exactly parallel account can be told, of course, for souls and their modes (perceptions, thoughts and feelings). The crucial premise here is that of complete modal determinacy, i.e. that, as a matter of metaphysical necessity, the creation of a body (or a soul) requires its creation with a fully determinate set of modes. This thesis granted, continuous creation does indeed seem to entail a thoroughgoing occasionalism.[23]

It is impossible, Malebranche insists, for God to communicate His power to creatures. His confidence rests, once again, on the doctrine of continuous creation. The reason is provided in Book Six of the *Recherche*. Only omnipotence can create bodies (or souls), and omnipotence is incommunicable: 'God cannot even communicate His power to creatures, He cannot make them gods' (*OCM* II 318, LO 451). Not even the most enlightened of the angels can be a true cause. God sometimes establishes the will of an angel as an occasional cause (i.e. He decides that He will execute the angel's volitions), which may explain the frequent miracles of the Old Testament,[24] but this is not a genuine transfer of causal power. Since God cannot create more gods, and only a god can possess the power of creation, the thesis of continuous creation rules out any communication or transfer of power from God to His creatures.

In the *Méditations Chrétiennes*, the Word spells out this doctrine in its purest form. No finite spirit, the meditator is informed, can so much as move an atom by as little as a hair's breadth (*OCM* X 49). For a body to continue to exist, God must continue to will its existence: creation and conservation are one and the same for God. The only way in which a finite spirit could move a body, it follows, is if it could oblige God to recreate the body at Y rather than at X. So to be a true cause, a finite spirit would have to prevail over God, which is self-contradictory. God may, of course, establish for Himself a general rule making the volitions of certain finite spirits occasional causes, but that is a different matter altogether.

The most formal and explicit statement of Malebranche's argument can be found in the seventh of the *Entretiens*. It is the will of God, Theodore explains to Ariste, that gives existence to all bodies.

> Thus it is this same volition that puts bodies at rest or in motion, because it is that volition which gives them being, and because they cannot exist without being at rest or in motion. For, take note, God cannot do the impossible, or that which contains a manifest contradiction. He cannot will what cannot be conceived. Thus He cannot will that this chair exist, without at the same time willing that it exist either here or there and without His will placing it somewhere, since you cannot conceive of a chair existing unless it exists somewhere, either here or elsewhere.
>
> (*OCM* XII 156, JS 111–12)

This argument is perfectly general, applying to minds as well as bodies. Just as God cannot create a body without determinate values for its size, shape, and position, so He cannot create a mind without a corresponding set of psychological modes, i.e. perceptions and inclinations. Theodore's pupil Ariste admits that, in the original creation of bodies, God must determine not just their existence but also their location and state of motion or rest. But, he continues, this is no longer the case. Now that the moment of creation has passed, he thinks, bodies dispose themselves 'haphazardly, or according to the law of the strongest'. But, retorts Theodore, the moment of creation does not pass!

> For the world assuredly depends on the will of the Creator. If the world subsists, it is because God continues to will its existence. Thus, the conservation of creatures is, on the part of God, nothing but their continued creation.
>
> (*OCM* XII 156–7, JS 112)

Ariste suggests that God would require a positive volition to annihilate His creation, but Theodore corrects him. To suppose that the physical universe will continue to exist unless God explicitly wills its annihilation is to represent the creature as independent of its creator. For some creator–creature relations (parent and child, builder and house) the creature can survive the absence or non-existence of its creator, but the relation between God and His creatures is not of this kind. The builder can emigrate, or die, and the house remain, but if the sun were to cease-to-be, its light would be extinguished and all would be dark. The relation between God and the world is of the latter kind: if He were for a moment to withdraw His sustaining hand, the whole of His creation would instantaneously cease-to-be.[25]

The lesson, Theodore concludes, is perfectly clear. Once we understand continuous creation, we see that it is simply self-contradictory to assume any causal powers either in bodies or in finite (created) spirits:

> Creation does not pass, because the conservation of creatures is – on God's part – simply a continuous creation, a single volition subsisting and operating continuously. Now, God can neither conceive nor consequently will that a body exist nowhere, nor that it does not stand in certain relations of distance to other bodies. Thus, God cannot will that this armchair exist, and by this volition create or conserve it, without situating it here, there, or elsewhere. It is a contradiction, therefore, for one body to be

113

able to move another. Further, I claim, it is a contradiction for you to be able to move your armchair. Nor is this enough; it is a contradiction for all the angels and demons together to be able to move a wisp of straw. The proof of this is clear. For no power, however great it be imagined, can surpass or even equal the power of God. Now it is a contradiction that God wills this armchair to exist, unless He wills it to exist somewhere and unless, by the efficacy of His will, He puts it there, conserves it there, creates it there. Hence, no power can convey it to where God does not convey it, nor fix nor stop it where God does not stop it, unless God accommodates the efficacy of His action to the inefficacious action of His creatures.

(*OCM* XII 160, JS 115–16)

An exactly similar proof could of course be provided for every mode of every finite and created mind.

Continuous creation and *volontés générales*

According to the doctrine of continuous creation, for every substance S and every mode M of S, the questions 'Why does S exist?' and 'Why does S have M?' must be answered 'Because God wills it so'. But this suggests – quite misleadingly – that God's volitions extend to all the particular details of His material and spiritual creation. This Malebranche emphatically denies, notably in the *Traité de la Nature et de la Grâce*, and in the ensuing controversy with Arnauld. To say that God does everything, Malebranche argues, does not entail that anything is arbitrary or idiosyncratic[26]. In establishing occasional causes, God binds Himself to acting in accordance with *volontés générales*. He wills that, for example, the collision of one body with another serves as an occasion for Him to redistribute motions in accordance with a set of universal rules, and that the modes of a human mind stand in a regular one-to-one correspondence with the modes of the human brain.

When Malebranche writes of God's *volontés générales*, does he mean that the content of such divine volitions is itself universal in form? Or does God will particular events, but do so in accordance with universal rules? Does God will, for example, 'Let it be the case that whenever X occurs Y occurs'? Or does God will, whenever X occurs 'let Y occur'? Most of the critics and commentators, from Arnauld to Desmond Clarke, have assumed that Malebranche takes the former view.[27] Recently, however, this established reading has been challenged by Steven Nadler,[28]

114

who argues that God exercises particular acts of will in accordance with general rules. On the traditional interpretation God doesn't need, strictly speaking, to intervene in the course of nature: a few timeless acts of will express His power once and for all. If this is right Leibniz's account of occasionalism, with its picture of God forever intervening in the course of nature,[29] is a gross caricature, and Malebranche's actual position is closer to Leibniz's own pre-established harmony. On Nadler's interpretation God, by contrast, is forever active in the physical and psychological realms alike, albeit exercising particular volitions in accordance with general rules. Nadler suggests that the reason God must execute His own designs is that He does not give His creatures 'natures', in the Aristotelian sense of 'nature' as internal principle of motion and rest. If creatures have no natures, Nadler argues, the laws of nature need to be actively executed by God, not merely laid down by Him in the act of creation. On this sensitive issue the texts are inconclusive. Nadler's reading seems better to capture Malebranche's keen sense of the immediacy of the dependence of all things on God. On the other hand, Malebranche does sometimes write as if the laws themselves are efficacious, which suggests that our talk of a 'law' is not mere shorthand for a regular and reliable pattern of particular volitions.

A recent paper by Andrew Pessin returns to this vexed question.[30] Pessin admits that the textual evidence is inconclusive, with some passages that lend themselves to each of the opposed readings. He finally comes down on the side of Nadler, arguing that the theory of particular volitions in accordance with general laws makes better sense of Malebranche's position than the standard view. He shows how – with a little ingenuity – this interpretation can meet the standard objections: that God is now said to be 'at rest', and that God seeks to minimise the number of His volitions. But he admits, in conclusion, that the issue is one that Malebranche himself seems never to have explicitly addressed, and may not even have been aware of. What concerned Malebranche was the lawlikeness of God's operations, not how, precisely, that lawlikeness is brought about.

If God does everything, how are we going to defend the notion of Divine Providence against obvious objections? How, as Milton would have put the question, are we to justify the ways of God to man? The problem is addressed in *Éclaircissement* VIII of the *Recherche*, in the context of Malebranche's explanation of original sin and its transmission. If God acted by particular volitions, says Malebranche, we would have to say that He willed every physical and moral evil that defaces and devalues our world.[31] But this overturns all religion and morality (*OCM*

III 84, LO 586). If we are to continue to describe God as 'just', 'wise', and 'benevolent', and mean anything at all by what we say, we cannot assume that He wills every detail of the world we experience. Rather, we must say that His will is in accordance with some principle of order. Order requires that God act by means of general laws, and this mode of operation permits the occasional lapse. In the realm of organic nature, for example, we come across monsters, i.e. animals with too many or too few limbs, or with members ill-adapted to their lifestyles. Why are there monsters?

> Order demands that the laws of nature by which God produces this infinite variety found in the world be very simple and small in number, as they in fact are, for this conduct bears the mark of an infinite wisdom. Now, the simplicity of these general laws produces in certain particular cases, due to the disposition of the subject, irregular kinds of motion, or rather, monstrous arrangements of them, and consequently, it is because God wills order that there are monsters. Thus, God does not will positively or directly that there should be monsters, but He wills positively certain laws of the communication of motion, of which monsters are necessary consequences.
>
> (*OCM* III 88–9, LO 589)

Continuous creation in accordance with *volontés générales* was not a dangerous or controversial doctrine when confined to the realm of nature. What proved much more provocative, and sparked the vitriolic exchanges with Arnauld, was Malebranche's explicit extension of the same doctrine to the theological realm of grace.[32] The Catholic Church requires us to believe that God sincerely wills that all men be saved, but orthodoxy also accepts that many are damned. This seems – at least at first sight – inconsistent with God's omnipotence. Jansenists such as Arnauld claim that God's grace is always efficacious, so the reason many are damned is that God has not given them sufficient grace, which seems to imply that God does not sincerely will to save all sinners. Malebranche's doctrine of *volontés générales* helps him to see an exit from this seeming theological impasse.

Experience suggests, says Malebranche in *Éclaircissement* XV, that grace is given to many, but that it is often inefficacious, like rain falling on stony ground (*OCM* III 220, LO 666). The analogy suggests that the distribution of grace, like that of rain, takes place in accordance with general laws rather than being given with an eye on the details of each particular case.

God's actions are always in accordance with order, but order requires Him to act in a manner that is worthy of His attributes of wisdom and immutability. This argument, only sketched in *Éclaircissement* XV (1678), becomes the central pillar of the *Traité de la Nature et de la Grâce* (1680), and the heart of the bitter polemical exchanges with Arnauld.

When we speak of God, says Malebranche in the *Traité*, we must not do so according to the ideas of the vulgar, but in accordance with our idea of an infinitely perfect Being (*OCM* V 26). Such a Being must be wise and immutable, and must act in such a way as to express these attributes. In sustaining the physical universe, He must act by a few simple and universal laws, as experience confirms. But the argument from the idea of God to His manner of action is *a priori*, not empirical, and must be equally valid in matters moral and spiritual as in matters physical (*OCM* V 32–3). This is the central argument of the entire *Traité*. God, according to Malebranche, has established the (human) soul of Jesus Christ as the occasional cause of the distribution of grace to humans, and acts Himself in accordance with the general principle 'If Jesus wills that X receive grace, X will receive grace'. But the soul of Jesus, although united with the divine wisdom of the Word, does not have *actual* knowledge of all that God knows, with the result that the distribution of grace is not, in general, proportioned to the specific needs of particular sinners.

That grace is distributed in accordance with general laws can be demonstrated, claims Malebranche in the first *Éclaircissement* to the *Traité*, both *a priori* and *a posteriori*. Arguing *a priori*, one starts with a divine attribute such as wisdom or immutability, which is necessarily contained in the notion of a perfect Being. One then demonstrates that acting by general laws betokens greater wisdom than acting by lots of particular volitions. (A watchmaker who can design a timepiece that will run without intervention shows greater skill than one who is continually obliged to tinker with his creation.) Only a being with limited intelligence and foresight needs to act by particular volitions (*OCM* V 165–6). Arguing *a posteriori*, we notice that grace sometimes falls on hardened hearts, as rain on stony ground. But the wilful rejection of grace by the sinner increases his guilt. It follows that, if God acted by particular volitions, either His will is frustrated, or He is malicious, i.e. He deliberately and cruelly wills to make a particular sinner more culpable. But His will cannot be frustrated. So the opponent, it seems, is committed to a representation of God as cruel and partial in His operations.

This line of argument is incessantly repeated in the correspondence with Arnauld. My *Traité*, Malebranche explains, is directed against two sets of opponents. On the one hand, there are the libertines and atheists; on the other, there are those Christian theologians who deny that God has a sincere will to save all men (*OCM* VI 35). The Catholic Church requires us to believe both that God wills the salvation of all men, and that many men are damned. How is this possible? Only God can resist God, so the reason why many men are damned must be found in the divine attributes. A perfect being must act by *volontés générales* rather than by *volontés particulières*. That God does so can be proved *a priori* (from the idea of a perfect Being), *a posteriori* (from experience), and by *reductio* (refutation of the rival theory). If God governed the world by particular acts of will, it would be a sin to run for cover when it rained, and we could re-instate trial by combat in place of the law courts, confident that God would intervene to vindicate the righteous (*OCM* VI 42–3). And we would be forced to conclude that God wills the salvation only of those who are in fact saved. Arnauld, according to Malebranche, may pretend to be a good Catholic, but his Jansenist principles are in fact just Calvinism in disguise (*OCM* VII 525ff).

Is this the best of all possible worlds?

Is the physical and moral universe that God has created the best world that He could have created? There are powerful reasons pressing Malebranche to answer both 'no' and 'yes'. Let us examine the negative answer first. God could have created a world in which rain always falls on cultivated ground, and is never wasted by falling on stony ground or into the sea. Likewise, God could have given to each man precisely the amount of grace needed for his salvation. But to achieve such ends God would have had to employ more complex means, either in terms of more, and more complex, general laws, or in terms of a greater number of particular interventions. If we just consider the physical universe, it is 'founded on laws of motion that are so simple and natural that it is perfectly worthy of the infinite wisdom of its author' (*OCM* V 29). From the infinity of possible universes, God has chosen, we are told, the one that 'could have produced and conserved itself by the simplest laws, or that had to be the most perfect in relation to the simplicity of the means necessary for its production or conservation' (*OCM* V 28).

If we consider the universe in abstraction from the laws by which God creates and sustains it, it will be judged manifestly imperfect. Just as monsters are blemishes in the Order of nature, so are hardened sinners in the Order of grace. Arnauld objects that it is rash – not so say presumptuous – to take it upon ourselves to find fault with the work of God

(*OCM* IX 767). What we call 'faults' and 'blemishes' must, he insists, merely reflect our ignorance of God's intentions. Monsters, as well as perfectly formed organisms, equally manifest God's will. If every detail of the world is the result of a particular volition on God's part, the inference is inescapable.

Arnauld's opinion, says Malebranche, threatens to overturn the very foundations of morality and religion (*OCM* IX 766). If we can't trust the objectivity of our judgements of perfection (physical and moral), a terrifying prospect looms before us. Maybe our value judgements reflect only our human desires and feelings, not to say our prejudices. If every monstrous birth and every unrepentant sinner is exactly as God willed – in every particular and detail – then God's ways are not our ways, and His ends may be utterly distinct from ours. But this is incredible. That a monster is imperfect, a *failed* copy of a divine plan or archetype, is simply apparent to us. To deny it is to reject the argument to design for the existence of a wise and benevolent Creator.[33] If we can't find faults in the works of God, we can't admire His handiwork or praise His wisdom either (*OCM* IX 769).[34] If a creature is perfect simply because it is as God willed it, and all creatures – perfectly formed and monstrous alike – are the product of particular divine volitions, it becomes completely meaningless to praise God's wisdom in achieving His ends.

> I do not fear to say it again: the universe is not the most perfect that could exist in an absolute sense, but only the most perfect that can exist, in relation to the means most worthy of the divine attributes. There are visible defects in the works of God – in His works I say again, but not in His conduct. It is a visible defect, that a child should come into the world with superfluous members which prevent it from living.
>
> (*OCM* IX 768)

To suppose that God had a particular volition to create this particular malformed infant would be, for Malebranche, a blasphemy. Rather, God owes it to Himself to act in accordance with His attributes of wisdom and immutability. His actions are always in accordance with Order, and Order requires that He care more about His own perfections than about His creatures. It is, after all, a mark of Order to love things in strict proportion to their objective degrees of perfection.

An all-perfect being must, Malebranche argues, act by the simplest of means to bring about its designs. Reliance on unnecessarily complex or cumbersome means to bring about a desired end is a mark of imperfection.

This serves to introduce the famous principle of the *simplicité des voies*. The picture here is of *simplicité des voies* as a side-constraint, limiting God's freedom to choose among the possible universes He could create. On such a picture, the degree of perfection of each universe is independent of the means used to create it, and the *simplicité des voies* principle serves merely to exclude many possible universes (including some of the best), leaving only a small subset for God to choose from. This, however, is not Malebranche's final view of the matter.[35] In the 'Letter against Prejudice' of 1704, Malebranche provides a synopsis of his *Traité*, and an enlightening picture of the nature of God's choice. It follows from my principles, Malebranche explains, that:

> God has not made, and did not have to make this world the most perfect that was possible, but only the most perfect that was possible with regard to the simplicity and fruitfulness of the means which He employed to produce it. Let me explain. A work with a degree of perfection of eight, or which expresses the character of the divine attributes to degree eight, produced by means which only express them to degree two, only expresses those attributes in total to degree ten. But a work with a degree of perfection of six, or which expresses the divine attributes to degree six, produced by means which also express them to degree six, expresses the divine attributes to degree twelve. Therefore, if God were choosing one of these two works, He would choose the less perfect, since the less perfect one, when combined with the means, would better display the character of His attributes, and His inviolable law is only, and can only be, the immutable order of His attributes. In a word, God honours Himself as much by the wisdom of the means as by the excellence of the works.
>
> (*OCM* IX 1085)

This explains why many aspects of creation, physical and moral alike, appear imperfect to us – we tend to notice the intrinsic perfections and imperfections of the work and to overlook the simplicity of the means employed. A little reflection, however, should serve to enlighten us. It would be contrary to Order for God not to care about His own wisdom, and not to intend to express it in His work. We can't, perhaps, see how to do the calculation, nor how to render the various divine attributes mutually commensurable, but this merely reveals our limitations.

If the *simplicité des voies* is thus reconstrued as part of the goal rather than as a side-constraint, Malebranche can reply to the objection of

Fontenelle that he represents God as a poor workman, unable to achieve His ends.[36] God's true aim, for Malebranche, is the best weighted expression of His own attributes, not any particular arrangement of the created universe. This also helps Malebranche with the thorny subject of miracles. God owes it to Himself, says Malebranche, to express His wisdom and immutability in His creation. This in turn requires that He minimise the number of miracles. But the minimum number of miracles (creation aside) is zero. So if the *simplicité des voies* were a side-constraint, we seem to have all the premises in place for an argument terminating in pure deism.[37] Malebranche's opponents, starting with Bossuet and Arnauld, levelled just this accusation against him, i.e. that he was denying – at least implicitly – the miracles of scripture. But on Malebranche's final account of the subject, this conclusion does not follow. If *simplicité des voies* is a part of God's goal in creation, to be balanced against other competing desiderata, it remains at least conceivable that Order (the most balanced total expression of all the divine attributes) could permit, or even require, the occasional miracle.[38]

Objections and replies

The non-existence of bodies

The most obvious objection to occasionalism is that, by making the material universe causally redundant, it leads directly to idealism. In his *Examination of Père Malebranche's Opinion of Seeing all Things in God*, Locke raises just this charge. How, on Malebranche's principles, Locke asks, can he know that the sun exists at all?

> Did he ever see the sun? No, but on occasion of the presence of the sun to his eyes, he has seen the idea of the sun in God, which God has exhibited to him; but the sun, because it cannot be united to his soul, he cannot see. How then does he know that there is 'a sun which he never saw? And since God does all things by the most compendious ways, what need is there that God should make a sun that we might see its idea in him when he pleased to exhibit it, when this might as well be done without any real sun at all.[39]

Locke's *Examination* is of course a critique of the Vision in God, so it might be thought inappropriate to introduce it here. But Locke's objection – that the Vision in God leaves Malebranche trapped in the 'palace of ideas' – turns precisely on the lack of any causal role for bodies in the production of our perceptions. For Malebranche, ideas are 'in' God and it is ideas that cause our perceptions, leaving no causal role for tables and chairs, trees and houses. It is because Locke allows such a causal role that he thinks his theory of ideas doesn't fall into the veil-of-ideas scepticism that threatens Malebranche.

If God produces all my sensations Himself, why should He need the prompt or reminder of an occasional cause (usually the presence of a body to my sense organs)? Since He does nothing in vain, surely it would be more economical and elegant to do without bodies altogether?[40] The Jesuits of the *Mémoires de Trévoux*, no friends of Malebranche, described Berkeley as a 'Malebranchiste de bonne foi' (*OCM* XIX 834) for explicitly accepting the idealism that they saw as implicit in Malebranche's principles.[41]

The objection is first voiced in *Éclaircissement VI* of the *Recherche*, and receives its fullest treatment in the sixth of the *Entretiens*. In the former work, Malebranche admits frankly that it is very difficult to prove that bodies exist (*OCM* III 53, LO 568). In philosophy, Malebranche has instructed us, we should only believe what has been demonstrated with geometrical rigour, propositions we cannot doubt without suffering 'the secret reproaches of Reason', as he puts it. But the existence of a material world is not demonstrable. The direct or immediate object of my acquaintance when I open my eyes is not the material universe but an 'intelligible' world, with its own 'intelligible' space, filled with 'intelligible' bodies (*OCM* III 61, LO 572–3). I find myself, of course, as Descartes reminded us in the *Sixth Meditation*, spontaneously believing in an external world of material things, but this *penchant extrême à croire* is a matter of conviction rather than of evidence. And we know that our natural judgements lead us astray in other matters, such as our tendency to 'project' sensible qualities such as red and hot and sweet, to suppose that these mere sensations are objective qualities of bodies.

Our erroneous judgements about secondary qualities, Malebranche replies, can readily be corrected by reason, whereas it is impossible to demonstrate by reasoning that bodies do not exist. The balance of probabilities must therefore favour belief: God has given us a strong propensity to believe in bodies, and it would be hard to absolve Him of the charge of deceit if such natural judgements were all erroneous. But this reasoning, which is a variant on Descartes' proof of the external world in *Meditation Six* (albeit deprived of its causal element) is still a matter of plausibility rather than a strict proof. Given that God was not obliged to create the material universe, its existence can only be contingent, and therefore not demonstrable *a priori*. So if the existence of bodies can be proved neither *a priori* (from the idea of God) nor *a posteriori* (from experience) it remains, as far as unaided reason is concerned, merely plausible. It is to faith, i.e. to scripture, that we must turn at last for full assurance that God created the heavens and the earth, and that the Word was made flesh (*OCM* III 64, LO 574).

In the sixth of the *Entretiens*, Theodore explains to Ariste that God, and not material things, is the true cause of all our sensations. The quick-witted young pupil promptly replies that he has just had a very strange thought:

> I almost dare not suggest it to you, for I fear that you will consider me a visionary. It is that I am beginning to doubt that bodies exist.
> (*OCM* XII 136, JS 94)

When Ariste demands a strict demonstration of the existence of bodies, Theodore responds that this is asking too much:

> 'An exact demonstration'! That is a little too much, Aristes. I confess I do not have one. On the contrary, it seems to me that I have an 'exact demonstration' of the impossibility of such a demonstration.
> (*OCM* XII 136, JS 95)

The notion of an absolutely or infinitely perfect being, Theodore explains, does not include the notion of creation. Since God is sufficient to Himself, creation is a free act of His will rather than a necessary emanation from His essence. So the existence of the material universe is a contingent fact that cannot be demonstrated *a priori*. Our confidence in the real existence of bodies must rest ultimately on revelation.

Revelation, Theodore continues, comes in two varieties, 'natural' and 'supernatural'. The natural revelation of the material world is provided by my senses. The senses do, admittedly, give rise to errors and confusions – we do sometimes confuse mere phantasms with real things – but this gives us no reason for a *general* doubt of the existence of bodies. On the contrary, says Theodore, my sensations of the external world pass a coherence test: they are 'so consistent, so linked together, so well ordered, that it seems to me certain that God would be deceiving us if there were nothing in everything we see' (*OCM* XII 142, JS 99).

Our sensations come with built-in natural judgements concerning the real existence and properties of external objects. These natural judgements are only plausible, never evident. But in the case of our judgements of sizes, shapes and distances we have no general reason to doubt them, and we find that (with a few exceptions, dismissed as 'dreams' and 'hallucinations') they pass a coherence test. Given these natural facts, says Theodore, no actual person entertains a genuine and sincere doubt of the existence of bodies (*OCM* XII 143, JS 100). But for complete certainty we still need to turn to faith. Our confident certainty of the existence of bodies thus rests, for Malebranche, on two different forms of revelation (sensation and scripture) and on two different coherence tests (of sensory beliefs with one another, and of sensory beliefs with the revealed Word of God).

Locke, we have seen, had a point. By denying the supposed causal connection between bodies and minds, Malebranche takes away the naïve, common-sense route to belief in an external world. In place of a simple inference from effect (sensation) to cause (external object), Malebranche leaves us with a web of natural judgements, coherent with one another for the most part but drawing external support only from the supernatural revelation of scripture. Small wonder that Malebranche was one of the ancestors of various idealist strands in modern philosophy.

Is occasionalism incompatible with mechanism?

In Cartesian physics, there is a powerful element of philosophical rationalism, a pressing *a priori* demand that all explanations in physics be couched in terms of our clear and distinct ideas. This appeal to clear and distinct ideas was taken to rule out action at a distance as unintelligible. Bodies, the Cartesians tell us, are moved only by impulse and pressure. This Cartesian physics is explicitly endorsed by Malebranche in Chapter Eight of Book Six of the *Recherche* (*OCM* II 400ff, LO 498ff). He goes on to apply it to the phenomena of magnetism and of muscular contraction, both of which are explained in terms of the mechanical action of currents of subtle matter.

But this Cartesian physics seems to depend on our possession of some kind of rational insight into real causal powers. The Cartesian mechanist thinks that only the impact of another, moving body *can* set a previously resting body in motion. It is far from obvious that Malebranche, given his commitment to occasionalism, can endorse this argument. If the true cause of all bodily motions is the will of God, why should He be under any obligation to establish laws of motion in which contact invariably plays the role of the occasional cause? Why not some form of action at a distance? This objection is voiced by Fontenelle in his response (1686) to Bayle's reply to his *Doutes sur le système physique des causes occasionelles.*[42] If, asks Fontenelle, there is nothing in the moving body that qualifies it to be the real cause of the ensuing motion of the struck body, why should contact be required at all?

> I shall suppose therefore that God, instead of establishing collision as the occasional cause of the communication of motions, has established as the occasional cause the passage of two bodies to a certain distance from one another, for example to a line which is the mean proportional between their diameters. The entire order of the material universe would then depend on this new principle.[43]
>
> (*OCM* XVII–1 588)

Let body A, of 1 inch diameter, approach body B, of 2 inches in diameter. Then, on this proposed principle, they will rebound as soon as the distance between them reaches $\sqrt{2}$ inches. But, says Fontenelle, we see no 'liaison naturelle et nécessaire' in such a case, in sharp contrast to the case of collision, in which the impenetrability of the colliding bodies necessitates some redistribution of their motions. When A strikes B, says Fontenelle,

> … I see that it is absolutely necessary that some change or other must take place; and the necessity of this change is not derived from the will of God, for according to the hypothesis He would still move A and B in the same way if nothing external to Him opposed this, but it is derived from the nature of bodies and from their impenetrability, which is absolutely opposed to the continuation of the movement of A and of B as it was previously.[44]
>
> (*OCM* XVII–1 589)

There is then, in Fontenelle's eyes at least, a necessary connection between the natures of bodies A and B (their impenetrability), and contact–action, which connection is lacking for action at a distance. The nature of bodies, he infers, plays a real causal role which the occasionalist cannot account for.

This is a powerful argument against occasionalism. The occasionalist, it seems, will be forced to say that the two types of action are essentially the same, and that impenetrability itself is only an 'institution', i.e. the consequence of a divine decree rather than a real causal power. Ariste comes close to this in the seventh of the *Entretiens*:

> Thus one body cannot move another by an efficacy belonging to its nature. If bodies had in themselves the force to move

themselves, the stronger would – as efficient causes – overcome those bodies they encountered. But, as a body is moved only by another body, their encounter is only an occasional cause which, in virtue of their impenetrability, obliges the mover or creator to distribute His action. And because God must act in a simple and uniform manner, He had to formulate laws which were general and as simple as possible, in order that when change was necessary He changed as little as possible and, at the same time, produced an infinity of different effects ...

(OCM XII 164, JS 119)

The suggestion here is that the impenetrability of bodies obliges God to make some change or other to the motions of colliding bodies, but that nothing in the intrinsic features of the bodies determines God's precise choices.[45] But this can only be part of the story. Even impenetrability cannot, for a strict occasionalist, be a real power residing in bodies and compelling God to act in certain ways. On the contrary, occasionalism requires that impenetrability itself be only an 'institution', a consequence of a divine decree and nothing more. But then, Fontenelle can ask, what exactly is a body, over and above a mere geometrical figure? Does it have any intrinsic nature of its own? This line of enquiry would lead Leibniz – another perceptive critic of Malebranche – towards a genuine dynamics of moving bodies.[46]

The most acute and incisive reply to Fontenelle was provided by Pierre Bayle. If God had established Fontenelle's imagined law then, says Bayle, men would simply have come to believe that the approach of A was the true cause of the motion of B. We are led by our nature, as if 'instructed by a natural lesson', to judge that regular succession indicates real causation (OCM, XVII–1 591). So whichever system of laws God chooses to establish, the occasionalist can continue to insist that God is the only true cause, while acknowledging that we will spontaneously find ourselves attributing natural powers to creatures – contact action in one case, action at a distance in the other.

In contact action, it seems, the change of state of the colliding bodies follows necessarily from their nature (impenetrability). This, says Bayle, the occasionalist can grant. But Fontenelle wants us to conclude that the collision is the real cause of the redistribution of motions, not just the occasion for that change. This, replies Bayle, does not follow. In creating impenetrable bodies, God establishes certain rules for Himself:

> It is therefore quite possible that the collision, or the nature of bodies, is at the same time the occasional cause, and nothing more, of the communication of motions, and that God is obliged by such an occasion to move bodies in a certain manner.
>
> (*OCM* XVII–1 592)

As regards the ontological issue of the real existence or otherwise of natural powers, Bayle's defence of occasionalism against Fontenelle seems conclusive. What it is for bodies to be impenetrable is simply for God to have established certain rules for His continuous re-creation of bodies and the re-distribution of the modes of local motion. The epistemological issue, however, remains unresolved. Given that occasionalism seems to place no *a priori* constraints on the rules God could choose to employ,[47] how can we be so confident that He has in fact chosen contact–action rules alone? Malebranche exudes confidence on this point, and his disciples were prominent in the French resistance to Newtonian physics,[48] but the principles of occasionalism seem to rule out any attempt to exclude action at a distance from physics on *a priori* grounds. It is true, of course, that we find contact–action easier to comprehend than action at a distance, but this may be only a matter of human psychology.

A theological parallel may help to reinforce this point, that occasionalism places no *a priori* constraints on (occasional) causes. Our intuitions tell us that an effect cannot precede its cause. But, as Malebranche sees, the occasionalist is at liberty to deny this. On Malebranche's account of grace, the prayers of Jesus Christ are the occasional cause of God's distribution of the gift of grace. But what of the grace received by the Old Testament patriarchs? On occasionalist principles, Malebranche replies, this objection is deprived of all force (*OCM* V 158). Since the cause (occasion) has no power or efficacy of its own, and no necessary connection with the effect, why should it not be the case that Abraham receives grace in 1000 BC because Christ prays for him in 30 AD? Since God is omniscient, He knows, at the former time, that Christ will pray for Abraham at the latter time, and God wills timelessly to distribute grace in accordance with Christ's prayers. Malebranche admits that such backwards causation seems 'contrary to order', and doesn't insist on the truth of this bizarre hypothesis, but on his principles it remains perfectly possible. The example serves to illustrate the tension between occasionalism and causal rationalism, as applied to occasional causes. The doctrine of occasionalism as we have seen, results from the application of causal rationalism to real (metaphysical) causation. But if occasionalism is correct, everyday 'causal' laws are just divine institutions, which need not fall under any *a priori* constraints. Unless we can lay down rules for God, we may have to make greater and greater concessions to Humean empiricism.[49]

God is the author of sin

In *Éclaircissement* XV of the *Recherche*, Malebranche lists a battery of arguments for the reality of second causes and against occasionalism. The sixth of these 'proofs' of second causes is based on morality. Human moral responsibility, we are told, requires the existence of a real causal power in the will; the occasionalist, by denying any such power, makes God the author of sin (*OCM* III 224, LO 668). Malebranche's reply to this charge will be discussed in detail in Chapter Nine; here, we shall just sketch the outline of his defence. Let us take an undoubtedly criminal action such as a wilful murder, and consider the implications of the doctrine of continuous creation. God re-creates the murderer's body from moment to moment, including the hand that holds the knife. But the mere positions and motions of bodies are morally neutral; in them alone there can be no sin. God also re-creates the killer's soul from moment to moment, including the modes that are his rage and his desire to kill. But, Malebranche insists, the sin lies not in the inclination *per se*, but in the sinner's acceptance and endorsement of it, in his failure to resist the temptation. It is only this second-order state that is the criminal's responsibility, and this state is not itself a mode of the soul and contains, as Malebranche puts it, 'rien de physique'. So God re-creates the murderer's soul with all its modes, but He does not create, and is therefore not responsible for, the murderer's giving way to an evil temptation.

Everything is miraculous

The fifth of the 'proofs' of second causes listed and rebutted in *Éclaircissement* XV is that, on Malebranche's principles, all events would be miracles:

> If bodies did not have a certain *nature* or *force* to act, and if God did all things, there would be only the supernatural in even the most ordinary effects. The distinction between the natural and the supernatural, which is so widely accepted and which is established by the universal assent of the learned, would be extravagant and chimerical.
>
> (*OCM* III 222–3, LO 667)

If the distinction between natural and supernatural events rested properly on the assumption of natural powers, Malebranche admits, this objection would be well-founded. Define a supernatural event as one that transcends the powers of creatures and it will evidently follow from occasionalism that, since there are no such powers, everything that happens is supernatural.[50] But the correct conclusion to draw from this is that the distinction had not been well drawn in the first place. The events we call 'natural' are those brought about by God in accordance with general laws, while those we call 'supernatural' require particular volitions.[51] The 'nature' of the pagans, so prominent in the philosophy of Aristotle, is indeed a chimera. But the distinction between natural and supernatural, properly drawn, remains in force.[52] We shall return to this issue in Chapter Ten.

Scripture acknowledges natural powers

The seventh supposed 'proof' of natural causes starts from scripture (*OCM* III 229–30, LO 672). It is easy enough, of course, for opponents of occasionalism to cite passages from scripture that speak of second causes as if they possessed genuine powers. When the Bible speaks of the earth bringing forth fruit, or of animals being commanded to increase and multiply, the most natural reading of such passages is in terms of delegated powers. But, Malebranche retorts, there are also many passages in scripture that attribute natural events directly to the will of God. How are we to resolve this apparent inconsistency?

Where scripture speaks with the vulgar, i.e. in accordance with the prejudices of the ordinary unreflective man, we should, Malebranche recommends, employ the doctrine of accommodation. In such passages the Word is accommodating itself to vulgar opinions. On the other hand, where scripture flatly contradicts vulgar opinions and prejudices (e.g. by ascribing natural events directly to God) it must be read literally.

This argument is repeated in the correspondence with Arnauld, where Malebranche sets out his view about the relation between the first cause and second causes (*OCM* VII 543–4). There are, Malebranche explains, three possible accounts. One could believe (1) that creatures act by their own delegated powers, independently of God; (2) that God's 'concourse' is necessary for the operation of all second causes; or (3) that God is the only true cause (occasionalism). Account (1) is rejected by theologians as un-Christian, and can be shown by philosophical argument to be impossible. Account (2), the 'concourse' theory, is commonly endorsed by Christian theologians, but is dismissed by Malebranche as both unintelligible and contrary to scripture. It is unintelligible because a creature cannot be said to have a causal power if it can't act independently. But if God's willing X is both necessary and sufficient for X, what does the supposed power of the creature amount to? The 'concourse' theory, in Malebranche's view, is unstable, and must collapse either into deism or into occasionalism. It is un-scriptural for two reasons. In the first place, it is nowhere found in the pages of scripture. More importantly, however, it is inconsistent with those passages of scripture in which natural events are attributed directly to God's will. (*OCM* VIII 700–3). The only account of the relation between the first cause and (so-called) second causes which is both intelligible in its own right, and compatible with the most plausible reading of scripture, is occasionalism.

6

MALEBRANCHE'S MODIFICATIONS OF CARTESIAN PHYSICS

Our concern in this chapter is not to provide a detailed account of all of Malebranche's contributions to physics, but to investigate the role of his philosophy in shaping his answers to the questions of physics. With this in mind, we shall regretfully set aside Malebranche's sophisticated and insightful modifications of the Cartesian theory of light and colour,[1] and concentrate exclusively on the most fundamental of all the questions of physics – the content and epistemological status of the laws of motion. Here, if anywhere, we might expect to see Malebranche's rationalist epistemology, and his occasionalist metaphysics, doing important work, serving to direct the research programme of Cartesian mechanism. But before discussing Malebranche's evolving views on this subject, we must retrace our steps a little and fill in the Cartesian background.

Malebranche's Cartesian inheritance

The essence of bodies, says Descartes, is three-dimensional extension and nothing more. All the modes of material substance are just modifications of extension, and intelligible in terms of it. There are no 'substantial forms', no 'real qualities', and no animal and vegetable souls. The mutual impenetrability of bodies, Descartes thinks, follows straightforwardly from their extension, together with a conservation principle. For two bodies to interpenetrate would involve the annihilation of extension. As for the mobility of bodies, this is simply their capacity for local motion, which is nothing more than a change of their spatial relations vis-à-vis other bodies. Descartes famously rejects the traditional definition of motion as an action, and replaces it with a purely kinematic definition (AT IX 76, CSM I 233–4).

We can now introduce the notion of the 'quantity of motion' of a moving body, defined simply as the product of its bulk and its scalar speed. This quantity of motion is a mode of the moving body, and is, as such, conceptually inseparable from it. This notion remains a purely kinematic one: it tells us nothing about what, if anything, moves bodies, nor about what happens, and why, when two bodies collide. Does Descartes possess anything that we would recognise as a theory of dynamics?

Descartes, as we have already seen in Chapter Two, accepts that created beings have no power to sustain themselves in existence from one moment to the next. Their continued existence is the result of continuous re-creation by God. This doctrine of continuous creation might seem to settle the issue once and for all against a Cartesian dynamics. The 'force' of moving bodies might simply be God's almighty will, as Descartes suggests in his letter of 1649 to Henry More (AT V 403–4, CSMK III 381). This is the burden of Gary Hatfield's argument in his well-known paper.[2] On the other hand, Alan Gabbey has argued that Descartes does have a dynamics, and that we can't understand his rules of motion unless we assume that talk of a 'force of motion' and a 'force of rest' is no mere *façon de parler*, but refers to something physically real.[3] Let's take a close look at the crucial texts – from *Le Monde* and Part Two of the *Principles* – to see whether they can help us to resolve this issue.

In *Le Monde*, written around 1630, but published only in 1664, Descartes constructs an imaginary world, and asks what laws of nature would hold in such a world (AT XI 36ff, CSM I 81ff). By 'nature', he immediately explains, I do not understand some mysterious inner power; I understand matter itself and the rules established by God governing the motions of bodies. An immutable God, Descartes argues, must operate by uniform laws, of which the following three are the most fundamental:

L1   Every mode of a body stays the same from one moment to the next unless changed by some external cause.
L2   The total quantity of motion in the physical universe is conserved.
L3   Bodies tend to continue moving in straight lines.

L1 is, for Descartes, simply a corollary of extending to local motion a principle all philosophers already accepted for other modes of bodies such as size, shape, and, crucially, rest (AT XI 38, CSM I 93). After emphasising the novelty of this idea, and directing a few well-aimed *ad hominem* barbs against the rival Aristotelian conception of local motion (as a mode that tends to self-destruct!), Descartes goes on to L2:

> I suppose as a second rule that when one body pushes another
> it cannot give the other any motion unless it loses as much of its

own motion at the same time; nor can it take away any of the other's motion unless its own is increased by as much.

(AT XI 41, CSM I 94)

This rule, Descartes admits, appears to be violated by experience, but such sensory appearances are misleading. Motion gained or lost by visible bodies may be compensated for by motion lost or gained by invisible ones. Reason thus over-rules experience here, and convinces us that L2 holds universally. After all, what firmer basis could one require than the immutability of God?

But does L2 follow from the two premises that (1) God created and sustains the motion in the physical universe, and that (2) God is immutable? Descartes' argument leaves a lot to be desired. Supposing, he says, 'that God placed a certain quantity of motion in all matter in general at the first instant he created it, we must either admit that he always preserves the same amount of motion in it, or not believe that he always acts in the same way' (AT XI 43, CSM I 96). But what counts as 'acting in the same way'? The theologian will reply, 'acting in accordance with the same immutable plan or design'. And why should an immutable design require an immutable 'quantity of motion'? Many critics pointed out the gap in Descartes' argument at this point. Pardies, for example, comments that Descartes' *non sequitor* is regarded as a joke by theologians.[4] Boyle objects that the argument presupposes some familiarity with God's ends or purposes in creating the physical universe, something Descartes has explicitly denied.[5] Why should an immutable design not best be served by a universe that is running down and heading for destruction? Such signs of decay might be a sort of warning from God, an indication to humans of the destruction that is to come. The millenarians might be mere enthusiasts, but they surely weren't guilty of an elementary misunderstanding of the concept of God?

This casual presentation of a lame *a priori* argument must lead us to ask how seriously Descartes intended us to take it. It may even lead us to sympathise with Desmond Clarke, who has argued that Descartes' physics is fundamentally empiricist in spirit.[6] On Clarke's reading, the supposed derivation of L2 from God's immutability is mere window-dressing (at best, a rational explanation for a theorem that derives its evidential support from elsewhere); our real reason for believing L2 to be true is empirical, grounded in its explanatory power. This seems to me to be a more radical re-interpretation than the texts can bear. It doesn't explain how Descartes can say, with such confidence, that reason over-rules experience, that we can be justifiably certain that L2 does indeed hold universally. Even Malebranche, no slavish disciple, admits that he was taken in by the plausibility of Descartes' derivation of L2 from God's immutability. So we simply have to accept that the invalidity of Descartes' derivation of L2 wasn't obvious to many of his disciples.

But let's move on from *Le Monde* to the more detailed discussion of the same issues in Part Two of the *Principles,* articles 36–52 (AT IX 83– 93, CSM I 240ff),[7] beginning with article 36:

> God is the primary cause of motion; and he always preserves the same quantity of motion in the universe.
>
> (AT IX 83, CSM I 240)

The first cause of motion, Descartes explains, is the omnipotent action of God, who created matter, along with its modes of motion and rest, and who conserves, by His ordinary concourse, as much motion and rest as He initially created:

> Admittedly motion is simply a mode of the matter which is moved. But nevertheless it has a certain determinate quantity; and this, we easily understand, may be constant in the universe as a whole while varying in any given part.
>
> (AT IX 83–4, CSM I 240)

This quantity of motion is measurable by bulk times scalar speed, so Descartes' conservation principle might be expressed, symbolically, as $\Sigma(m \times v) = k$, where m = bulk or volume and v = scalar speed. Once again Descartes claims that this principle follows from God's immutability. Not only does God not change in Himself, Descartes explains, but His manner of operating in the physical universe is equally unchangeable. So He re-creates, at any given instant $t(n)$ the precise quantity of motion that existed at the immediately preceding instant $t(n-1)$. This conservation principle tells us nothing, however, about how this constant quantity of motion is distributed (or redistributed) between bodies. To discover this, we must read on – I now translate from the French text rather than follow the CSM translation from the Latin.

> 37. The first law of nature: each thing remains in the state it is in, so long as nothing changes it.
>
> (AT IX 84)

From our knowledge of God, we can derive certain rules or laws of nature:

The first is that each particular thing ... continues to be in the same state, as much as it can, and never changes state except by the encounter of others.

(AT IX 84–5)

Just as a square body will remain square unless something acts on it to change its shape, and a resting body will remain at rest unless something acts on it to set it in motion, so too a moving body will continue moving with constant speed and direction unless some external force acts on it. Thus, says Descartes,

... if a body has once started to move, we must conclude that it will continue afterwards to move, and that it will never stop of its own accord.

(AT IX 85)

The rival Aristotelian view is dismissed as a mere prejudice, a mistaken inference from the testimony of sense. Of course projectiles do visibly slow down, but this is because of the retarding influence of the medium, not because motion tends spontaneously to decay. A moving body, Descartes continues, tends to continue moving not just anyhow, but always in a straight line:

The second law of nature: Every moving body tends to continue its movement in a straight line.

(AT IX 85)

This rule too, Descartes explains, depends on God's immutability, and on the simplicity of the rule by which He sustains motion:

This rule, like the preceding one, depends on the fact that God is immutable, and that He conserves movement in matter by a very simple operation; for He does not conserve it as it may have been some time before, but as it is precisely at the same instant that He conserves it.

(AT IX 86)

It is not, of course, that motion can actually exist in an instant; rather, the nature of a rectilinear motion is such that it can be characterised in a single moment, whereas that of a curvilinear motion cannot. A body whirled in a sling thus tends always to fly off in a straight line at a tangent to the curve of its actual path. Experience, says Descartes, confirms this analysis.

What exactly is the role played here by experience? The text suggests that it is being used as a check on the accuracy of a piece of *a priori* reasoning – much as I might count the money in my pocket to see if I had done my sums right. This doesn't show that arithmetic is an empirical matter, just that humans sometimes miscalculate. This would imply that Cartesian physics is purely *a priori*, and that empirical checks are needed only to ward off the risk of miscalculation. But has Descartes given us any rational principles strong enough to derive the law of rectilinear inertia? He tells us that God re-creates the material universe by a 'very simple' operation, that at instant $t(n)$ He looks only to $t(n-1)$, not to $t(n-2)$, $t(n-3)$ and so on. But Descartes gives us no reason why an omnipotent and omniscient God must choose such a rule. After all, an omniscient being won't forget the states of the moving body at earlier times. So God could have chosen a 'circular inertia' as a fundamental law of motion.[8] Descartes tells us that He hasn't done so, but He gives no *a priori* reason why God has to prefer one possible rule to the other. Once again, the interpreter faces a difficult choice between a rationalism so feeble as to be broken-backed and a surrender to empiricism. It was, presumably, the perceived feebleness of the rationalist interpretation that led Desmond Clarke to seek to re-interpret Descartes as an empiricist.

The *Principles* go on to introduce the 'third' law of motion:

> if a moving body encounters another stronger than itself, it loses none of its movement; if it encounters a weaker body which it can move, it loses as much [movement] as it gives to it.
>
> (AT IX 86)

In the first case, says Descartes, the moving body retains its quantity of motion but changes its 'determination' (i.e. its direction); in the second case, it gives as much motion to the weaker body as it loses itself. It is this metaphor of combat, with its explicit opposition between 'stronger' and 'weaker', each striving to change the state of the other, that led Gabbey to attribute to Descartes a genuine dynamics. The fact that Descartes' rules of impact violate mechanical relativity is grist to Gabbey's mill – it suggests that the distinction of 'weaker' and 'stronger' is physically real, not an artefact of our arbitrary choice of a reference frame. If the 'force' of a moving body is given by bulk times speed, and speed is something purely relative, then the distinction of 'weaker' and 'stronger' collapses – by the choice of an appropriate frame of reference, either of two colliding bodies can arbitrarily be represented as the 'stronger'.

To understand the first part of his rule, Descartes continues, we must learn to distinguish 'movement' from 'determination'; the latter can be changed while the former remains the same. When a ball collides with a rigid wall, for example, the wall compels the ball to alter its determination; nothing compels it to alter its quantity of motion, which is thus conserved. As for the second part of the rule, it follows from the manner in which God conserves the physical universe, by re-creating from one instant to the next the same total quantity of motion. Since collisions are inevitable, the conservation principle requires God to 'transfer' motion from one body to another. Strictly speaking, this is nonsense – no mode can be transferred from one substance to another. All Descartes can consistently mean is that body B gains in the collision as much motion as body A loses.

Descartes now goes on to try to explain the 'force' of moving bodies to act on others, and of resting bodies to resist being moved by others. This 'force', he says, consists only in the tendency of each body to remain in its previous state (AT IX 88). A resting body thus tends to remain at rest; a moving body tends to retain its motion and its determination. The contrary of motion is rest; the contrary of a given determination is an opposite determination (AT IX 88–9). In any collision, the stronger body will act and produce its effect on the weaker, whose resistance to change will be overcome (AT IX 89). Granting some idealising assumptions (perfectly hard bodies colliding *in vacuo*) we can now derive, from these principles, the rules of impact for colliding bodies.

Descartes now goes on to present his seven rules of impact, but we must pause a moment to reflect. Given extended and impenetrable bodies, tending to move indefinitely in straight lines, we can expect collisions to occur. That is, there will be occasions where it is impossible for both bodies to remain in their prior states. The conservation principle puts a rather weak constraint on possible outcomes. But whence does Descartes derive his determinate set of rules? Not from rectilinear inertia, mutual impenetrability, and the scalar conservation principle alone; those principles are so weak and so permissive as to be compatible with any number of outcomes. And the combat metaphor doesn't help much: it tells us that the 'stronger' will overcome the 'weaker', but not how, exactly, this will take place. A further assumption, not explicitly stated in the text of the *Principles*, is needed to derive the detailed rules of impact. But what is this assumption, and where does it come from?

The answer to this question has been provided by Alan Gabbey.[9] Citing an important letter to Clerselier of 17 February 1645 (AT IV 183–8, CSMK III 246–8), Gabbey suggests that Descartes' rules of impact depend on a Principle of Least Modal Mutation (PLMM). As Descartes explains to Clerselier, the basic principle of his rules of impact is that:

> ... when two bodies collide, and they contain incompatible modes, then there must occur some change in these modes in order to make them compatible; but this change is always the least that may occur. In other words, if these modes can become compatible when a certain quantity of them is changed, then no larger quantity will change.
>
> (AT IV 185, CSMK III 247)

This raises a multitude of further questions. How does Descartes propose to weigh a change of motion against a change of determination? Is there always a unique least change, and what happens if there isn't? Are the rules as they are presented derivable from PLMM or even always compatible with it?[10] But most importantly, for our purposes:

Q1 What is the supposed ground for PLMM?
Q2 Why does Descartes conspicuously omit PLMM from the *Principles*, when it is needed to deduce the laws of impact?

I can see no clear answer to the first of these questions, no clear derivation of PLMM from the divine attributes. The most plausible route would be via a principle of economy of divine effort, but there seems no reason why an omnipotent being should worry about economy – it's not as if He is liable to get tired! As for Q2, Gabbey's answer is highly plausible – Descartes omits PLMM from the text of the *Principles* because it seems to violate his own strictures against teleological principles.[11] But suppressing PLMM leaves the rules of impact isolated, deprived of their main rational support, neither self-evident in themselves nor derivable from the principles explicitly stated in the text. But let us look at the rules, and see what they tell us about Cartesian dynamics.

Rule 1. Two bodies A and B collide, with equal bulk b and equal but opposite speeds (AT IX 89). After colliding, each will return whence it came, with the same speed but in the opposite direction. There is, says Descartes, no cause that can alter the quantity of motion of either, but there is an evident reason why the determinations of one or both must alter. Since this reason is the same for both alike, there is no reason for one to rebound rather than the other, so both will rebound symmetrically. Already, we see, Descartes has departed from PLMM – allowing both bodies to continue with the original speed and direction of either would involve less 'modal mutation'. It seems that PLMM is not so much abandoned here as 'trumped' by a symmetry condition stemming from some version of the principle of sufficient reason.

Rule 2. If A is a little greater than B, and they collide with equal and opposite speeds, only B will rebound, and they will continue together with the original speed and direction of A. Since A has more 'force' than B, it triumphs over B and is therefore not compelled to rebound by B – its speed and direction are unchanged (AT IX 90).

Rule 3. If A and B have the same bulk but A moves somewhat faster than B (in an opposite direction) not only will B rebound but A will transfer half its excess motion to B. Clearly, A, having reversed the determination of B, cannot continue to move faster than B on pain of interpenetration. So A must transfer some motion to B. How much? Here PLMM comes into play: A must transfer to B as little of its excess motion as is required to prevent interpenetration (AT IX 90).

Rule 4. If B is bigger than A and at rest, then however fast A moves, A cannot set B in motion, but will simply rebound (AT IX 90–1). This, says Descartes, is because the 'force of rest' of B must always exceed the 'force of motion' of A, however fast A is moving. How does Descartes seek to justify this counter-intuitive result? How is the 'force of rest' determined? This takes a little explaining. The basic idea is to consider a *counterfactual* situation in which A does move B, imparting to it enough of its own motion to set B in motion too. Then calculate the 'force' of this hypothetical motion of B – this gives the 'force of rest'. The opposed force, the 'force of motion' of A is estimated not from its original bulk times speed, but from its bulk times speed in this counterfactual situation. But then, since B is *ex hypothesi* greater than A, the 'force of rest' of B will always exceed the 'force of motion' of A. It doesn't matter how fast A moves initially, nor how much greater B is than A – the result stands. No moving body can impart more than half of its 'force of motion'; rather than do so, it simply rebounds.

Descartes is fully aware that his Rule 4 is counter-intuitive and seems to contradict the testimony of experience. His response is simply to say that experience is not to be trusted. All observed bodies are floating in subtle fluid media of various kinds; his rule would only be observed *in vacuo*. But his conclusion stands: given the combat metaphor, the 'force of rest', and PLMM, it does indeed seem that Rule 4 follows as a consequence.

Rule 5. If the moving body A is larger than the resting body B that it strikes, by however little, then A, however slowly it moves, will have sufficient 'force' to move B, and to transfer to it a part of A's motion (AT IX 91–2). If A is twice B, for example, it must transfer to B $\frac{1}{3}$ of its initial quantity of motion, enabling the two bodies to move off together at the same speed and in the direction of A's original motion.

Rule 6. If B is at rest, and of equal bulk with the moving body A that strikes it, it is necessary that B be 'in part' propelled by A, and that it 'in part' compel A to rebound (AT IX 92). Here there is no clear distinction of 'weaker' and 'stronger', as there is for rules 4 and 5. We can therefore describe the following pair of scenarios. In the first, we declare A to be the 'victor' and envisage the case as akin to that of rule 5: A transfers exactly half its motion to B, and the two bodies move off together with half A's original speed. In the second, we declare B the 'victor' and envisage the case as akin to rule 4: B is unmoved, and A rebounds with its original speed. Now there is, says Descartes, no sufficient reason to choose one of these outcomes over the other. So there must result a 'mixed' state, a sort of compromise between them, in which A transfers $\frac{1}{4}$ of its motion to B, and rebounds with the remaining $\frac{3}{4}$. This use of the principle of sufficient reason (again over-ruling PLMM) is ingenious, but scarcely convincing. It is easy to imagine the response of Leibniz to the manifest discontinuities involved in these rules.[12]

Rule 7. Where A overtakes B, two cases are possible (AT IX 92). Either A transfers some of its motion to B, or it rebounds from B with all of its original motion. The former will occur whenever A is greater than B, or even if A is smaller, so long as its quantity of motion is greater. If, however, B's excess bulk over-compensates for A's excess speed, A must rebound without communicating any motion to B. (If A's excess speed is exactly counterbalanced by B's excess bulk, we get another 'mixed' or compromise state, as in rule 6.)

Descartes ends with a confident endorsement of these rules, even in the face of the contrary testimony of experience:

> And the demonstrations of all this are so certain, that although experience seemed to us to show the opposite, we would nevertheless be obliged to give more faith to our reason than to our senses.

> (AT IX 93)

It would be all too easy to poke fun at Descartes for this excess of confidence in the power of reason, even perhaps to portray him as some kind of charlatan. With hindsight, we can see so many things wrong with these rules. They violate the principle of continuity, as Leibniz was to point out: an infinitesimal variation in initial conditions can produce an immense difference in the outcome of a collision.[13] They violate the principle of conservation of the vector quantity momentum, and fly in the face of mechanical relativity, soon to be established by the work of Huygens.[14] And they seem to have at best a tenuous connection with our experience of moving bodies.

But I have no wish to poke fun at Descartes. Since his was the first attempt to establish the laws of motion on a rational basis, and the starting-point for all who came after him, it would be more fitting to understand before we condemn. What concerns me is the supposed rational basis for Descartes' rules, and their tenuous relation to the world of experience. Are we entitled simply to take the 'high priori road' and dismiss the testimony of experience where it doesn't fit our rational intuitions? Or is all this theory just a hypothetico-deductive construct, ultimately to be validated by experience? These questions, of the validity of Descartes' reasoning, and of the relation between theory and experience in this domain, are fundamental for Malebranche's philosophical physics.

Malebranche's philosophical physics

This section examines the relations between philosophy and physics in Malebranche's work. Does his philosophy drive and direct his physics, or does it merely provide *post hoc* rationalisations of results arrived at independently, e.g. by empirical methods? With this question in mind, let us examine the implications for physics of Malebranche's rationalist epistemology and his occasionalist metaphysics.

On the surface, Malebranche's rationalism seems akin to that of Descartes. Like Descartes, Malebranche starts from a theory of ideas. Having a clear and distinct idea of X enables us to determine *a priori* the properties X must possess. If our clear and distinct idea of X represents it as F and not as G, we can be certain that X is F and is not G. And like Descartes, Malebranche is clear that these ideas are not derived from sensory experience, neither imprinted passively on the mind by external objects nor derived from such sensory impressions by a process of abstraction. Here, however, the similarities end. For Descartes, ideas are modifications of the substance of the human soul, modes which (mysteriously) represent external objects. Malebranche finds this intellectually unsatisfying. In the first place, he objects, this Cartesian account of ideas (as found in, e.g. Arnauld and Régis) doesn't explain how a mode of our souls can represent an external object. Not, surely, by any kind of resemblance?[15] Worse still, this theory leaves the Cartesian with no response to the sceptic, no principled way of bridging the gap between 'my idea of X represents it as F' and 'X really is F'.

At this point Malebranche invokes his celebrated Vision in God.[16] Our clear and distinct ideas, he argues, are not modes of our souls at all. They are, rather, God's ideas, the archetypes or blueprints for creation. And it is logically impossible that a creature should fail to conform to the omniscient and omnipotent Creator's idea of it. The Vision in God thus bridges the epistemic gap between thoughts and things, and leaves no purchase for sceptical doubts. Only the Vision in God, Malebranche argues, makes science (demonstrative knowledge) possible.

But what clear and distinct ideas do we have of the material world? In the final analysis, Malebranche thinks, all our ideas of matter reduce to one, *étendue intelligible* or 'intelligible extension'.[17] Whatever is truly a property of bodies can be explained in terms of *étendue intelligible*; whatever cannot be so explained is no property of bodies (*OCM* I 456–67, LO 241–7). Starting from *étendue intelligible*, we can derive size and shape, infinite divisibility, mobility and impenetrability – it is self-contradictory that two feet of extension should become one foot (*OCM* II 325, LO 455).

Given size and shape and infinite divisibility, we can develop the science of geometry. Given size, shape, infinite divisibility and mobility, we can develop the science of rational kinematics, the pure study of motion as such, of its formal cause, to put it in Aristotelian terms. But what becomes of dynamics? If we allow Malebranche his derivation of impenetrability,[18] then we can know *a priori* that two moving bodies can't simply pass freely through one another, each continuing serenely on its path. But at this point our rational insight appears to run out. We can't see precisely what will happen to prevent interpenetration of dimensions – many possibilities remain open.

Do we have any rational insight into the 'force' of a moving body? The answer, Malebranche insists, is a flat and decided negative. Strictly speaking, no such force exists – the notion of such a force, he tells us in Book One of the *Recherche*, is not a clear idea but an obscure one, based on prejudice and misunderstanding of sensory experience (*OCM* I 101–2, LO 37). We can of course speak of the quantity of motion of a moving body, but this is still a kinematic concept, yielding no insight into questions of dynamics. Malebranche can argue for this conclusion from two different sets of premises. He can start with the idea of *étendue intelligible*, an idea so determinate as to exclude all that it does not explicitly contain. Since motive force is not 'contained' in *étendue intelligible*, it is excluded by it – bodies possess sizes, shapes and motions, but no forces. Alternatively, Malebranche can proceed as he does in Book Six of the *Recherche*, starting from the idea of causal agency as involving a necessary connection between cause and effect, and denying that the impact of one body necessitates the motion of another (*OCM* II 312–14, LO 448–9).

If Malebranche is to develop a rational dynamics, it can therefore be derived neither from the notion of *étendue intelligible*, nor from any rational insight into the nature of the 'moving force' of bodies. The only remaining source for such a science of dynamics is our knowledge of God. God is known, according to Malebranche, not by way of an idea but immediately and in Himself, since it is He who is directly present to the mind in all its cognitions. God, we know, is a Being with all possible perfections. Does anything follow from this regarding the manner of His operation in the physical world?

We have already discussed, in Chapter Five, Malebranche's arguments for occasionalism. In his later works, his occasionalism is presented as a simple corollary of the metaphysical theory of continuous creation. In the correspondence with Arnauld, for example, he writes that 'it is evident that if God creates a body successively in certain places, or always in the same place, no power will be able to take it from there and put it in other places' (*OCM* VII 569). In the seventh of the *Entretiens sur la Métaphysique* the full implications of the doctrine are stated as forcibly as one could wish. The continued existence of a material object such as a chair is, says Malebranche's spokesman Theodore, just a matter of God's continuing to will it to exist. But not even God can will something that is in itself inconceivable. So He must recreate the chair in some definite place or other. It is thus self-contradictory, Theodore continues, that any body should possess the power to move another. But that isn't all. The same argument will show that no finite spirit can move a body.

If God is the only cause operating in the physical universe, can we know anything *a priori* about the manner of His operation? God must act, Malebranche replies, in a manner that expresses His attributes. One crucial consequence of this is that He acts (with a few important exceptions) by means of general laws, laws that can be executed by *volontés générales* rather than *volontés particulières*. But can we say anything more definite about the content of these general laws? This is where Malebranche's difficulties start to arise.

Must God maintain the 'quantity of motion' in the universe? The young Malebranche thought so, and accepted Descartes' derivation of the scalar conservation principle from God's immutability. The later Malebranche abandoned both the derivation and the theorem, accepting instead the modern principle of conservation of a vector quantity, momentum. But it is far from clear why any conservation principle should be logically implied by the immutability of God.

Malebranche even has difficulty defending the Cartesian insistence on contact action. It is evident, he writes in *Éclaircissement* XVI, 'that a body is moved only because it is impelled, and it can be impelled only by the one immediately touching it' (*OCM* III 270, LO 696). But why should this be evident to an occasionalist? If a natural cause is no more than an occasion for God to act, why shouldn't this occasion be the presence of one body at some arbitrary distance from another? Fontenelle, as we saw in Chapter Five, raises just this question. If, he asks, nothing in the moving body itself qualifies it to be the real cause of the subsequent motion of the body it strikes, if all is effected by the almighty will of God, then why should contact be required at all? Malebranche has no obvious reply consistent with his principles. As Bayle explained in his defence of Malebranche, we have a natural propensity to confound regular succession with true causation. This explains our readiness to judge that collision is the true cause of the motions of bodies, not just the occasional cause. In creating impenetrable bodies, God doesn't invest creatures with real causal powers; He merely obliges Himself to go on acting in a certain regular manner. If God successively re-creates two bodies on convergent paths, He cannot also will that each continues its motion uninterrupted after they have come into contact. Some redistribution of motion will be required. Does it follow that impenetrability is a real causal power? No. The impenetrability of bodies is simply a self-imposed constraint on God, obliging Him to make some change or other in the motion of one or both of the colliding bodies. But can we say nothing more definite? How does Malebranche regard Descartes' seven rules of impact?[19]

Malebranche's first revision of Descartes: drop the force of rest

From the outset, Malebranche flatly rejected Descartes' force of rest. For a body to remain at rest, he claims, it is sufficient that God continues to will its mere existence; for motion, an extra divine volition is required. As a mere privation, rest is devoid of causal efficacy – even as an occasional cause, it is inert.[20] Why, precisely, God cannot use a privation as an occasional cause Malebranche does not tell us. But if we reject the force of rest, we must also reject those of Descartes' rules of impact (rules 4 and 6 above) which depend on it. So what rules should Descartes have arrived at from his assumptions, but without the force of rest? The question is addressed in Malebranche's 'petit méchant traité' of 1692.[21]

The occasional cause of the communication of motion, Malebranche begins, is always impact. For one body to move another, it must collide with it; the motion imparted is then proportional to the strength of the impact (*choc*). How is this impact measured? Take the relative velocity of the colliding bodies, says Malebranche, and multiply it by the bulk of the smaller body. In this type of collision, the 'stronger' pushes the 'weaker' only as hard as it must to prevent interpenetration (*OCM* XVII–1 61). This looks like Gabbey's Cartesian PLMM, resurfacing to provide determinate solutions to Malebranche's problems.

If, in a head-on collision, the smaller body is the more powerful, the quantity of the impact is simply the sum of the forces of the two colliding bodies. So for a head-on collision, one first imagines the weaker as coming to rest, before being pushed back by the strength of the blow. For a catch-up collision, the increase in the speed of the weaker is proportional to the impact.

In this thought-experiment, Malebranche explains, I am assuming that the colliding bodies are perfectly rigid, and that therefore all changes of motion are instantaneous. I am also assuming Descartes' scalar conservation principle (*OCM* XVII–1 56). In such collisions, the weaker body can't lose any of its own motion, so it must instantaneously rebound with all its original motion, plus whatever it receives from the stronger.

Some philosophers think that perfectly hard bodies would come to rest on collision because there is no cause (elasticity) for them to rebound. Malebranche disagrees. If, he says, a moving body A strikes a resting body B of equal bulk, A will come to rest and transfer all its motion to B. So much, he thinks, is incontestable (*OCM* XVII–1 62). But if B is immovable, then when A pushes it, it must push back as powerfully as it is pushed. If so, A must rebound with its original speed.

But, replies the critic, there is here no elasticity *(ressort)*, and it is elasticity that causes A to spring back in such a collision. In elastic bodies, Malebranche replies, the colliding bodies impart their motion – briefly – to the subtle matter in their pores; this subtle matter then surrenders its excess of motion back to the gross bodies to produce the rebound. But in the collision of perfectly rigid bodies this mediation is omitted and the original forward motion is immediately replaced by a backward motion (*OCM* XVII–1 64). If this assumption is wrong, Malebranche admits, all the laws of motion derived from it will be equally mistaken.

It is time to take a close look at Malebranche's first modification of Descartes' rules. We assume the following:

1   Perfectly rigid bodies colliding *in vacuo*.
2   No force of rest.
3   The scalar conservation principle $\Sigma(m \times v) = k$.
4   Force of impact or 'choc' = $m(v1 \pm v2)$.
5   Divide this force by the bulk of the body struck, and one has its final speed.
6   The striking body retains whatever motion it does not impart; divide this quantity by its bulk, and one has its final speed.

This is clearer from examples.

Case One: the struck body is at rest:

In these tables, the figure before the m represents units of bulk (no figure indicates a bulk of 1 unit); the figure after the m represents units of speed; the arrow represents direction.

BEFORE IMPACT		AFTER IMPACT	
m1 →	m0	m0	m1 →
m2 →	m0	m0	m2 →
m3 →	m0	m0	m3 →
2m1 →	m0	2m½ →	m1 →
m1 →	2m0	m0	2m½ →

(Note the deviation from Descartes' Rule 4 in this final example)

Case Two: for 'catch up' collisions:

BEFORE IMPACT		AFTER IMPACT	
m2 →	m1 →	m1 →	m2 →
2m2 →	m1→	2m³⁄₂ →	m2 →
m2 →	2m1 →	m1→	2m³⁄₂ →

Case Three: for head-on collisions:

BEFORE IMPACT		AFTER IMPACT	
m1 →	m1 ←	← m1	m1 →
m2 →	m1 ←	← m1	m2 →
2m1 →	m2 ←	← 2m1	m2 →
2m1 →	m1 ←	← 2m½	m2 →
2m2 →	m1 ←	← 2m1	m3 →

These rules may appear strange, Malebranche admits, but they are necessary consequences of the principles established. Two further examples may help to fix these principles in our minds.

(1) In a head-on collision, m12 strikes 3m2. The 'force' of m12 = 12, that of 3m2 = 6. So the smaller is also the stronger. In this case, says Malebranche, it comes to rest and transfers all its motion to the weaker body. So the final speed of the smaller body = zero, and that of the larger body = $^{18}/_3$ = 6 units. So we have:

BEFORE		AFTER	
m12 →	3m2 ←	m0	3m6 →

If the stronger body is the larger, we imagine the weaker first brought to rest, then sent backwards with a speed proportional to the shock. The stronger body retains whatever motion it does not impart, albeit now with its direction reversed. Imagine a head-on collision between 4m3 and 3m2. The shock, in this case, is given by the relative velocity (5 units) multiplied by the bulk of the smaller body (3 units) = 15 units. So the smaller body rebounds with a speed of $^{15}/_3$ = 5 units, leaving only 3 of the original 18 units of motion for the rebound of the larger body, giving it a speed of ¾, thus:

BEFORE		AFTER	
4m3 →	3m2 ←	← 4m¾	3m5 →

In this first modification of Cartesian physics, Descartes' rules 4 and 6 (and 7) are rejected; rules 1, 2, 3 and 5 are retained. But we still seem, in hindsight, far from having a credible set of rules. Most obviously, the combat metaphor, with its clear violation of mechanical relativity, is still dominating the discussion. The lessons of Huygens and his barges have yet to be absorbed.

Malebranche's second revision of Descartes: abandon the scalar conservation principle

In the early editions of the *Recherche*, Malebranche endorsed Descartes' derivation of his scalar conservation principle from God's immutability, and was prepared to take the 'high line' with regard to experience, dismissing experimental methods of enquiry (e.g. those of Mariotte) as misleading (*OCM* XVII–1 55). In the *petit méchant traité* Malebranche rejects Descartes' derivation of his scalar conservation principle, but still thinks the principle itself may be true. Later still, under the constant pressure of Leibniz's criticisms, Malebranche found himself obliged to rethink. There may, he now suspects, be no unique rational solution to the question of the rules of colliding bodies – different assumptions may simply yield different results, and there may be no *a priori* method for determining which assumptions are true.

In the 1700/1712 version of this material, Malebranche is still more explicit:

> Mr Descartes believed that God always conserved in the universe an equal quantity of movement. He supported his opinion on this incontestable principle, that the action of the Creator must bear the mark of His immutability, and that therefore, His will being the moving force of bodies created or conserved in motion, it was necessary that that force remained always the same.
>
> (*OCM* XVII–1 71–3)

That God's conduct must express His attributes is for Malebranche incontestable – he uses the principle again and again in his philosophy, from the laws of nature to the workings of grace. But Descartes' rules are erroneous. It follows that his inference, however plausible (*vraisemblable*) it might appear, is invalid. The statement that God conserves the same quantity of motion in the universe is, Malebranche now sees, ambiguous between a falsehood (the old scalar conservation principle) and a truth (conservation of a vector quantity, our 'momentum'). This true conservation principle, Malebranche insists, still bears the mark of the divine attributes, since it entails a certain sort of balance or equilibrium in the universe, a fitting expression of the divine wisdom (*OCM* XVII–1 75).

Two comments are in order at this point. The first is that, although Malebranche insists that the new principle bears the marks of God's wisdom, there is no attempt to derive it *a priori* from that particular divine perfection. In terms of its epistemological grounds, the principle we know as conservation of momentum must be regarded as empirical; the theological argument is little more than a *post hoc* rationalisation. The second comment is that a vector conservation principle is perfectly consistent with a universe that is running down.[22] Leibniz saw this clearly and argued, in his *Brief Demonstration* and elsewhere, for a new scalar conservation principle, namely the conservation of *vis viva* or living force.[23] But Leibniz's dynamism remained completely alien to

Malebranche's thought. Here, perhaps, his occasionalism, with its insistence on the radical impotence of all creatures, is misdirecting his physics.[24]

But let us return to the rules for the collision of hard bodies. If we reject the scalar conservation principle, says Malebranche, we must reject all those rules that depend on it. The supposition that contrary motions destroy one another affects, however, only the case of head-on collisions, so we can expect the rules for all other cases to be unaltered. For head-on collisions, we must first find the quantity of motion in each body. Subtract from each the quantity of motion of the weaker. Then regard this as being at rest, and think of the stronger as striking it with whatever remains, after the subtraction, of its original motion. We can now apply the rules cited earlier for the collision of a moving body with a resting one. If the smaller is the stronger, it will communicate all its motion and come to rest; if the larger is the stronger, it will impart some motion to the weaker, and continue itself with whatever motion remains to it (*OCM* XVII–1 77). Once again, examples make this clearer:

BEFORE IMPACT		AFTER IMPACT	
$m1 \rightarrow$	$m1 \leftarrow$	$m0$	$m0$
$m2 \rightarrow$	$m1 \leftarrow$	$m0$	$m1 \rightarrow$
$2m1 \rightarrow$	$m1 \leftarrow$	$2m\frac{1}{4} \rightarrow$	$m\frac{1}{2} \rightarrow$
$3m1 \rightarrow$	$m1 \leftarrow$	$3m\frac{4}{9} \rightarrow$	$m\frac{3}{4} \rightarrow$
$3m1 \rightarrow$	$m2 \leftarrow$	$3m\frac{2}{9} \rightarrow$	$m\frac{1}{3} \rightarrow$
$2m2 \rightarrow$	$m1 \leftarrow$	$2m\frac{3}{4} \rightarrow$	$m\frac{3}{2} \rightarrow$

These rules are arrived at by re-applying the earlier rules for the collision of a moving body with a resting one. So the method is: subtract contrary motions, then treat as before. The striking body has a counterfactual speed at the hypothetical phase one: this speed is imparted to the body struck. One then subtracts that quantity of motion from the quantity of motion of the striking body at this counterfactual phase one to find its actual motion after collision.

Unfortunately, the lessons of Huygens have still not been learned. Although Malebranche talks of contrary motions destroying one another, he still hasn't fully taken mechanical relativity on board. Imagine performing one of the above experiments on one of Huygens' barges. The viewer from the canal bank sees:

$$2m1 \rightarrow \quad m1 \leftarrow \quad \text{------} \quad 2m\frac{1}{4} \rightarrow \quad m\frac{1}{2} \rightarrow$$

But suppose the barge is moving with unit velocity in the direction of the second body. Then, to a viewer on the barge, what we have is the following case:

$$2m2 \rightarrow \quad m0 \quad \text{———} \quad 2m1 \rightarrow \quad m2 \rightarrow$$

The relative velocity of separation of the two bodies after impact is ¼, according to the viewer on the canal bank, and 1, according to the viewer on the barge. But this is impossible. Our two viewers are just providing alternative descriptions of what is physically the same state of affairs. The two observers can't observe completely different outcomes to the experiment. Like his master Descartes, Malebranche is still assuming a real ontological distinction between rest and motion; his talk of 'weaker' and 'stronger' presupposes that this distinction makes sense and corresponds to something physically real. It is striking that Huygens arrived at his clear vision of mechanical relativity by concentrating on the kinematics, and that he never developed a worked-out dynamics of moving bodies.[25]

In any case, Malebranche now tells us, these laws for the collision of perfectly hard bodies, whether based on Descartes' scalar conservation principle or on the new vector conservation principle, are of interest only as intellectual exercises (*OCM* XVII–1 79, 112). It is time to turn to the true laws of physics, and to do that we must abandon the notion of perfectly rigid bodies.

Malebranche's third revision of Descartes: reject hard bodies

In the *petit méchant traité* (*OCM* XVII–1 225), there still remain clear signs of Malebranche's Cartesian inheritance. Descartes' derivation of his scalar conservation principle is rejected, but Malebranche still thinks the principle may be true – we do not, after all, live in a universe that is visibly running down (*OCM* XVII–1 202). Malebranche also retains rigid bodies, and retains Descartes' crucial distinction of 'weaker' and 'stronger', a distinction we have seen to be incompatible with mechanical relativity. Although many Cartesians were happy with the *petit méchant traité*, Leibniz remained unsatisfied. He continued to press Malebranche on a number of crucial points – on the rational basis of the laws of motion, on the conservation of *vis viva*, and on the existence or otherwise of hard bodies.[26] The very existence of perfectly rigid bodies would, according to Leibniz, violate the rational order of nature: we can be certain *a priori* that God has created no such things.

Once again, Malebranche is forced to rethink. Having already abandoned the force of rest, he now comes to reject Descartes' scalar conservation principle as false (not merely unproven), and to regard the existence of hard bodies as extremely doubtful. God could, doubtless, have created hard bodies, but experience seems to show that He has not in fact done so. The experiments of Mariotte reveal that even steel balls flatten somewhat on impact.[27] The laws of collision of perfectly rigid bodies are henceforth described as mere intellectual exercises, of no relevance to physics. All real bodies are either soft or springy; all real collisions, as Leibniz had argued, take time.

Malebranche's final and definitive treatment of the laws of collision can be found in a draft of 1700, the results of which were to be included in the latest editions of the *Recherche* (*OCM* XVII–1 81 and successive odd-numbered pages). An elastic body seeks to restore its original size and shape if bent or compressed. This 'force' must, Malebranche thinks, reside in some motion or other:

> In fact, if one wishes to reason about bodies and their properties only from the clear ideas that we can have of them, one will never attribute to matter any other force or action than that which it derives from its motion.
>
> (*OCM* XVII–1 83)

But, he continues, this motion is not in the parts of the springy body itself: they are, *ex hypothesi*, at rest at the moment of fullest compression or bending. It follows that the motion must reside in the subtle matter contained in the pores of the springy body.

It is not clear that Malebranche is entitled to this inference. A causal rationalist might help himself to the axiom 'only motion can cause motion' because he regards this as an *a priori* insight into the true cause. But for Malebranche, the natural cause is only an occasion, and it is not evident *a priori* that only a prior motion can be the occasion for a subsequent motion. Can there be any rational insight into patterns of occasional causation? Malebranche tells us to reason from clear ideas. That might serve to exclude Aristotelian pseudo-explanations in terms of real qualities or mysterious faculties. But it won't exclude bizarre laws like 'whenever a sphere is placed at a distance of less than two of its diameters from a cube, the cube will move away with a velocity of one of the sphere's diameters per second'. God presumably could have established such a law.

Malebranche seems to be aware of this difficulty, and suggests that we regard the above account of elasticity as a supposition, the

151

consequences of which can be tested against experience (*OCM* XVII–1 83). We seem already to be moving towards an explicitly hypothetico–deductive physics.

Imagine a body A placed on an anvil and struck with a hammer. The parts of A directly struck by the hammer recede immediately, compressing the subtle matter in the neighbouring pores. If this subtle matter can flow freely away, the parts of A will approach one another – that is, A will be flattened. But if the outflow of the subtle matter is resisted, A will only flatten a little. If the subtle matter is forced to flow back into the pores it was expelled from by the shock, the body is elastic and will tend to spring back to its former figure. On this model, the whole process of flattening and restoration takes time: nothing happens in an instant. The collision is only complete when the rearmost part of the colliding body has come, perhaps momentarily, to rest – this is the point of maximum compression of the subtle matter, and a sort of equilibrium point.

We can now see what was wrong with Descartes' rules. On Descartes' model, the 'stronger' body could never receive any force from the 'weaker'. But for real bodies, no such conclusion follows. The 'weaker' may not overcome all the 'stronger' body, but it can overcome the first parts of the stronger, before being itself pushed back by the combined effect of the others. In the following situation, for example:

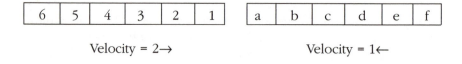

6	5	4	3	2	1

a	b	c	d	e	f

Velocity = 2→   Velocity = 1←

In this collision of the compound bodies 654321 and abcdef, the part a by itself cannot overcome 1, but ab can balance 1, and abc can drive 1 back into 2, before being pressed back by 21, which in turn can be balanced by abcd and driven back by abcde, and so on. Eventually, a point of equilibrium is reached, at which the subtle matter receives its maximum compression. This then presses back equally on the two bodies, producing effects inversely proportional to their masses.

To calculate the results of an elastic collision, says Malebranche, one must first regard the two bodies as if they were perfectly soft. Such bodies adhere on impact; the vector conservation principle (our 'conservation of momentum') gives the resultant velocity. For an elastic collision, one then calculates the change of motion of each of the colliding bodies Δmv, and doubles it, thus:

E.g.	m24→ meets	3m0
hypothetical mid-state	m6→	3m6→
'shock'	−m18	+3m6
resultant	m12←	3m12→

The rule here is sufficiently clear (and reversible), but its physical rationale seems at first to be puzzling. Why should we first treat elastic bodies as if they were soft, and then re-introduce elasticity at a later stage? And why is the force of the 'shock' only m18, in the above example, while the motive force of the moving body is 24 units? If, in the above example, A struck B with a force of 24, and this force was then redistributed in inverse proportion to the masses of the bodies, we would find A rebounding with m18 and B moving off with 3m6 – a force of elasticity of 36. This has to be wrong. The force of the subtle matter can't exceed the force by which it was initially compressed. This, says Malebranche, is evident to reason and confirmed by experience – a rubber ball dropped on a hard floor never bounces higher than the height it was dropped from. At first, says Malebranche, I tended to doubt the experiments (e.g. those performed by Mariotte). But my attempts to derive other laws of elastic collision were bound to come into conflict with experimental results. Ultimately, he concedes, 'We must not merely conform to the rule, but seek to discover the physical reasons for the operations which it prescribes' (*OCM* XVII–1 125).

In themselves, Malebranche now explains, all bodies are soft. Since rest has no opposition to motion, the parts of such a body simply recede when struck – the conservation of momentum yields the velocity. So phase one of our rule is perfectly intelligible – it simply makes abstraction of the compression of the subtle matter and its elasticity (*OCM* XVII–1 129). In the second operation, we distribute the effects of this compression of the subtle matter, which pushes back equally on the colliding bodies, producing effects inversely proportional to their masses (*OCM* XVII–1 133). All this is in perfect conformity to reason. The compression of the subtle matter in the above case is not the total force of A before collision (= 24 units) but the force A expends before equilibrium is reached (= 18 units). The compression of the subtle matter only continues until this equilibrium point is reached – after that, elasticity takes over (*OCM* XVII–1 143).

These results can now be stated in algebraic form. Let m and n be the masses of the colliding bodies, v and r their respective velocities, and let mv > nr. For contrary motions, the total quantity of motion (our momentum) = mv – nr. So the phase one velocity = (mv – nr) / (m+n). For the velocity of m after collision, we now have

(mv – nr + 2nr) / (m + n)

And for the velocity of n after collision, we have

(nr – mv + 2mv) / (m + n)

This analysis, and these formulae, can be found in a paper by Carré in the *Mémoires de l'Académie des Sciences* of 1706,[28] and is repeated in the final editions of the *Recherche*. At last, it seems, we have something that looks recognisably modern. There is no force of rest, the principle of conservation of momentum plays a fundamental role, and the abandonment of hard bodies allows Malebranche finally to take mechanical relativity on board and admit that the 'weaker' pushes the 'stronger'. (In fact, of course, the whole distinction of 'weaker' versus 'stronger' can now be seen to be an absurd irrelevance.) For elastic collisions, Leibniz's *vis viva* (mv^2) will be conserved, although Malebranche, like Huygens before him, is far from according any fundamental theoretical significance to this result. At last, it seems, we have a body of rational principles capable of facing the tribunal of experience. We have laws for the collision of perfectly soft bodies, and laws for the collision of perfectly elastic bodies; only experience will tell us how elastic the bodies made of any given material actually are.

Is Malebranche an empiricist *malgré lui*?

Have these successive modifications of the laws of impact been driven by reason or by experience? Has Malebranche seen that some of Descartes' axioms are false, his deductions invalid, or his principles inconsistent with one another? That would be a rational critique. Or is it the insistent demand that we reconcile the supposedly rational laws of collision with the testimony of experience that has forced the revisions? Is the late Malebranche still a rationalist in his physics, or has he tacitly surrendered to empiricism?

Costabel vigorously rejects the claim that the late Malebranche was a closet empiricist.[29] Certainly Malebranche was no Baconian inductivist. He continues to reproach the experimentalists for their wrong-headed approach: they pile up experiments, he complains, and establish rules 'which provide, so it seems to me, no opening for the intellect, because they do not reveal the natural principle from which they must be derived' (*OCM* XVII–1 124). Malebranche continues to insist that reason must make sense of what is given in experience, that nothing can be accepted in science unless it satisfies the intellect as well as the senses. For Costabel, experience forced Malebranche to rethink, and this rethinking led him to his successive modifications of Descartes' rules. Experience, says Costabel, cannot by itself show which laws are true; all it can do is supply answers to rationally formulated questions. reason tells us that either X or Y must be true; we then ask of experience 'is X true, or Y?', experience tells us that X is true and Y false. But if we approached experience without the rational schema in mind, it would teach us nothing.

This is an attractive reading of Malebranche, and one that does justice to many of the texts, while preserving some tincture of rationalism. But it already involves a major departure from the strong programme of Cartesian rationalism. Malebranche no longer thinks that the laws of collision can be uniquely determined *a priori* on the basis of first principles. Rather, we can set out different assumptions about colliding bodies; which sets of laws hold in the physical universe will then depend on which sort(s) of bodies God has chosen to create (*OCM* XVII–1 53).

The crucial point is this: for Malebranche, creation is a free act on God's part. The reason for God's creation of our universe (or indeed, any universe at all) is to be found in His will rather than His intellect. Now our minds are united, via the Vision in God, to the divine intellect. It is 'in God' that we see the eternal and necessary truths of logic, mathematics and morality. But we have no such epistemic access to God's will. Whether or not a given law (e.g. a conservation principle) holds is, therefore, a contingent matter, to be settled only by experience:

> For, since we cannot grasp the Creator's designs, nor understand all the relations which they have to His attributes, whether to conserve or not to conserve an equal quantity of movement seems to depend on a purely arbitrary volition of God, of which in consequence one could only be assured by a type of revelation such as experience provides.
>
> (*OCM* XVII–1 55)

It is experience, not reason, which tells us that the scalar conservation principle is false. But our lack of rational insight into the springs of motion is still more radical than this. It might happen, Malebranche admits, that the feeblest body could change the determination of the strongest, or that it could be repulsed by the stronger (without elasticity) faster than that body is in fact moving. Such things may seem incredible, but 'I admit that this could be, for this is arbitrary, and depends on the will of God' (*OCM* XVII–1 45).

Malebranche cannot, of course, mean that the will of God is itself arbitrary, independent of His intellect.[30] He flatly rejects Descartes' voluntarism about the necessary truths, insisting that not even God could make $2 + 2 = 5$. He maintains against Arnauld that God's will does not of itself constitute justice and righteousness: God wills something because He sees that it is right, not *vice versa*. In creating the universe, God seeks the best overall expression of His attributes, as we explained in Chapter Five. What he must mean in the above passage is that there is not the remotest prospect of our carrying out for ourselves this complex weighted sum, arguing *a priori* from God's attributes to the laws of motion He has established.[31] Since all God's actions are subject to Order, we can be confident that this is how the laws have been established (and not by an arbitrary act of will), but we cannot proceed in this manner. In place of such an ambitious *a priori* demonstration, we must have recourse to the revelation of God's will provided by experience.

If Malebranche takes this limited concession to voluntarism seriously, there can be for us no rational dynamics. We have rational sciences of geometry and kinematics because these sciences are deducible from *étendue intelligible*, which we 'see' in the divine intellect itself. But how the motions of colliding bodies are redistributed on impact depends on what type of bodies God has chosen to create. This in turn depends on His will, which we learn only through the revelation that is experience.

It follows, surely, that even such rational principles as continuity and contact action can only be justified empirically. If God chooses to create a body at one place at instant t1, and then at a distant place at t2, it doesn't follow that it must have passed continuously through all the intermediate places to get from one to the other. Malebranche's discussion of the Eucharist shows that he doesn't regard discontinuity as self-contradictory, nor as violating the identity-conditions of bodies (*OCM* XVII–1 491–5). There can even be backwards (occasional) causation: God can give a sinner grace at t1 because He foresees that Jesus will ask for it at a later time t2 (*OCM* IV 158). If this is possible in the domain of grace, why not in that of nature? And if God had so chosen, He could have established Fontenelle's action-at-a-distance, with bodies springing back before ever coming into contact. As we showed in Chapter Five, the occasionalist is in a very weak position when it comes to laying down *a priori* constraints on (occasional) causation. It is only experience that tells us that these bizarre possibilities are not realised. But does experience tell us this? What should we say about gravity and magnetism? The *a priori* demand for contact-action forced the Cartesians to invent vortices of subtle matter, but there is no independent evidence of their existence. If one combines the metaphysics of continuous creation with this new concession to voluntarism, there seems no principled reason why Malebranche and his followers should not accept action-at-a-distance. Malebranche's disciples in France were, it seems, in a particularly weak position to resist the Newtonian invasion.[32]

I am not arguing that Costabel is simply wrong, and that Malebranche became, in his later years, a card-carrying empiricist. But I do think the thrust of his argument is in that direction. The driving force behind his successive revisions of the laws of collision is the need to reconcile reason with experience, but in the end the reconciliation is virtual surrender. Reason ceases to be a source of *a priori* knowledge of the laws to which nature must conform, and becomes instead a search for intelligible reasons for the laws experience has revealed. This surrender is justified by the partial theological shift to voluntarism. Malebranche perhaps didn't see it; he continued to insist, for example, that contact-action is based on a clear idea whereas action-at-a-distance is not. But this intuitive claim is now devoid of all rational ground. If the laws of motion stem from God's will which, although not arbitrary in itself, must always appear opaque to us then – as far as *a priori* reasoning is concerned – anything can be the cause of (i.e. occasion for) anything else. In this area, at least, Malebranche really is an empiricist *malgré lui*, and a close intellectual ancestor of Hume.[33]

7

MALEBRANCHE'S BIOLOGY

Although the title of this chapter is 'Malebranche's biology', it could as easily have been entitled 'Malebranche on the generation of plants and animals'. The chapter is concerned with biology only to the extent that it reflects Malebranche's over-riding metaphysical and theological concerns. Only one biological issue – generation – forced Malebranche into a radical rethink of the mechanical philosophy he inherited from Descartes. For the most part, he takes mechanism, even in its more contentious aspects, to have been established by Descartes. He is, for example, one of the most stalwart defenders of the *bête-machine*.[1] But when it comes to the question of the origin of plants and animals, whether of the individual or the species, Malebranche departs radically from Descartes and devises a completely new version of mechanical philosophy. It is this shift, within the tradition of mechanism, which provides the focus for our chapter.

Nature and supernature

In an important paper, Keith Hutchison has argued that the mechanical philosophy constituted a shift away from naturalism and towards super-naturalism in natural philosophy.[2] Strip matter of its forms and qualities, he argues, and you strip it of its active powers, leaving it merely passive, moved around only by external forces. For the mechanists, no body has a 'nature' (*physis*) in its Aristotelian sense, an inner principle of motion and rest.[3] A particular body moves as it does because it was pushed by another, but there is nothing in the nature of body as such that accounts for motion, nor does the body have any inclination of its own to move in any one direction rather than another. To explain why bodies move at all we need to have recourse to immaterial agents, and ultimately to God. The so-called 'laws of nature' are just the rules that God observes in moving bodies around. The mechanists, it seems, are committed by their conception of matter to a thoroughgoing super-naturalism.

On the other hand, Aram Vartanian has argued that the mechanical philosophy, at least in its Cartesian version, was the precursor of Enlightenment naturalism.[4] Descartes, we are told, was the intellectual ancestor of Maupertuis and Diderot, and ultimately of Darwin. His naturalistic cosmogony, a grandiose attempt to explain the origin of stars and planets, plants and animals from a primeval chaos, by the laws of motion alone, marks Descartes out as among the pioneers of evolutionary naturalism. When Descartes says, in a letter to Henry More, 'I have not yet met anything connected with the nature of material things for which I could not very easily think out a mechanistic explanation' (AT V 340, CSMK III 375), we are to assume that he includes the generation of plants and animals in the scope of the project.

It should be clear that Hutchison and Vartanian are using the terms 'natural' and 'supernatural' to mark different distinctions.[5] Hutchison is mainly concerned with the metaphysical issue of the powers of matter. Do bodies possess 'natures', i.e. intrinsic sources of active power, or is matter passive and inert, moved around only by an immaterial agent (God)? Descartes' endorsement of the latter viewpoint marks him as a metaphysical supernaturalist.[6] On the other hand, a scientist might use the nature/supernature distinction to separate those phenomena explicable in terms of natural laws alone from those that are not. Are all events in the physical world explicable in terms of 'matter and motion', without invoking special providences; or will we come across some (perhaps many) phenomena in nature which cannot be accounted for except by special acts of divine craftsmanship? Here Descartes' clear endorsement of the former answer marks him as a physical naturalist. The apparent opposition between Hutchison and Vartanian turns out to be merely verbal.

Our topic in this chapter is not metaphysical but physical super-naturalism. There is no doubt that Malebranche, with his occasionalism and his doctrine of continuous creation, is a complete supernaturalist in his metaphysics. But he is also, unlike his master Descartes, a physical supernaturalist. That is, he abandons some of Descartes' more ambitious claims, and limits the scope of naturalistic explanation. If we ask Descartes 'why are there giraffes?', he will try to explain both how there came to be giraffes in the first place, and how existing giraffes propagate their kind. If we ask Malebranche the same question, he will reply 'because God made them'. The naturalist must know his limitations: faced with some questions, as Réaumur famously said, 'il faut admirer et se taire'.[7]

This chapter discusses the shift, within the mechanical philosophy, from physical naturalism to supernaturalism. Among the mechanists, Malebranche plays a prominent role in providing the philosophical rationale for this shift. But before discussing Malebranche's own views, we must say a few words about the Cartesian programme he was rejecting.

Descartes' naturalistic cosmogony

In constructing a cosmogony, writes Descartes in Part 3, Article 47, of his *Principles*, the assumption of initial conditions is irrelevant:

> Hardly anything can be assumed from which the same effect cannot be derived, though perhaps with greater trouble, for due to these laws matter takes on, successively, all the forms of which it is capable. Therefore if we considered these forms in order, we would eventually arrive at that which is our present world, so that in this respect no false hypothesis can lead us into error.
>
> (AT IX 126, CSM I 258)

Matter takes on, successively, all the forms of which it is capable. Starting from any chaotic arrangement of corpuscles, the unaided laws of motion would suffice – given enough time – to give rise to our present cosmos and all its bodily inhabitants – everything, in fact, apart from human souls. God has a metaphysical role (sustaining the existence of matter and motion) but no physical role: to the eyes of astronomers and biologists, worlds and organisms alike will appear to be products of nature.

Descartes' official position, of course, is that the naturalistic cosmogony he presents in *Le Monde* and in the *Principles* is a fiction, an account of an imaginary new world and its origins. This is stressed both in *Le Monde* (AT XI 31, CSM I 90) and again in the *Principles* (AT IX 123–4, CSM I 255–7). But this fiction, he insists at the start of Book Four of the *Principles*, still possesses explanatory power in the real world. Even if God created everything in its perfect state, we will understand more about the workings of a plant or an animal when we see how such things could have emerged from the play of corpuscles (AT IX 201, CSM I 267).

In an important sense, indeed, Descartes does believe that actual organisms arise from the play of corpuscles. Even if the naturalistic cosmogony is a fiction, it must be (given *Principles* 3, 47) a possible account of how things came-to-be. So the mere play of corpuscles can fashion a plant or animal from formless matter. It is then no surprise to find Descartes a partisan of epigenesis, arguing that all animals have arisen from a mixture and condensation of two seminal fluids, male and female. In his unpublished *First Thoughts on Animal Generation* he even endorses so-called spontaneous generation (*abiogenesis*) with a casual remark: 'since therefore so few things are necessary to make an animal, it is assuredly not surprising to see so many animals, so many worms, so many insects form spontaneously in all putrefying matter' (AT XI 50).

In the unpublished manuscript, *de la formation de l'animal*, Descartes attempts to complete his mechanical philosophy by describing this process of epigenesis in more detail. The attempt was ambitious but premature: he provides no credible account of the specificity of generation (why do tigers beget tigers?), of the staggering complexity of animal bodies (how can so much structure emerge from none at all?), and of the adaptation of structure to function (why do all the parts of the animal seem to serve a unifying design or purpose?) His ambitious programme of mechanistic epigenesis found few followers.

The last of the three difficulties listed above is connected, of course, with Descartes' well-documented hostility to teleology in natural philosophy. He famously claims in Book One of the *Principles* that we should not invoke final causes in the study of nature, on the grounds that it would be presumptuous of us to claim to know God's purposes in creation (AT IX 37, CSM I 202). We should seek to uncover the efficient causes (how things came to be as they are) but should eschew purported explanations in terms of final causes (why things are as they are). On this point he is challenged by Gassendi, who comes down firmly in defence of finalism.[8] According to Gassendi, we cannot hope to know how, e.g. the valves in the heart were formed; but if we begin by asking what they are for we shall be led to useful knowledge (in this case, Harvey's discovery of the circulation of the blood[9]). *De la formation de l'animal* takes up Gassendi's challenge: the cardiac valves are, Descartes thinks, deposited at the interface between two opposed currents of blood (AT XI 279). But his explanation is sketchy at best, and offers no credible account of how structures in plants and animals are so well adapted to serve their functions. Malebranche was by no means the only Cartesian to follow Gassendi rather than Descartes on this issue.

Worlds and organisms in Malebranche

In Book Six of the *Recherche*, Malebranche presents a beautifully lucid exposition of Cartesian cosmogony (*OCM* II 321ff, LO 453ff). Descartes' theory of vortices is, he insists, the world-system that results if one simply follows the light of reason. When we turn to consult experience, we find that it confirms our rational cosmogony:

> If we are to follow the lights of reason, then we are obliged to arrange the parts of the world, which we imagine to have been formed in the simplest ways, in just this way. For everything that has just been said rests only on our idea of extension, whose parts supposedly tend to move with the simplest motion, which is rectilinear motion. And when we investigate through effects, if we do not err in wanting to explain things by their causes, we are surprised to see that the phenomena of the heavenly bodies are in rather close harmony with what has just been stated.
>
> (*OCM* II 334, LO 459)

The principal objection to Descartes' cosmogony, Malebranche continues, is that it is said to contradict scripture, which, we are told, teaches that the physical universe was created in its present state. To this objection, Malebranche replies, different responses are possible. One might reply that it is not obvious that the Cartesian world-making programme does contradict scripture. Some Cartesians, including Cordemoy,[10] had already taken this line, which Malebranche is not prepared to reject outright. He is thus prepared to write to Arnauld in the following terms:

> For what Moses tells us in Genesis is so obscure that it could perhaps be equally well reconciled with Cartesian principles as with the opinions of other philosophers. Several people have already written books on this subject, and although they may not have had great success, I do not know that others may not do better,
>
> (*OCM* VIII 780)

Alternatively, one can adopt Descartes' own explicit fictionalism, building cosmogony on an admittedly false hypothesis (*OCM* II 340, LO 463–4). But what is the use of a fictional cosmogony, an account of how some imaginary world came to be? Descartes thought that an admittedly fictional account could still possess explanatory value, that we can understand our actual cosmos and its inhabitants better if we see them as products of a fictional evolutionary history. Malebranche agrees with this claim. Consider, he says, the stability of the solar system. If God had

162

chosen a different arrangement for the system than one that could have arisen from the unaided laws of motion, the system could not be stable (*OCM* II 341–2, LO 464). If, for example, God had created a cubic sun, displaced from the centre of its vortex, the laws of motion would have tended to wear away its corners and shift it back to its 'proper' place in the centre.

Even the natures of living things, Malebranche continues, can be illuminated by a genetic approach. Suppose a man wants to discover the nature of the chicken:

> To do this, every day he opens all the eggs it lays. In them he notes a vesicle that contains the embryo of the chicken, and in this vesicle a projecting point that he discovers to be its heart; that from there, blood-carrying conduits that are the arteries go out in all directions, and that this blood returns toward the heart via the veins; that the brain also appears at an early stage, and that the bones are the last parts to be formed. By this means he is delivered from a great many errors, and he even draws many conclusions of considerable use in the understanding of animals from these observations. What can one find to criticize in the conduct of this man? Can we say that he would persuade us that God formed the first chicken by immediate creation of an egg to which He gave a certain degree of heat in order to make it hatch, just because he tries to discover the nature of chickens in their formation?
>
> (*OCM* II 342, LO 464)

Why then, Malebranche continues, do people reproach Descartes for contradicting scripture? Descartes tells us frankly that he does not doubt that the solar system was created in its present state, and that Adam and Eve were created as mature adults. The Christian religion teaches this, and reason concurs: an all-wise and all-powerful God must create a perfect universe, not a formless chaos out of which a cosmos will in the course of time emerge.

It is at this point, however, that Malebranche makes a crucial departure from Descartes. The solar system, Malebranche thinks, could have arisen out of chaos; a plant or an animal could not have done so. Why not? The reason is this:

> An organised body contains an infinity of parts that mutually depend upon one another in relation to particular ends, all of

which must be actually formed in order to work as a whole. For it need not be imagined with Aristotle that the heart is the first part to live and the last part to die. The heart cannot beat without the influence of the animal spirits, nor these be spread throughout the heart without the nerves, and the nerves originate in the brain, from which they receive the spirits. Moreover, the heart cannot beat and pump the blood through the arteries unless they as well as the veins that return the blood to it are already complete. In short, it is clear that a machine can only work when it is finished, and that hence the heart cannot live alone. Thus, from the time this projecting point that is the heart of the chicken appears in a setting egg, the chicken is alive; and for the same reason, it is well to note, a woman's child is alive from the moment it is conceived, because life begins when spirits cause the organs to work, which cannot occur unless they are actually formed and connected. It would be wrong then to pretend to explain the formation of animals and plants and their parts, one after the other, on the basis of the simple and general laws governing the communication of motion; for they are differently connected to one another by virtue of different ends and different uses in the different species. But such is not the case with the formation of vortices; they are naturally born from general laws, as I have just in part explained.

(*OCM* II 343–4, LO 465–6)

This is a very important passage, marking a sharp and decisive break with Descartes' physical naturalism. For Malebranche, in contrast to Descartes, many things are necessary to form an animal, and, crucially, these things are all functionally specific and functionally interdependent. But if no organ of the body can function without all the others, it follows that an organism cannot come-to-be gradually, one part after another. Epigenetic theories, whether Aristotelian or Cartesian in inspiration, can be ruled out as impossible. Descartes' project, says Theodore in the *Entretiens sur la Métaphysique*, was 'very foolhardy' (*OCM* XII 264, JS 205), and was abandoned by Descartes himself. Descartes started with the heart, but how can the heart function without arteries, veins, nerves and brain? In the light of modern physiological knowledge, we could go on to add liver and kidneys, and no doubt numerous other organs. The heart could presumably function in the absence of arms and legs, so the argument doesn't strictly entail that the foetus must already be fully-formed, but it does entail that all the vital organs, all the organs necessary for life itself, must be present *ab initio*, i.e. from conception. If conception is the beginning of life, this argument will not apply before that moment: one could assemble a machine piece by piece and only set it in motion once assembled.

In the *Méditations Chrétiennes* we find essentially the same argument repeated, but with an even greater emphasis on teleology. This is how the Word of God puts the point:

> When one considers organised bodies, the purpose and wisdom of the work appear in part in the construction of the machine. One sees clearly that it is not at all the work of chance. Everything in it is formed in accordance with a definite plan and by particular acts of will. Everything in it is formed in accordance with a definite plan: for it is evident by the situation and by the construction of the eyes that they were made for seeing, and that all the parts that compose the bodies of animals are destined for certain uses. And everything in it is formed by particular acts of will, for organised bodies could not be produced by the laws of communication of motion alone. The laws of nature can only give them, little by little, their ordinary growth.
>
> (*OCM* X 721)

Since the laws of nature cannot give rise to a chicken or a partridge, it follows that these animals must be already formed in the eggs from which they hatch. When it comes to inanimate things, however, even the entire solar system, the message is quite different:

> But all the rest of the visible world has been conserved for so many years, and could have been formed precisely as it is by the general laws of communication of motion, supposing that the first impressions of motion had had certain determinations and a certain quantity of force that God alone knows.
>
> (*OCM* X 72)

It is not complexity as such but functional complexity, and particularly functional interdependence of parts, which furnishes evidence of design. As we are reminded in Book Four, Chapter Seven, of the *Recherche*, mere size counts for nothing at all:

> The smallest fly better manifests the power and wisdom of God to those who will consider it with attention, and without being

prejudiced by its size, than everything the astronomers know about the heavens.

(OCM II 61, LO 296–7)

Every organism, we are told, is a particular product of divine craft, something that could not have arisen from any other cause. It could not have arisen from the unaided laws of motion, for the reasons just given; and there are no subordinate agents (animal and vegetable souls, 'plastic nature') available for the task.[11] Every cabbage and mushroom, every beetle and mosquito is the product of a particular providence. But if we admit a God who is continually intervening in the course of nature for the generation of every plant and animal, have we not abandoned natural philosophy altogether? It is to avoid this objection that Malebranche has recourse to his theory of pre-existence.

The theory of pre-existence

To appreciate the novelty of the doctrine of pre-existence, it is important to distinguish it clearly from the rival theory of preformation.[12] Preformation postulates a process, governed by the soul of the parent, in which the future organism is fashioned in the testicles of the father or the ovaries of the mother. Generation can be said to have taken place when the egg or seed has been sufficiently 'elaborated' by the soul of the parent. (To admit a genetic role for both parents, i.e. a double preformation, raises obvious difficulties.) By contrast, pre-existence postulates no such process of elaboration, and no vital role for the soul of the parent. The future organism pre-exists in the egg or sperm, but owes its origin to a special act of creation. Preformation is therefore a naturalistic theory involving the generous attribution of causal powers to creatures; pre-existence is pure supernaturalism.[13]

Malebranche introduces the theory in Chapter Six of Book One of the *Recherche*, a chapter ostensibly devoted to errors of vision. He begins with the observation of micro-organisms under the microscope:

> With magnifying glasses, we can easily see animals much smaller than an almost invisible grain of sand; we have seen some even a thousand times smaller. These living atoms walk as well as other animals. Thus, they have legs and feet, and bones in their legs to support them (or rather on their legs, for the skin of an insect is its skeleton). They have muscles to move them, as well as tendons and an infinity of fibres in each muscle; finally, they

166

have blood or very subtle and delicate animal spirits to fill or move these muscles in succession. Without this, it is impossible to conceive how they should live, nourish themselves, and move their tiny bodies from place to place according to the various impressions of objects ...

(*OCM* I 80, LO 25–6)

The inference here is from function to structure, structure which must be present (albeit invisibly) to sustain vital activities. Even if the senses and the imagination fail us here, says Malebranche, reason retains its rights:

Our vision is very limited, but it must not limit its object. The idea it gives us of extension has very narrow limits; but it does not follow from this that extension is so limited. Undoubtedly, it is in a sense unlimited; and this small section of matter, which is hidden from our eyes, can contain an entire world in which would be found as many things, though proportionately smaller, as are found in this larger world we live in.

(*OCM* I 80, LO 26)

Given the infinite divisibility of matter, nothing prevents there being smaller and smaller organisms *ad infinitum*:

For the tiny animals of which we have just spoken, there are perhaps other animals that prey upon them and that, on account of their awesome smallness, are to them as imperceptible as they themselves are to us. What a mite is compared with us, these animals are to a mite; and perhaps there are in nature things smaller and smaller to infinity, standing in that extreme proportion of man to mite.

(*OCM* I 81, LO 26)

Our imagination may boggle at this thought, but so much the worse for the imagination. Since matter is infinitely divisible, nothing prevents the existence of organisms within organisms *ad infinitum*; indeed, this seems a fitting manifestation of the power and wisdom of God. There is then no reason at all to believe that the latest microscopic discoveries will be the last:

On the contrary, it is much more plausible to believe that there are many things yet smaller than those already discovered, for in

167

the final analysis, there are always tiny animals to be found with microscopes, but not always microscopes to find them.

(*OCM* I 81, LO 26)

So far, this emphasis on infinite divisibility, and on the possibility of organisms within organisms without end, has just been a softening up exercise on Malebranche's part. Now, however, he moves onto the attack:

When one examines the seed of a tulip bulb in the dead of winter with a simple *magnifying lens* or convex glass, or even merely with the naked eye, one easily discovers in this seed the leaves that are to become green, those that are to make up the flower or tulip, that tiny triangular part which contains the seed, and the six little columns that surround it at the base of the flower. Thus it cannot be doubted that the seed of a tulip bulb contains an entire tulip.

(*OCM* I 81, LO 26)

The next step in the argument is a simple generalisation:

It is reasonable to believe the same thing of a mustard seed, an apple seed, and generally of the seeds of every sort of tree and plant, though all this might not be seen with the naked eye or even with a microscope; and it can be said with some assurance that all trees are in the seeds of their seeds in miniature.

(*OCM* I 82, LO 26)

What drives this generalisation? Not, it should be clear, the evidence of our senses. We see that some plants are pre-existent in their seeds, and promptly judge that this is true of them all. Why should we thus generalise so hastily? Because structures, particularly complex functional structures, cannot emerge out of nothing. The oak tree must already be present in the acorn, as the tulip is in its bulb.

But this, of course, only displaces the search for explanation. We can now explain how an oak tree emerges from an acorn (it is just unpacking and growth), but how was the acorn formed in the first place? Does the oak tree somehow possess the power to assemble mini-replicas of itself? That, for a good mechanist like Malebranche, is literally unthinkable. But the only alternative is pre-existence:

Nor does it seem unreasonable to believe even that there is an infinite number of trees in a single seed, since it contains not only the tree of which it is the seed but also a great number of other seeds that might contain other trees and other seeds, which will perhaps have on an incomprehensibly small scale other trees and other seeds and so to infinity. So that according to this view, which will appear strange and incongruous only to those who measure the marvels of God's infinite power by the ideas of sense and imagination, it might be said (1) that in a single apple seed there are apple trees, apples, and apple seeds, standing in the proportion of a fully grown tree to the tree in its seed, for an infinite, or nearly infinite number of centuries; (2) that nature's role is only to unfold these tiny trees by providing perceptible growth for that outside its seed, and imperceptible yet very real growth in proportion to their size, for those thought to be in their seed ...

(*OCM* I 82, LO 27)

There are, we are told, apple trees within apple pips, and a further generation of apple trees within the pips of these mini apple trees, and so on for untold generations. What the naturalists have called 'generation' is just unpacking and growth. And what goes for plants goes for animals too:

Likewise, a chicken that is perhaps entirely formed is seen in the seed of a fresh egg that has not been hatched. Frogs are to be seen in frogs' eggs, and still other animals will be seen in their seed when we have sufficient skill and experience to discover them. But the mind need not stop with the eyes, for the mind's vision is much more extensive than the body's. We ought to accept, in addition, that the body of every man and beast born till the end of time was perhaps produced at the creation of the world. My thought is that the females of the original animals may have been created along with all those of the same species that they have begotten and that are to be begotten in the future.

(*OCM* I 82–3, LO 27)

The claim to empirical support here cannot be taken very seriously. The eggs of chickens and frogs would have been fertilised eggs, so the presence of fully formed structures would be compatible with any of the main theories of generation – pre-existence, preformation, metamorphosis, and epigenesis. To rule out metamorphosis and epigenesis one would need to detect fully formed organs in an unfertilised egg. Such claims were made in the late seventeenth century by Littré in France[14] and Croone in England,[15] but were never confirmed by their respective scientific communities. And even if one could observe such structures in an unfertilised egg, they would not support pre-existence against preformation.

Malebranche's argument, as is clear from the above quote, was never meant to be inductive. On the contrary, he insists that the intellect must outstrip the evidence of the senses and demand an intelligible account of the origin of plants and animals. The argument for pre-existence can then be formulated as an argument from elimination: once you have dismissed all those accounts that manifestly fail to satisfy the intellect, you will find that only pre-existence remains.

The same mixture of empirical evidence and *a priori* constraints reappears in the tenth of the *Entretiens sur la Métaphysique* (*OCM* XII 223ff, JS 170ff). Malebranche's spokesman Theodore begins by citing empirical evidence (this time a letter from Leeuwenhoek to Wren for the Royal Society in London) for the existence of micro-organisms.[16] There are, says Theodore, an untold number of animals still more minute than those Leeuwenhoek had discovered with his microscope: 'We are losing ourselves, Aristes, in the small as well as in the large. No one can claim that they have at last discovered the smallest animal' (*OCM* XII 228, JS 174).

Since nature acts only by the blind, mechanical laws of motion, it is clear that 'it is not the earth which produces plants and that it is not possible that the union of the two sexes forms a work as wonderful as the body of an animal' (*OCM* XII 229, JS 175). The laws of motion, Theodore continues, can explain the growth of animals but not their generation:

> We see, rather, that unless we wish to have recourse to an extra-ordinary providence, we must believe that the seed of a plant contains in miniature the plant which it engenders, and that in its womb an animal contains the animal which should come from it.
>
> (*OCM* XII 229, JS 175)

Either God is continually intervening in the course of nature, fashioning every new mosquito and mushroom, or each new organism is pre-existent in its germ. But where did this germ come from? The only conceivable solution, concludes Theodore, is that the organisms have been packed inside one another, generation inside generation, like Russian dolls, since the first creation. This is the notorious theory of *emboîtement*:

> We even understand it to be necessary that each seed contains the entire species it can conserve; that every grain of wheat, for instance, contains in miniature the ear it germinates, each grain of which contains in turn its own ear, all the grains of which can always be as fertile as those of the first ear.
>
> (*OCM* XII 229, JS 175)

Here we find the theory of *emboîtement*, argued for along lines that are essentially negative and *a priori*, i.e. from the inconceivability of rival accounts. The laws of motion cannot frame an organism:

> Surely it is impossible that the laws of motion alone can, in respect of certain ends, adjust together an almost infinite number of organic parts which comprise what we call an animal or a plant.
>
> (*OCM* XII 229, JS 175)

Given the non-existence of animal and vegetable souls, 'plastic nature', etc. (which Malebranche takes to have been established by Descartes), it follows that the only possible cause of animal and plant generation is God Himself. Faced with a choice between continual interventions and pre-existence, the natural philosopher must opt for the latter. Take this line of reasoning to its logical extreme, and one has the theory of *emboîtement*. The course of nature is mechanical, and hence intelligible; the ultimate origin of all things is supernatural.

Theodore now proceeds to admit one important qualification to the doctrine of pre-existence. The miniature plants and animals contained in their seeds need not, he tells us, resemble fully formed adults:

> Nonetheless, it is not the case that the tiny animal or the germ of the plant has precisely the same proportion of size, solidity, and figure among all its parts, as the animals and plants. But it is the case that all the parts essential to the machine of the animals and plants are so wisely disposed in their germs, that they will, in time and as a consequence of the general laws of motion, assume the shape and form which we observe in them.
>
> (*OCM* XII 229, JS 176)

Here Theodore turns for support to Malpighi's observations of chickens, dissected at various stages between fertilisation and hatching. The heads of these embryonic birds are relatively large, and their bones not fully formed. Similar phenomena can be observed in the grubs of insects: pre-existence does not entail that the imago or adult form is present in every last detail in the larva:

> I simply claim that all the organic parts of bees are formed in their larvae, and are so well proportioned to the laws of motion that they can grow through their own construction and through the efficacy of those laws, and can assume the shape suitable to their condition, without God intervening anew through extraordinary providence.
>
> (*OCM* XII 253, JS 195–6)

This concession, that the pre-existent germs need not be fully-formed plants and animals, resembling in all respects the adults they will become, will be important later in our story. For the moment let us simply note that Malebranche does not want his theory of pre-existence to rule out altogether any role for the environment in animal generation.

Theodore now advises his young pupil Ariste to examine the wonderful compound eye of a fly under a microscope. This fly could not emerge from the grub, Theodore insists, unless it were already contained in it, 'for that is inconceivable' (*OCM* XII 230, JS 176). The nature of Malebranche's argument – negative and *a priori* – could scarcely be clearer. He goes on, of course, to cite 'un savant Hollandais' (Jan Swammerdam) who, by a skilled dissection, can exhibit the butterfly in its pupa,[17] but he must be well aware that such empirical evidence provides only the weakest of support for pre-existence. Experimental biology (Leeuwenhoek's microorganisms, Malpighi's chicks, Swammerdam's butterflies) are used to illustrate the theory rather than to confirm it.

In *Entretien* XI the same line of argument is used against so-called 'equivocal' or 'spontaneous' generation. The topic is raised by Ariste:

> There are people who claim that insects come from putrefaction. But if a fly has as many organic parts as an ox, I would rather say that this large animal can be formed from a mound of clay, than maintain that flies are produced from a piece of rotten flesh.
>
> (*OCM* XII 252, JS 195)

The grubs that hatch in rotting meat emerge simply from eggs laid by adult flies. Here Theodore refers us to the famous experiments of Francesco Redi.[18] As for the supposed 'proofs' of spontaneous generation, they are dismissed as feeble:

> I cannot understand how such a large number of people of good sense have been able to commit such a blatant and palpable error for similar reasons. For what is more incomprehensible than an animal forming itself naturally out of a little rotten meat? It is infinitely easier to conceive of a piece of rusty iron being turned into a perfectly good watch; for there are infinitely more parts of greater delicacy in a mouse, than in the most complex clock.
>
> (*OCM* XII 263, JS 204)

The theory of *emboîtement* may not be easy to grasp, Theodore admits, but at least one can see (given the infinite divisibility of matter) that it is not impossible; whereas the generation of an animal from unaided matter and motion is literally inconceivable.

Malebranche seems to have conflated two distinct lines of argument here. What is inconceivable, by his lights, is the emergence of an organism from anything but a suitable pre-existent seed or germ. But whether God has in fact seen fit to place all these seeds within the bodies of mothers of the same species is a further question. If God wanted flies to be generated, without mothers, from rotting meat, He could simply place the 'germs' of flies into the bodies of the higher animals, there to await the right stimulus to develop into grubs and eventually into (parentless) flies. To rule out this possibility, the *a priori* argument is useless; here, at least, one must rely on the empirical arguments of Redi. But in the late seventeenth century this empirical argument was still less than conclusive: there were still organisms (e.g. parasitic worms in the guts of higher organisms) that seemed to be products of spontaneous generation.[19]

Creation and special providence

As we saw in Chapter Five, at the heart of Malebranche's philosophy is his distinction between *volontés générales* and *volontés particulières*. Since God is the only causal agent, it is true to say of everything that happens that it was caused by the will of God. There remains, however, this crucial distinction: some events are brought about in accordance with general laws; others result from particular volitions. The laws of motion, for example, result from *volontés générales* – in reassigning motions to corpuscles on the occasion of a collision, God acts by a sort of habit, without any special concern for the particular case.

In the *Traité de la Nature et de la Grâce* Malebranche offers an ingenious and original theodicy. The explanation for the existence of so much evil lies – paradoxically – in the very perfection of God. God must act, Malebranche insists, in a manner worthy of Himself, i.e. in a manner that expresses His perfections, most importantly, His wisdom. This in turn implies, we are told, that He will always act by the simplest means to bring about any given effect. In choosing between possible universes, God weighs the perfection of the final product against the simplicity of the means by which it is brought about, producing the optimum weighted sum of these two *desiderata* (*OCM* V 28, *OCM* IX 1085).

But simplicity is achieved by means of *volontés générales*, by bringing about as many effects as possible in accordance with general rules. In choosing between possible universes, then, God picks 'the one which could have been produced and conserved by the simplest laws, or the one which would be the most perfect in relation to the simplicity of the means necessary to its production or its conservation' (*OCM* V 28). So God is obliged, by His own wisdom, to achieve as much as possible by general laws, minimising the number of *volontés particulières*.

One might imagine that the minimum number of *volontés particulières* would be zero, and that Malebranche's God will find Himself obliged to bring about all things by means of general laws. This, Malebranche retorts, is logically impossible. The creation of the physical universe in the first place was a free act on God's part – it was not necessary for Him to create a world at all. But God cannot create bodies and set them in motion without particular volitions, i.e. without creating bodies of particular sizes, shapes, and motions. This, he explains in his extended controversy with Arnauld, 'could not occur in any other way. For particular volitions were necessary to commence the determinations of movements' (*OCM* VIII 759). A deist may think that God should act only by general laws, but:

> This freethinker does not notice that he subjects his account to this condition which makes it impossible, namely that God gives to the particles of matter a suitable movement to form the world, *without acting by particular volitions*. For it is evident that it is necessary to start with such acts of will to determine the first movements, which at first must be all different, some to the

right, others to the left, these upwards, those downwards, in order to divide matter into an infinity of parts.

(*OCM* VIII 779)

Since special providences are logically required for creation, God was evidently not required to cut their number to zero. Here the fecundity of the effect outweighs the simplicity of the means. In fact, Malebranche's argument doesn't seem to be a straightforward matter of minimisation at all. If it were just a matter of minimising the number of *volontés particulières*, the time factor would be irrelevant. If every mosquito is, quite literally, a miracle, then pre-existence requires the same number of miracles as continuous miraculous interventions to create each insect individually. This objection would be pressed against the theory of pre-existence by Maupertuis in his *Vénus Physique*.[20] For Malebranche, it is clear that the time factor does matter, that all the little miracles are lumped together into the great miracle of creation. This is how he explains it to Arnauld:

… no more particular volitions were needed to form animals than to divide matter into an infinity of parts. But even if an infinite number more had been needed, besides the fact that they were necessary in the formation of the universe, they would not at that time disturb the simplicity of God's ways, because they precede the general laws, and the encounters of bodies which are the occasional cause of them. But those laws being established God must not, without great reasons, cease to follow them.

(*OCM* VIII 781)

Prior to the establishment of the general laws, special providences do not disturb the *simplicité des voies*; after the establishment of those laws, special providences are to be cut to a minimum. So Malebranche's argument doesn't actually turn on minimisation (though this is what he says); what matters is the all-encompassing miracle of creation. If one can provide independent grounds for believing in creation, one can then say that, at the moment of creation, God fashioned the seeds of all plants and animals that were ever to see the light of day. In the first few days of creation, Malebranche writes to Arnauld that God

was obliged to act in this lowly and for Him as it were servile manner. The formation of organised bodies, and the relation which He wanted to establish between the physical and the moral, could not have been established without His acting by particular volitions. But at present He is resting.

(*OCM* VII 594)

This 'repose' is not, of course, the cessation of God's activity; it is the cessation of particular volitions, leaving the universe to unfold according to the laws of nature established by *volontés générales*.

What follows from all this for biology? Every organism is the result of a special providence, something impossible without a particular divine volition. It is not literally a miracle, as Swammerdam had suggested,[21] because its creation violated no laws of nature, for the elementary reason that the laws of nature had not yet been established at the moment of creation. But it transcends naturalistic explanation. The naturalist can study the 'packaging' of each generation within another (illustrated by parthenogenesis in aphids, where females can be born already pregnant), and can investigate the phenomena of growth and maturation, but generation must forever remain beyond his grasp. Faced with the mystery of generation all that remains for us is an awed silence. There is such a thing as natural history, but natural science in the sense sought by Descartes, that is, an understanding of all things through their causes, will forever remain beyond us.

The problem of monsters

The existence of monsters was routinely cited, throughout the sixteenth and seventeenth centuries, as providing decisive evidence in support of naturalism.[22] If every organism were the product of a particular divine volition, it was argued, then there would be no monsters. Since there manifestly are monsters, God must have delegated the generation of animals and plants to subordinate agents – e.g. the souls of the parents, or an all-embracing 'plastic nature'.

As a metaphysical supernaturalist, Malebranche will have none of this. To assume the existence in nature of real causal powers is, he insists, bad philosophy as well as bad theology. It is 'the most dangerous error of the philosophy of the ancients' (*OCM* II 309ff, LO 446ff). But if God is the cause of all things, does it not follow that He is also the cause of monsters? And if so, might it not follow that His values are not our values – a disturbing thought for ethics and theology. In *Éclaircissement* VIII Malebranche addresses the difficulty:

Likewise, we know that God is wise, and that everything He does is good. We also see monsters or defective works. What is one to believe? That God has erred or that these monsters are not His work. Surely if one has any sense or strength of mind, one will believe neither one nor the other, for it is evident that God does everything and that He can do nothing that is not as perfect as it can be in relation to simplicity and the small number of means He employs and must employ in the formation of His work.

(OCM III 88, LO 588)

God wills Order; Order requires that He act by a few simple laws. Working in accordance with these laws will produce, on odd occasions, monstrous results. God could of course intervene to prevent this, but that would require Him to act in a manner unworthy of Him, i.e. by particular volitions. In the last of the *Éclaircissements*, Malebranche discusses defects of vision in the human eye. Although such defects are common, we should not conclude from them that our eyes are the craftsmanship of any other cause than God Himself:

And resorting to a blind nature, plastic forms, the soul of the mother or of those who have these defects in order to explain them is of good intention, but it is to form chimeras. It would be better to believe that these defects in individuals contribute to the perfection of the entire work, or that God always makes use of them for the good of those who have them.

(OCM III 341, LO 743)

But this is inconsistent with Malebranche's considered opinion on the subject of natural evil. The 'aesthetic' justification of natural evil likened such evils to the shadows in a painting or dissonances in a piece of music, which contribute to the beauty and harmony of the whole. The outlines of such an account can be found in Augustine; it became a commonplace in the tradition of natural theology; Leibniz gave it a famous expression in his *Theodicy*. Malebranche however rejected it as false and blasphemous:

Shadows are necessary in a picture, and dissonances in music. Therefore it is necessary that women miscarry, and an infinity of monsters are born. 'What a consequence!' I will boldly reply to the philosophers. Such monsters are only seen by midwives, and only live a few days, so necessary are they to the beauty of the universe.

(OCM VIII 765)

Monsters, Malebranche insists in the controversy with Arnauld, are emphatically not necessary to the beauty of the universe: 'Fundamentally, I think that such things do not make God's work more perfect. On the contrary, they disfigure it, and make it disagreeable to all those who love order' (OCM VIII 765). A universe without monsters would be better, in itself, than one with them.[23] Our world, Malebranche reiterates, does contain blemishes:

> I do not fear to repeat it: the Universe is not the most perfect which could exist in an absolute sense, but only the most perfect which could exist in relation to the means which are most worthy of the divine attributes. There are *visible flaws* in the work of God, in His work I say once again, not in His conduct. It is a visible flaw that an infant should come into the world with superfluous members, which prevent it from living. I have said this, and I maintain it. I would rather leave this flaw in the body of the unfortunate infant, and consequently in the universe, than ascribe it to the sinister designs of its Author.

(OCM VIII 768)

To suppose, as Arnauld does,[24] that God created this malformed infant by a particular volition would be, on Malebranche's view, truly blasphemous. If God acted by particular volitions, there would be no monsters. Since there are monsters, it follows that God does not act by particular acts of will.

This dispute about nature is, for Malebranche and Arnauld, a precise parallel to their theological dispute about grace. There are two parallel paradoxes that Malebranche is hoping to evade. For nature, we have:

> God wills that all organisms be well-formed.
> God is omnipotent.
> Many organisms are defective.

In theology, we have the following:

> God wills that all men be saved.
> God is omnipotent.
> Many (most) men are not saved.

178

Can one, in either case, consistently accept all three propositions? Yes, says Malebranche, so long as one bears in mind that God loves His own perfections more than He loves His creatures. His concern that His conduct should express His attributes (His love of Order) over-rides His concern for the well-being of mere creatures, and requires that He act by means of general laws.

But hasn't Malebranche explicitly told us that every plant and animal is the product of a particular divine volition? If so, his 'solution' to the problem of monsters looks in flat contradiction to his theory of pre-existence. Malebranche seems only half-aware of the difficulty, but does sketch the beginnings of a reply. The development of an organism from its germ is not, it seems, to be thought of as simply a matter of growth; the growing plant or animal is still susceptible to environmental influences:

> I maintain that all organized bodies have been formed since the beginning of the world in a manner sufficient to derive their growth and to acquire their entire formation in consequence of the law of communication of motions; and that it is even because of this, and because of the relations which God then established between the brain of the mother and that of her child (it will be clear that I am only speaking of primitive parts which have no names, and which are unknown to us); it is because of this, I say, that there are among animals so many irregularities and so many monsters.
>
> (*OCM* VIII 781)

The pre-existent seeds of animals are not fully formed, not perfect miniatures of their parents. Only the nameless *parties primitives* are pre-existent; the final form of the organs remains to be determined – in part at least by environmental factors. But this is now a difficulty for the advocate of pre-existence. Since creation has to involve particular providences, why didn't God create the seeds of all things as perfect miniatures, immune to external damage? Why did He bother to create, by particular acts of will, the seeds of organisms that would fail to develop properly? Without intervening in the natural processes of development (which are all, of course, subject merely to natural laws, and thus fall under *volontés générales*) God could have pre-empted the existence of monsters in the first act of creation. It therefore seems that He could have created a universe with no monsters, at no extra 'cost' in terms of particular volitions. Malebranche's answer leads us into another of the labyrinths of his philosophy, the problem of original sin. As so often in life, it turns out that our mothers are to blame.

The maternal imagination and original sin

Among the external factors that can affect the development of the foetus, one in particular is emphasised by Malebranche. This is the supposed 'rapport' between the brain of a pregnant mother and that of the foetus in her womb. Here Malebranche departs radically from the rules of his own methodology, simply endorsing without question one of the old wives' tales of traditional medicine. No one denies that the psychological state of the pregnant mother can affect her growing child, but that these effects should be precise and iconic – e.g. that a pregnant mother lusting after strawberries should produce a baby with a strawberry birthmark – was supported only by the feeblest of anecdotal evidence, and that mostly *post hoc*.[25] If we enquire after the proposed mechanism for such a transmission, Malebranche is on still shakier ground: there seems to be no nervous communication to transmit the (corporeal) images.

So why does Malebranche endorse the old wives' tale? The empirical evidence in its favour is only anecdotal (of a kind that in other contexts he would dismiss with scorn); there is no remotely plausible mechanism to convey the supposed influence; the theory of pre-existence seems to render such an influence redundant. Everything, it seems, should militate against endorsing the old wives' tale.

When we turn to the relevant chapter of the *Recherche* (*OCM* I 232ff, LO 112ff) we find Malebranche citing, most uncharacteristically, a couple of the standard anecdotes, and claiming that the supposed 'correspondence' between the mother's brain and that of the foetus can account for such iconic effects. This 'correspondence', he continues, is not useless; on the contrary, it can serve to transmit valuable instincts, e.g. the fear of wolves in sheep. It might even, he suggests, account for the specificity of animal generation:

> For although one can give some explanation of the formation of the fetus in general, as Descartes has tried successfully enough, nevertheless it is very difficult, without this communication of the mother's brain with the child's, to explain why a mare does not give birth to a calf, or a chicken lay an egg containing a partridge or some bird of a new species; and I believe that those who have meditated on the formation of the fetus will be of this opinion.
>
> (*OCM* I 242–3, LO 117)

But Malebranche is a partisan of the supernatural theory of pre-existence. Given pre-existence, there is no problem of accounting for specificity, such as faced Descartes' epigenetic theory. God can pack generation after generation of calves into cows, and foals into mares, *ad infinitum*. Malebranche does at least see the objection:

> It is true that the most reasonable thinking, that which conforms most closely to experience in this very difficult question of the formation of the fetus, is that infants are already almost completely formed even before the action by which they are conceived, and during the gestation period their mothers do nothing but provide them their normal growth. However, this communication of the mother's animal spirits and brain with those of the infant seems to serve to regulate this growth, determining the particles used to nourish it to be arranged gradually in the same way as in the mother's body; which is to say, this communication of the spirits renders the child like its mother, or of the same species.
>
> (*OCM* II 242, LO 117–18)

This, if Malebranche means us to take it seriously, would mark a radical modification of the theory of pre-existence. On this view, the pre-existent seed or germ is not yet a seed or germ of any definite species until the maternal imagination gets to work on it. But this would raise problems both conceptual and empirical. Can there be organisms that don't belong to any species? If the same embryo could become a pig (if lodged in the womb of a sow) or a horse (if lodged in the womb of a mare), what is it in itself? Can it have a determinate (and functional) arrangement of parts? As for the empirical dificulties, they are if anything more obvious. Plants generate their kind, but here the maternal imagination is conspicuous only by its absence. Small wonder then that Malebranche begins to backtrack:

> However, I do not deny that God could have disposed all things necessary for the propagation of the species throughout the infinite ages in a manner so precise and regular that mothers would never abort, but would always give birth to children of the same size and colour or, in a word, so similar that they would be taken for one another, without this communication of which we have just spoken.
>
> (*OCM* I 243, LO 118)

The maternal imagination thus need not be invoked to account for the specificity of generation. God could easily dispense with it. Plants breed true without any such role for the imagination. Even in the animal kingdom, there is a mass of evidence against the hypothesis. If a hen sits on duck eggs, Malebranche knows that it is ducklings that hatch and not chickens. So perhaps the maternal imagination should be invoked to explain not something as basic as specificity but more minor resemblances between parent and child. (The theory can, of course, easily account for resemblances between children and their fathers.) Even here, however, the theory of pre-existence seems to render any such account redundant: foresight and pre-packaging can explain any observed degree of resemblance between parents and their offspring.

So why does Malebranche endorse the old wives' tale? His rationalism militates against it: the *Recherche* is full of warnings against superstitious beliefs resting on nothing more than anecdotal evidence. His mechanism militates against it: there is no credible mechanism for transmitting corporeal images from one brain to another. And the biological facts of specificity and resemblance to parents don't require it, but are easily handled by the theory of pre-existence without assuming any role for the maternal imagination.

In the final analysis I think we have to accept that this is one of those occasions on which Malebranche abandons philosophical rationalism for dogmatic theology. He is looking for an explanation of the transmission of original sin, and thinks that this widely accepted theory of the maternal imagination provides it. If the growing foetus shares its mother's thoughts and passions, it partakes in her fallen state. It is indeed an *enfant de colère*, born to sin and – without the sacrament of baptism – bound for the flames of hell.[26]

Conclusion: reason and experience in Malebranche's biology

Malebranche's final position is thus an uneasy compromise between pure pre-existence and the admission of some role for the environment. There must always be a pre-existent germ for every organism, created at the moment of the creation of the universe, but this germ does not fully determine all the features of the eventual organism. If Malebranche really wants the maternal imagination to account for specificity, this miniature germ is not yet even a mini-dog or a mini-cat. But Malebranche seems reluctant to commit himself so far. Given the nature of his earlier argument (from complexity and functional interdependence of organs to pre-existence), the germ must be sufficiently determinate to function. Even growth requires a certain number of basic metabolic functions. The logical position for Malebranche to adopt would be to say that environmental factors can explain failures and lapses (hence monsters), but not perfection of design. If Malebranche really thought that the maternal imagination could take a mass of formless matter and turn it into a cat or a dog, he would have abandoned the theory of pre-existence for the rival theory of preformation.

So what Malebranche ought to say is that the germ is already pre-formed in all vital respects – since its organs are all interdependent, no one can be formed before the others. Given suitable materials, this little germ will grow into a cat, or a dog, or whatever. External factors (e.g. the maternal imagination) may be invoked to explain superficial resemblances, and also to account for monsters. But why doesn't God, at the moment of creation, foresee and prevent such accidents? Malebranche has no principled answer. Since he admits that every organism is a special providence, he can't appeal to the *simplicité des voies*. Without any extra special acts of providence, there could be a universe without monsters. So Malebranche has no principled reply to critics such as Arnauld and Régis who insist that each and every monster must be intended as such, no doubt for some mysterious purpose of God's inscrutable will.

What is rapidly becoming clear about Malebranche's biology is the extent to which it is driven by his metaphysics and theology. Malebranche is very well informed about developments in biology – the *Entretiens* contain references to the work of Swammerdam, Leeuwenhoek, Malpighi, and Redi – and he clearly thinks the weight of the new experimental evidence is on his side. He sometimes suggests that the argument for pre-existence is essentially empirical, but he must have been well aware that this was stretching the point. With the one striking exception of parthenogenesis in aphids, empirical evidence for pre-existence and *emboîtement* was virtually non-existent. More realistically, empirical research might be seen as providing support for an argument that is essentially *a priori*, as follows:

P1 Organisms are enormously complex and apparently 'designed' things, with their parts functionally interdependent on one another.

P2 It is impossible for such things to come-to-be by means of epigenesis (e.g. by the mixing of fluids as Descartes thought), with organs appearing one after another.

P3 Such things (because of the functional interdependence of their parts) can only come-to-be all at once.

P4 There are no plant and animal souls, no 'plastic nature', etc. (from the mechanical philosophy).

P5 Only God can create a plant or an animal.

P6 God is now 'resting', i.e. acting by means of general laws rather than particular acts of will.

C. All organisms that are ever to be were created all at once, as germs or seeds, in the creation of the universe.

What is the structure of this argument, and what role does empirical biology play within it? In the first place, of course, biological research lends powerful support to P1: microscopes reveal new and more complex structures; physiologists discover more and more complex functional interdependence of parts. But P1 in turn supports P2: the more complex and functionally integrated an organism turns out to be, the less plausible any theory of epigenesis will seem. No biologist from the end of the seventeenth century would have endorsed Descartes' offhand 'il faut si peu de choses pour faire un animal'. Now P3 is supposed to follow from P2: if no part can exist and function without the others, the organs can't appear successively. The key word here is of course 'function' – one could imagine a mechanism producing heart, liver, kidneys, lungs, etc. successively, but not 'switching them on' until all are ready and connected up. This is a possibility Malebranche seems to overlook. More fundamentally, his argument seems to assume that a given function can only be served by one specific organ. Suppose a biologist were to argue as follows: the heart cannot function without a supply of oxygen; the lungs supply oxygen to the heart; therefore, the heart cannot function without the lungs. The fallacy here is clear. In the embryo, something or other must supply oxygen to the heart, but it need not be the lungs. A given function may pass from one organ to another. And if we imagine the organism scaled down enough, it may need no special organs at all to supply oxygen to the miniature organs.

But let us grant Malebranche the plausible P3, and see where it leads him. P4 he simply takes from the mechanical philosophy of Descartes, which recommends itself to Malebranche for reasons both epistemological (the reliance on clear and distinct ideas) and theological (the banishment of natural powers). But of course there remain lesser spirits such as angels and demons. So the step to P5 is still not obvious. Why can't a subordinate agent create a flea, or a beetle, at least as an occasional cause? If *emboîtement* is true, of course, every fertile female is infinitely complex, so no finite cause could have the required knowledge, but this looks suspiciously like arguing in circles.

An intriguing question arises at this point. Does *every* female contain eggs within eggs within eggs *ad infinitum*? Or does God only do what is needful, i.e. create the seeds of those organisms that will actually come to maturity? On the former view, God does a great deal in vain, and most of His *volontés particulières* are thwarted. On the latter view, microscopic examination on the ovaries of females might in principle reveal how many children, grandchildren, etc. they will have. Malebranche nowhere faces this rather obvious dilemma.

Given P5 and P6, we can derive the conclusion C. This conclusion, of course, far outstrips any conceivable empirical evidence we could possess. Malebranche must have been aware of this – his biology is more rational than empirical. Pre-existence could, I suppose, be construed as involving two empirical claims, one negative and one positive. The negative claim is that all naturalistic attempts to explain the generation of animals and plants are doomed to fail. The successful completion of a research programme such as that of Descartes would thus undermine pre-existence. The positive claim is simply that (at least within fertile females) there is infinite structural complexity waiting to be found by more and more powerful microscopes. In principle one might go on discovering such structures *ad infinitum*. But failure to observe such structures does not entail their non-existence. So this programme is weakly verifiable but not falsifiable by experience.

But perhaps I am making too much of the significance for Malebranche of empirical biology. How, we must ask, would he have responded to negative empirical findings – structures apparently emerging out of seemingly homogeneous fluids, or the failure of microscopists to find seeds within seeds within seeds? We can anticipate his probable answer. He would, one suspects, simply repeat the above argument and insist that the pre-existent structures *must* be present, albeit invisibly, in both cases. In the end, the senses must yield to the voice of reason.

8

MALEBRANCHE ON
THE SOUL AND
SELF-KNOWLEDGE

Descartes' arguments for the immateriality
of the soul

Malebranche is usually described, in histories of philosophy, as a disciple of Descartes. In many respects, this is unproblematic and undeniable: the influence of Descartes can be felt throughout Malebranche's strictly philosophical writings. On a number of important points, however, Malebranche takes care to distance himself from his illustrious predecessor, while maintaining that this dissent is itself Cartesian in spirit. The true Cartesian, he teaches in the *Recherche*, uses the writings of Descartes to stimulate his own meditations; to believe anything merely because 'the master has said it' would be not discipleship but betrayal (*OCM* I 412, LO 215).

Our topic in this chapter is one of Malebranche's most significant modifications of Cartesian metaphysics: his denial that we possess a clear idea of the soul. My central claim is that this denial undermines the spiritualistic metaphysics that Malebranche is explicitly concerned to defend. He may not have been aware of it, but he was demolishing rational psychology from within. The philosophical morals were pointed out by Kant in the *Paralogisms of Pure Reason* of the first *Critique*, but by that time the demolition job had already been done. The edifice of Cartesian rational psychology had been pulled down by its own defenders.

Descartes offers his readers three distinct types of argument for his belief in the immateriality of the soul. I shall label them the positive *a priori* argument, the negative *a priori* argument, and the *a posteriori* argument respectively. The basic outlines of these three distinct strategies are as follows.

The positive *a priori* argument presupposes that we possess some rational insight into the nature of the soul itself. Intellectual intuition reveals it as a simple spiritual substance, the essence of which is to think

– i.e. to be conscious. In the *Fourth Meditation*, for example, Descartes tells us that his idea of the mind is more clear and distinct than any idea of material substance. 'And indeed the idea I have of the human mind, in so far as it is a thinking thing, which is not extended in length, breadth, or height and has no other bodily characteristics, is much more distinct than the idea of any corporeal thing'.[1] The existence of a clear and distinct idea of thinking substance is defended in the replies to Arnauld and Gassendi. Against Gassendi, Descartes argues that I must have a clear idea of the soul because I can list its attributes – thinking, willing, feeling, etc.[2] This idea of the soul, Descartes replies to an important objection of Arnauld, is no mere abstraction but a sufficiently adequate idea, i.e. one that contains all that is required for the real existence of the thing.[3] Malebranche refers to this Cartesian claim in *Éclaircissement* XI of the *Recherche* (*OCM* III 163, LO 633), only to dissociate himself from it. If I were in possession of such an idea, all I would then need to do to demonstrate the immateriality of the soul is to show that this idea does not contain that of extension.

According to the negative *a priori* argument, we have a clear and distinct idea of matter (three-dimensional extension), and can see by inspection of this idea that no material thing can think and feel. From this point of view, the notion of a spiritual substance is purely negative (something distinct from matter), and the soul is conceived of simply as 'whatever it is that thinks and wills and feels'. The substance–mode metaphysic is preserved, but the substance just becomes an unknown X 'supporting' the familiar modes of thinking, willing and feeling. This, as we shall see, is the line of argument favoured by Malebranche. He also suggests – with some plausibility – that it is the argument that Descartes himself should have deployed, i.e. the one most consistent with his own principles.[4]

According to the *a posteriori* argument, prominent in one of Descartes' replies to Henry More,[5] it is the limits of mechanism that provide the grounds of dualism. Whatever is material, Descartes thinks, is mechanisable, i.e. capable of being realised by a sufficiently complex machine. But whereas the (supposed) souls of brutes are mechanisable, those of humans are not. We could in principle create and programme machines to perform all the actions of dogs, but not those of intelligent language-users such as ourselves. (The potential infinity of sentences that the user of a natural language can deploy and understand is crucial here for Descartes, as later for Chomsky). So the immateriality of the human mind emerges, on this strategy, from the anticipated limits of a programme of mechanistic reduction.

Descartes, I suggest, only resorted to the two negative arguments, *a priori* and *a posteriori*, to supplement and buttress his positive metaphysical claims. He confidently affirms in the *Sixth Meditation* that the soul is a simple substance, the essence of which is to think.[6] These seem to be straightforwardly positive metaphysical claims: it is far from clear how either could be supported by a mere *via negativa*. Even if such arguments could show that the soul is not extended (and thus not divisible into spatially separate parts) this would not rule out other sorts of complexity. An emotion or a musical chord can be complex, without consisting of spatially distinct parts. And how could negative methods show that thinking is the essence of the soul rather than – as Locke was to claim[7] – merely one of its activities?

But if we have a positive, clear and distinct idea of the soul, representing its nature or essence to the reflective gaze of the meditator, a rather obvious question immediately and pressingly arises: why is there no 'spiritual geometry' and no 'spiritual kinematics'? From the very idea of three-dimensional extension I can derive, by a combination of rational intuition and demonstrative reasoning, the twin sciences of geometry and pure kinematics. (We have already seen in Chapter Six that our hopes for a pure rational dynamics are much more problematic.) There seem to be no such demonstrative sciences of the soul.[8] We can't state a few self-evident axioms, 'the soul is F, and G, and H', and then rigorously deduce an indefinite number of theorems following from these axioms. The only remotely plausible candidates to fill the role of FGH are unity and simplicity, and these seem to generate further problems. As Kant would later explain with characteristic acuity, the attempt to base rational psychology on the unity and simplicity of the soul involves a crucial confusion.[9] The unity of consciousness is a necessary formal feature of our thought, not a special property of the noumenal thinker.

We lack a clear idea of the soul

The conspicuous absence of a spiritual geometry is evidence, for Malebranche, that we have no idea of the soul. Remember that, for Malebranche, ideas are not modes of the soul but divine models or archetypes, eternally present in the divine intellect and intermittently revealed to finite minds. This conception of ideas is derived from Augustine rather than from Descartes, as is emphasised in the replies to Arnauld (*OCM* IX 916) and in the preface to the 1696 edition of the *Entretiens* (*OCM* XII 14–18, not in JS). All knowledge, on this theory, is revelation: the attention and concentration of a finite mind is a natural analogue of prayer.

The distinction between ideas on the one side, and modes of the soul on the other, is made in Book Four of the *Recherche*, where Malebranche argues that ideas and modes of the soul must be distinct things, because they have quite distinct properties:

> For it is clear that the soul's modes are changeable, but ideas are immutable; that its modes are particular, but ideas are universal and general to all intelligences; that its modes are contingent, but ideas are eternal and necessary; that its modes are obscure and shadowy, but ideas are very clear and luminous ...
>
> (*OCM* II 103, LO 322–3)

The same distinction is made, and the same lesson drawn, in several of Malebranche's later works. In the *Conversations Chrétiennes*, for example, Aristarque affirms that the first principle of all reasoning is that we may affirm of any object whatever is clearly and distinctly perceived in its idea. That Cartesian thesis itself, replies Theodore, depends on the prior principle that ideas are archetypes in the divine intellect, not merely subjective states of our own souls (*OCM* IV 68–9). If ideas were merely modes of our souls, Malebranche insists in his controversy with Arnauld, we could never know whether they accurately represented external objects, and scepticism would be inescapable (*OCM* IX 924). But if ideas are divine archetypes, we have complete assurance that the inference from idea to object is valid: it is contradictory that a creature should fail to conform to the creator's plan or blueprint for it. The doctrine of continuous creation will of course buttress this argument by eliminating any doubts that might have arisen from the passage of time. As Theodore puts it in the *Entretiens*, the moment of creation does not pass.

Malebranche thinks that it is evident that we don't have an idea of the soul in this sense. (In a weaker sense, it may be said, we need an idea of the soul in order to think about it at all. The term 'notion' sometimes gets pressed into service to mark this weaker sense.) One has a clear idea of X when one can simply 'see', by direct intellectual intuition, the properties X must possess – and, correspondingly, those that it cannot possess (*OCM* VI, 160). We know the properties of matter this way, Malebranche claims, but not those of the soul. If I consult my idea of matter (*étendue intelligible*), I see clearly both *that* a square and a circle are modifications of matter (extension), and *how* matter (extension) is modified to produce them. Given a little basic geometry, I could provide constructive definitions of such figures. But as regards the soul, writes Malebranche in his reply to Arnauld's *Vraies et Fausses Idées*, the situation is completely different:

> I do not know the soul at all, neither in general, nor my own in particular, by its idea. I know that I exist, that I think, that I will, because I sense myself. I am more certain of the existence of my soul than of that of my body; that is true. But I do not know at all what my thought, my desire, and my pain are.
>
> (*OCM* VI 161)

If I had a clear idea of the soul, I could know all its possible modes *a priori*, i.e. I could grasp the essential nature of anxiety, say, or nostalgia, by rational insight: I wouldn't have to experience them to know that the human mind was capable of such states. I would 'see' how the mind is modified to produce anxiety, or nostalgia, enabling me not merely to feel but to understand these states. But this, Malebranche reminds us, is not the human condition. Our knowledge of the soul, he explains in Book Three of the *Recherche*, is experiential, not rational:

> If we had never sensed pain, heat, light, and such, we would be unable to know whether the soul was capable of sensing these things, because we do not know it through its idea. But if we saw in God the idea corresponding to our soul, we would at the same time know, or at least could know all the properties of which it is capable – as we know, or at least could know all the properties of which extension is possible, because we know extension through its idea.
>
> (*OCM* I 450, LO 237–8)

Our lack of a clear idea of the soul explains some facts that would otherwise seem puzzling. We knew before that there was no spiritual geometry; we now understand why there is no such science, at least for human beings as we currently find them (for Adam before the fall, or for ourselves in a future state, things might be very different). We can also explain how certain philosophical errors and confusions are possible. The status of sensible qualities and the nature of the relation between mind and body provide Malebranche with his key examples.

One striking error concerns sensible qualities such as red, hot and sweet.[10] Ordinary people (and Aristotelian philosophers) frequently ascribe to bodies what are really states of their own souls such as colours, tastes and smells. If we had a clear idea of the soul, Malebranche explains in Book One of the *Recherche*, we would be able to see that such sensible qualities as red, hot and sweet were among its modifications, and would never fall into the vulgar error of confusing such subjective states with objective properties of bodies (*OCM* I 139–40, LO 58). Lacking such a clear idea of the soul, we have to employ a more tortuous and indirect *via negativa*, i.e. we have to show that colours and tastes are not among the possible modes of material substance. This, Malebranche thinks, can be demonstrated, but it is like a complex and indirect mathematical proof, hard for us to grasp and to keep in mind. In such cases, error is rather to be expected, and it should come as no surprise that the most popular school of philosophy actually endorses the misconceptions of the vulgar.

Another vulgar error of crucial importance for metaphysics and morals concerns the relation between the human soul and its body. Since the fall, Malebranche tells us in Book One of the *Recherche*, the soul itself has become 'carnal', liable to confuse itself with the body (*OCM* I 136–7, LO 57). An indication of this confusion is that it even seeks to represent itself by means of an image (*OCM* I 146, LO 62). The point is repeated in Book Four (*OCM* II 98, LO 320) and in *Éclaircissement* XI (*OCM* III 170–1, LO 637–8). If we had a clear positive idea of the soul, such fundamental errors of metaphysics would not be possible.

Divine and human knowledge

According to Malebranche, God possesses the ideas both of matter and of the human soul: that is, both of these archetypes exist timelessly in the divine understanding. (Presumably there are ideas of particular human souls as well as the blueprint of the human soul in general, although Malebranche never explicitly affirms this.[11]) Only one of these ideas, however, is revealed to us. When I think about matter (e.g. when I do geometry), God reveals the archetype of material substance to me; when I reflect on the nature of the soul, I receive no such illumination. I feel pain, and know that pain is a modification of the (unknown) substance of my soul, but I can't tell how that substance is modified to produce pain. This is taught in Book Four of the *Recherche*, where Malebranche draws a sharp contrast between God's knowledge of my mental states and my own knowledge of those same states:

> Certainly the soul has no clear idea of its substance, according to what I mean by clear idea. It cannot discover by examining itself

whether it is capable of this or that modification it has never had. It truly experiences its pain, but it does not know it; it does not know how its substance must be modified in order to suffer pain, and to suffer one pain rather than another. There is a great difference between sensing and knowing itself. God, who continually acts in the soul, knows it perfectly; He sees clearly, without suffering pain, how the soul must be modified to suffer pain, whereas the soul, on the other hand, suffers pain and does not know it. God knows it without feeling it, and the soul feels it without knowing it.

(*OCM* II 97, LO 319)

The point is developed and further defended in *Éclaircissement* XI. If we had such an idea of the soul, Malebranche there explains, many things that are currently obscure would become clear to us – e.g. the relation between green and red, and whether there can be a purely spiritual memory, independent of brain-traces. As regards the former, we sense the differences between colours but do not understand them, because we are unable to grasp any intelligible relations between the modes of the soul that we call 'seeing red' and 'seeing green' (*OCM* II 168, LO 636). As regards the latter, our ignorance of the soul's dispositions means that 'through reason we cannot ascertain whether the soul when separated from the body or taken in isolation from the body is capable of having any habits or memory' (*OCM* II 169, LO 636–7).

There is therefore a sharp contrast between divine and human knowledge of the soul. God knows (understands) pain, fear and lust, without feeling them; He knows exactly what intelligible modifications of the human soul constitute those states. He has this knowledge of the human soul because, as its Creator, 'He finds in Himself a clear and representative idea of it' (*OCM* II 97, LO 319). We, by contrast, feel pain, and fear, and lust, from time to time, but without understanding them. The soul, Theodore explains to Ariste in the *Entretiens,* remains a mystery to itself.

In turning inward I cannot recognise any of my faculties or capacities. The inner feeling I have of myself teaches me that I am, that I think, that I will, that I suffer, etc., but it does not let me know what I am, the nature of my thought, of my will, of my feelings, of my passions, of my pain, nor the relations all these things have to one another. For, once again, not having an idea of my soul, and not seeing its archetype in the divine Word, in

contemplating it I can discover neither what it is nor what the
modalities are of which it is capable, nor finally what the relations
are between its modalities …

(*OCM* XII 66, JS 34–5)

As the meditator admits in the ninth of the *Méditations Chrétiennes*,
'je ne suis que ténèbres a moi-même', I am but shadows to myself (*OCM*
X 102). The Word explains that this will remain the case unless and until
the idea or archetype of the soul is revealed to the gaze of the meditator.

Whereas we know bodies by means of their common idea (*étendue
intelligible*), we know our own mental states only by *sentiment intérieur*.
Malebranche uses the French words *connaître* and *sentir* to stand for
these two quite distinct forms of awareness.[12] The distinction plays a
crucial role in the dispute with Arnauld about the nature of ideas. Arnauld
thinks that he knows the soul because he is aware of its modifications,
but this is to fail to make the distinction between '*sentir*' and '*connaître*'
(*OCM* VI 54). For Arnauld, mere subjective awareness reveals the soul to
itself as it is,[13] but this is to ignore the distinction between mind as
subject and mind as substance.[14] On the slender basis of mere sensitive
awareness, Arnauld seeks to build substantive metaphysical claims. He
tells us, writes Malebranche, that the modes of the soul are essentially
representative, that the soul thinks because it is its nature to think. In
Éclaircissement X of the *Recherche* Malebranche had already dismissed
this as a lapse, on the part of certain Cartesians, back into Aristotelian
obscurantism (*OCM* III 86, LO 622). He now challenges Arnauld to provide
a proof of his claim that ideas are modes of the soul (*OCM* VI 91). If you
had the clear idea of the soul you claim to possess, Malebranche argues,
you would be able to demonstrate that its modes are, by their very
nature, representations of an external world. But the facts of the matter
are quite otherwise. On Malebranche's view, of course, the states which
are truly modes of the soul (e.g. feeling pain, seeing red) do not represent
anything external to themselves. Intentionality is not 'the mark of the
mental'.[15] Indeed, no mental state has representative content.[16] Just as
the problem of causation demands a supernatural solution (occasionalism) so too does the problem of intentionality (the Vision in God).

The study of the soul, Malebranche warns us, is and must remain a
'*science expérimentale*'. This doctrine will play a central role in the *Traité
de Morale* (*OCM* XI 67). By an 'experimental science' Malebranche is
not, of course, talking about laboratory experiments; what he has in
mind is a mixture of introspection and observation. The implied contrast
is with the unattainable ideal of a rational or demonstrative *a priori*

science of the soul.[17] Introspection can reveal some of the modes of the soul, and perhaps some empirical regularities linking our thoughts, feelings and volitions; what it cannot reveal are any necessary connections. Even if such necessities exist, it seems that, without a clear idea of the soul, we could never come to know them.

A number of problems arise here. It seems as if Malebranche is suggesting that the various modes of the human soul are all like Humean impressions, 'loose and separate', capable in principle of occurring in any combination and any order. But it surely isn't just a contingent and empirical matter that we tend to think well of people we love, or to avoid people we loathe? Both our emotions and our volitions seem to be so intimately linked to thoughts (i.e. to judgements) that they could not intelligibly be divorced from those thoughts. And thoughts, in virtue of their content, do stand in logical relations to one another. We must return to these problems later.

Until God decides to reveal the idea of the soul to our rational inspection, we will remain a mystery to ourselves. There is such a model or archetype in the divine intellect, analogous to the idea of matter (*étendue intelligible*) that God has chosen to reveal to us. Our ignorance is therefore a contingent matter,[18] subject to the divine will, as Malebranche tells us in Books Three and Four of the *Recherche* (*OCM* I 416, LO 218, *OCM* II 98, LO 320) and again in the controversy with Arnauld (*OCM* IX 956). But why, we ask, did God decide not to reveal the archetype of the soul to us? The fact is certain; the explanation is problematic.[19] At different times, Malebranche offers a variety of tentative explanations. The clearest answers appear in his reply to Arnauld's *Vraies et Fausses Idées* (*OCM* VI 155–6), and in the *Méditations Chrétiennes* (*OCM* X 103–4). The following three lines of thought emerge:

1   The loss of this self-knowledge is part of the punishment for the Fall.
2   God actually wants us to be 'carnal' beings, at least in the sense of caring about our own bodies. The lack of a clear idea of the soul facilitates this by helping us to think of ourselves – confusedly and erroneously – as essentially embodied beings.
3   If we had a clear idea of the soul, we might become lost in admiration of our own perfections and lose sight of our Creator.

None of these explanations is very convincing.[20] The first fits neatly with other things Malebranche says about the Fall, and with his opinion that theology can illuminate some questions that philosophy leaves mysterious, but it makes the Fall itself still more incomprehensible. If

Adam had a clear rational insight into the nature of his soul and hence of its distinction from his body, how could he ever have been led astray by worldly goods?

The second explanation fares, if anything, still worse. On such a view Malebranche's own philosophy (which is, like Plato's, a sort of preparation for death) might actually be in opposition to the will of God. If God wants us to be confused about the mind–body problem, and to have a tendency to slide into materialism by identifying ourselves with our bodies, what justifies Malebranche in preaching a strict dualism? In any case, if the 'goods' of the body are not our true goods, why should God want us to desire them? The best Malebranche can offer in this context is the suggestion that we are to regard our own bodies as *objects of sacrifice*, and that this attitude requires us to care about, and feel emotional attachment, to the flesh.[21] Anything I can give up with complete indifference wouldn't be a genuine sacrifice.

The third explanation fares no better. After all, what would the archetype of the soul reveal to me? In the first place, it would have to have something analogous to the highly complex and functional structures we find in organised bodies, and this complex 'structure' would presumably show manifest traces of intelligent design. I should therefore not admire it but its Maker, as I do when I examine fleas and lice under the microscope. In the second place, without God's sustaining power, my soul is like a piece of electrical apparatus without a battery or a connection to the mains. Looking at the archetype or blueprint, I would see clearly that my soul is by its nature capable of such and such thoughts and feelings (as a body is by its nature capable of a variety of motions), but would see equally clearly that it is not self-moving. All its powers are passive and receptive powers. Separate a spirit from God, says Malebranche in the *Traité*, and you have something without intelligence, without reason, without desire, and without love (*OCM* V 117). So if God had wished to enlighten us about these truths of metaphysics, and thus to elevate our minds to Him, He could have done no better than to reveal to us the idea (archetype) of the human soul. It would reveal to us not so much our perfections as our limitations, and our essential dependence on Him.[22]

The *via negativa* route to dualism

However lame Malebranche's explanations, the fact remains: God has not revealed to us the archetype of the human soul. Given this fact, it follows that any argument for dualism must be by means of a *via negativa*, in which the soul is characterised negatively, as something that is not bodily in its nature. The clear idea of matter (*étendue intelligible*) does not include thought, and a clear idea excludes whatever it does not include.[23] This is, from the start, Malebranche's explicit position. The distinction between soul and body is emphasised throughout the *Recherche* (e.g. at *OCM* I 122–3, LO 49), but it is always body that is the positive notion. The soul is whatever I call myself, whatever has a particular set of thoughts and experiences. I can know that it is not extended – and therefore not dispersed around the members of the body – but I cannot say positively what it is like in its own right.

It is therefore only by means of the clear idea of matter (*étendue intelligible*) that the immateriality of the soul can be proved. This is clearly spelled out in *Éclaircissement XI* of the *Recherche*, and again in the *Méditations Chrétiennes*. In *Éclaircissement XI* Malebranche consults the clear idea of matter (three-dimensional extension) in order to determine that sensible qualities are not possible modifications of matter, and must therefore 'belong to the soul'. The lesson is obvious:

> Since we have to consult our idea of extension in order to discover whether sensible qualities are modes of our mind, is it not evident that we have no clear idea of the soul? Would we otherwise ever bother with such a roundabout way?
>
> (*OCM* III 166, LO 634)

It is only indirectly, the Word explains in the ninth of the *Meditations*, that the spirituality of the soul can be proved (*OCM* X 105). Having a clear idea of matter enables us to see that thoughts and feelings could not be modes of material substance. This requires a little reasoning, but is sufficiently evident if we take care to reason only from our clear (Cartesian) idea of matter rather than from confused (Aristotelian) ideas.

We thus have the makings of an argument for the claim that the soul must be an immaterial substance. I think and feel, Theodore explains to Ariste in the *Entretiens*, but thoughts and feelings must inhere in some substance. (Mere nothingness has no properties.) But this cannot be a material substance, since matter is just three-dimensional extension, and this excludes thought.

> Nothingness has no properties. I think. Therefore I am. But what am I, who think, at the time when I think? Am I a body, a mind, a human being? As yet I know nothing of all this. I know only that, at the time I think, I am something that thinks. However, let

us see. Can a body think? Can a thing extended in length, width, and depth reason, desire, sense? Undoubtedly not, for all the ways of being of such an extended thing consist only in relations of distance; and it is evident that these relations are not perceptions, reasonings, pleasures, desires, sensations – in a word, thoughts. Therefore this *I* that thinks, my own substance, is not a body, since my perceptions, which surely belong to me, are something entirely different from relations of distance.

(*OCM* XII 32–3, JS 6)

When Ariste challenges the crucial assumption that three-dimensional extension exhausts the essence of matter, Theodore replies with a long-established metaphysical argument that can be traced back to Occam. What can be conceived separately, says Theodore, can exist separately, and is therefore a true substance. But there is no problem in conceiving three-dimensional extension without conceiving of anything else (*OCM* XII 33–4, JS 7). So, since material substance is just three-dimensional extension, and thoughts and feelings cannot be properties of this substance, it follows that they must be properties of some non-material substance.

As yet, however, this is a purely negative concept, without any positive content. Can we grasp such a notion? And can we, lacking as we do any idea of it, make any intelligible claims about the soul?

Malebranche is not at his best in facing up to this obvious challenge. In the *Réponse à M. Arnauld* he states explicitly that by 'idea' he means clear idea, one which allows a person to deduce *a priori* the properties of the corresponding object (*OCM* VI 160). In *Éclaircissement* III, however, he says that the word 'idea' is equivocal, and that in one weaker and looser sense we do have an idea of the soul, whereas in another stricter and stronger sense we do not (*OCM* III 44, LO 561). What he needs, it seems, is something like the distinction that Berkeley was later to draw between ideas and notions.[24] He needs to be able to say that he has a notion of the soul as a non-material substance, in order to make intelligible claims about it, while continuing to deny that he has an idea of it in his own technical sense.

Let us suppose for the moment that the *via negativa* argument achieves its end, and that Malebranche has established, by means of his rational insight into the essence of material substance, that the soul is non-material. No material thing, however complex its organisation, can think and feel. If one grants this metaphysical thesis, and accepts the traditional substance –mode metaphysic, one must infer that the 'something' in me that thinks and feels is not my body or any part of it. But will this weak, and essentially negative, notion of a non-material substance suffice for Malebranche's metaphysical and theological purposes? The answer seems to be that it will not.

Personal immortality under threat

It was required of Catholic philosophers by the Lateran Council that they teach the spirituality and natural immortality of the soul, and refute the corresponding 'errors' of materialists and mortalists.[25] Descartes had cited this requirement in his prefatory letter of the *Meditations*, which promised the theologians of the Sorbonne new proofs of the existence of God and of the immortality of the soul.[26] (They were to provide the sugar coating on the bitter pill of his anti-Aristotelian metaphysics and epistemology.) After a fashion, the *Sixth Meditation* redeemed the second promise, purporting as it does to provide proofs both of the real distinction of mind and body, and of the simplicity of the soul. A simple substance cannot disintegrate into parts, but could perish only by annihilation. God could, of course, annihilate it if He chose, but it is of its own nature imperishable and thus (DV) immortal. Add God's own guarantee (from revelation) that He will not annihilate our souls, and one has as complete a proof as could be hoped for.

Malebranche refers to these arguments as 'sound', but is he entitled to endorse them so glibly? Remember that Descartes claims to have a clear and distinct idea of an immaterial substance; for Malebranche it is merely a negative and relational notion, a 'something' that stands to thoughts and feelings in the same relation as three-dimensional extension stands to shapes and local motions. Malebranche, however, remains confident. The immortality of the soul, he writes in Book Four of the *Recherche*, can be easily demonstrated, once its status as an immaterial substance has been established (*OCM* II 22, LO 273). If we grant the existence of a non-material substance then, he writes in one of his replies to Arnauld, we must accept that it is imperishable, 'for it is only modes which perish' (*OCM* VI 163). For a substance to cease-to-be is 'impossible by the ordinary forces of nature'.

Let us give the matter a little reflection, and see how well founded this confidence is. If my only notion of my soul is as whatever it may be that is currently having these experiences, it seems hard to find grounds for claiming either (a) that it is a metaphysically simple substance, or (b) that the identity of this substance constitutes my identity.[27] Even if every substance is (DV) imperishable, a number of possibilities remain open. My soul could be a complex of spirit-atoms; on my death they separate and then recombine to form a new and distinct human soul. They would be immortal; I would not. Or my soul could be just a portion of the universal common soul-stuff, perennially being recycled to produce new but ephemeral subjects of consciousness. Maybe the pantheists were right after all?

Malebranche's problems are gradually becoming clear. Like so many other metaphysicians down through the ages, he is trying to extract too much from too little, strong conclusions from weak premises. He denies that we have a clear idea of the soul (thus disabling some of Descartes' arguments for dualism) while simultaneously maintaining that his weaker premises can still yield the desired theological conclusions.

The only resources available to Malebranche in his attempt to flesh out his notion of the soul are those provided by *sentiment intérieur*. In Book Six of the *Recherche* he tells us plainly that all our knowledge of the soul is derived from this source. One knows the soul 'only by the inner sensation one has of it'. This knowledge is immediate and experiential, not discursive and rational. It provides certainty, but no insight. 'Thus, one will know by simple perception or inner sensation all one can know of the soul, without having to construct arguments in which error might be found' (*OCM* II 369–70, LO 480). The point is repeated in a letter to Régis of 1693. The soul, says Malebranche,

> … senses only that it is, and it is evident that it can sense only what it is in itself. It sees itself and knows itself if you will, but exclusively through inner sensation, a confused sensation that discovers to it neither what it is nor what is the nature of any of its modalities.
>
> (*OCM* XVII–1 298)

Malebranche is confident that such limited knowledge is sufficient for the great ends of religion and morality, and seeks to reassure his readers in Book Three of the *Recherche*:

> Although our knowledge of the soul is not complete, what we do know of it through consciousness or inner sensation is enough to demonstrate its immortality, spirituality, freedom, and several other attributes we need to know.
>
> (*OCM* II 453, LO 239)

But is it possible to base ontological theses on the deliverances of phenomenology? There are a number of passages in his works where

Malebranche suggests such a strategy. Let us run briefly through these passages. Introspection reveals each soul to itself as something capable of thinking, willing, and feeling. But can this merely abstract and relational characterisation be filled out to give a richer and fuller notion of the soul as it is in itself?

Metaphysics and introspection

The one thing I know with most certainty, says Malebranche in Book Six of the *Recherche*, is the existence of my soul as a centre of experience. I also know by introspection my current thoughts and feelings – no room for doubt or error can arise here. With regard to my *dispositions intérieures*, however, there is room for error and for lack of self-knowledge.[28] In an exchange that would have amused Gilbert Ryle, Arnauld swears an oath that he has not written against Malebranche out of chagrin; Malebranche replies that he doubts whether this is true; Arnauld flies into a rage because he takes Malebranche to be accusing him of lying. Malebranche's second reply is rather more careful. With regard to your current, actual, thoughts and feelings, he replies, you have privileged access and your word has absolute authority: there is room for deceit but no room for honest error. With regard to the *dispositions intérieurs* of your soul, however, the situation is quite different (*OCM* VIII 628). Every soul has its habits, known by God in his capacity as *scrutateur des coeurs*, but known to men only by their manifestations. I judge of Arnauld's dispositions, says Malebranche, by his books, which tell me clearly that he is a man of choleric temperament (*OCM* VIII 629). I don't need to search his heart to see this.[29] Indeed, such is our ignorance of our own *dispositions intérieurs* that an external observer may understand them better than the agent himself, who may be merely the dupe of his passions, an important theme in the *Traité de Morale* (*OCM* XI 52). Our knowledge of other minds is thus, in large part, a matter of inferring *dispositions intérieurs* from manifest behaviour, and then using our hypotheses regarding these dispositions to predict and explain further behaviour.

All this, however, clearly belongs to empirical psychology. I feel anger, and immediately infer that my soul is capable of such a modification. I study the passions of the soul, and learn how to detect the manifestations of anger in others, and how to recognise people of choleric temperament from manifestations (some obvious, some more subtle) of this inner disposition. But this seems to get me no further in my search for metaphysical insight into the nature of the soul. The study of man seems to remain exclusively an experimental science rather than a rational one.

There are, however, a number of passages in Malebranche's works where he appears to cheat, i.e. to make metaphysical assertions about the soul which, by his own lights, he is not entitled to make. Let us list and examine such apparent lapses.

1   At a number of places in the *Recherche*, Malebranche endorses the Cartesian thesis that thinking is the essence of the soul, together with its obvious corollary, that the soul always thinks, and does not do so more at one time than another (*OCM* I 381, LO 198; *OCM* II 282, LO 431). Fainting, for example, consists not of the absence of thought but of a vast and confused mass of micro-thoughts, the opposite of concentrated attention. But on what basis can Malebranche sustain such a claim? Alquié[30] notes a passage at the end of *Éclaircissement* II in which Malebranche says that, if we had a clear idea of the soul, we would see that its essence consists in thinking. He comments ironically how remarkable it is that Malebranche can see, without the idea, what we *would* see if we had it! Why should thinking not be, as Locke was to enquire,[31] an operation of the soul rather than its essence? An immaterial soul might have a completely unknown essence, and merely have the power of thinking, a power that may only intermittently be exercised. Lacking a clear idea of the soul, how is Malebranche to rule this out?

2   Malebranche firmly states that the soul is a simple substance (*OCM* XVI 28), and that it is one and the same simple substance that thinks and wills and feels (*OCM* III 40, LO 560). I know this, he writes, although I don't understand how it is so. Once again, however, doubts must arise. Does anything in introspection testify to the absolute unity and simplicity of the soul? Locke would have denied it. A century later, Kant diagnosed the fallacy of this form of rational psychology.[32] The disciples of Descartes, according to Kant, are guilty of confusing the purely formal unity of apperception (the 'I think' which must be capable of accompanying all my perceptions to make them mine) with the supposed unity of the noumenal self. Insofar as I am a self-conscious being, I must conceive myself as a unity; it doesn't follow that I possess any sort of rational intuition of the soul as a sort of metaphysical monad. To suppose so is to fall victim to a transcendental illusion.

3   I know, Malebranche argues, that I am not the cause of my own perceptions. This is an important part of the argument for the Vision in God. Once again, however, we find him in difficulties. On what grounds can he base such a claim? He can't consult the idea of the

soul to deduce its lack of sensation-producing powers, but must proceed by a more roundabout route. He can of course have recourse to the perfectly general metaphysical doctrines of occasionalism and continuous creation. If God is the cause of everything, then *a fortiori* He is the cause of all my experiences. But Malebranche appears to think that the mind's passivity in sensation is known immediately, without any need for such a metaphysical detour. This in turn requires him to assume the Cartesian thesis of the transparency of the mental: if the sensation-producing power were in me I would be aware of it. But it seems difficult if not impossible for Malebranche, given his denial that we possess a positive idea of the soul, to provide any grounds for the Cartesian thesis. Why shouldn't the soul have hidden depths, and powers not accessible to introspection?

4 Another crucial problem concerns free will. Once again we find Malebranche claiming, in *Éclaircissement* 1 (*OCM* III 27, LO 552) that free will is something we know from experience, which can no more be doubted that we can doubt our very existence. *Sentiment intérieur*, he insists in the controversy with Arnauld, is sufficient – even in the absence of an idea of the soul – to demonstrate liberty (*OCM* VI 163). This claim must, however, stand on its own merits, without the rational support that might in principle be provided by insight into the nature of the soul (see *OCM* XVI 29). But the sentiment of liberty may be an illusion, a product of our ignorance of the hidden causes determining our choices.[33] A further problem arises here for Malebranche, in that on this issue his own metaphysics can be used against him. Towards the end of his life he found himself embroiled in a controversy with one Père Boursier, who took the doctrine of continuous creation one crucial step further even than Malebranche had done. Malebranche had always insisted (against the Jansenists) that the human soul remains free to reject the gift of grace, i.e. that God requires our free assent to His promptings. This act of assent, Boursier argues, is a mode of the soul, and hence something real. Therefore, by the doctrine of continuous creation, it too can only have been created by God. So, Boursier concludes, God not only provides the gift of grace; He also makes the souls of those He wants to save accept the gift (*OCM* XVI 36–7). To introspection, of course, this would appear indistinguishable from free and spontaneous assent. Malebranche attempts to refute Boursier, but finds himself lacking crucial argumentative resources to do so. If I have no idea of the soul, I can't deduce its intrinsic powers *a priori*. But the phenomenology of the experience would be the same

on either hypothesis. Any subjective experience Malebranche can cite Boursier can accept, and merely add the inevitable rider that it too is produced – of course – by God in His successive re-creation of the human soul. So how can Malebranche be so confident that he is right and Boursier is wrong? Once again, he needs an indirect and roundabout route, this time by way of the notion of the Divine perfections. God cannot be Himself the author of sin, and only an unjust God could behave as Boursier describes – i.e. punish us for our sins if He were Himself the cause of them (*OCM* XVI 39; see also *Éclaircissement* I, *OCM* III 30, LO 554).

5   Another place at which Malebranche seems to violate his own rules occurs in Book Five of the *Recherche*, in his discussion of the passions. All the passions, he says, 'seek their own justification' (*OCM* II 225, LO 397). If I fall in love with Mary, I will tend to idealise her, i.e. to think of her as possessing all manner of admirable qualities. This reinforces the preliminary judgement that excited the passion in the first place. There is a positive feedback loop from initial favourable judgement (a mode of the soul), via the laws of mind–body union to an agitation of the blood and animal spirits (a mode of the body), and thence, once again by way of the laws of mind–body union, back to another more exaggerated set of thoughts. We know that this takes place, says Malebranche, both by experience (*sentiment intérieur*) and by reason (*OCM* II 226, LO 397). Gaining such knowledge by experience is unproblematic; it is Malebranche's claim that such knowledge is attainable by reason that raises difficulties. Reason tells us, for example, that we can't think very badly of someone we love. But this suggests that rational psychology is not absolutely impossible, if even the emotions have a rational structure that is at least in part intelligible to us.

The sciences of psychology

Malebranche denied the possibility of a rational psychology on the grounds that we lack a (clear) idea of what the soul is in itself. He posits a fundamental disanalogy between our knowledge of matter and our knowledge of the soul. But, a critic might respond, when we examine our concept of matter, it is its key attribute of extension that takes centre stage. The substance of matter, in Descartes and Malebranche, seems just to resolve into three-dimensional extension itself. Could we not do for thought what we can do for extension,[34] i.e. deduce a set of theorems from our intuitive grasp of what *thinking* is? In Book Three of the

Recherche, Malebranche gives a blunt response: 'we have no clear idea of thought as we do of extension (*OCM* I 381, LO 198). We can, nevertheless, pursue the analogy a little further, and ask what such a rational psychology would be like.

This superficially simple question turns out to conceal hidden depths. In the first place, there are certainly two (and maybe, more problematically, three) distinct sciences based on our clear idea of extension.[35] There is the synchronic science of geometry, which shows us the timeless relations between the modes of extension, and there are the two diachronic sciences of kinematics and dynamics. The former simply 'unpacks' what is analytically contained in the concept of motion, abstracting all questions about causality and agency; the latter attempts to lay down the laws of moving and colliding bodies. Whether there can be a rational science of this latter kind, i.e. a rational dynamics, was a vexed question for the Cartesians, and troubled Malebranche throughout his career. We have already seen, in Chapter Six, that as he grew older he became increasingly convinced that the laws of dynamics depend on God's will rather than His intellect, and therefore cannot be known by us *a priori*.

Are there parallel sciences of the mind that we could label 'psychogeometry', 'psycho-kinematics' and 'psycho-dynamics'? Let us examine each in turn. The geometer starts with the idea of extension, states some self-evident axioms concerning it, and proceeds to deduce theorems, e.g. that a certain mode of matter (a triangle) is necessarily connected with a certain property (having angles equal to two right angles). It may look at first sight as if there is something similar concerning the soul. If, for example, two concepts are necessarily connected, it might be considered impossible to think one without thinking the other. For Malebranche, however, ideas are not modes of the human soul; they exist eternally in the divine intellect.[36] What follows for human minds is, at best, a proposition of hypothetical necessity. If F and G are necessarily connected, then, if I am attending to F, and thinking clearly, I will 'see' its connection with G. (Even this is too simple: geometry is *a priori*, but it remains a difficult science, requiring considerable pains and attention. There are necessary connections between concepts that are anything but obvious.) The corresponding modes of my soul, however, can readily come apart, e.g. when I find myself wondering whether 47 is prime, and perhaps even doubting or denying it. So what might look at first sight to be logically necessary connections between modes of the soul turn out, on closer scrutiny, to be logically necessary connections between ideas in the divine mind, and contingent truths about how closely my mind is attuned to God's. Similar remarks will apply to the possibility of a science of psycho-kinematics.

There is, for Malebranche, no phenomenology of pure thought or intellection (see *OCM* III 167, LO 635–6).[37] There is of course a characteristic phenomenology of attention, distraction and mental effort, but that is a different matter. The absence of such phenomenology helps to explain why his point is hard to grasp and to accept. Malebranche draws a sharp distinction between sensations, which penetrate the soul, and ideas, which only touch it superficially, producing what he calls 'pure perceptions'. When he denies that ideas are modes of our souls, he cannot be denying that there are modes of our souls that are such pure perceptions. What he says is that these modes are as if perfectly transparent, so all we ever become aware of in pure thought are the contents of the thoughts (the ideas), not the perceptions themselves. But then, since the contents are necessarily connected, it is easy to fall into the error of supposing that the same is true of the modes.

Psycho-dynamics raises yet further difficulties. Here we must say something about Malebranche's views on the passions and their relation to value judgements. Malebranche is quite clear that there is a perfectly objective hierarchy of degrees of perfection in the universe, from God down to the basest matter. God, of course, loves everything in strict proportion to its degree of perfection – i.e. Himself most of all. Anything else would be a violation of the principle of Order. This claim, we have already noted, plays a central role in the argument of the *Traité de la Nature et de la Grâce*. If I were sufficiently clear-sighted, this objective hierarchy of degrees of perfection would impose certain constraints (e.g. transitivity) on my value judgements. But ignorance and error will remain as possible in axiology as they are in mathematics. Again, if I were a perfectly rational being, order would be similarly imposed on my desires: I would necessarily desire more what I judge to be better. But again, this supposed necessity is merely hypothetical: we can make sense of the notion that I could judge X better than Y, but simultaneously desire Y more than X. Such disorder is, for Malebranche, one more proof of our fallen condition. Since we don't know our own *dispositions intérieurs*, we can't be certain whether the loves of our souls are in conformity with order or not. Even Saint Peter fell famously short of such self-knowledge (see *Éclaircissement* XI, *OCM* III 170, LO 637).

So even if we know what someone is thinking in a given situation (in particular, what value judgements they are making), we cannot yet predict even their occurrent desires and passions (far less their all-important abiding dispositions) and hence can only guess at their eventual actions. We can of course make rationalising assumptions, but the predictions based on such assumptions remain hypothetical.

There may be a science of psycho-dynamics, but it is reserved for God in His capacity of *scrutateur des coeurs*. Knowing our *dispositions intérieurs* gives Him an insight into our motives, passions, and actions that we ourselves can never attain.

So what becomes of psychology, if Malebranche is right? It seems that we are left with four distinct disciplines, as follows:

Ψ1 = rational psychology. This is not really psychology at all, since it is in no way concerned with the human mind, or indeed with any finite minds. This discipline studies the eternal and immutable relations between ideas, which exist timelessly in the divine intellect, and between the divine perfections, which provide the basis for objectivity in value judgements. It can be applied to psychology only with the aid of idealising assumptions, and then gives rise to disciplines like logic and perhaps decision theory.

Ψ2 = introspective psychology, the mind's knowledge of its own modes or subjective states through introspection. Based as it is on *sentiment intérieur*, it provides no rational insight into the nature of these modes or the relations between them. From this perspective, all the modes of the soul must seem 'loose and separate', as Hume was to say, and all relations between them merely contingent. Note that this psychology is silent about pure intellection, the modes of which have no phenomenology.

Ψ3 = physiological psychology, which is prominent in the *Recherche*. This discipline seeks to study empirically the divinely established laws of the mind–body union, e.g. the dependence of traits of character on the condition of our brains, and hence on such factors as sex, age, climate and nutrition. It can provide important and valuable insights into the hindrances that our embodied condition places in the path of rational knowledge in mathematics, metaphysics and morals. People of a certain temperament will turn out to be constitutionally liable to certain characteristic types of error or sin, and should thus be on their guard against them.

Ψ4 = depth psychology, the *a priori* investigation of the *dispositions intérieurs* of our souls and the relations (synchronic and diachronic) between them. There are necessary connections here, for Malebranche, but we cannot know them. So this sort of psychology is not a science for us, at least not in our present state, although it remains possible in principle. Maybe the angels practise it, in which case they might know in advance of experience that one man will resist a temptation to which another will succumb.

Two final questions

Let us conclude this chapter by addressing two questions. Can Malebranche, given his explicit denial that we possess a (clear) idea of the soul, still provide plausible arguments for Cartesian metaphysics, and for Christian orthodoxy? And given that his preferred strategy rests firmly on his bare conception of matter as three-dimensional extension and nothing more, should we re-examine that Cartesian premise?

The answer to the first of these questions should by now be clear. Arnauld was right: without a clear idea of the soul, we can't demonstrate its immortality, spirituality and liberty (*OCM* VI 162). Malebranche's departure from Descartes leaves him wide open to sceptical attack. If my notion of the soul is just 'whatever it is in me that thinks and feels', even if I can show that it is non-material, it is hard to provide plausible grounds for the orthodox theological conclusions. If my mind is an immaterial substance only in this negative sense, why should it be immortal? Admittedly, it can't break into spatially distinct parts, but is that the only way in which something can cease to exist? Why should it not simply fade out? And if something does survive my bodily death, why should that something be me? After all, Malebranche tells us that our lack of a clear idea of the soul prevents us from answering the question whether a purely spiritual memory is possible. But if it is not – if all personal memory depends on brain-traces – won't the dissolution of my brain mean (miracles aside) the end of me? If one wants to argue for personal immortality, Malebranche's foundations simply won't bear the weight he puts on them.

All of this, of course, has taken for granted the soundness of what I have labelled the negative *a priori* argument. This was, around 1700, far and away the most popular proof of the immateriality of the soul. (It is prominent, for example, in several of the sets of Boyle Lectures.[38]) But this argument rests firmly on Descartes' assumption that three-dimensional extension is an adequate idea of body. Arnauld had suggested in his criticisms of the *Meditations* that Descartes' idea of the mind might be a mere abstraction, not an adequate idea. Maybe the same is true of the idea of body as three-dimensional extension?[39] This is the opinion of Locke, who followed Arnauld on a number of crucial points. Who can take it upon himself to say, Locke asks with beguiling innocence,[40] whether God might not have 'superadded' to some complex material systems the power of thought? But if the essence of matter may consist of more than we are aware of, all that will follow from Cartesian or Malebranchian arguments is that we are not in a position to understand how a material thing could also be a subject of thought. The proper conclusion from this argument then becomes much weaker than Malebranche wants. We might conclude with Thomas Nagel[41] that we can't understand how physicalism could be true. We might say, with Colin McGinn,[42] that there is a true account of the mind–body relation, but we're not intelligent enough to grasp it. We would not, however, be in the position to be able to claim that materialism is demonstrably false. In the final analysis, Malebranche's arguments won't work, and serve only to undermine the position he is seeking to defend. While trying to derive Descartes' orthodox conclusions from a weaker set of premises, he arrives – without so much as realising it – at a position, as regards our knowledge of our own souls, not far removed from the scepticism of Hume.[43]

9

MALEBRANCHE ON FREEDOM, GRACE AND THE WILL

Philosophical background: continuous creation and the Vision in God

This chapter deals with what is perhaps the most intractable problem in Malebranche's philosophy, the problem of free will.[1] Why does the issue of freedom raise particular difficulties for Malebranche, difficulties that do not arise – or at least, do not arise in the same form – for other philosophers and theologians? The answer stems, I suggest, from the combination of two of his most fundamental metaphysical theses: continuous creation and the Vision in God. Both doctrines lie at the heart of Malebranche's philosophy: it is unthinkable that he could abandon either of them. But their combination raises a formidable difficulty for Malebranche's philosophical theology.

According to the theory of continuous creation, which we discussed at some length in Chapter Five, the continued existence of any creature is simply its continuous (re)creation by God. No body, and no finite spirit, continues to exist by its own power; without divine sustenance, all things would simply cease-to-be. If this thesis of continuous creation is extended from all created substances to include all their modes, we have Malebranche's principal argument for occasionalism. If it is logically impossible for a finite substance to exist without a determinate set of modes (a body can't exist unless it exists in some particular place, a mind can't exist unless it thinks some particular thoughts), then even God cannot create or sustain indeterminate creatures. Malebranche's departure from scholastic and Cartesian tradition, we suggested, lay in his willingness to accept the continuous creation of all modes CC(AM) and of determinate modes CC(DM), and then to try to come to terms with the startling implications of such a doctrine.

If Malebranche does indeed accept CC(AM) and CC(DM), and applies those theses to the continuous creation of human souls, an obvious problem arises regarding human free will. The modes of the soul include on the one hand its occurrent thoughts and inclinations, and on the other its habits or *dispositions intérieurs*. If each and every such modification of every human soul owes its existence to the direct action of God, it seems impossible to find any room for human freedom. This in turn raises two obvious problems regarding the compatibility of this doctrine with (a) introspection and (b) divine justice.

As we saw in Chapter Eight, Malebranche never doubted the evidence of introspection or *sentiment intérieur* in establishing the freedom of the will. Like his joint mentors Augustine and Descartes, he regards this freedom as a *given*, not something that can be reasoned away. One cannot philosophise against experience. But if CC(DM) is true, and universal in its application (i.e. applies to souls as well as to bodies) this inner sentiment of liberty seems to be a mere illusion. God could, of course, have established for Himself a law to consult the modes of my soul at t1 when (re)creating it at t2, which would make the modes at t1 occasional causes of those at t2, but this only generates a regress. It doesn't establish any genuine freedom of the will.

The problem of theodicy – of justifying the ways of God to man – was particularly pressing for Malebranche. The reason for this is simple. In the Vision in God, he thinks, our minds partake of God's ideas. We come to see things – at least in part – as it were with God's eyes.[2] This Vision in God takes in, of course, the eternal and necessary truths of mathematics, forever present in the divine intellect. Equally important, however, are the eternal and necessary truths of morality, grounded in the Order that is also part of God's mind.[3] Just as I can see that $2 + 2 = 4$ is necessarily true, and is true for all minds, so likewise I can see that God is (infinitely) more valuable than a man, and a man is more valuable than a horse. Such truths of Order constitute a perfectly objective axiology or doctrine of value, a body of truths just as absolute, eternal and necessary as those of mathematics.[4] God acts as He does, Malebranche explains, because Order requires it (or at least permits it).[5]

It follows from this doctrine that all forms of voluntarism about the necessary truths must be utterly rejected.[6] Descartes was wrong to say that God could make $2 + 2 = 5$, or a triangle with angles that do not add to 180°, even though we can't understand how He could do so.[7] God cannot violate His own wisdom. And in the realm of ethics, we can't say that a particular course of conduct is just because willed by God; on the contrary, God must will it because it is just.[8] Voluntarist theology, Malebranche insists again and again,[9] provides no weapons to use against the *libertins*. The Christian theologian describes God's conduct towards man in a way that seems – at least on the face of it – grossly and manifestly unjust, e.g. selecting a particular people for special favours, or condemning all humanity for the remote crime of a distant ancestor. The freethinker protests that the Christian God is unjust. If the voluntarist theologian merely responds by saying 'God willed it, and His willing it makes it just', he empties the notion of justice of all intelligible content. To answer the freethinker, Malebranche insists, we need to justify the ways of God to man in a way that humans can understand and appreciate, i.e. in terms of the universally intelligible norms of conduct prescribed by Order itself.

It should now be clear why it is the combination of continuous creation and the Vision in God that raises special problems for Malebranche. Believers in real causal powers in creatures can accommodate a robust notion of free agency in man, and a corresponding notion of our responsibility for how we use or misuse our delegated powers. The metaphysics of continuous creation seems to rule out any such causal powers in creatures. One could, of course, combine continuous creation with voluntarism. In a theology of this kind, God places certain demands on His creatures, makes some of them conform to His orders and others disobey them, and then rewards the former and punishes the latter. This, as we shall see, is how Malebranche interprets Jansenism. If this conduct seems irrational and unfair to us, we are simply told that it is not for us to judge our Maker. The Vision in God, by allowing us to share with God an insight into Order itself, rules out any such voluntarist reply to the freethinker. Malebranche must provide a justification of the ways of God to man that humans will find both intelligible and worthy of acceptance. If God is to distribute rewards and punishments in an *orderly* manner, it is only natural to suppose that He does so in accordance with our deserts. And this in turn seems impossible without some genuine freedom on our part. If continuous creation excludes human freedom, while the Vision in God (by way of the perception of Order) requires human freedom, Malebranche's philosophy is profoundly – indeed irreparably – inconsistent.

Theological background: Augustine against the Pelagians

The crucial background for Malebranche's theory of grace is the campaign of orthodox Christians, led by Augustine, against Pelagianism. Pelagius (*c*.360–*c*.420) was a British monk and an almost exact contemporary of Augustine (354–430). Pelagius rejected the doctrine of original sin, arguing that humans possess free will, and hence have the power to lead morally perfect lives by their own unaided efforts, without the supernatural gift of grace.[10] The implications of this doctrine for Christian theology are as profound as they are revolutionary. If there is no original sin, there is no need for the sacrament of infant baptism as practised in the Church. If a man can become just by his unaided efforts, simply through the exercise of his natural powers, then Socrates or Confucius may have been as righteous as Saint Peter, and as deserving of salvation. The divine gift of grace, on such a view, may make it easier for a man to do his duty, but is in principle dispensable. A virtuous pagan, it would seem, has no need in principle of a mediator and a redeemer. It is easy to see why such a doctrine was attacked with such vigour as not merely un-Christian but anti-Christian, inconsistent with central aspects of Christian faith and practice.

Augustine's writings against Pelagius have become, over the course of the centuries, fundamental documents of Christian theology. In these polemical writings Augustine takes himself both to be defending existing Christian belief and practice against an un-Christian heresy and to be articulating a proper Christian anthropology, an account of man consistent with the testimony of inner experience. The reader of Augustine's *Confessions* is struck by his vivid picture of a young man mired in a life of sin, knowing the life he was called upon to lead, but unable to abandon the worse life for the better. In our fallen state, he tells us, we can see the good but we cannot love it – or, more plausibly, cannot love it with sufficient firmness and resolution to put aside our habitual sins and pursue it. Experience informs us not of our powers but of our incapacity to live the life we would choose in our clear-headed moments. The state of *akrasia* described in Book Seven of Aristotle's *Nicomachean Ethics* (seeing the better and choosing the worse) is not, for Augustine, a mere puzzle for rationalistic theories of ethics. It is the universal condition of fallen humanity, of natural man without the supernatural gift of grace. By the natural light of reason we can see how we should live, but our will does not find itself desiring what our reason represents as good. So we feel remorse, and self-dissatisfaction, and sense our urgent need for a saviour and redeemer who by the gift of grace makes possible what would otherwise be impossible. Hence Augustine's famous prayer, which so offended Pelagius, 'Give what Thou enjoinest, and enjoin what thou wilt'.[11] If for example chastity is commanded, and a man finds himself unable to obey, he must pray for the gift of grace rather than assume that he can achieve such moral perfection by his own unaided efforts.

Pelagianism was quickly condemned as a heresy and suppressed within the Christian community. But at the heart of Pelagius' heresy was his emphasis on free will and moral responsibility. This moral insight could not be suppressed, any more than Augustine's agonising over our dependence and powerlessness. Our moral responsibility seems unintelligible without some notion of agency. Even if grace is required for justification and salvation, surely there is something we can do to earn the gift? This natural thought gives rise to the heresy of semi-Pelagianism. On this doctrine, no man can become just by his own unaided efforts, without the gift of grace, but a man can at least make the first move, and thus merit the gift. This theory still leaves some room for our own efforts, and makes the gift of grace itself less mysterious. If God distributes graces in response to our autonomous efforts, we can begin to apply familiar human notions of distributive justice to the difficult theological issue of predestination.

Augustine had no more sympathy for this compromise theory than for full-blooded Pelagianism. Both theories, he felt, represent the creature as independent of the creator, and are therefore presumptuous and un-Christian. *All* our merits without exception are to be regarded as gifts, so there can be no merit in man prior to and independent of the gift of grace. 'What hast thou', as Saint Paul asks, 'that thou hast not received'?[12] There can be no reason or ground in the creature for being chosen, so from the human point of view the selection of some human souls and not others for the gift of grace remains a mystery.[13] All men are sunk in original sin, so no man *deserves* such a gift, which remains – as the name implies – gratuitous. No man gets less than he deserves; a few receive much more.[14] The gift of grace, according to Augustine, does not destroy liberty. On the contrary, it restores liberty by making it possible for us to delight in good rather than in evil, and thus to love and gladly to do what before we had found beyond our powers.[15] But this in turn raises worries about divine justice. If the sinner cannot do as he is commanded, it seems unjust to condemn him for his failure. And if the recipient of the gift of grace simply comes to take such delight in his duty that he can do no otherwise, why does he deserve any reward?

Augustine's polemical writings against the Pelagians were fundamental documents during the theological debates of the Reformation, much cited by Luther and Calvin and their disciples. The reformers found it impossible to reconcile the Augustinian doctrine of grace with any robust sense of free will, and were thus led to deny free will altogether. If God's predestination of some to share the glory of the saints and of others to eternal damnation seems unjust to us (because not dependent on our merits), this only shows, they will argue, that we go astray when we attempt to apply human standards to God. In the French Catholic Church of the seventeenth century, the Jansenists also pored over the volumes of Augustine, and developed in response their own doctrine of 'efficacious grace'. The gift of grace, they argued, must always be efficacious in converting the soul of the sinner and drawing it to God. This seems to entail the denial of free will on our part, since it implies that the sinner contributes nothing to his conversion.

If grace is always efficacious, the Jansenists reasoned, it must be sufficient for salvation. So all and only those are saved who receive the gift of grace. Two dangerous corollaries seem to follow from this doctrine. In the first place, Christ did not die for all men but only for those predestined to salvation, perhaps a small proportion of the human race. And furthermore, if it is impossible to resist the workings of grace there can be no merit in being moved by it to love God and to do one's duty. Unless we can co-operate with grace, we are just puppets in the hands of God, with no liberty or moral responsibility. Jansenist theology, according to its many opponents, is indistinguishable from Protestantism, although the Jansenists strove to find verbal formulae that preserved at least the outward semblance of orthodoxy. It is therefore no surprise to find Malebranche citing against Arnauld the edits of the Council of Trent against Protestantism (*OCM* VI 277).

Catholic theologians debating the tangled issues surrounding grace and free will had to steer a perilous course between Scylla and Charybdis. On the one side, there is the heresy of Pelagianism, which has a clear and robust sense of human freedom and moral responsibility, but makes of grace a mere optional extra. This flies in the face both of orthodox Christian doctrine and of the sort of Christian experience so vividly depicted by Augustine in his *Confessions*. On the other side, there is the hard line interpretation of Augustine offered by the reformers, which emphasises human worthlessness and powerlessness without the gift of grace, and our utter incapacity to earn that gift in any way. This represents predestination as the ultimate mystery, and offends our natural sense of justice. How, we ask, could God have established a system of rewards and punishments that bears no relation to our deserts? And how could we deserve reward or punishment unless we have moral responsibility, and hence some control over our actions? The two extreme views – Pelagianism on one side, and Calvinism on the other – are each perfectly intelligible. The problem facing Catholic theologians is to navigate a path between these extremes, i.e. to construct an account of freedom and grace that is self-consistent and intelligible in its own right, but doesn't fall into either extreme position. This, as the Arnauld–Malebranche controversy shows, was a difficult and delicate task. Arnauld thinks that Malebranche falls into Pelagianism or semi-Pelagianism; Malebranche retorts that Arnauld is a Calvinist in all but name.

Freedom and grace in the *Recherche*

Much of the *Recherche* can be read as a sort of extended commentary on Descartes' *Fourth Meditation*. If my clear and distinct ideas are given to me by an all-perfect Being, omnipotent, omniscient, and benevolent, how is it, the meditator asks, that I can still fall into error? The answer is that there is more to judgement than the passive reception of ideas: there is an act of the mind, an exercise of the faculty of volition. An obvious analogy might be the deliberations of a jury. They weigh the evidence, perhaps at some length; but ultimately they must decide 'Smith is guilty as charged' or 'Smith is not guilty'. And it is always possible to decide on insufficient evidence or on the basis of merely confused ideas, and thus to risk falling into error. In everyday practical contexts we often have to do this, Descartes knows,[16] but in what Bernard Williams has called 'The Project of Pure Enquiry' we should never commit ourselves to a judgement until we have a clear and distinct perception of its truth.

In Chapter Two of Book One of the *Recherche*, Malebranche sets out this Cartesian view of the will and the intellect, and derives from it two rules for the avoidance of (1) error in the sciences and of (2) sin in morals. In the sciences, he says, 'We should never give complete consent except to propositions which seem so evidently true that we cannot refuse it of them without feeling an inward pain and the secret reproaches of reason.' The corresponding rule for the moral domain is that 'We should never absolutely love some good if we can without remorse refuse to love it' (*OCM* I 55, LO 10). It is important that we clearly distinguish delectation from love. The former is passive (simply finding something pleasing); the latter involves an action of the soul, a sort of commitment to something as a true good. Just as we should subject our judgements to the test of the first rule, so too we should subject our loves to the test of this second rule. Only God passes this test, so only God is to be loved absolutely and unconditionally.

The *Recherche* is, as Robinet has shown in great and painstaking detail,[17] a stratified text, its final version resembling an archaeological site like the ruins of Troy. In its six (seven) editions,[18] dating from 1674 to 1712, Malebranche made very substantial revisions and additions to the text. This sometimes makes it hard for the modern reader to discern the development of Malebranche's thought and to isolate his final and considered opinion on a number of important topics.

Nowhere is this difficulty more acute than in the discussion in the *Recherche* of freedom and the will. Malebranche sometimes suggests that he doesn't believe in CC(DM), or at least that he is not prepared to extend it to spirits. His opening definitions of the will and of freedom suggest that God merely creates each soul willing the good in general, i.e. with an indeterminate inclination only, and that it is up to us how we direct this inclination towards particular ends. Here are his definitions:

> Consequently, I propose to designate by the word WILL, or capacity the soul has of loving different goods, *the impression or natural impulse that carries us toward general and indeterminate good*; and by FREEDOM, I mean nothing else but *the power that the mind has of turning this impression toward objects that please us so that our natural inclinations are made to settle upon some particular object*, which inclinations were hitherto vaguely and indeterminately directed toward universal or general good, that is, toward God, who alone is the general good because He alone contains in Himself all goods.
>
> (*OCM* I 46, LO 5)

There is, of course, a problem for Malebranche regarding how God is to be conceived. Is He 'the general good', in which case even sinners love God (albeit confusedly), or is He a particular good, requiring a particular and directed love? Malebranche, I presume, must answer 'both'. God is the good in general for the reason Malebranche gives ('He contains in Himself all goods') but is also a good in particular because He wants us to love Him as He is, and not through clouds of sensuality and ignorance.

The picture we are offered here attributes considerable causal power to the will. God remains the motor, but the steering wheel remains in the hands of the soul itself. If God merely creates in us the will itself, i.e. the indeterminate impulse towards the good in general, and leaves it up to us how to direct this desire towards particular ends, then CC(DM) is false in its application to spirits.[19] The model Malebranche is drawing on is one of the weakest aspects of Cartesian physics.[20] Faced with the problem of how the immaterial mind can move the animal spirits in the brain, Cartesians like La Forge suggested that the mind can alter the direction of flow of the animal spirits in the pineal gland, without altering the total quantity of motion.[21] Such an action, La Forge suggests, is physically null, because it doesn't add or subtract any 'quantity of motion' to the animal spirits. A comparable view of the mind would allow God to successively re-create it with a given 'quantity of striving', as it were, but permit the mind itself to determine its own inclinations.

In Book Six of the *Recherche*, the difficulty crops up again, this time in the context of Malebranche's argument for occasionalism. The noblest minds, he insists, are in a state of impotence:

> They can know nothing unless God enlightens them. They can sense nothing unless God modifies them. They are incapable of willing anything unless God moves them towards good in general, i.e. toward Himself. They can determine the impression God gives them toward Himself towards objects other than Himself, I admit; but I do not know if that can be called power.
>
> (*OCM* II 314, LO 449)

Malebranche's indecisiveness here is clear, and its underlying reason is easy to discover from the text. He is arguing in the chapter for the radical occasionalist thesis that God is the only true cause, and that finite spirits lack all causal powers. But he still wants to say that our sins are our own fault, not God's, i.e. that we are never compelled to fall into sin. An obvious way to reconcile those two claims would be to endorse only CC(S) for souls, to reject CC(DM), and to allow souls to have the genuine power to redirect their own inclinations, in accordance with their own perceptions or misperceptions of the good.

Although some commentators, including even Gueroult,[22] have ascribed this view to Malebranche, it is not his considered opinion, as is evident from many other passages in the *Recherche*. His final view, as we shall see, is that God doesn't just re-create each soul with its indeterminate striving for the good in general but also with its inclinations towards particular goods. Thus in Chapter One of Book Four, after introducing the love of the good in general, irresistibly impressed on us by the Author of nature, Malebranche goes on to discuss our love of particular finite goods. Is it up to us which finite goods we love? Malebranche now proceeds to offer, in two successive paragraphs, two strikingly different accounts of the relation between the indeterminate love of the good in general and the love of particular things and people. We begin with the picture of the soul's power to steer itself towards particular ends:

> It certainly need not be imagined that this power of loving we have comes from, or depends on, us. Only the power of loving

badly, or rather of loving well what we should not love at all, depends on us, because as free beings we can and do in effect determine towards particular, and consequently false, goods the good love that God unceasingly imprints in us, so long as He continues to preserve us.

(*OCM* II 12, LO 267)

This is the familiar picture of an indeterminate love of the good directed towards particular limited goods by the soul's own choices. The next paragraph, however, paints a very different picture:

But not only our will (or our love for the good in general) comes from God, but also our inclinations for particular goods (which inclinations are common to, but not equally strong among, all men), such as our inclination toward the preservation both of our own being and those with which we are naturally united are impressions of God's will on us for by the term natural inclination, I mean all the impressions of the Author of nature common to all minds.

(*OCM* II 12–13, LO 267)

Of these two inconsistent accounts, the former leaves a greater power of self-determination to the soul, while the latter ascribes more to God. *Éclaircissement* I comes down firmly on the side of the latter view. Its topic is the soul of the sinner; its thesis is that God produces whatever is real in the mind's impulses (including those of the sinner), but is nevertheless not the author of sin. God's role, Malebranche explains, is the following:

First, God unceasingly impels us by an irresistible impression toward the good in general. Second, He represents to us the idea of some particular good, or gives us the sensation of it. Finally, He leads us toward this particular good.

(*OCM* III 18, LO 547)

It is true that in a sense God leads the sinner to love the object of his sin; for, as practically all theologians put it, whatever matter, act, or impulse there is in sin comes from God.

(*OCM* III 21, LO 549)

A man's choices, Malebranche explains, never produce in his soul any 'new modifications that materially change or modify his substance'.

So it can be true *both* that God re-creates the soul with all its modifications, *and* that we are responsible for our own sins. The modifications that God creates include all our first-order inclinations, which we experience in our souls but do not choose;[23] the sin lies in a second-order act by which we as it were 'endorse' some of these inclinations. All that is needed to render the two positions consistent is a sharp distinction between the 'physical' and the 'moral' aspects of what the sinner does. The problem is, of course, that our actions (and inactions) give rise to habits, and these *dispositions intérieurs* are modifications of our souls. But this is a problem to which we must return later.

So what does the sinner do? Malebranche's answer is startling in its simplicity: 'nothing at all'. Augustine's paradoxical account of evil, it will turn out, was right after all: whatever exists is good to the extent that it exists; evil is a mere privation. The sinner's fault is not the fact that he finds a particular fruit tasty, or a particular person sexually attractive; such natural inclinations are from God, and are as such good. His error is that he has not stopped to think and to reflect; he lets himself go and reaches for the particular good that is offered to him, without stopping to ask whether it will really satisfy him, or whether some better thing might be available. Here we see another striking example of Malebranche combining Augustinian and Cartesian themes. The Augustinian doctrine that evil is a mere privation fits neatly with the Cartesian account of error in *Meditation Four*. Given Malebranche's second rule, the only way to be sure of avoiding moral error is to submit each proposed good to a searching scrutiny, to ask 'will it really make me solidly and securely happy?' Since none of the finite goods of this life will pass this test, it follows that we should be forever dissatisfied with worldly goods (*OCM* II 17, LO 269), never content until our love is given unconditionally to God alone, and to creatures only in accordance with God's will.[24]

All the above, says Malebranche, should be apparent by the light of reason, the universal '*grâce du créateur*' distributed to all men. This grace, called *lumière* by Malebranche in self-conscious imitation of Augustine, enables us to see that worldly goods can never satisfy us, and that our true happiness lies in God alone. But, Malebranche adds, again following closely in Augustine's footsteps, the light of reason has moral authority but no motivational strength. It enables us to see the good, but not to love it or to pursue it. In one of his most Augustinian passages, he writes as follows:

> The mind's perception by itself is never enough to make us resist the urges of concupiscence as we should; besides

219

perception, a sentiment of the heart is required. This illumination of the mind by itself is, if you will, a grace sufficient only for condemning us, for making us aware of our weakness and of our need for appealing through prayer to Him who is our strength. But this sentiment of the heart is a living, functioning grace.

(*OCM* I 409, LO 213–14)

It is not clear from this quote whether the mere perception of the good, without the gift of grace, has zero motivational force, or merely insufficient motivational force to overcome the temptations of concupiscence. If Malebranche were to take the former line, he could follow Augustine's own hard line on the supposed moral virtues of the pagans, dismissing them as mere pride and vainglory.[25] There are chapters of the *Recherche* which echo this Augustinian theme.[26] But Malebranche also admits that the mind's perception of its own ordered (or disordered) state causes an 'intellectual joy' (or sadness) which is a true emotion, and as such capable of moving the soul (*OCM* II 156, LO 356). Likewise in the *Traité de Morale* he tells us not just that the pagans have the ineffaceable idea of Order but that they also have some residual love of Order (*OCM* XI 54). He asserts in the *Recherche* only that this love, and these resulting intellectual emotions of joy and sadness, are too feeble to enable us to overcome sin:

It is nonetheless true that without the grace of Jesus Christ, the delight the soul takes in yielding to its passions is greater than that which it experiences while following the rules of reason, and it is this delight that is the source of all the disorders that have resulted from Original Sin and that would make us all slaves of our passions if the Son of God had not delivered us from their servitude through the delight of His grace.

(*OCM* II 157, LO 356)

The pagan, he suggests, can see the good, and can even love the good, albeit perhaps feebly and fleetingly. But these intellectual emotions are always weaker than the passions arising from our embodied state (*OCM* II 155–6, LO 355). Moreover, these perceptions and inclinations are merely occurrent states of our souls, and it is a stable virtuous *disposition* that justifies (*OCM* III 80, LO 584; *OCM* XI 98–9). So perhaps Malebranche's final position is a sort of *contingent* anti-Pelagianism. On this view, there are intellectual pleasures and pains resulting from our perception of the requirements of Order and of our own compliance and non-compliance with those requirements. Since these pleasures and pains are true emotions, capable of moving the soul, it will not be logically impossible that a man could achieve moral virtue by reason alone, without the supernatural assistance of grace. But in fact the pleasures and pains of concupiscence are, let us suppose, a whole order of magnitude greater than those of the intellect. So no man has ever arrived at genuine moral virtue by such an arduous route.[27] I am not sure whether this still concedes too much to the Pelagian to be considered orthodox by theologians.

The *Traité de la Nature et de la Grâce*

Malebranche's early relations with Arnauld had been cordial, and Arnauld clearly had entertained hopes of drawing the young Oratorian into the Jansenist camp.[28] The publication in 1678 of the *Éclaircissements* to the *Recherche* put an end, once and for all, to any such hopes. What was it that Malebranche said that so scandalised Arnauld? The crucial claim was the assertion in *Éclaircissement* XV that God *must* act, in the domain of grace as in that of nature, in a manner that is worthy of His attributes. This meant, according to Malebranche, by means of *volontés générales* rather than *volontés particulières*. So there are 'very simple laws in the order of grace' as in the order of nature (*OCM* III 221, LO 666–7). Since the argument is *a priori*, not based on experience but on the idea of an all-perfect Being, we can be certain that God does not act differently in the distribution of grace than He does in the governance of nature.

The central analogy at the heart of the *Traité* is that of the rain. God wills, we may be sure, that all seeds be fertile, but we know that many never germinate for lack of water. How is this possible? The reason, says Malebranche, is simple. Reason and Experience equally testify that rain is distributed by means of universal laws of nature, not in accordance with the needs of particular seeds. So rain sometimes falls on the sea or in the deserts, and is wasted, and sometimes fails to fall on cultivated ground, leaving the seeds to shrivel and die. If God had a particular concern for the individual members of His vegetable creation, He would give each seed the rain it needed to germinate and grow, but we see that He does not do this. To act in such a manner would be 'base' and 'servile', beneath His dignity and inconsistent with His wisdom.

If we shift from the realm of nature to that of grace, we find a similar picture. God wills that all souls be saved, but we know (through the authority of the Church) that many fall into damnation. How is this possible? The reason, says Malebranche, is that grace, like the rain, is distributed in accordance with general laws (*OCM* V 38, R 121). Reason

221

tells us that God must act in a manner worthy of His attributes, i.e. by means of general laws, not descending to individual cases. Experience tells us that the gift of grace is sometimes wasted on the souls of hardened sinners. If God did have a special concern for each and every soul, He would send it precisely the amount of grace necessary to lead it to salvation, but we see that He has not acted in this way. God quite rightly regards the expression of His own attributes (in this case, His wisdom) as incomparably more important than the fate of individual human souls.[29] Such a judgement is objectively correct (in accordance with Order); to wish that He should think and act otherwise would be to wish that God were not God.

Malebranche's central claim in the *Traité* is that the occasional cause God has appointed for the distribution of grace is the human soul of Jesus Christ (*OCM* V 65–7, R 138–40). Such a finite soul can have concerns for, and thus pray for, particular human souls. His prayers are the occasional causes of God's distribution of grace. God thus says to Himself 'For all X, if Jesus prays for X, I shall send grace to X'; this saves Him from stooping to particulars.[30] But what determines the prayers of Jesus? Malebranche's answer to this question takes us into one of the most idiosyncratic parts of his theology, his attempt to explain God's reasons for creating our universe.

God, Christians believe, is absolutely perfect in all conceivable respects. As such, He is self-sufficient unto Himself. So why did He create a universe of bodies and finite spirits at all? Not, we must assume, for any benefit He could hope to gain from it. From the point of view of Order (= the objective hierarchy of value) any finite creature, matter or spirit, is infinitely inferior to God. The same can be said of the entire creation, which must be – considered in itself – quite simply beneath God's notice. Was the creation then an aberration on God's part, an irrational violation of His own perfection? Surely not. Order requires that God always acts for good reasons. The only way in which the created universe could become worthy of God is by the incarnation of the Word, i.e. through Christ.[31] So the entire universe only exists, Malebranche concludes, because of God's design for the incarnation of the Word.[32] Christ's role on earth is the establishment, by the gifts of grace of which his will is the occasional cause, of the living temple of his Church.

Christ, in his role as head of the Church, is instructed to select the bricks (= souls) that will form the temple (= the mystical body of the Church). His ultimate concern is not for the souls of individuals as such but for the construction of the building. Just as the builder needs a hundred stones of a particular size and shape, so Christ needs a hundred souls of type X. If there are a thousand to hand, he may not care which hundred he picks up first (*OCM* V 82).[33] Since Malebranche continues to insist that God has a sincere will to save *all* men, Christ is presumably acting under instructions to make the temple as extensive as he can, consistently with its overall design. If the temple required only a hundred souls of type X, but there were a million to hand, the rest would be simply superfluous to requirements.[34] For consistency, we must assume that Christ's instructions are not just 'build a temple to such-and-such a design out of that stuff' but 'build a temple to such-and-such a design out of that stuff, using as much of it as you can without wrecking the design'.

The principles according to which grace is distributed relate, according to Malebranche, to the requirements of the temple, not the needs of individuals. It follows that they often appear bizarre and inexplicable to us, and bear little or no relation to our notions of justice. In particular, grace is not distributed equally to all men, nor is it distributed in accordance with our merits (that would be Pelagianism), nor again is it distributed in accordance with our individual needs (if it were, no one would be damned). Nor does Jesus anticipate the uses to which grace will be put by each individual receiver. By its union with the Word, the soul of Christ has access to God's omniscience, but in the distribution of grace this potential source of fore-knowledge is not actually drawn upon (*OCM* V 79–81). So he frequently picks a stone up (gives an individual soul a gift of grace) but has to put it down again (the gift is wasted on an already hardened heart). There are 'disorders' and 'irregularities' in the order of grace as in the order of nature (*OCM* V 84).

Having explained the theological background of the *Traité*, we are now in a position to look more closely at Malebranche's account of free will. The effects of the fall, he agrees with Augustine, have left us mired in concupiscence, unable through our own efforts to achieve anything of value. To counterbalance the effects of the Fall we need the *délectation prévenante* of grace, which comes to us of course through the prayers of Jesus Christ. This provides a pleasure in doing our duty, a pleasure that can weigh against concupiscence. Malebranche quite explicitly introduces a balance model at this point, and insists that both weights are efficacious:

> For example: there is in one of the bowls of a scale, a weight of ten pounds. One places in the other bowl a weight of only six pounds. This second weight will truly weigh something: for if one added as much again, or if one took enough out of the

other bowl, or if finally one suspended the scale closer to the bowl which is the more weighted, this weight of six pounds would tip the balance.

(*OCM* V 132, R 182)

But a crude balance model of the will is plainly inconsistent with freedom. If the more powerful force simply triumphs, it looks as if we have the makings of a perfectly deterministic psychology, akin to the picture of the will familiar to us – and to Malebranche – from Hobbes.[35] Malebranche continues to insist, however, that we remain free to resist the pleasures of the senses, and even (against the Jansenists) that we can resist the workings of grace. Even in our fallen condition, we have the power to suspend judgement and thus to regulate our loves:

This power of suspending the judgement which actually governs love, this power which is the principle of our liberty, and through which pleasures are not always invincible, is very diminished since the advent of sin, though it is not annihilated.

(*OCM* V 126, R 177)

Liberty, for Malebranche, is a matter of degree, and can be strengthened by its exercise.[36] If the soul of a sinner is in such a condition that this power has been weakened, this deficiency is his own fault:

But having had to, and having been able to, accustom himself to resist pleasure, to fight for the preservation and for the augmentation of his liberty, even a sin committed by a kind of necessity makes him culpable and worthy of being punished; if it is not because of the sin, it is at least because of the negligence which is at the root of it.

(*OCM* V 130, R 180)

How then are we to incorporate a role for free will into the balance model? Malebranche has three different attempts at this task. I shall call them (1) Perfect equilibrium plus pure rational choice, (2) Balance plus locking mechanism, (3) Balance plus sliding fulcrum. Let us see what consequences can be derived from each in turn.

(1) Malebranche often writes as if the role of grace were simply to provide a counterbalance to the weight of concupiscence, leaving the soul as it were freely suspended and able to make an unfettered rational choice based simply on its clear perception of the good:

Pleasure is the balance of the soul: it inclines naturally towards it; sensible pleasures pull it down to earth. It is necessary, for it to be able to determine itself, either that these pleasures dissipate, or that the delectation of grace raise it towards heaven, and put it nearly back in equilibrium.

(OCM V 97, R 151)

The qualification 'nearly' here is important. If, says Malebranche, the soul received an amount of grace precisely equal in its motivational force to the 'weight' of concupiscence, it would then be bound to choose rightly:

Thus the grace of Jesus Christ is stronger than concupiscence. One can call it victorious grace, because it is always the mistress of the heart, when it is equal to that of concupiscence. For when the balance of our heart is perfectly in equilibrium through the equal weights of contrary pleasures, the pleasure which is the most solid and the most reasonable always carries the day, because light favours its efficacy, and because the regrets of conscience are opposed to the action of false pleasure.

(OCM V 137–8, R 186–7)

So if the gift of grace is greater than, or equal to, the 'weight' of concupiscence, it will always triumph. This seems to leave no room for freedom and merit on our part. But there is one further possibility, not explicitly discussed. Suppose the gift of grace is almost but not quite as great as the weight of concupiscence. Can we do the rest – i.e. make up the small deficit – by our own powers? Malebranche's admission that there are genuine intellectual joys and pains, resulting from the perception of our souls' ordered or disordered states, suggests a positive answer. But this would leave him wide open to Arnauld's accusations of Pelagianism.

(2) The model of a simple balance with a locking mechanism is Malebranche's most common picture of the operations of the will. On this model, we need a very sharp distinction between acts and omissions. In our natural (fallen) state we can do nothing of value, because the weight of concupiscence is always our most powerful motivation. But we retain the power to suspend judgement, i.e. not to give our consent to the apparent good. So we are at fault when we sin, because we have failed to use a natural power left in our souls despite the fall. If the weight of concupiscence is powerful and constant and that of grace negligible,

this model will of course give only a feeble and purely negative sort of freedom. But if the weight of concupiscence is variable, and there are occasional gifts of grace, a balance with a lock can allow for the possibility of some genuinely good deeds. We only have to release the brake at the right times. It is still hard to see how this avoids the charge of Pelagianism. If 'letting go' or 'going with the flow' are cases of inaction, as the privation theory of evil suggests, then 'slamming on the brakes' looks like a clear case of an action on our part, and as such something meritworthy.

(3) Malebranche's most sophisticated version of the balance model is that of a balance with a sliding fulcrum. On such a model, a smaller weight may of course overcome a greater one:

> The effects of pleasure and of all the feelings of the soul depend in a thousand ways on the actual dispositions of the mind. The same weight does not always produce the same effects: it depends, in its action, on the construction of the machine by which it is applied to the contrary weight. If a balance is unequally suspended, the lighter ones may outweigh the heavier. It is the same with the weight of pleasure …
>
> (*OCM* V 144, R 192)

This version of the balance allows us to make the best sense of Malebranche's incessant recommendations of prayer and fasting and the mortification of the flesh. Nothing we do can guarantee or earn the gift of grace, which is not given to us for any merits we may possess. Nor can we overcome the weight of concupiscence by our own efforts. But if we can, as it were, shift the fulcrum of the balance, we can improve our chances by altering the state of our souls in such a way that a small gift of grace may triumph over a great weight of sinful desires.

Is this Pelagian? If orthodoxy merely requires us to believe that no one is saved without the gift of grace, Malebranche's position remains perfectly orthodox. But if we want to explain why Smith is saved and Jones is damned, the explanation may lie in Smith's efforts and Jones' negligence – they may well, on this model, have received equal gifts of grace. The analogy of the rain and the farmers may help. No one thinks that the farmer, by carefully preparing the ground, can make it rain. No one believes that the most diligent ploughing and manuring can produce a crop without the gift of rain. A good farmer is no more likely to receive rain than a bad one. But suppose there are two farmers with neighbouring farms, in a country where adequate rainfall is the norm. If we want to explain why Smith has a good crop and Jones does not, we may find ourselves taking the rain for granted as a background condition, and focusing our explanation on Smith's labours and Jones' negligence. It is this thought, I suspect, that leads Arnauld to accuse Malebranche of Pelagianism.

The controversy with Arnauld

Volumes Six to Nine of Malebranche's *Oeuvres Complètes* are given over to his seemingly interminable controversy with Arnauld, conducted through an exchange of broadsides in the form of public letters. Neither of the antagonists, it has to be said, appears at his best. The letters of both protagonists are full of sarcasm, bitterness, wilful misunderstanding and mere point-scoring. But beneath the antagonism, two serious issues are at stake.[37] The first of these issues – the nature of ideas – was the topic of Chapter Four. But it was the second topic – grace and freedom – that was the real heart of the controversy.[38] What Arnauld could never accept in Malebranche was the incursion of philosophical rationalism into theology.

Arnauld, of course, was the great partisan of Jansenism in the French Catholic Church of the late seventeenth century. Following Jansen, who in turn claimed to be following Augustine, he championed so-called 'efficacious grace', grace that, once given, always has its proper effect of converting the soul of the sinner. Those who receive this gift, according to the Jansenists, consent 'freely' to its operation, but in fact they cannot do otherwise. Their liberty is merely an absence of external constraint, not an absence of necessity.[39] Those who lack this grace are irretrievably lost. To suggest that the soul can do anything on its own account either to earn or to assist the gift of grace is to fall into Pelagianism. On Malebranche's account, says Arnauld, the human soul can both prepare itself to receive the gift of grace, and can assist the working of the gift once it has been received. These are meritworthy acts of the soul prior to and independent of the gift of grace. So Malebranche is a Pelagian, and must be sent back to school to re-learn the teachings of Augustine.

Malebranche has a three-pronged response to the charge of Pelagianism. He seeks to show (a) that his position is not Pelagian; (b) that the Jansenists cannot silence the freethinkers; and (c) that Jansenism is Protestant in all but name, and thus falls under the anathema of the Council of Trent. Let us consider these points in turn.

(a) In the first of Malebranche's *Four Letters* of 1687 (*OCM* VII 345–75) he sets out his views of the Jansenist doctrine of efficacious grace, and seeks to distinguish his position from Pelagianism. The human soul, he thinks, is 'naturally Pelagian', i.e. we tend naturally to fall into the error of assuming that God rewards us according to our merits.[40] It takes serious thought to realise that He must act as Order requires, and that Order requires Him to act as a general cause only of the distribution of grace. The pleasure of grace is always efficacious, says Malebranche, in the sense that it moves the soul, counterposing a '*sainte concupiscence*' to the '*concupiscence criminelle*' resulting from the corruption of our nature. But, he continues, 'this natural or necessary movement that grace produces never invincibly transports the will. It is not efficacious with regard to its consent' (*OCM* VII 353). It is evident, he says, that grace is always efficacious in one sense (we feel it, it 'moves' the soul), but that it cannot of itself produce the act of assent of the will. If it did, there could be no rational choice, no free will, and hence no merit or demerit on our part. Nothing is more certain from observation and introspection, Malebranche insists, than that we sometimes withhold our assent to grace and refuse to act in the manner to which we are being prompted. The Jansenist doctrine of efficacious grace is thus inconsistent both with the requirements of justice and with the evidence of introspection.

As for the accusations of Pelagianism, they result from a misreading of Augustine, and a refusal to recognise the context in which he was writing. Pelagius, Malebranche explains, denied original sin and the corruption of our nature, and hence claimed that a man could be saved without the gift of grace. Others admitted the need for grace but held that a man could earn the gift by his own efforts. These two errors were the targets of Augustine's polemics. But my principles, Malebranche insists, involve neither error. I accept original sin, and agree with Augustine that the light of reason alone does not suffice to enable us to will the good and to do it. And on my theory, Christ's gifts of grace are distributed in accordance with the needs of the Church, and not in accordance with our merits. So, Malebranche concludes, my principles are not Pelagian (*OCM* VII 375).

(b) My *Traité*, writes Malebranche in his 1684 *Réponse* to Arnauld's *Vraies et Fausses Idées,* was written to silence the freethinkers by proving that God's conduct was in accordance with Order, wise and just and good. When one says that God is wise and just and good, 'one does not pronounce words empty of sense, but one awakes ideas which are common to all those who enter into themselves' in reflection (*OCM* VI 24). If Arnauld simply says that God saves those He chooses, and rejects the rest, acting in every case by particular volitions, he represents God's conduct as arbitrary and unjust. Arnauld's voluntarism is worthless in this apologetic context. To silence the freethinkers we need to show that

God's actions manifest wisdom and justice in the plain sense of those terms.

(c) When Arnauld accuses Malebranche of being a Pelagian, Malebranche responds by branding Arnauld a Protestant in all but name. It is a dogma of the Catholic Church that God wills that all men be saved, but Arnauld must on his principles deny this (*OCM* VI 35). If God distributes grace by particular volitions, it seems clear that He wills to save only those who are in fact saved. So Christ died for the saints and not for mankind as a whole. And if the gift of grace compels the assent of the will, the just have no free will and can thus acquire no true merit by their co-operation with the workings of grace.[41] This is precisely the Protestant heresy condemned by the Council of Trent (*OCM* VI 277). On one point at least, Luther is compared favourably with Arnauld. Luther, we are told, denied free will 'because he said frankly what he thought, and called things by their names' (*OCM* VII 382). Arnauld wants to sustain the doctrine of Luther and Calvin – that all grace is irresistible – without falling into their heresy. To this end he declares roundly that the invincibility of grace destroys neither freedom nor merit. But this, Malebranche insists, is mere sophistry (*OCM* VII 399).

On one very important point, Malebranche feels obliged to correct Arnauld's misinterpretation of his doctrine. In an unguarded moment in the *Traité* (*OCM* V 138, R 187), Malebranche had intimated that the soul can acquire merit by going, 'as it were' further than it was pushed.[42] This suggested an obviously Pelagian model to the keen critical eye of Arnauld. Grace impels the soul towards the good with an impulse I, which is natural and necessary (i.e. without freedom or merit); the soul freely adds an increment ΔI from its own resources, which is free and therefore meritorious. Malebranche's admission that there are pure pleasures and pains of the intellect, resulting from the perception of Order and of our souls' conformity or otherwise with Order, does seem to provide further evidence that such a model had crossed his mind. If these pleasures and pains are, say, an order of magnitude less than the pleasures of concupiscence (or for that matter of the *sainte concupisence* of grace) then we have the position I labelled 'contingent anti-Pelagianism' at the end of the earlier section on 'Freedom and Grace in the *Recherche*'.

Any such model, Malebranche sees, would violate continuous creation, and involves too great a concession to Pelagianism. He now takes pains to disavow such a model, arguing that he nowhere claimed that the soul could advance (however minimally) by its own efforts (*OCM* VII 393–5). On the contrary, the assent of the soul, whether to grace or to concupiscence, is a kind of rest:

Now here is what is mine: it is that I consent to this movement towards such a good. But what do I do in this? I remain; I rest; I stop with such a good. This is, unless I am mistaken, all that I do. My consent is an immanent act of my will which produces nothing beyond itself, and which does not even change the modifications of my substance, or which does not produce there either ideas or sensations or movements, and I have no need for that of any efficacy proper to myself.

(*OCM* VII 566–7)

To consent, to let oneself go, is not an act at all. But what of resisting temptation? To introspection, this appears to be something I do rather than something I merely let happen. Yes, replies Malebranche, but even here my action produces '*rien de physique*'.

But supposing that I do not succumb to a temptation, or that I do not consent to the natural movement which carries me towards a particular good; then, one will say to me, you act, and you make use of the veritable and real power which you have of resisting. I reply that I act, but that I produce nothing real in myself, neither sentiments nor ideas. Doubtless I act: but my immanent act produces nothing physical.

(*OCM* VII, 567)

The *prémotion physique*

The publication in 1713 of Père Boursier's *L'Action de Dieu sur ses Créatures* provoked the elderly and ailing Malebranche into one last articulation and defence of his position. Boursier had argued for a *prémotion physique*, an action of God on the will of an individual human soul, necessarily determining its volitions. In other words, the soul does consent to the operation of grace, but this act of the soul is itself brought about by a particular and irresistible act of God. Boursier's argument for this theory turns on the metaphysical doctrine of continuous creation. God recreates every soul, he argues, with a complete and determinate set of modes. But the act of consent to the operation of grace is a mode of the soul. Therefore it too falls under the scope of continuous creation (*OCM* XVI 7–8). It would be self-contradictory for a soul to receive the *prémotion physique* and not give its consent to the workings of grace.

Malebranche felt obliged to reply to Boursier, not because his work raised any new issues of principle but because it 'fait beaucoup de bruit',[43] and because its principles were inconsistent with human freedom, and represented God's actions as arbitrary and unjust.[44] Malebranche completed his reply, the *Réflexions sur la Prémotion Physique*, shortly before his death in 1715. The issues raised by Boursier are fundamentally the same as those discussed at some length in the controversy with Arnauld. If God produces by His own almighty and irresistible power the act of assent of the will, it would be logically impossible for the soul to receive the *prémotion physique* and not give its consent. But this destroys liberty, and has all the frightful consequences that follow from the denial of liberty (*OCM* XVI 8). The implications of Boursier's theory 'overturn religion from top to bottom' (*OCM* XVI 16).

To illustrate this point, Malebranche tells the following story (*OCM* XVI 85). Imagine a sculptor who creates a dozen fine statues, each with a thread linking the head to the body in such a way as to enable them to nod when someone pulls on the thread. The sculptor pulls on the threads as he enters the room, and the statues bow low and salute him. Then one day he pulls on only some of the threads; these statues salute him, while the others of course do not. The sculptor is outraged, and smashes the offending statues. An observer would regard such behaviour as capricious and irrational at best, cruel and unjust at worst (*OCM* XVI 88). But this is exactly how Boursier represents the conduct of God towards His creatures. Boursier continues to say that God is good and wise and just, but when he tells us explicitly that His choice among His creatures is 'purely arbitrary' we must ask whether he means anything at all by such words (*OCM* XVI 90–1).

The crucial distinction Boursier has overlooked, according to Malebranche, is that between *sentir* and *consentir*. We *sense* the workings of grace in our souls, as we sense the effects of concupiscence, but we need not *consent* to either (*OCM* XVI 17). There is a corresponding distinction between *délectation* (which occurs in us but is not of us) and *love* (which requires our assent). God can produce in our souls, by the gift of grace, a *plaisir prévenante* capable of counter-balancing the effects of concupiscence. But to suppose that God brings about the act of consent itself is as inconsistent with theology as it is with philosophy. The Council of Trent re-affirmed human free will against Luther and Calvin (*OCM* XVI 8); philosophy requires us to think of God as a perfect Being, acting in accordance with Order, not as an arbitrary and capricious tyrant.

How does Malebranche respond to Boursier's use of the doctrine of continuous creation? He needs to defend the counter-intuitive claim that the soul's acts of consent are not in fact modes of the soul at all. This is what he says:

I agree that God is the sole author of all substances, and of all their modalities ... But one must take care here; I understand by modality of a substance only what cannot change without there being some real or physical change in the substance, of which it is the modality, and it is thus that it is ordinarily understood.

(*OCM* XVI 40)

I have always maintained that the soul was active: but that its acts produce nothing physical, or do not of themselves produce, by their own proper efficacy, any new modalities, any physical change, either in bodies or in itself. I say by their proper efficacy; one must take care here. For it is certain that there occur many physical changes in the soul following its morally good or evil acts.

(*OCM* XVI 41)

The acts of consent and dissent (suspension of judgement) are not modifications of the substance of the soul. Why does Malebranche say this? Presumably he will say that they produce no new thoughts or inclinations. Malebranche stoutly denied any perfect liberty of indifference to the soul; it cannot create new motives, or choose without a motive. If it decides at any given moment to release the brakes, the then strongest existing motive will always prevail (*OCM* XVI 47–8). So all the soul does is to allow the currently strongest inclination – be it one of concupiscence or of grace – to have its way. The inclination is a modification of the soul, and as such is caused by God; the 'letting go' is an act of mine, but is not a modification of my soul, and as such doesn't fall under CC(DM).

Can this account be made to work? The glaring problem is that, as Malebranche knows full well, our acts give rise to habits. The fundamental truth of ethics, we are told in the *Traité de Morale*, is that acts produce habits, and habits produce acts (*OCM* XI 51). And there can be no doubt that our habits, our *dispositions intérieurs*, are modifications of our souls. So if our acts are so much as occasional causes of our dispositions, they are as 'physically real' as any of the other modifications of our souls. Of course our acts of assent do not act by their own efficacy on the substance of our souls – that would be inconsistent with continuous creation. But if they serve as reliable, lawlike occasional causes of modifications that are 'physically real' in Malebranche's sense, it is hard to see how he can consistently maintain that they contain in themselves 'rien de physique'.

Malebranche, it is clear, needs a sharp conceptual distinction between the moral and the physical. But how are the moral 'acts' of the soul to be conceived? With the aid of some later authors, we might see what we can make of his doctrine. Perhaps the moral acts of the soul stem from Kantian imperatives of pure practical reason, grounded in a noumenal self that somehow escapes ordinary causality? Or perhaps they are second-order volitions in the manner of Harry Frankfurt?[45] The Kantian owes us an account of moral character, of how it is that people 'internalise' the demands of pure practical reason in such a way as to render their first-order volitions compatible with the moral law. As for Frankfurt's non-Kantian theory of second-order volitions, it is hard to see why we shouldn't regard them too as simply part of nature, i.e. as part and parcel of the empirical psychology of complex and reflective beings like ourselves. But as parts of nature they would be, for Malebranche, further modes of the soul, and would therefore fall under CC(DM).

My reluctant conclusion is that Malebranche can't have it both ways, and that his account of free will, for all its undoubted ingenuity, falls into inconsistency.[46] If Malebranche is to accept – in accordance with good Aristotelian wisdom and common sense – that our moral acts produce dispositions, it is hard to see how he can simultaneously continue to claim that such acts produce 'rien de physique', bring about no new modifications of our souls. One might ask him whether he believes there is such a thing as character. The model of a balance with a shifting fulcrum suggests a positive answer. One man can resist a stronger temptation than another, or can do good works with a smaller gift of grace, because of the position of the fulcrum in the balance of his soul. Is the position of the fulcrum something that is up to us? We cannot, of course, shift it by an isolated act of will – if we could, virtue would be easy, even for the habitual sinner. But we can, Malebranche thinks, take steps both to weaken the grip of sin and to aid the operation of grace when it arrives. This looks like a *bona fide* natural power, and leads us back into paradox. To admit natural powers, Malebranche has told us, is to fall into idolatry. But to deny this particular natural power is to portray God as a cruel and arbitrary tyrant. There seems to be no consistent position available for Malebranche.

10

THE DOWNFALL OF MALEBRANCHISM

The aim of this concluding chapter is to document some of the unresolved tensions and contradictions in Malebranche's thought, and thus to shed light on the way in which his work was received in the eighteenth century. Malebranche himself was a conservative thinker, but in seeking to propound rational arguments for opinions that had previously rested on faith and authority, he exposed those opinions to intense critical scrutiny. Arguments tend to take on lives of their own, independent of the intentions of their creators. One philosopher thinks he has good grounds for a proposition p, sees that p entails q, and infers q by *modus ponens*. Another philosopher finds q incredible (perhaps in the plain literal sense of the word), sees that p implies q, and infers not-p by *modus tollens*. This, as we shall see, is more or less the relation between Malebranche and Hume.

Malebranche's role in the early enlightenment would make an interesting case study. Intellectual historians of the period[1] portray him as a conservative figure of the 'moderate' enlightenment. This seems broadly correct, at least as regards his intention of constructing a philosophy both truly Christian and compatible with the new science. But the same intellectual historians emphasise the role of Pierre Bayle as one of the founding fathers of the 'radical' enlightenment. Yet the debt of Bayle to Malebranche is immense, and would be very easy to document in detail. It was Malebranche who took the bold step of subjecting Christian dogma to close rational scrutiny, insisting that God must act in accordance with an Order that is – at least in principle – accessible to all minds.[2] On Malebranche's principles, laymen can ask Churchmen why God has acted in the manner described by Christian dogma, and can demand intelligible replies. Sceptical thinkers like Bayle pointed out the weaknesses of traditional Christian apologetics, concluded that faith and reason are incompatible, and recommended a retreat into sceptical fideism.[3] As genuine conservatives like Bossuet saw, the intellectual independence of the Cartesian tradition posed a threat to the authority of the Church.[4]

In this chapter, we shall pick up just a few of the unresolved tensions and outstanding difficulties left by Malebranche for the ongoing meditation of his readers. He tells us clearly, after all, that one should never take an author at his word, but should use his works as a stimulus to one's own meditations.[5] We shall therefore take up some Malebranchian themes – in epistemology, metaphysics, ethics and theology – with a view to seeing if his insights and arguments always support his own stated conclusions.

Epistemological difficulties

The limitations of a priori *knowledge*

Historians of philosophy have often divided seventeenth and eighteenth century philosophers into two warring camps, setting the 'Continental Rationalists' against the 'British Empiricists'. This is, of course, a grossly oversimplified picture, and one that may well have outlived its usefulness. It might be better to start with the traditional notion of a *science* as a body of knowledge capable of *a priori* demonstration from self-evident axioms or first principles, and then to ask, of any given philosopher, how many *sciences* in this strong sense he believes in. How much can be demonstrated *a priori*; how much must be left to the teachings of experience? At one extreme, we have the universally acknowledged paradigm of a *science*, Euclidean geometry. At the other extreme, we have the study of history, the empirical nature of which no rationalist would be so foolish as to deny. The interesting and contentious cases lie in between these extremes. A philosopher of rationalist persuasion might be characterised as one who is optimistic about the prospects of a *science* of, say, dynamics or psychology.

If we pose the problem in these terms, a case begins to emerge for seeing Malebranche as a closet empiricist, even as a precursor of Hume. The crucial passages are in the discussion of truth in Book Six of the *Recherche*. Truths, according to Malebranche, are relations, and these relations are of three kinds:

> There are those between ideas, between things and their ideas, and between things only. It is true that twice two is four – here is a truth between ideas. It is true that the sun exists – this is a truth between a thing and its idea. It is true that the earth is larger than the moon – here is a truth that is only between things.
>
> (*OCM* II 286–7, LO 433)

Of these three types of truths, Malebranche continues, only those of the first type (relations of ideas) are eternal and immutable. Ideas are timelessly present in the divine intellect, and are therefore themselves eternal and immutable. All creatures are however liable to change. So relations between ideas are eternal and immutable; relations between ideas and things, or relations between things, are changeable. It follows, says Malebranche, that only those sciences dealing exclusively with relations of ideas can be *a priori*:

> Thus, we use the mind alone to try to discover only truths between ideas, for we almost always employ the senses to discover the other sorts of truths. We use our eyes and our hands to assure ourselves of the existence of things, and to recognise the relations of equality and inequality between them. Relations of ideas are the only ones the mind can know infallibly and by itself without the use of the senses.
>
> (*OCM* II 287, LO 434)

Geometry, arithmetic and algebra provide our existing paradigms of *sciences* based on relations of ideas, but Malebranche foresaw an enormous expansion of such knowledge, and played a prominent role at the heart of a group of French mathematicians who were teaching the new differential and integral calculus of Leibniz and Jean Bernoulli.[6] He also predicted that a vast new territory of 'relations of relations' was opening up to mathematical investigation. None of these disciplines, however, deal with what Hume would later call matters of fact and real existence.

What other *sciences* does Malebranche envisage as either existent or at least possible in principle for humans? The disciplines of metaphysics and axiology (theory of value) spring to mind. As regards the former, Malebranche is in no doubt that we possess at least the rudiments of such a *science*.[7] In Book Four of the *Recherche*, for example, he complains that metaphysics is so neglected that some people are foolish enough to deny even common notions:

> There are even some who deny that we can and should assert of a thing what is included in the clear and distinct idea we have of it; that nothingness has no properties; that a thing cannot be reduced to nothing without a miracle; that no body can move itself by its own forces; that an agitated body cannot communicate to bodies with which it collides more motion than it possesses,

and other such things. They have never considered these axioms from a viewpoint clear and focused enough to discover their truth clearly.

(*OCM* II 90, LO 315)

These axioms would never suffice to ground a *science* of real existence; they serve rather as *a priori* constraints on intelligible theorising about the real. Of the five axioms Malebranche cites here, the first four can plausibly be regarded as concerning relations of ideas, and hence as analytic, in our terms. Only the fifth looks suspiciously like an act of trespass on the empirical domain.[8] If 'communicate' is read in occasionalist terms, there seems no reason why the supposed axiom must be true. God could presumably create super-elastic bodies, and thus produce a universe that speeds up through the collisions between such bodies.

As for axiology, Malebranche is perfectly explicit that there are objective relations of value (degrees of perfection) between things, and that these are in principle knowable by us. We can see that God is (infinitely) more valuable than an individual human soul, and that a human soul is more valuable than its body. It would be a violation of Order, therefore, if God were to care more about His creatures than about His own perfection, e.g. if He were to work miracles to save particular sinners from either physical or moral evil. It would equally be a violation of Order for a human soul to submit itself entirely to the needs of its body, e.g. to assume that we have minds in order to find food and drink for our bodies.[9] Once again, however, the science of axiology tells us nothing about real existence. Having the ideas of a man and a dog, I can see that a man is more valuable than a dog, but only experience teaches me that men and dogs exist at all.

When we ask questions concerning real existence, according to Malebranche, we are addressing questions that concern not just God's intellect (in which we participate through the Vision in God) but also His will.[10] In the third of the *Méditations Chrétiennes*, the Word explains to the meditator which of his questions will be answered and which will not. Attention is a sort of natural prayer, and a prayer of this kind is always answered, provided certain conditions are met:

... provided that it is made with attention and with perseverance; provided they [men] ask of me what they are in a condition to receive from me; and finally, provided they ask what I possess in my capacity of wisdom and eternal truth.

(*OCM* X 30)

The final clause rules out any attempt on our parts to discover contingent truths *a priori*. Contingent truths depend on God's will, not just on His intellect. There is therefore no possibility of our coming to know them simply by interrogating the Word in meditation. We can do mathematics in this way, but not physics or psychology.[11] Malebranche thus consistently denies the possibility of a rational *science* of psychology, and gradually comes to see the impossibility of a corresponding *science* of physics. As we saw in Chapter Six, he eventually abandoned the Cartesian programme of deriving the laws of motion from first principles. The laws of motion of our world, he came to realise, depend on the type of body God has chosen to create. We can proceed by a hypothetico-deductive method, setting out the laws for, e.g. perfectly elastic bodies, but ultimately we must consult experience to confirm that God has made bodies of this kind. It will be the same for psychology: the infinite intellect of God will doubtless contain blueprints for many types of created soul; which type He has chosen to actualise is determined by His will rather than His intellect alone.

Malebranche even goes so far, at one point, to call God's choice (of one type of body rather than another) 'purely arbitrary' (*OCM* XVII–1 55). This offended Leibniz, and cannot represent Malebranche's considered view.[12] God always acts for reasons, and in accordance with the requirements of Order. The creation of our universe is, for Malebranche, the best expression of the divine attributes, like a maximisation problem in the calculus. So there will be an *a priori* derivation of our actual universe from the divine attributes – it will be a better expression of God's perfections than any possible rival. Nowhere in Malebranche's work, however, is there the slightest hint that such an *a priori* route from God's perfections to the details of His creation is accessible to us. He would say, presumably, that for mere humans to propose such a method would be presumptuous. We don't know, perhaps, all of God's perfections, nor exactly how each would best be expressed in creation, nor again the principles determining how the expression of each divine perfection is weighed against the expression of others. If God's wisdom and immutability require that He act by universal laws, while His benevolence extends to individual creatures, we can ask how much potential suffering on the part of His creatures would prompt Him to work a miracle on their behalf, but we should not expect an answer.

Natural judgements

The chapters on the senses in Book One of the *Recherche* present a detailed and carefully worked out account of sensation and its relation to judgement. We see things, according to Malebranche, not as they are in themselves but in accordance with the needs of our bodies (*OCM* I 77–8, LO 24). The proper function of the senses is to inform the soul regarding the needs of the body by means of the 'short way' of sensation, without any need of tedious and difficult calculations on our part. So the sweet taste of a fruit is a reliable sign that it will be good for us to eat, so long as our tastes remain simple and uncorrupted. A man in good health would do better to trust his own senses, when it comes to questions of diet and exercise, than to consult the most learned physicians (*OCM* III 182, LO 645). In creating my organs of taste and establishing the laws of the mind–body union God has given me, as it were, the conclusions of a process of chemical analysis without the premises.[13] Likewise when I see the sizes, shapes, distances and motions of surrounding bodies, God provides me with visual sensations which contain such 'natural judgements' as integral parts of the sensation itself. I don't calculate sizes and distances from information about the images of bodies on my retinas; the calculations are all, as it were, done for me. God doesn't, of course, perform billions of such calculations every second. He merely creates human sense organs and brains, and establishes a law to the effect that whenever human brains are stimulated in manner Φ, the associated human mind will have sensation Ψ. I simply open my eyes and find myself spontaneously making natural judgements about the bodies around me. Just as my sense of taste gives me the conclusions of a chemical analysis without the premises and the reasoning, so my sense of vision gives me the conclusions of a lot of complex optics and geometry without my needing to do any of the calculations myself.[14]

Malebranche's theory of natural judgements is highly sophisticated and perceptive in its own right, and consistent with much of what we now know about perception from evolutionary biology and cognitive psychology. He notices, for example, the phenomenon now known as size constancy. Suppose a man walks towards me, advancing from a distance of 10 feet to a mere 5 feet away. The image of the man on my retinas will double in size. But I don't see him as twice as tall; my perceptual system 'corrects' for the assumed reduction of distance (*OCM* I 97, LO 34). Malebranche also gives an account of the moon illusion – why the moon appears larger at the horizon than when directly overhead – which anticipates much modern thinking on the topic.[15] But our purpose in this section is not to praise Malebranche but to criticise him, and criticism must begin with his account of the role of the will in these natural judgements of sense.

In one sense, it must be obvious that the natural judgements of sense are involuntary. They occur, as Malebranche says again and again, 'en nous', but 'sans nous, et même malgré nous' (*OCM* XV 15). My soul, he insists, doesn't perform dizzying feats of calculation or chemical analysis every time I hit a cricket ball or taste an apple. In the first place, introspection reveals no such processes. In the second place, I know that my soul simply doesn't have the necessary mathematical and chemical competence. The sensations – and their inherent natural judgements – are brought about in my soul by processes beyond my control, ultimately by God through the established laws of the mind–body union.

But if our natural judgements are involuntary, what are we to say about the cases – which are frequent – where they are erroneous? An essential part of Malebranche's message in the *Recherche* is the Cartesian account of error, borrowed from *Meditation Four*, which holds that our errors are our own fault, and result from our misuse of our free will. When we assent to a proposition not clearly and distinctly perceived to be true, says Descartes, we abuse our free will and risk falling into error. But if the natural judgements of sense are involuntary, this account is undermined and the wisest of men will have no way of guarding against error.

In answer to this objection, Malebranche seeks to distinguish four things present in each sensation, but often confused by sloppy and superficial thinkers. We must distinguish, he tells us, between (1) the action of the object on the sense organ, (2) the passion in the sense organ, (3) the sensation itself, and (4) the judgement(s) made by the soul. In fact, he goes on to explain, there are two judgements involved in most sensations:

> Now this natural judgement is only a sensation, but the sensation or natural judgement is almost always followed by another, free judgement that the soul makes so habitually that it is almost unable to avoid it.
>
> (*OCM* I 130, LO 52)

The word 'almost' is clearly important here. If we couldn't help but assent to the natural judgements of sense, we would have no protection against their in-built errors. What Malebranche has in mind, it seems, is a vision of a rational and autonomous self that can, as it were 'bracket' the deliverances of sense.[16] They are still recognised and acknowledged: introspection tells me clearly that no acquisition of theoretical knowledge eliminates natural judgement. (I could write a book on the psychology of the moon illusion and still find myself subject to it.) But my rational self refuses to commit itself to the truth (as opposed to the biological utility) of such judgements.

The obvious objection Malebranche faces at this point concerns the reality of this supposed power of refusing assent to natural judgements. He admits himself that it is extremely difficult to do this consistently, and that we are 'almost' unable to restrain ourselves. Delete the word 'almost', and Malebranche's theory of natural judgements is transformed into Hume's. If as Hume says 'nature, by an absolute and uncontrollable necessity has determin'd us to judge as well as to breathe and feel',[17] then any advice to the effect that I ought to refuse my assent and suspend judgement will be idle. The supposed power of the rational autonomous self will be an illusion, and the sort of doubts about the senses recommended alike by Malebranche and the sceptics will be unthinkable, except perhaps as amusing pastimes in the philosopher's study.

By way of example, let us consider one extremely important subject on which natural beliefs clash with philosophical reflection. Malebranche is a firm and committed advocate of the Cartesian doctrine that animals are insentient machines, supporting it with a variety of metaphysical and theological arguments. But he also notices that the contrary natural belief is impossible to eliminate altogether:

> I even suffer when a dog, which I believe to have no soul at all, says to my senses or to me by way of my senses, that it is suffering pain, and that it has need of my help: because God has connected all His works to one another for their mutual conservation, in a sure manner that one cannot too much admire.
>
> (*OCM* VI 104–5)

Although the belief in animal souls is a vulgar error, it can never be eliminated – even in philosophers, far less in the vulgar – because it is a natural belief resulting from the bonds of sympathy God has established between His creatures.[18] (Why God should have wished us to be prone to this error is a further question.) But a rational being cannot hold two contradictory opinions at the same time, while being aware of the contradiction. Malebranche will say that his firm opinion is that the dog is not feeling pain, and that the natural belief 'the dog feels pain' is present in his soul but only 'bracketed' and not endorsed. Hume, we can imagine, will ask which of the contrary beliefs affects Malebranche's emotions, and determines his resulting actions. If Malebranche is visibly distressed by the dog's howls, and takes the trouble to remove its paw from the trap, then he really believes the dog is in pain, his verbal protestations to the contrary notwithstanding.

Malebranche's doctrine of natural judgements was developed and articulated within the context of a supernatural metaphysics and morality. The natural man must be taken proper account of, for Malebranche, if we are to understand our limitations and our potential, but the natural man is not the whole man. His problem is that by admitting that natural judgements are involuntary and effectively ineradicable, he leaves a position that positively lends itself to a transformation into Humean naturalism. The fully autonomous rational self that can elevate itself above 'mere' nature is dismissed as a fantasy, and replaced by a more metaphysically modest vision of the human condition.

Metaphysical difficulties

The slide into idealism

Malebranche never tires of reminding his readers that the proper home of the soul is the *monde intelligible*, distinct from the world of bodies. When we open our eyes, it is an intelligible sun that is the immediate object of our experience, not the material sun. The experience of seeing the sun, he tells us clearly in Book One of the *Recherche*, is independent of the actual existence of any material object (*OCM* I 159, LO 69). The point is made still more forcefully in *Éclaircissement* VI, in which Malebranche discusses the difficulty of proving the existence of bodies. Of course, he admits in response to an obvious objection, I seem to perceive a world of bodies. But such experience – or rather, the natural judgements closely associated with it – may be deceptive:

> Let us be careful here: the material world we animate is not the one we see when we look at it, i.e. when we turn the body's eyes toward it. The body we see is an intelligible body and there are intelligible spaces between this intelligible body and the intelligible sun we see, just as there are material spaces between our body and the sun we look at.
>
> (*OCM* III 61, LO 572–3)

Likewise when we are aware of our own bodies in sensation it is intelligible arms and legs that we experience, not material ones. The argument is most clearly set out in the second of the *Entretiens sur la Mort* (*OCM* XIII 385–415). A man who has lost an arm or leg can still feel pain there, and thus still possesses an 'ideal' arm or leg which is the object of his experience. The ideal arm cannot be nothing at all – *qua* direct or immediate object of experience, it must possess some reality. To perceive nothing is not to perceive at all. So the ideal arm has a real existence in its own right. This argument from phantom limbs proves that the soul is not immediately united to its body or to the material world but rather to the idea of its body, and thus to the intelligible world:

> It is an intelligible or ideal arm which causes pain not only to an amputee, but which caused your own pain when I grasped your arm roughly.

> (*OCM* XIII 409)

We have already discussed, in Chapter Three, Nadler's attempt to rescue Malebranche from the accusation that he holds a theory of indirect or representative realism, and is thus vulnerable to veil of ideas scepticism. Nadler's interpretation of the Vision in God, we concluded, was ingenious, and had some notable virtues. (Nadler is surely right to emphasise the intellectual nature of Malebranche's ideas, and thus to distance his theory from the sense data theories of the empiricist tradition). But his account as a whole fails to do justice to too many of the texts,[19] and flies in the face of the universal interpretation of Malebranche's own contemporaries.

Bodies, Malebranche insists time and time again, can never act on our minds, can never be a source of light to us. In *Éclaircissement* X he tells us frankly that he would rather be ridiculed as a 'visionary' than admit either that bodies can act on the mind, or that the mind can be the source of its own ideas (*OCM* III 128, LO 613). But if bodies never act on souls, and all our sensations are directly caused by God, why does He need to bother with bodies at all? It is this lack of any causal action of bodies on minds that leads Locke, in particular, to accuse Malebranche of idealism. It is not that he thinks indirect or representative realism in general liable to collapse into idealism; it is a particular objection against Malebranche's occasionalist version of indirect realism. How, asks Locke, does Malebranche know that there is any such real being as the sun?

> Did he ever see the sun? No, but on occasion of the presence of the sun to his eyes, he has seen the idea of the sun in God, which God has exhibited to him; but the sun, because it cannot be united to his soul, he cannot see. How then does he know there is a sun which he never saw? And since God does all

things by the most compendious ways, what need is there that God should make a sun that we might see its idea in him when he pleased to exhibit it, when this might as well be done without any real sun at all.[20]

Why did God bother to create a world of bodies, if it is completely redundant? This question is posed in the eleventh of the *Méditations Chrétiennes*. God must act, the Word replies, in a manner that expresses His attributes. Bodies serve as occasional causes of our perceptions, and it is fitting for God to act by general laws rather than by particular volitions (*OCM* X 120). But this doesn't get to the heart of the problem. Why should a general law be a psychophysical law rather than a purely psychological one? Surely God could equally act by simple and universal laws by ordaining that the experiences of souls will follow regular and mutually co-ordinated patterns, without needing to create bodies at all? A body cannot act on God to prompt Him to act on our souls. An omniscient Being needs no reminders. It is hard to see, then, what bodies actually do, and why God should have any use for them. The God of Berkeley is no less regular and lawlike in His operations than the God of Malebranche.

To this reader, Malebranche seems actually to flirt with idealism. He insists that our experiences are of a *monde intelligible*, distinct from the *monde matériel* of vulgar belief. He employs textbook versions of the argument from illusion to illustrate his position (e.g. *OCM* IV 72–3, *OCM* XV 9). He admits frankly that it is very hard to prove the existence of bodies, and is not unhappy to be ridiculed as a 'visionary'. He tells us that an exact knowledge of ethics and even of physics is possible without a proof of the existence of bodies (*OCM* II 373, LO 482). He vigorously denies that bodies can act on souls, and provides them with a role in perception – as occasional causes only – which can easily be seen to be redundant. He addresses the objection explicitly, but provides only the feeblest of replies. In Britain, where Malebranche's works were widely read in the 1690s and 1700s, George Berkeley and Arthur Collier both arrived – independently – at idealist conclusions. The coincidence appears less striking, as Stuart Brown remarks, if we remember that both men were heavily influenced by Malebranche.[21] The Jesuit editors of the *Journal de Trévoux* – no friends of Malebranche – were quick to spot the connection:

Mr Berkeley, Malebranchist of good faith, has bluntly advanced the principles of his sect far beyond common sense, and he has concluded from them that there is no body, no matter, and that minds alone exist.

(*OCM* XIX 834)

244

Impenetrability and the powers of matter

In the course of Fontenelle's *Doutes* about occasionalism, he emphasised the role of impenetrability in our conception of the nature of bodies. In contact action, he argued, our minds perceive a 'natural and necessary connection' between contact and impulsion (*OCM* XVII–1 588). The special intelligibility of this type of causal relation (as contrasted with action at a distance) shows, he argues, that our minds have insight into at least one genuine power of bodies. In virtue of its impenetrability, any body has the power to resist the motion of another. Such a power, Fontenelle suggests, is conceptually inseparable from our notion of a body.

In our discussion of this problem in Chapter Five we sketched two different occasionalist responses. The first admits that impenetrability is a genuine power, but adds that mere impenetrability does not suffice to determine the laws of collision. Two colliding bodies cannot both continue to move undisturbed and pass smoothly through one another, but their mutual impenetrability alone doesn't determine how the motion of each body will alter in speed and direction. On this view, impenetrability in itself is a strangely indeterminate power until supplemented by the divinely established laws of collision.

The more robust and rigorous reply for the occasionalist is to insist that impenetrability itself is only an 'institution', i.e. a product of the divinely established laws of motion and collision. On this view, our conception of what it is to be a body may include impenetrability, but the existence of bodies at all depends on God's ordinance of those laws. It is not that bodies have this power by their nature, if by 'nature' we mean something like the Aristotelians' 'inner principle of motion and rest'. Such a 'nature' is a mere chimera. Rather, we can talk about the 'nature' of bodies only because God acts in regular and reliable ways. But this occasionalist account of bodies faces two profound objections.

In the first place, there is the obvious problem regarding the consistency of occasionalism with our natural beliefs. Long before Hume, Malebranche notices our tendency to confuse regular succession with necessary connection, and laments the errors into which such habits lead us.[22] Bayle too, in his defence of Malebranche against Fontenelle, notes the same habit or tendency. We are, he says, drawn by nature to confuse concomitants with true causes (OCM XVII–1 591). But if such natural beliefs are ineradicable, occasionalism may be literally incredible. Malebranche warns his readers that God, and not the apple, is the true cause of the pleasant sensation of sweetness. But if we have always experienced that sensation when eating an apple, and never otherwise, we may find ourselves with a powerful conviction that the apple is the true cause. Malebranche, of course, is perfectly aware that his message will often fall on deaf ears. He knows that the voice of nature is strong, and that it is hard for fallen humans to resist it. In the final analysis, we find ourselves back with the problem already discussed in the previous section. Is there a rational autonomous self, capable of 'bracketing' the natural judgments of sense; or is such rational autonomy a mere delusion?

The other profound difficulty raised by Fontenelle's objection concerns the relation between a substance and its powers. Bodies, in Malebranche's metaphysics, *are* something but don't *do* anything. God, it seems, could create a world of bodies (portions of three-dimensional extension) and then wonder what to do with them, i.e. what laws to impose on them to govern their motions. After God has established a system of laws we can talk about the powers of bodies (e.g. inertia, impenetrability). We can even, at this stage, say that it is in the 'nature' of a body to continue moving in a straight line, and to resist penetration by other bodies, but this 'nature' is merely a *façon de parler*, a shorthand way of talking about God's operations. But this only raises in the most acute form the question of what a body *is* in itself, independent of such operations. This helps to make sense of Leibniz's accusation that Malebranche's theory involves a 'perpetual miracle'. Without an intelligible connection between what a thing is and what it does, Leibniz argues, the very notion of a created substance makes no sense.[23]

Ethical difficulties

Disinterested love

For Malebranche, as we have seen, there is a perfectly objective science of axiology. This objective order of relations of perfection, he explains in *Éclaircissement* X, is precisely analogous to the objective order of relations of magnitude that provides the ontological ground for the necessary and eternal truths of mathematics:

> … just as there are necessary and eternal truths because there are relations of magnitude among intelligible beings, there must also be a necessary and immutable order because of the relations of perfection among these same things. An immutable order has it, then, that minds are more noble than bodies, as it is a necessary truth that twice two is four, or that twice two is not five.
>
> (*OCM* III 138, LO 618)

God perceives the precise degree of perfection of each of His creatures, and loves each – as Order requires – in precise proportion to its absolute worth. The intellectual perception of Order is therefore not merely something speculative; it has the force of law for the divine will:

> It must be considered, then, that God loves Himself with a necessary love, and that thus He loves what in Him represents or contains greater perfection more than what contains less – so much so that if we wish to suppose an intelligible mind to be a thousand times more perfect than an intelligible body, the love by which God loves Himself would necessarily be a thousand times greater for the intelligible mind than for the intelligible body; for God's love is necessarily proportionate to the Order among the intelligible beings He contains, since He necessarily loves His own perfections.
>
> (*OCM* III 138, LO 619)

The requirements of Order, one might naturally infer, *should* govern our loves as they *do* govern God's. If God does love everything in direct proportion to its worth, the obvious implication for human ethics is that we should do so, that we should make His will the model for ours[24]. In the *Recherche*, Malebranche seems content to accept this inference. In Book Four, for example, we find him claiming that 'God cannot will that the wills he has created should love a lesser good more than a greater good, i.e. that they should love more what is less lovable than what is more lovable' (*OCM* II 12, LO 266). And again in *Éclaircissement* X, the inference is explicitly endorsed:

> Now, this immutable Order that has the force of law with regard to God Himself clearly has the same force with regard to us. For, since God has created us in His image and likeness, He cannot will that we love more what deserves to be loved less – He wills that our will conform with His and that here below we freely and hence meritoriously render things the justice that He necessarily renders them.
>
> (*OCM* III 138–9, LO 619)

But can our finite minds ascend to the dizzy heights of God's absolute point of view? Is such an ascent possible – or even desirable? God, we must presume, loves His creation as the fullest and most perfect expression of His attributes. But this creation includes the eternal damnation of the majority of mankind, including perhaps myself. Can I continue to love

God and His works while caring no more about my own salvation than Order requires? And if every human soul is of roughly equal worth, it is surely better that 100 men are saved than that one man is. Should I then be willing to commit a mortal sin myself in order to prevent 100 other men falling into such a sin? If God loves everything in proportion to its worth, and His love is to be the model for mine, it seems that the answer must be affirmative.

Thoughts such as these led the Spanish mystic Miguel de Molinos (1640–97) to develop the doctrine of Quietism, with its central notion of a sort of spiritual selflessness, a love of God so intense and so overwhelming that it leads to a 'holy indifference' to one's own fate. Although Molinos was arrested for heresy, forced into a public retraction, and imprisoned by the Inquisition, his teachings spread through Spain and into France, where they made influential converts.[25] Although the 'excesses' of Quietism were denounced by the French bishops, Fénélon was converted, as was Malebranche's friend Lamy, who argued, in his *Connaissance de Soi Même*, for a 'disinterested' love of God, a love independent of any desire for one's own happiness. Lamy also claimed that Malebranche's principles were congenial to Quietism, and cited textual evidence in support of this claim. Malebranche thus found himself drawn into the public furore over Quietism, and was obliged to disassociate himself from what he regarded as a dangerous error. The result was his *Traité de l'Amour de Dieu* (1697–98). The Quietists' 'disinterested love', Malebranche there argues, is (a) chimerical, (b) morally dangerous, and (c) inconsistent with scripture.

We all, Malebranche begins, have an invincible desire for our own happiness, and are only capable of loving what we believe – rightly or wrongly – contributes to that happiness. Such self-love is natural and necessary, and of itself blameless; we become culpable only if we seek pleasure in the wrong things.[26] As for the love of happiness, that must be simply accepted as a given: 'Do not ask me why I want to be happy, ask that of Him who made me, since that does not depend at all on me. The love of blessedness is a natural impression: enquire of the Creator' (*OCM* XIV 16). This desire of happiness is the wellspring of all our loves, even those that are 'disinterested' in the common sense of the word. (I take pleasure in the virtues of my friend, and am willing to make sacrifices for his sake; the saints enjoy their contemplation of the divine perfections.) When Lamy speaks of a love that is perfectly disinterested he thus flies in the face of *sentiment intérieur*, and invents a mere chimera (*OCM* XIV 158).

Although the 'disinterested' love of the Quietists is non-existent, their teachings must still be denounced as dangerous. The disciple of the Quietists, Malebranche argues, is in peril of his soul:

> ... indifference for his blessedness, for his perfection, and for his happiness, is not only impossible, but it is very dangerous to pretend to it, because that can only inspire an infinite carelessness for his own salvation, which one must seek, as the Apostle said, with fear and trembling.
>
> (*OCM* XIV 27)

Scripture, Malebranche sees, is clearly against the Quietists, since it is full of threats and promises. It therefore presupposes self-love rather than seeking to abolish it. We are indeed told that we must be prepared to sacrifice our lives, but only with the promise of something better by way of recompense (*OCM* XIV 53).

God's will, Malebranche explains, is in accordance with the objective requirements of Order. But the rule for my will is not God's will; it is what God wills that I will:

> I say moreover that what God wills is not always the rule of what we must will. For example, God wills a hundred just men a hundred times more than a single one. However, I must will to be just preferably to a hundred [others]. For as the Apostle says, one must not do evil in order that good come of it. What God wills that we will, there is precisely our rule.
>
> (*OCM* XIV 17)

God, it appears, doesn't want us even to try to see things from His point of view, and has actually created us in such a way that it is impossible for us to do so.[27] The desire for happiness that governs all our loves is not something we can overcome; all we can do is regulate it in such a way that we find our happiness in our own perfection, i.e. in ever-greater union with God Himself. We must, Malebranche argues, love God with all our hearts, and this is strictly inconsistent with preferring the salvation of other men – even of all other men – to our own (*OCM* XIV 20). God wills that each human soul be perfect, but it can only achieve this perfection through union with Him; so each human soul must will such union above all else. In the realms of the spirit, it seems, selfishness is not a vice but a necessity.

The love of God

Christianity teaches us, according to Malebranche, that the great majority of human beings will be damned. He even goes so far as to suggest that only about twenty people in one thousand will be saved.[28] In the correspondence with Arnauld, he suggests the even lower figure of one in a hundred (*OCM* VII 493). From God's point of view, of course, all this is in accordance with Order, and thus acceptable. Our creation, encompassing the drama of the Fall and the Incarnation, is the best overall expression of the divine attributes. The temple will be built, and if some bricks are wasted, that is not a matter of sufficient importance to warrant special intervention. Christ's concern, in his capacity as architect of the temple, is for the building, not for the bricks (*OCM* V 82).

This is how things look from the absolute perspective of God. If we could adopt such a point of view, we would see why it is better that millions of men and women should suffer damnation than that God violate the *simplicité des voies* (*OCM* IV 46–7). No one can reproach God for loving His own wisdom more than He loves us – this is simply an objective requirement of Order (*OCM* V 187). God has done all that He can do – consistently with His attributes – for our benefit (*OCM* IX 1091–2). God is not merciful or benevolent in the vulgar sense of those terms, which lend themselves to anthropomorphism.[29]

The problem is, of course, that Malebranche has already told us that we can't see things from this exalted point of view. Each of us naturally and necessarily desires his or her own happiness, and will thus tend inevitably to love what promotes our well-being and to hate what frustrates it. Malebranche wants to help us to love God, he tells us in the prefatory letter to the *Traité de la Nature et de la Grâce* (*OCM* V 3–4), but his principles are almost as little conducive to that purpose as those of the Jansenists. Suppose you are offered a ticket in a lottery. There are a hundred tickets, and only one prize. Holders of the other ninety-nine tickets are subjected to intolerable torture. No one in their right minds would want a ticket. If forced to play the game, we would naturally come to hate its creator. Better not to play (i.e. never to exist at all) than to play on those terms.

If Pelagianism or semi-Pelagianism were true, the situation would be significantly better. Here, instead of a lottery, I am offered a prize for good behaviour, and know that I can win the prize by my own efforts. But Pelagianism is a heresy. On the Augustinian theory, I am offered a prize for good behaviour, but the task I am set to perform is beyond my powers. I can't perform my duty without divine assistance, and nothing I can do guarantees such assistance. Who would not hate to be put in such a situation? And if God has put such a burden on us against our will, how can we avoid hating God? Can Malebranche find a credible answer to this question? Does the account of providence in the *Traité* help us to love God?

On Malebranche's theory, Christ distributes grace according to the requirements of the temple, not the needs of individual men. I can prepare the ground, as it were, and co-operate with whatever gifts of grace I may receive, but I might still be passed over. If the temple requires ten thousand souls of type X, and my soul is of that type, my chances will depend on two factors: how many souls of type X there are altogether, and how many of those are suitably prepared and willing to co-operate. Suppose there are one hundred thousand souls of type X altogether. Then if all are willing, my chances are one in ten. If only half are willing, my chances go up to one in five. If only one in ten are willing, there is a sort of pre-established harmony between the supply of suitable souls and the demands of the temple, and I can effectively guarantee my own election. But Malebranche never hazards a guess about these numbers, and never gives his readers the least reason to suspect that this optimistic scenario is the true one. For all I could know, my soul might be one of a very common type, millions of which will be ignored in the building of the temple.

There is, it seems, little comfort or consolation for us in Malebranche's philosophical theology. God must act as Order requires. If we could ascend to His level, and appreciate the reasons – objectively good reasons, no doubt – we would see why so much human suffering in this life, and the eternal damnation of most men in the next, are all part and parcel of His creation. But Malebranche has told his readers explicitly that we can't adopt God's point of view, and that we should not try to do so. We all inevitably desire our own individual happiness, but this seems of little consequence to God. Ariste makes the objection, rather plaintively, in the twelfth of the *Entretiens*. Theodore has just set out Malebranche's account of providence, and explained that God makes use of general laws to shower blessings on His creatures. Ariste is not impressed:

> God made all the creatures for us, but some people have no bread. A providence which would furnish all equal natures equally or which would distribute good and evil exactly according to merit would be a true providence.
>
> (*OCM* XII 293, JS 229)

Such anthropomorphic notions of God, Theodore responds sternly, are inconsistent with the idea of a perfect being. Ariste is humbled and rebuked, but his objection won't go away. In the final analysis, we would prefer a God who cared less about His own perfections and more about the suffering of His creatures. The God of Malebranche may be admirable, but He is scarcely lovable.

Animal souls again

If Malebranche's God is not amiable, surely at least He is just? The sufferings of humans are all, we are told, the results of sin, and so deserved. But what of animal pain? Here Malebranche sees a further argument for the Cartesian doctrine of the *bête-machine* (*OCM* II 104, LO 323; *OCM* XIII 337).[30] The proof goes as follows:

1   There is a just God.
2   Animals are innocent of sin.
3   A just God would not permit the innocent to suffer.
∴4 Animals do not suffer.

Malebranche thinks that the demonstration is conclusive, but acknowledges that it will not be persuasive because its conclusion contradicts a natural belief. But the situation is worse than that. His argument actually lends itself to the following transformation by the atheist Baron d'Holbach.[31]

Not-4. Animals do suffer (natural belief).
2   Animals are innocent of sin.
3   A just God would not permit the innocent to suffer.
∴ Not-1: There is no just God.

If the natural belief in animal sentience is the genuine belief of all men – metaphysical and theological arguments to the contrary notwithstanding – then Malebranche has provided the atheists of the eighteenth century with a ready-made weapon to use against the belief in a just God.

Theological difficulties
The efficacy of prayer

Malebranche's conception of a God who is bound by His own perfections to act only – or almost only – by *volontés générales* provoked a storm of protests from more traditional Christians. One obvious point of attack was the efficacy of prayer. Bossuet, in his funeral oration for the Queen, takes the opportunity to launch a fierce denunciation of the recently-published *Traité de la Nature et de la Grâce*:

> How I despise those philosophers who, measuring the designs of God by their own thoughts, make Him only the author of a certain general order from which the rest develops as it can! As if He had, like us, general and confused views, and as if the sovereign intelligence could fail to understand in its designs particular things which, alone, truly exist.[32]

The same charge can be found in Chapter Fifteen of Fénelon's *Réfutation* of Malebranche's *Traité*. If, Fénelon argues, Order permits God only a limited (and small) number of interventions in the course of nature, prayers for natural goods will be futile.[33] The practice of prayer presupposes that God is free to grant or to refuse our petitions; but Malebranche tells us that a God who did thus intervene would be no God at all. The notion that God sends physical goods and evils as particular providences is, Fénelon warns, at the heart of Christian doctrine. 'If it is a vulgar error, it is an error that Scripture, that the entire tradition of the holy fathers has taught us, and that piety has rooted in all hearts'.[34]

Malebranche seeks to counter the objection in the first of the *Éclaircissements* added to later editions of the *Traité*. Some people, he notes, accuse me of denying the efficacy of prayer. On the contrary, he replies, if we are just, our prayers will be worthy ones; if they are worthy, Order requires that they be granted. As for sinners, they must pray to Christ for the gift of grace (*OCM* V 170–1). But this response is feeble.[35] It overlooks the all-important distinction between what God wills and what God wills that we will. Order requires that God establish Jesus Christ as head of the Church and occasional cause of the distribution of grace. But this grand design is indifferent to the needs of individual souls. What I will is not just that the temple be completed, but that I be part of it, and thus that I receive the necessary gifts of grace. Such spiritual selfishness, Malebranche has told us, is natural and necessary. So I naturally pray for myself, but Order requires only the salvation of a certain number of souls like mine. The objection stands.

As for public prayers within the Church, Malebranche's attitude is ambivalent. It was still, of course, common practice within the Church to pray for rain, for good harvests, for relief from the plague, and so on. In the eighth of the *Méditations Chrétiennes*, the meditator seeks some light on the dark topic of divine providence. It is tempting God, the Word replies, to pray for a miracle when natural means are at hand to relieve distress (*OCM* X 88). The sick man must go on a diet or consult his doctor; the farmer must cultivate his land. We honour God rightly when we honour His wisdom and His immutability, not when we think of Him in naïve and anthropomorphic terms. We must therefore seek His aid through the universal laws of nature, not through miracles. Only when all natural means have been exhausted, and one is in such peril that without a miracle all would be lost, is one permitted to pray for divine intervention (*OCM* X 86). There may be occasions on which God will intervene, but these will be 'assez rares', and will normally be for reasons connected with the order of grace, to which nature is subject (*OCM* V 34). Nowhere, Malebranche replies to Arnauld's objection, do I say that God never intervenes in the course of nature (*OCM* VII 503; *OCM* IX 1116).

The term 'miracle', the Word goes on to explain, is ambiguous. What we are praying for during a severe drought or in a medical crisis need not be a direct intervention by God Himself. We know from the Old Testament that He has appointed angels as vice-regents over parts of nature, their volitions serving as occasional causes of physical good and ill to humans. What He has done in the past He may continue to do. The point is repeated in the *Traité de Morale* (*OCM* XI 110), where it is used to justify public prayers within the Church. If there are many such divinely appointed occasional causes God could seem to answer our prayers without needing to stoop to particulars Himself.

Malebranche nowhere tells his readers whether he thinks the establishment of angels as occasional causes of natural goods and evils is widespread in our world. His emphasis, however, is perfectly clear, and was not lost on his readers. It is always on God's establishment of universal laws. He admits angels as occasional causes to accommodate the frequent miracles of the Old Testament (*OCM* V 197ff) not because he thinks our present world is similarly governed. The establishment of angels as occasional causes is admitted as a theoretical possibility only, a defensive bulwark against objections. The admission of many such second causes, although not strictly inconsistent with Malebranche's principles, is clearly contrary to the spirit of his system. The impious, says the Word, deny the existence of miracles; the pious seek, out of a proper respect for the divine wisdom, to diminish their number (*OCM* X 81).

The sacraments

Malebranche's account of the efficacy of the Christian sacraments reveals him at his weakest. It is hard sometimes to believe that the philosopher who could debate so boldly with Arnauld about the nature of ideas, or with Leibniz about the laws of motion, could be so timid and so conservative in his attitude to Catholic dogma. Voltaire's Quaker was exactly right: Malebranche was a bit of a Quaker, but not enough of one.[36] He was confident, of course, that reason and faith come from the same source – the Word of God – and therefore cannot contradict one another. Apparent contradictions must therefore be shown to be misunderstandings, taking something to be the voice of reason, or the deliverance of faith, when in fact it is only a fallible human opinion or authority. But this confidence in a harmony of faith and reason can lead in either of two opposite directions. One can seek to blunt one's own moral and metaphysical intuitions, and use all the intellectual resources at one's disposal – including sophistry and blatant special pleading – to bring 'reason' into line with faith. Or one can use one's rational insights as a way of purifying faith, rejecting as merely human accretions whatever elements of religion appear unintelligible or morally indefensible. Fénélon accuses Malebranche of taking the second path, of subordinating Christian theology to philosophy.[37] I would accuse him of exactly the opposite fault, of trying vainly to rationalise too much of Christian dogma. His discussion of the sacraments amply illustrates this contention.

We have already discussed, in Chapter Seven, Malebranche's account of the transmission of original sin from mother to child. The soul of every new-born baby, Malebranche tells us in the lengthy *Éclaircissement* VIII of the *Recherche*, is in a 'disordered' state, its thoughts turned towards the needs of its body rather than to its Creator (*OCM* III 71–118, LO 579–606). In the sacrament of baptism, the grip of sensuality is weakened, and the soul becomes capable of a free – and hence meritworthy – love of God. There is therefore a 'true regeneration' and 'real justification' (*OCM* III 82, LO 586) of the infant's soul, which in turn can give rise to a virtuous habit or disposition. God could, of course, produce this habit or disposition directly, but Malebranche clearly prefers his own hypothesis – of an actual love of God in the infant's soul rather than a mere change in its dispositions. It is only prejudice, he replies to an objection, which tells us that the souls of infants are incapable of such an actual love of God (*OCM* III 116, LO 605). As for the unbaptised infant, its thoughts are all of the body; it has no love of God to counter concupiscence. Such an infant, we are told in the *Conversations Chrétiennes*, is a 'child of wrath', bound inevitably for damnation (*OCM* IV 100). The message is softened a little in the *Méditations Chrétiennes*, where we are told that the souls of new-born infants, although forever deprived of the heritage of the elect, will at least suffer no pain (*OCM* X 220).

Malebranche is keen to insist that the soul of the infant is justified before God by its own actual love – he rejects any account which relies on a merely 'imputed' virtue (*OCM* III 82–3, LO 586). But what relation can there be between the splashing of water on the baby's head by the priest, and the supposed changes in its soul? How could a just God, the freethinkers will ask, operate in such an arbitrary and palpably unjust manner? Baby A dies immediately after baptism; baby B dies on its way to church. Why should B be punished for a misfortune that was clearly not its fault? Charles and Christine are Catholics (though vain and worldly at heart, conforming merely for reasons of convenience); Derek and Deborah are Anabaptists, devout Christians who believe that undergoing baptism must be the action of a responsible adult. Both couples lose their babies. Why should baby C do any better than baby D? Is God going to punish infants for the theoretical beliefs of their parents?

A similar story is told of the efficacy of communion in Chapter Eight of the *Traité de Morale* (*OCM* XI 91–106). When one takes communion, Malebranche explains, the actual love of Order is changed into a habitual love as a result of the standing volition of Jesus Christ. To bring about the remission of sins and make the soul of the sinner agreeable to God, a fleeting mental act (perception and love of Order) is not sufficient; only a permanently virtuous disposition can justify a man before God. Absolution must therefore change the act into a habit; it is this power of absolution and the remission of sins which was possessed by Christ and transmitted by him to his disciples – i.e. to the Church.

Unfortunately for Malebranche, this account seems liable to many of the same objections as we levelled against his discussion of baptism. Admittedly, one major difficulty is set aside if we suppose we are dealing with adults coming to church of their own free will, rather than with babies being brought for baptism by their parents. But even here we can imagine one man being killed going into church and another on his way out. Or we can contrast the merely conventional and worldly Catholic who takes communion frequently with someone of more doubts and scruples, who takes communion more rarely. Or again we can ask the fate of non-Catholic Christians, or even of non-Christians. A God who would favour Tartuffe over Socrates or Akbar because of accidental reasons of history or geography is not a God worthy of our worship. The idea that the clergy – specifically, the Roman Catholic clergy – have in their hands this tremendous power of remission of sins is simply not one that reason can endorse.

Malebranche's influence

Malebranche's fame and reputation reached its highest point around 1700.[38] The persecution suffered by the young Cartesian philosopher at the hands of his superiors in the Oratory was now behind him. The Oratorians knew that they were dealing with an international celebrity, and treated him accordingly. Malebranche's modest cell attracted visits from foreign scholars and dignitaries – even the exiled King James II paid a courtesy call. To be sure, Malebranche's major works found themselves on the index of prohibited books,[39] but this was simply due to the machinations of his enemies, and in any case the power of the Roman Inquisition in France was strictly limited.

Meanwhile, his influence continued to spread throughout the learned world. In England, two translations of the *Recherche* and two of the *Traité* appeared in the 1690s, and one might almost speak of a school of English Malebranchians. John Norris (1657–1711), Thomas Taylor (1669–1735?), and Arthur Collier (1680–1732) all drew heavily on the work of Malebranche.[40] In Ireland, we can find a reading group at Trinity College discussing Malebranche's works.[41] It would not be hard to document similar lines of influence in Holland, Germany and Italy.[42] Malebranche was one of the central figures in what has been called the 'moderate' enlightenment,[43] building on the 'clear and distinct ideas' of Descartes, but seeking to use a broadly Cartesian philosophy to defend Christianity rather than to undermine it.

By 1750, the picture had changed dramatically. Philosophers had become sceptical about the pretensions of *a priori* metaphysics, and suspicious of the great system-builders of the previous century. The empiricism of Locke and the science of Newton were all the rage. Meanwhile, the more radical currents of the enlightenment were gathering in strength, and giving rise to deism and even to atheism. To such thinkers, Malebranche could only be a transitional figure, useful perhaps as a source of arguments that could be turned against Christian orthodoxy (e.g. Holbach on animal suffering) but not to be taken seriously in his own right. Let us take a moment to document these changes.

In England, the backlash can be said to begin with publication of Locke's *Examination* of *Père Malebranche's Opinion of Seeing all Things in God*. Originally intended as a chapter of the *Essay Concerning Human Understanding*, the *Examination* eventually appeared in 1706 in a posthumous collection of Locke's works.[44] Locke dismisses the Vision in God as completely unintelligible, and rejects Malebranche's eliminative argument for it as broken backed, resting as it must on the assumption that we have listed all possible ways in which we can have ideas of objects.[45] There are, Locke concludes, 'enthusiasms' in philosophy as there are in religion; Malebranche's fame will prove, he predicts, just a passing fashion.

The influence of Malebranche on Berkeley has already been documented in some detail by scholars such as Luce[46] and McCracken.[47] Some of Berkeley's arguments – e.g. for the causal redundancy of matter – owe a manifest debt to Malebranche. Berkeley took some pains, however, to deny that he was a mere disciple, notably in Philonous' explicit disclaimer in the *Second Dialogue*:

> I shall not therefore be surprised if some men imagine that I run into the enthusiasm of Malebranche; though in truth I am very remote from it. He builds on the most abstract general ideas, which I entirely disclaim. He asserts an absolute external world, which I deny. He maintains that we are deceived by our senses, and know not the real natures or the true forms and figures of extended things; of all which I hold the direct contrary. So that upon the whole, there are no Principles more fundamentally opposite than his and mine.[48]

A similar pattern emerges when we turn from Berkeley to Hume. It would be easy to show in detail the influence of Malebranche on Hume's views on causation, on the self, and so on. The crucial difference, as we have seen, concerns their respective attitudes to natural beliefs. Malebranche wants us to pay close attention to them because they are the source of important errors in metaphysics and in morality; Hume thinks that nature is (fortunately) too strong for reason. In Section Seven of the *Enquiry*, for example, he dismisses occasionalism as literally incredible:

> First, it seems to me that this theory of the universal energy and operation of the Supreme Being is too bold ever to carry conviction with it to a man, sufficiently apprized of the weakness of human reason, and the narrow limits to which it is confined in all its operations. Though the chain of arguments which conduct to it were ever so logical, there must arise a strong suspicion, if

not an absolute assurance, that it has carried us quite beyond the reach of our faculties, when it leads to conclusions so extraordinary, and so remote from common life and experience. We are got into fairy land, long ere we have reached the last steps of our theory; and *there* we have no reason to trust our common methods of argument, or to think that our usual analogies and probabilities have any authority.[49]

Turning back to the French-speaking world, we find a similar pattern. Malebranche is still widely read, and his works are frequently pillaged for arguments that could be put to the uses of other authors. He is admired for his lucidity, but his system, with its delicate and elaborate balance of elements drawn from Augustinian Christianity and Cartesian rationalism, was regarded as a mere house of cards. Bayle, for example, owed a great debt to Malebranche, and was never slow to express his admiration for the author of the *Recherche* and the *Traité*. In the article 'Paulicans', however, he denies that any philosopher or theologian – including Malebranche – has provided a satisfactory solution to the problem of evil.[50] And in the article 'Manicheans' and the following *Éclaircissement* he casts doubts on the attempts of Malebranche and others to rationalise Christianity.[51] What is above reason, he warns, cannot be comprehended and explained by reason; the proper attitude for the Christian should be a sort of sceptical fideism.

The *philosophes* of the French enlightenment had little time for Malebranche. In Condillac's *Traité des Systèmes* (1749) he merits a chapter, but it is mostly devoted to accusations of unclarity and equivocation, sophistry and word-play. Malebranche knew the human condition, Condillac admits, but was more poet than philosopher:

Malebranche was one of the finest minds of the last century: but unfortunately his imagination had too much sway over him. He saw only by its means, and believed he was hearing the responses of uncreated wisdom, of universal reason, of the Word. Granted, when he gets hold of the truth, no one can be compared to him. What sagacity in disentangling the errors of the senses, the imagination, the intellect and the heart! What touches when he paints the different characters of those who go astray in the search for truth! Did he go wrong? It is in a manner so seductive that he appears clear even in those passages where he was unintelligible.[52]

A strikingly similar opinion was expressed by Diderot, with more than a hint of chauvinism. The British empiricists may turn out to have been right about many things, but they can never match the flair of the French:

A page of Locke contains more truth than all the volumes of Malebranche, but a line of Malebranche contains more subtlety, imagination, finesse, and perhaps even genius than Locke's whole fat book.[53]

Voltaire dismisses the unfortunate Malebranche in a single paragraph of the *Siècle de Louis XIV*:

MALEBRANCHE (Nicolas), born at Paris in 1638, Oratorian, one of the most profound meditatives who has ever written. Animated by that powerful imagination which makes more disciples than the truth, he had followers: in his time there were Malebranchists. He showed admirably the errors of the senses and of the imagination; and when he wanted to sound the nature of the soul he got lost in that abyss like the others. He is, like Descartes, a great man from whom one learns little, and he was not a great geometer like Descartes. Died in 1715.[54]

But it would be unfair to leave the last word to a critic like Voltaire who, hostile as he was both to speculative metaphysics and to Christianity, could not have been sympathetic to Malebranche's philosophical aims. Justice demands a more charitable verdict on Malebranche's work and its influence. By 1750, to be sure, few philosophers would have called themselves Malebranchists. His influence lived on, however, both in academic philosophy and in the intellectual currents of the 'moderate' enlightenment. In philosophy, his views on the soul and self-knowledge, on the objectivity of thought, on causation, on sensation and natural judgement, and on the rational foundations of ethics all proved both insightful and influential. And within the enlightenment as a whole, there is a long and honourable tradition of thinkers seeking to reconcile the Christian tradition with the new philosophy. Thinkers in this tradition drew freely on Malebranche's work.

Malebranche's position in the history of philosophy was a matter of some contention in the twentieth century. In France, his place in the canon was beyond doubt, as a succession of great commentaries (Gouhier, Gueroult, Dreyfus, Rodis-Lewis, Alquié) amply testify. Among anglophone historians, he enjoyed a less exalted status. Russell, for example, mentions him three times, but only once as a serious thinker. In recent years, however, his star has been on the rise, with the publication of a number of commentaries that combine sound scholarship with intellectual rigour. He has even become the subject of a *Cambridge Companion*, a collection of essays showing the breadth and depth of recent scholarship in France, Britain and the USA.[55] At last, it seems, Malebranche is ready to resume his rightful place – along with Descartes, Spinoza and Leibniz – as one of the greatest of the seventeenth-century rationalists.

NOTES

1 Introduction

1 Voltaire, *Siècle de Louis XIV*. For Voltaire's (negative) assessment of Malebranche, see vol. 2, 252–3.

2 For the life of Malebranche, see André. For briefer biographical notes, see Fontenelle's *Éloge* (*Oeuvres*, vol. 1, 201–16), Robinet (in Nadler, ed., 2000) 288–304, and Rodis-Lewis 5–20.

3 This combination of Descartes and Augustine was by no means unusual at the time. Augustine's philosophy was widely disseminated by means of the five-volume *Philosophia Christiana* of André Martin (writing under the pseudonym of Ambrosius Victor). See Dijksterhuis, ed., and Gouhier (1978).

4 Gueroult, vol. 1, 10.

5 Alquié 60.

6 The *Recherche* received two English translations in Malebranche's lifetime. See Stuart Brown in the *Cambridge Companion to Malebranche* (Nadler, ed., 2000) 262–87.

7 Robinet (1965) makes much of developments in Malebranche's thought. In this work I shall assume that Malebranche himself was correct in saying that he did not – at least after the *Éclaircissements* of 1678 – change his mind about anything of fundamental importance, and that his later works provide only clarifications, extensions and defences of essentially unchanging positions.

8 Foucher 32, *OCM* II 493.

9 For the clearest example of this hostility, see the controversy with the Jesuit Louis la Ville about the Eucharist (*OCM* XVII–1 445ff).

10 Arnauld, *Vraies et Fausses Idées*. English translations by Elmar Kremer and Stephen Gaukroger are available. I have made use of Kremer's translation.

11 For illuminating commentary, see Denis Moreau, 'The Malebranche–Arnauld Debate' (in Nadler, ed., 2000, 87–111). See also Alquié 186, 401 who thinks that Arnauld was within his rights to attack Malebranche in this way, because he saw some of the consequences of Malebranche's importation of philosophical rationalism into theology. For a much fuller discussion of the issues at stake, see Moreau's *Deux Cartésiens*.

12 For some insights into seventeenth-century rationalism, see Edward Craig.

13 For background on this debate, and its implications for natural philosophy, see Margaret Osler.

14 See Robinet (1965) for details.

15 Connell shows in some detail the dependence of Malebranche's doctrine of the Vision in God on scholastic sources, most notably Suarez's *De Angelis*. Malebranche's account of human knowledge, it appears, is closely modelled on scholastic accounts of angelic knowledge. As Connell admits, however, this dependence is perfectly consistent with sustained hostility to the Aristotelian elements in scholastic philosophy.

16 Gueroult, vol. 1, 18.

17 Descartes, *Meditation* 4, AT IX 42–50, CSM II 37–43.

18 Descartes, Letter to Princess Elizabeth of May 21, 1643, AT III, 663–8, CSMK III, 217–20.

19 For this 'trialist' reading of Descartes, see Cottingham.

20 See Gueroult, vol. 1, 142–3.

21 For Malebranche on the *bête-machine*, see Rosenfield, 41–6.

22 For an account of supernaturalism in seventeenth-century thought, and especially in the Mechanical Philosophy, see Keith Hutchison

23 See Gouhier (1948) Part 3, Chapter 3, 'L'Union à Dieu par la Raison', 279–311.

24 Descartes, Letter to Mersenne of May 27, 1630, AT I 152, CSMK III 25.

25 Descartes, *Principles*, Part 1, Proposition 28, AT IX 37, CSM I 202.

26 For a very similar argument, see Robert Boyle's *Disquisition about the Final Causes of Natural Things* in his *Works*, vol. 5, 392–443, especially 397.

27 Kant is often credited with having undermined the pretensions of the pseudo-science of rational psychology. But that honour, it should be clear, belongs by right to Malebranche.

28 There is of course the letter to Mesland of February 9, 1645 about the Eucharist. See AT IV 161–72, CSMK III 241–6.

29 Arnauld, 'Fourth Replies' AT IX 153–4, CSM II 138.

30 Foucher 32, *OCM* II 493.

31 Fontenelle, *Oeuvres*, vol. 1, 208. 'It is surprising and perhaps annoying', remarks Fontenelle, 'to find oneself led by philosophy alone to all the most rigorous obligations of Christianity; people generally think that it is possible to be a philosopher at less cost.'

32 For the role of his religion in shaping Malebranche's philosophy, see Gouhier (1948).

33 See Descartes' Letter to the Sorbonne, prefaced to the *Méditations* AT IX 4–8, CSM II 3–6.

34 Bayle, article 'Manichaeism', 144–53.

35 Hazard, 165.

36 Malebranche was thus sympathetic with Burnet's *Theoria Telluris Sacra*, which represented our earth as the wreck of a previously perfect creation. He received a copy from the author, with a complimentary letter and a request for criticisms, in 1681. See *OCM* XVIII 196–8. For commentary on Burnet, see Kubrin.

37 For the most illuminating account of the sceptical argument of the criterion, see Richard Popkin's classic work.

38 See Popkin, especially Chapter 1, 1–17.

39 See Voltaire, *Letters from England*, 28. When Voltaire's Quaker says 'Your Malebranche was a bit of a Quaker, but not enough', he is making a serious point.

40 Robinet (1965) makes much of Malebranche's intellectual development, stressing his ever-increasing rationalism.

41 Descartes to Mesland, February 9, 1645, AT IV 161–72, CSMK III 241–6.

42 Bossuet, *Lettre à Huet*, May 18, 1689, quoted from Hazard 249.

43 Alquié 408.

44 Hazard 164–5.

2 Tensions in Cartesian metaphysics

1 Watson (1966).

2 See Watson (1987), Watson (in Brown, ed., 1991) 22–34, Watson (in Nadler, ed., 1993) 75–91.

3 For a sympathetic account of Descartes on mind–body union, and on how some mental powers may be dependent on embodiment, see Cottingham.

4 Chappell.

5 See Costa, Cook (1987), Yolton (1984) Chapter 1 'Perceptual Cognition of Body in Descartes', 18–41.

6 Chappell 193.

7 See Cook (1974) and Radner (1976).

8 Jolley (in Nadler, ed., 2000) 38.

9 The contained quote is from *Meditation* 3 (AT IX 31, CSM II 25).

10 La Forge 90.

11 La Forge 88–9.

12 La Forge 82.

13 La Forge 92.

14 La Forge 96. The 'storehouse' theory of innate ideas, here raised and dismissed by La Forge, would also be among Malebranche's targets in his eliminative argument for the Vision in God.

15 La Forge 91.

16 Arnauld *Art de Penser* 29. All translations from Arnauld are mine.

17 *Ibid* 30. The example is of course familiar from reading Descartes.

18 *Ibid* 31.

19 *Ibid* 36.

20 *Ibid* 37.

21 Arnauld, *True and False Ideas* 19. For comments, see also Nadler (1992) 134.

22 Arnauld, *True and False Ideas* 20.

23 Régis, *Métaphysique* I.2, *Système général*, vol. 1 72–3.

24 See André 246–55.

25 See Régis, *Métaphysique*, *Système général* Book 2, Part 1, Chapter 18 194–5.

26 For a recent overview of the arguments, and a different interpretation from his own earlier view (Garber 1987) see Garber (in Nadler, ed., 1993) 9–26.

27 See Hatfield for a classic occasionalist reading of Descartes' physics.

28 Loeb 139–40, Richardson.

29 See Radner (1985) for a convincing response to Loeb and Richardson.

30 Radner (1985) 42.

31 Watson (in Nadler, ed., 1993) 75–91.

32 Nadler (1998) 229, Clatterbaugh 39–40, 58–9.

33 See Gabbey (1971 and 1980) and Garber (1992) for detailed accounts of Descartes' dynamics.

34 Hatfield.

35 See Nadler (1994) 40.

36 Scott (2000).

37 Nadler (1993) 65–6.

38 Radner (1985) finds this unacceptable, arguing that a partial cause must be responsible for part of the total effect, and must thus contain part of the total effect. But this, she says, cannot be the case for mind–body interaction (43). This strikes me as the weakest part of an otherwise admirable paper. If a complex of eight causal factors C1–8 are jointly responsible for an effect E, it doesn't generally make sense to ask what part of E was due to factor C5.

39 Garber (1987).

40 Garber (in Nadler, ed., 1993) 9–26.

41 Scott (2000).

42 Nadler (1993) 65–6 and (1994) 40.

43 Clatterbaugh (58–60) thinks that Descartes is a 'concurrentist' rather than an occasionalist. Malebranche will of course dismiss the 'concourse' theory as unintelligible.

44 For an illuminating overview with a focus on La Forge, see Desmond Clarke's paper in the collection edited by Gaukroger, Schuster and Sutton, 131–48.

45 The views of Guelincx, Clauberg and Le Grand – to cite but three – might all demand inclusion in a fuller treatment of this subject. For Le Grand, see Clatterbaugh 100–12.

46 It was of course his discovery of Descartes' *L'Homme* in 1664 that had turned the young Malebranche into a philosopher.

47 See Desmond Clarke's introduction to La Forge xv, and Nadler (1993) 58.

48 La Forge 143.
49 La Forge cites Descartes' relativistic definition at *Principles* 2, 25 (AT IX 76, CSM I 233).
50 La Forge 145.
51 La Forge 146–7.
52 Nadler (1998) 215.
53 La Forge 148.
54 La Forge 150.
55 La Forge 150.
56 La Forge 151.
57 La Forge 105.
58 La Forge 97.
59 La Forge 124. See Nadler (in Nadler, ed., 1993) 67–9.
60 Cordemoy 122. See also Balz.
61 Cordemoy 136–7.
62 Cordemoy 137. Translation mine.
63 Cordemoy 139.
64 Cordemoy 143–4. This thought takes Cordemoy very close to Malebranche.
65 Cordemoy 149.
66 Cordemoy 283–6.

3 The Vision in God

1 See Bardout 201.
2 Radner (1978) 13.
3 We need the qualification to cope with seeing such things as shadows and rainbows.
4 This is the strategy of modern 'disjunctive' accounts of perception. The visual experience, on this account, is either a perception or an experience phenomenologically indistinguishable but really distinct from a perception.
5 Nadler (1992) 83–4.
6 Arnauld, for example, takes Malebranche's argument to depend on a conflation of local with ontological presence (*True and False Ideas*, Chapter 4, 16–17, Chapter 8, 35–40), and on a mistaken analogy with optical images. Yolton (1984) 3–17 takes the analogy with optical images to underlie many of the errors of seventeenth-century accounts of ideas as representative entities.
7 For helpful commentary on this important point, see Rodis-Lewis 100, Gueroult vol. 1 83–7, and Nadler (1992) 76–7.
8 See our discussion of Watson's Causal Likeness Principle (CLP) in Chapter 2.
9 Arnauld, *True and False Ideas*, Chapter 11, 50–2.
10 See Gueroult, vol. 1, 160, Connell 154, Nadler (1989) 60, Radner (1978) 107.
11 Nadler (1989) 60.
12 Nadler (1992) 177. Beatrice Rome (300–2) had also argued that Malebranche's theory is a form of direct realism.
13 The parallel is emphasised by Nadler (1992) 5.
14 Locke raises just this objection, that we have no way of knowing that we have listed all possible hypotheses. But without that assumption, he argues, an eliminative argument proves nothing. See Locke, *Examination*, 214.
15 This is Foucher's objection. Malebranche's argument simply assumes, he objects, that we are capable of knowledge of external objects. Without that assumption, his argument for the Vision in God proves nothing. See Gouhier (1948) 238.
16 Malebranche describes his list as 'une division exacte' at *OCM* VI 198. See Rodis-Lewis 56–7.
17 Connell 162–5.
18 Connell 162.
19 Nadler (1992) 138–40.

20 See also Chapter 14 of Book 1 of the *Recherche*, where Malebranche had already launched a polemic on the unintelligible and non-explanatory theory of species (*OCM* I 157, LO 68).
21 Nadler (1992) 108–14.
22 This charitable reading of Malebranche's attack on H1 is offered by Rome (78). On Cartesian (mechanistic) principles, she insists, the scholastic theory of *species* has to be assimilated to the Epicurean theory of *eidola*. See also Connell 170.
23 *OCM* III 144, LO 622. For comments, see Rodis-Lewis 63, Nadler (1992) 120. The production theory could certainly be read into La Forge's discussion of Descartes' *Notes on a Programme*, which we discussed briefly in Chapter 2. Some of the commentators ascribe this theory to Regius.
24 Herbert of Cherbury might be suggested, but the 'infinite storehouse' theory was generally rejected in Cartesian circles as a crude misunderstanding of innatism.
25 See Rodis-Lewis 67, Nadler (1992) 130–1.
26 Gueroult, vol. 1 102.
27 It is also a plausible source for Leibniz's theory of monads, each of which, although windowless, nevertheless mirrors all the other monads.
28 Further arguments against the *monde intelligible* can be found in Chapter 7 of Book 3 of the Recherche (*OCM* I 452, LO 238), in Éclaircissement X (*OCM* III 147–51, LO 624–6), and in the third of the *Conversations Chrétiennes* (*OCM* IV 62–3).
29 Malebranche's question, says Rome (67), is not 'is knowledge possible?' but 'how is knowledge possible?' We thus have the makings of a transcendental argument for the Vision in God as a necessary condition of objective knowledge.
30 See Gareth Matthews' paper, 'Knowledge and Illumination' in Stump and Kretzmann, eds, 171–85, especially 180–1. As Matthews says, the image of knowledge as illumination occurs frequently in Augustine's writings.
31 For this adverbial account of sensation see Nadler (1992) 64.
32 See Rodis-Lewis 79–80, Gueroult, vol. 1, 38. The argument from properties, according to Gueroult (vol. 1, 63), is absent from the first edition of the *Recherche*, and appears only in Malebranche's later works.
33 For further commentary, see Gueroult, vol. 1, 76–9.
34 For this Platonic–Augustinian reading of Malebranche on ideas, see Nadler (1992) 10.
35 Regrettably, this preface is omitted from the translation of Jolley and Scott as being 'of minor philosophical interest' (xlii).
36 Nadler (1992) 51, 102–3.
37 See Gouhier 222–3.
38 Nadler (1989) 63–5.
39 Jolley (1990) 60.
40 Arnauld, *True and False Ideas*, 65. To deny that God has ideas of each and every individual creature, however humble, is, Arnauld maintains, to deny His omniscience.
41 Gueroult, vol. 1, 234.
42 Gueroult, vol. 1, 217.
43 Arnauld, *True and False Ideas*, Chapter 13, 63–7.
44 Robinet (1965) 215, Gueroult, vol. 1, 212.
45 Gouhier (1948) 354–6, Alquié 221–2, Nadler (1992) 58.
46 Alquié 221–2.
47 Radner, 83, Alquié, 223.
48 For a similar account, stressing the role of intelligible extension as providing the conditions of constructibility of possible bodies, see Bardout 87–8.
49 See Gueroult, vol. 1, 174–5.
50 See Gueroult, vol. 1, 157, Alquié 215.
51 For helpful commentary see Radner (1978) 117.
52 Locke finds himself wrestling with exactly the same confusion in *Essay* Book 2, Ch XV, Section 9 (*Essay* 164–5). Although whatever is extended is complex, he still

thinks that the idea of extension may be called simple because it is not divisible into distinct ideas.

53 See Watson (1966) 40–63, Gouhier (1948) 250.
54 Arnauld, *True and False Ideas*, 78.
55 Locke, *Examination*, 219.
56 Alquié (506–7) is the most perceptive of the commentators on this topic. Some historians of philosophy might frown at the anachronism of reading Malebranche through the eyes of Kant, but in this case it does seem to shed real light on the sort of tangle Malebranche has found himself in and the steps that might be needed to extricate him.
57 Gueroult, vol. 1, 185–6.
58 Robinet (1965) 259.
59 Jolley (1990) 76–7.
60 Nadler (1992) 96–7, 149.
61 Radner (1978) 1–6, and Cook (1998), 526–7 emphasise Malebranche's allegiance to the substance-mode metaphysic.
62 See also Cook (1998) 528.
63 Gueroult, vol. 1, 110, Radner (1978) 55.
64 The preface to the *Entretiens* is not included in JS.
65 Arnauld, *True and False Ideas*, 97–8.
66 This section is heavily influenced by Cook (1998).
67 See Nadler (1992) 41–2.
68 Radner (1978) 51.
69 Nadler (1992) 8, 177.
70 For a somewhat different criticism of Nadler, see Scott (1996).
71 Nadler himself admits (1992, 158–9) that there are passages, e.g. in *Éclaircissement* VI and the first of the *Entretiens*, that lend themselves to the traditional interpretation of Malebranche as an indirect or representative realist, and that even invite an idealist reading. His attempt to explain away such passages is to my mind entirely unconvincing.
72 Nadler (1992) 51–2.
73 The most perceptive of the commentators on this difficult issue are Alquié and Radner. Without certain Kantian notions and distinctions, Alquié explains (226, 506–7) Malebranche cannot extricate himself from his difficulties over *étendue intelligible*. Radner (1978, 92) distinguishes between idea-meanings and idea-pictures, and argues – correctly – that Malebranche's theory requires both.
74 There is, as Radner (1978, 107) sees, no identity of intelligible object and material object. The intelligible circle is not a part or aspect of the material circle but an independent reality.

4 The dispute with Arnauld over the nature of ideas

1 For relations between Malebranche and Arnauld, see *OCM* VI i–xxvii.
2 For this alliance between Cartesian philosophy and Augustinian theology, see Gouhier (1978) and several of the contributors to Dijksterhuis ed., (1950).
3 Robinet (1965) 17–26.
4 See Moreau 107–8.
5 Arnauld, VFI 1.
6 Arnauld, VFI 26–7. Descartes, says Arnauld, did not think of ideas as distinct from perceptions; rather, he defines an idea as 'our thought itself, insofar as it contains objectively what is formally in the object'. See also Nadler (1989) 126–9.
7 Arnauld, VFI 22.
8 Arnauld, VFI 44–8.
9 Arnauld, VFI 44.
10 Arnauld, VFI 6.

11 Arnauld, VFI 33. Malebranche could of course admit that we are spontaneously inclined to believe this, and can posit a 'natural judgement' which overlooks the idea and attaches belief directly to the thing itself. But since the phenomenology of non-veridical experience is indistinguishable from that of veridical experience, it will follow that a significant minority of such natural judgements are false.

12 Arnauld, VFI 25.

13 Nadler (1989) 121–2 is good on this, providing a helpful account of how earlier commentators (e.g. Lovejoy and Church) were led astray.

14 Arnauld, VFI 20.

15 Arnauld, VFI 12–18 and 35–40. A strikingly similar analysis has been put forward three hundred years later by John Yolton. See Yolton (1984), Chapter III, 58–75, 'Direct Presence among the Cartesians'.

16 Arnauld, VFI 51.

17 Arnauld, VFI 172–6. See Descartes' *Meditation Six* (AT IX 63, CSMK II 55).

18 Arnauld, VFI 43.

19 In *Meditation Three* (AT IX 31, CSMK II 27) Descartes contrasts the astronomers' idea of the sun with that of the man in the street.

20 Arnauld, VFI 7.

21 In an unguarded moment, for example, Malebranche had seemed to identify intelligible extension with God's immensity. A charitable critic would dismiss this as a mere slip; Arnauld takes the opportunity to accuse Malebranche of Spinozism.

22 See also Malebranche's reply to the first objection in *Éclaircissement* X (*OCM* III 144–7, LO 622–4).

23 This makes it look as if resemblance is the crucial issue. In fact, however, Malebranche doesn't require literal resemblance. All he demands is that the idea be capable of making known the properties of the object.

24 See the refutation of the *monde intelligible* theory at *OCM* I 433–6, LO 228–9, discussed in Chapter Three. For Malebranche the soul is not, but God is, a *monde intelligible*.

25 The 'walking soul' argument, which makes it look as if mere spatial distance counted, is now dismissed as a sort of joke. See *OCM* VI 95–6.

26 It represents extension as infinite, but also represents an infinity of types of figures.

27 See Nadler (1992) 49–51, Radner (1978) 51.

28 See Nadler (1992) 41–3.

29 As a Cartesian, of course, Malebranche accepted the infinite divisibility of matter and denied the real existence of atoms or indivisible bodies. Hence his non-committal allusion to 'what is called an atom'.

30 Nadler (1992) 183–5.

31 Arnauld, VFI 38.

32 Arnauld, VFI 47–8.

33 Arnauld, VFI 53.

34 Arnauld, VFI 97–8.

35 Quoted from VFI 27. For the relevant passage from the *Second Replies*, see AT IX 127–8, CSMK II 113–14.

36 Arnauld, VFI 113.

37 Arnauld, VFI 15–17. See Nadler (1989) 173.

38 Arnauld's position is therefore close to that which has been articulated and defended in our own times by philosophers such as Roderick Chisholm and John Searle.

39 Nadler (1992) 184–5.

40 See *Éclaircissement* X (*OCM* III 140, LO 620), and *Entretien* III of the *Conversations Chrétiennes* (*OCM* IV 69–72). After 1700, when Coste's French translation of Locke's *Essay* appeared, Locke took pride of place for Malebranche among the Pyrrhonists. See *OCM* IX 899, and Malebranche's letter to Fénélon of June 1713 (*OCM* XIX 842).

41 See Descartes' *Fifth Replies* (to Gassendi), AT IX 212, CSMK II 275. To deny that we can reason from the clear and distinct idea to the properties of the ideatum is, says Descartes, 'the objection of objections'. Unless we can reason thus from ideas to

things 'we must entirely close the door to reason and content ourselves with being monkeys or parrots rather than men'.

42 See Nadler (1992) 145–9.

43 Arnauld's interpretation of Descartes is thus close to the reading offered in our own time by Harry Frankfurt.

44 See Gueroult, vol. 1 114, Rodis-Lewis 104, Radner 57.

45 For this way of presenting Malebranche's argument, see Rome 67. Like Kant, Rome suggests, Malebranche is not asking 'is knowledge possible?' which addresses scepticism directly. Rather, he is asking 'how is knowledge possible?'

46 Jolley (1990) 56.

47 Frege, 'On Sense and Meaning', quoted from Frege 59.

48 Jolley (1990) 63.

49 The best of the commentators on this topic is Denis Moreau (in Nadler, ed., 2000, 87–111). There is a discussion by Harry Bracken (in Brown, ed., 1991, 35–48) which doesn't seem to me to add much to our understanding of the controversy. Bracken regards it as 'ideological', without much philosophical interest, and dismisses Arnauld as being confused about the philosophical issues at stake. This strikes me as simply mistaken. Of course Arnauld was a theologian first and a philosopher second. But in his controversies with Descartes, Malebranche and Leibniz we can see a first-rate philosophical mind at work.

50 Alquié 186. My translation.

51 See Moreau, especially Chapter 10, 'Combat des Dieux', 268–301.

52 Moreau (in Nadler, ed., 2000) 104.

53 See Craig, Chapter 1, 'The Mind of God', 13–68. For Craig's views on Malebranche, see 64–8.

54 Moreau, 180–1. The quote is from Isaiah LV, 8.

55 See Robinet's preface to the *Conversations* (*OCM* IV xvi).

56 *OCM* IV, preface xviii.

57 See Bardout 123, 152 for Malebranche's insistence on the univocal and universal nature of rationality. All minds whatsoever (humans, angels, God) are subject to the same set of rationally binding norms.

58 Cf. Malebranche's dismissal in *Éclaircissement* XV of scriptural passages which seem to accept the reality of natural powers (*OCM* III 229–53, LO 672–85). Such passages, he tells us, are mere accommodations, i.e. concessions to the prejudices and the level of understanding of the vulgar.

5 Occasionalism and continuous creation

1 Leibniz, *New System*, in Ariew and Garber, eds, 143.

2 Fontenelle, in Chapter 2 of his *Doutes* (616–18) suggests just this origin for Cartesian occasionalism.

3 For a lucid overview of the subject, see Steven Nadler's own paper, 'Malebranche on Causation', in Nadler, ed., 2000, 112–38.

4 Jolley (1990) 105

5 Alquié 248–9.

6 Clatterbaugh 115–16.

7 Clatterbaugh 112.

8 Fontenelle, *Doutes*, in *Oeuvres*, vol. 1, 621.

9 Hume, *Treatise* Book 1, Part 4, Section 5, 248–9.

10 Church 92–3.

11 Watson (in Nadler, ed., 1993, 75–91) especially 83.

12 Fontenelle, *Oeuvres*, vol. 1, 621.

13 Hume, *Treatise* Book 1, Part 4, Section 5, 248–9.

14 For more sympathetic accounts of Malebranche's argument, see Rome 169–72 and Alquié 250–1.

15 See Descartes' Letter to Princess Elizabeth of May 21, 1643, AT III, 663–8, CSMK III 217–20. For more detailed discussion of Descartes' 'trialism', see Cottingham.
16 See Alquié 45.
17 The epistemic requirement that the cause of X must know how to bring X about is often ascribed to Guelincx and La Forge (see Gueroult, vol. 2, 224, and Clatterbaugh 99). Intuitively, it seems too strong, ruling out as it does the very possibility that anything but a spirit could even be a candidate for being a cause. Nadler (in Nadler, ed., 2000, 123–5) thinks that Malebranche holds this epistemic requirement for all genuine causes. If so, it was good tactics on his part to deploy other arguments that do not depend on it.
18 The issues arising here will be discussed in more detail in Chapter 8.
19 See Robinet (1965) 79.
20 For Malebranche's rejection of 'psychological immanence' see Gueroult, vol. III, 74–5.
21 According to Clatterbaugh (58–9) Descartes shared this scholastic view.
22 See Gueroult, vol. II, 226–7.
23 See Radner (1978) 3. For weaker versions of continuous creation that are compatible with the attribution of some causal powers to creatures, see Clatterbaugh 40.
24 See the final *Éclaircissement* of the *Traité de la Nature et de la Grace* (*OCM* V 197ff), written against Arnauld.
25 See Nadler (in Nadler, ed., 2000) 126 for this scholastic distinction between *causa secundum fieri* and *causa secundum esse*.
26 Gueroult, vol. 2, 215–16.
27 See Desmond Clarke (1995).
28 Nadler (1993 and 1995).
29 Leibniz, *New System*, in Ariew and Garber, eds, 143.
30 Pessin (2001).
31 Moreau makes much of Malebranche's audacity in taking evil at face value, granting that many of the things we experience as evils are indeed evils. See Chapter 4, 'Et Noluit Consolari', 110–26.
32 Malebranche defended this position at a famous meeting with Arnauld and others in 1679. No one else, we are told, took Malebranche's side in the ensuing argument. See Alquié 430.
33 The same argument appears in Robert Boyle. See his *Disquisition about the Final Causes of Natural Things* in his *Works*, vol. 5, 392–443, especially 397.
34 Arnauld, according to a sympathetic critic, claimed only that we can never know all of God's purposes in Creation, not that we can never guess some of them (see Moreau, 178–9). If this reading is correct, his position is less vulnerable to Malebranche's attack.
35 See Gueroult, vol. 2, Chapter 4, 99–113, Robinet (1965) Section 3, Chapter 1, 83–114, and Alquié 282 for more detailed accounts.
36 Fontenelle 625.
37 Bayle suggested that Malebranche's position would be more well-rounded and consistent if he claimed that God never troubles the *simplicité des voies*. See Moreau 117. See also Voltaire, *Philosophical Dictionary*, article 'Miracles', 311–17.
38 Gueroult, vol. 2, 184–5.
39 Locke, *Examination*, 221, 254.
40 This objection can be found in Fontenelle's *Doutes*, 630, where it is argued that God has no need of occasional causes and would therefore show His wisdom by simply dispensing with them. Only limited and imperfect beings need continual prompts and reminders.
41 It was not just Berkeley who came to espouse idealism. Arthur Collier's *Clavis Universalis* (1713) also argues explicitly for the non-existence of matter, drawing heavily on the work of Malebranche. See Stuart Brown (in Nadler, ed., 2000) 275–8.
42 See Fontenelle, vol. 1, 615–36

43 Fontenelle, vol. 1, 637.

44 Fontenelle, vol. 1, 638.

45 Gueroult, vol. 2, 248.

46 For Leibniz's dynamics see Costabel and Robinet, eds (1955).

47 Hume sees this point clearly. As far as *a priori* arguments are concerned, he says, anything can cause anything. See *Treatise* Book 1, Part 3, Section 15, 173. 'Any thing may produce any thing. Creation, annihilation, motion, reason, volition; all these may arise from one another, or from any other object we can imagine.' Note that Hume explicitly denies any real distinction between cause and occasion.

48 For the story of the Cartesian and Malebranchian resistance to Newton, see Brunet.

49 This will be discussed in much more detail in Chapter Six, where we shall indeed find Malebranche making a succession of concessions to the empiricist.

50 See Hutchison.

51 Alquié 267.

52 The correct definition of a 'miracle' is a central issue in the Leibniz–Clarke correspondence. Leibniz adopts what he takes to be the traditional definition of a miracle as an event that transcends natural powers. Clarke thinks that there is no real difference – from God's point of view – between miracles and so-called natural events, and that we simply call rare and remarkable events miraculous. For Malebranche, as for Clarke, there are no natural powers, so the definition of a miracle as an event that transcends the powers of creatures would be idle. But for Malebranche, as for Leibniz, there is a real distinction between divine action in accordance with a *volonté générale* and divine actions that require *volontés particulières*.

6 Malebranche's modifications of Cartesian physics

1 Malebranche was the first Cartesian to explicitly accept Newton's demonstration of the composition of white light and to incorporate it into a wave theory by associating different colours with different wavelengths. See *Éclaircissement* XVI of *the Recherche*, *OCM* III 257ff, LO 689ff.

2 Hatfield.

3 Gabbey (1971) and Gabbey (in Gaukroger, ed., 1980).

4 For Pardies, see Costabel's note to his discussion of Malebranche on the laws of motion (*OCM* XVII–1 203–4).

5 See Boyle's *Disquisition about the Final Causes of Natural Things* in his *Works*, vol. 5 392ff, especially 396. To derive his conservation principle from God's immutability, says Boyle, Descartes must be tacitly claiming to know something of God's designs in creating and sustaining the physical universe.

6 Clarke (1982).

7 The CSM translation unfortunately omits the seven rules of impact.

8 For the notion of a 'circular inertia' in Galileo, see Koyré.

9 Gabbey (1971) 263–5.

10 Gabbey thinks that Rule Six fails this test, i.e. is incompatible with PLMM.

11 Gabbey (1971) 265.

12 Leibniz would insist on a principle of continuity as an *a priori* constraint on any acceptable laws of impact. But on Descartes' rules the difference between the case where the two colliding bodies A and B are equal in bulk, and the case where A is greater than B by one part in a billion can be momentous.

13 For Leibniz's critique of Cartesian dynamics, see Costabel.

14 For Huygens, see Westfall 146ff.

15 For this line of criticism, see Watson (1966).

16 See the discussion in Chapter 3.

17 *Étendue intelligible* makes its first appearance in *Éclaircissement* X of the *Recherche* (*OCM* III 127–43, LO 612–32) and thereafter plays a prominent role in Malebranche's accounts of the Vision in God.

18 Strictly speaking, we should not permit this derivation. As Kant famously remarked, the law of non-contradiction never pushed anything.

19 For a more detailed study of Malebranche's successive modifications of Descartes' rules of impact, see Mouy (1927).

20 For Malebranche's explicit rejection of Descartes' 'force of rest' see *Recherche* Book 6, Part 2, Chapter 9, *OCM* II 420–49, LO 510–26.

21 The epithet '*petit méchant traité*' is Malebranche's own, applied retrospectively to a brief article on the laws of motion from what one might call his 'middle period'.

22 Newton of course noted this in the *Queries* to his *Opticks*. A universe in which motion is lost in the collisions of hard bodies (atoms) was compatible with Newton's physics and congenial to his theology. For a detailed study of this issue, see Wilson Scott.

23 For Leibniz's *Brevis Demonstratio* see L.E. Loemker, ed., 296–302. The famous article first appeared in the *Acta Eruditorum* of 1686.

24 See Costabel's commentary on Malebranche's failure to accommodate this aspect of Leibniz's critique (*OCM* XVII–1 23).

25 For Huygens' discovery of mechanical relativity, and his emphasis on kinematics at the expense of dynamics, see Westfall, 146ff.

26 Pierre Costabel provides very helpful editorial notes documenting Leibniz's ongoing critique of Malebranche's successive formulations of the laws of motion. See *OCM* XVII–1 23. For more details on the relations between Malebranche and Leibniz, see Robinet (1955).

27 See the memoir by Carré on this subject, reprinted in *OCM* XVII–1 182ff.

28 Reprinted in *OCM* XVII–1 181–97.

29 See Costabel's editorial comments at *OCM* XVII–1 84.

30 See Bardout 292, who interprets Malebranche's final position as almost Kantian. Reason guarantees lawlikeness, but does not fix the precise laws.

31 See Bardout 287. The laws of nature are not 'arbitrary', Bardout insists, in the sense that God could have established quite different ones; we can be certain *a priori* that their choice is grounded in Order. Bardout assumes without further argument that Order determines God's choice rather than merely imposing constraints on it.

32 For this resistance of Cartesians to Newtonian action at a distance, see Brunet.

33 See Hume, *Treatise* Book 1, Part 3, Section 15, 173. As far as *a priori* reasoning is concerned, says Hume, anything can cause anything. Note that Hume also denies any real difference between cause and occasion.

7 Malebranche's biology

1 For Malebranche's explicit defence of the *bête machine*, see the *Recherche*, Book 4, Chapter 11 (*OCM* II 104–6, LO 323–5) and Book 5, Chapter 3 (*OCM* II 150–2, LO 351–3).

2 Hutchison (1983).

3 For this definition of 'nature' (*physis*) see Aristotle, *Physics* Book 2, Chapter 1, 192b 20–2.

4 Vartanian (1953).

5 See Pyle (1987) for further clarification.

6 The case for seeing Descartes as a (metaphysical) supernaturalist has already been made by Hatfield and others. See our discussion of Descartes on causation in Chapter 2.

7 See Roger, especially 378–84.

8 See Gassendi 226, 237.

9 According to Boyle, Harvey made his famous discovery of the circulation of the blood by asking the function served by the valves in the veins. See Boyle's *Works*, vol. 5, 427.

10 Cordemoy 257ff.

11 The theory of 'plastic nature' was endorsed by Cambridge Platonists such as Ralph Cudworth. For more details, see Pyle (1987).

12 For this crucial distinction see Roger (325–6) and Bowler.

13 Pyle 246–50.

14 For Littré's claim, see Roger 191–2. The claim was queried by the sceptical Fontenelle, and was never widely accepted.

15 For Croone's claim, see Gunther, ed., vol. 7, 499. The Royal Society asked for further confirmation, but never formally endorsed the claim.

16 For Leeuwenhoek, see Dobell.

17 For Swammerdam, see Schierbeck's biography and Lindeboom's collection of his letters to his friend Thévenot. Malebranche was thoroughly familiar with Swammerdam's work and with the religious significance Swammerdam himself found in it.

18 See Redi's famous *Experiments on the Generation of Insects* (reprinted in T. Hall, ed.) 363. For an in-depth study of the spontaneous generation controversy, see Farley.

19 Some of the complex life-cycles of parasites took many years of painstaking research to unravel. For details of this long slow process, see Farley.

20 Maupertuis, vol. 2, 66–7.

21 Swammerdam's title *Miraculum Naturae* was of course deliberately paradoxical. In his letter of April 1678 to Thévenot he writes: 'Herewith I offer you the Omnipotent Finger of God in the anatomy of a louse: wherein you will find miracles heaped on miracles' (quoted from Lindeboom, ed., 105).

22 This argument can be found in any number of authors of widely different points of view. For documentation, see Pyle.

23 Malebranche is thus prepared to take our experience of natural evil at face value, i.e. to regard apparent blemishes in God's creation as real blemishes. See Moreau 94.

24 For Arnauld, God wills 'strictly, positively, and directly that there are monstrous animals'. See Moreau 222.

25 The sharpest objection comes from Maupertuis in his *Vénus Physique*. No one doubts, he writes, that the mental state of the mother can affect the development of the foetus, but no remotely plausible mechanism could be proposed to account for *iconic* effects. See his Works, vol. 2, 77–8.

26 The lengthy *Éclaircissement* VIII of the *Recherche* (*OCM* III 84ff, LO 579ff) is a sustained attempt to articulate and defend the doctrine of original sin and its transmission.

8 Malebranche on the soul and self-knowledge

1 *Fourth Meditation*, AT IX 42, CSM II 37.

2 *Fifth Replies*, AT IX 207, CSM II 245. For commentary see Jolley (1990, 116–17, Schmaltz 1996, 37).

3 *Fourth Replies*, AT IX 172, CSM II 156.

4 A number of the commentators agree with Malebranche on this point. Alquié (1974, 199) describes Malebranche's *via negativa* as 'fidèlement cartésien', Schmaltz (1996, 7) represents it as an 'internal' revision of Cartesianism, and reminds us that Descartes himself espoused such an argument in the *Fourth Replies*.

5 Descartes' Letter to More of February 5, 1649, AT V 267–79, CSMK III 360–7. Malebranche makes no use of this *a posteriori* argument, though as an orthodox Cartesian believer in the *bête-machine* he could have endorsed it.

6 *Meditation Six*, AT IX 62, 68; CSM II, 54, 59.

7 Locke, *Essay* Book 2, Chapter 1, Section 10, 81.

8 Alquié (97) denies that Malebranche's departure from Descartes is a radical one, noting that Descartes never attempted to articulate a 'spiritual geometry'. But the question remains: why not?

9 Kant, *Critique of Pure Reason*, Paralogisms of Pure Reason, 'B' version, 368–83.

10 Jolley (in Nadler, ed., 2000, 31–58) ascribes to Malebranche an 'adverbial' account of sensations. When I see something red, on such an account, my soul is not in some strange relation to a red object (a sense-datum, or whatever); rather, it should be described as sensing redly.

11 Schmaltz (1996, 70).

12 Descartes' 'clear and distinct perception' conflates these two quite distinct types of certainty, knowledge by idea and knowledge by immediate awareness. See Alquié 104–6, and Jolley (1990, 43).

13 Schmaltz (1996, 177) suggests that for Arnauld what has been called 'the subjective view' reveals the soul to itself as it is.

14 See Alquié 104. See also Gueroult on the 'déchéance du cogito' (Gueroult, vol. I, Ch II, 41–61). The cogito, Gueroult explains, ceases for Malebranche to be a paradigm of clear and distinct knowledge – it is certain, but it is not clear.

15 Jolley (1990, 31). For Malebranche, according to Jolley (39) sensations are 'cognitively empty'.

16 Jolley (1990, 60).

17 I thus find myself in agreement with Jolley (1990, 50–1) against Schmaltz (1996, 66), that the central issue at stake for Malebranche is the lack of *a priori* knowledge, of a 'science' of the soul in the strict sense. Schmaltz makes too much of the distinction between discursive and nondiscursive knowledge, and misses the central issue.

18 Rodis-Lewis (180) stresses the possibility – in Malebranche's eyes – of a *mathesis spirituelle*, and hence the contingency of our lack of such a science. Alquié (106) suggests that the non-existence of a science of the soul may be linked to issues about subjectivity, and hence be non-contingent.

19 Locke, *Examination*, 245–6 raises just this question, but doesn't seem interested in Malebranche's attempts to reply to it.

20 Jolley (1990, 121) comments that Malebranche offers 'a few lame remarks which show him at his worst'. This is harsh, but not unfair.

21 Gueroult, vol. III, 138–9, Alquié 49.

22 Gueroult, vol. I, 136–7.

23 See Nadler (1992, 28–9). The clearest statement of this exclusion principle is at *OCM* VI 160.

24 Berkeley, *Dialogues Between Hylas and Philonous*, 3rd dialogue, 195.

25 Malebranche cites this requirement in Book Three of the *Recherche* (*OCM* I 466, LO 247).

26 Descartes' letter to the Sorbonne, AT IX 5, CSM II 4.

27 Schmaltz (1996, 170) comments that neither Descartes nor Malebranche perceived this problem. Both men seem to have assumed that if the continued existence of immaterial substance could be assured, the problem of personal identity would also be resolved.

28 Our lack of knowledge of the *dispositions intérieurs* of the soul is discussed in *Éclaircissement* VII, (*OCM* III 67–9, LO 577–8).

29 See Rodis-Lewis 178.

30 Alquié 96.

31 Locke, *Essay* Book 2, Chapter 1, Section 10, 81. 'I confess myself', Locke writes with disarming modesty, 'to have one of those dull souls, that doth not perceive itself always to contemplate *ideas*; nor can conceive it any more necessary for the *soul always to think*, than for the body always to move …'.

32 Kant, *Critique of Pure Reason*, 'Paralogisms of Pure Reason', B version, 368–83.

33 See Schmaltz (1996, 205).

34 I owe this suggestion to Tom Sorell.

35 Jolley (1990, 122) thinks that Malebranche may only have psycho-geometry in mind. But kinematics is equally a purely rational science.

36 Jolley (in Nadler, ed., 2000, 44) speaks of Malebranche's 'resolute anti-psychologism' about ideas, and represents him as a significant intermediary between Plato and modern defenders of objective thought such as Frege. See also Jolley, 1990, 56.

37 See Radner (1978, 72, 100), Schmaltz (1996, 115).

38 Pyle, ed. (2000, introduction, xxvi–xxvii).

39 Arnauld, *Fourth Objections*, AT IX 158, CSM II 143.

40 Locke, *Essay* Book 4, Chapter 3, Section 6, 147.

41 Nagel, 'What is it like to be a Bat?', in Nagel, 165–80.

42 McGinn.

43 Hume's discussion 'Of the Immateriality of the Soul' (*Treatise*, Book 1, Part 4, Section 5, 232–51) shows traces of Malebranche's influence almost on every page.

9 Malebranche on freedom, grace and the will

1 For a lucid account and perceptive criticism of Malebranche's account of human freedom, see Kremer's article in Nadler, ed., (2000) 190–219.

2 See Edward Craig on 'the insight ideal', Chapter 1, 13–68.

3 See Moreau 154 and Bardout 152.

4 Gueroult, vol. 2, 33.

5 Whether Order determines God's actions or merely constrains them (ruling out some things but still permitting a range of options) is a difficult question for Malebranche. His own comments, e.g. on the creation, suggest the latter; critics such as Fénelon think he is committed by his own principles to the former hard-line position. Such a theory, Fénelon argues, effectively denies God's freedom. (See Fénelon Chapter 6, 37–44.) God becomes in effect the prisoner of His own moral perfection. Such an objection would, of course, later be raised against Leibniz.

6 This rejection of voluntarism is quite explicit in *Éclaircissement* VIII of the *Recherche* (*OCM* III 84, LO 586). Voluntarism, Malebranche tells us, 'overthrows everything', science, religion and morality alike.

7 For Descartes' voluntarism about the necessary truths, see his letter to Mersenne of May 27, 1630 (AT I 152, CSMK III 25). This position is often repeated in his later works and in his correspondence.

8 This dilemma goes back, of course, to Plato's *Euthyphro*. Malebranche's attack on voluntarism puts him squarely in the Platonist camp.

9 Cf. Malebranche to Arnauld (*OCM* IX 1090), where Malebranche alleges that Arnauld's voluntarist principles overthrow all of religion and morality.

10 For a clear (if unsympathetic) account of Pelagianism, see the introductory essay by Warfield to Augustine's Anti-Pelagian Writings.

11 Augustine, *Confessions*, Book 10, Section XXIX 250.

12 1 Cor 4, 7.

13 See Gilson 156.

14 Kirwan suggests (146–50) that Augustine has no grasp of *comparative* justice. If I have enough food to feed a thousand starving men, none of whom has any claim on my assistance, and I choose to give it all to just one of them, have I done an injustice to the others?

15 See Gilson 164.

16 Malebranche too is clearly aware that in practical contexts *vraisemblance* or plausibility will often have to suffice. See *Recherche*, Book 1, Chapter 3 (*OCM* I 64, LO 15).

17 Robinet (1965) provides the best account of the development of Malebranche's thought.

18 Actually there seem to have been seven editions of the *Recherche*. See LO xxv.

19 Pierre Bayle (generally an acute and sympathetic critic of Malebranche) adopted this reading in his review of Villemandy on the efficacy of second causes. See *OCM* XVIII 423.

20 Alquié 335, Gueroult, vol. 3, 392–4.

21 La Forge 151.

22 Gueroult, vol. 3, 177–8. Gueroult also notes (185) Malebranche's later view, and accuses him of inconsistency. It would be more accurate to say that the text of the *Recherche* contains inconsistencies because it has not been thoroughly reworked to eliminate all traces of this early (and discarded) account. See Robinet (1965) 373.

23 There is in Malebranche's psychology no pure indifference. The mind can neither make up motives, nor choose without a motive. See Rodis-Lewis 230.

24 Kremer (in Nadler, ed., 2000) is good on this. See especially, 200–5.

25 For this reading, see Gueroult, vol. 3, 243, 393.

26 Cf. Malebranche's attack in Book Two of the *Recherche* on Seneca's portrayal of the Stoic hero Cato (*OCM* I 345–54, LO 176–81).

27 In the *Traité de Morale* (*OCM* XI 56) Malebranche tells us that the most virtuous of the pagans *could not* be saved by good works alone without the gift of grace. So it seems that he has something stronger than a merely contingent anti-Pelagianism in mind.

28 Robinet (1965) shows in painstaking detail Malebranche's early attachment to the '*Dieu caché*' of Pascal, and documents the phases of his abandonment of Jansenism. See 64–5.

29 See Alquié 412. This *égoisme divin* may be objectively correct, but, as critics like Fénélon remarked, is not much comfort to us. Even Malebranche feels the force of this objection, which he puts in the mouth of the young Ariste in the *Entretiens* (*OCM* XII 293, JS 229).

30 There is of course one particular crucial to this account -- the soul of Jesus Christ himself. But I have already explained that Order requires God only to minimise His concern for particulars, not to eliminate it altogether. As a Christian, Malebranche is committed to a unique status for the soul of Christ.

31 Malebranche's opinion, that the Incarnation was not merely redemptive but was always an essential part of God's purpose in creation, was not original – it can already be found in Scotus and Suarez. See Moreau 108.

32 Fénélon (172) accuses Malebranche of turning scripture upside down here. Scripture tells us that God so loved the world that He sent his own son to redeem it; Malebranche tells us that God only cares about the world because of His plan for the incarnation of the Word.

33 Riley's translation of the *Traité* does not contain all the additions Malebranche made to the later editions of the work. A number of my references will therefore be to the *Oeuvres Complètes* alone, with no reference to Riley's translation.

34 For this objection, see Fénélon 226–33. But since Fénélon believed that grace was distributed by particular acts of will, he seems even worse placed than Malebranche to deal with this objection.

35 Malebranche was quite familiar with Hobbes' work, though of course utterly hostile to it. See the attack in the eighth of the *Entretiens* (*OCM* XII 192, JS 144).

36 Alquié 378.

37 Moreau insights rightly (against the dismissive judgement of Bracken) that there are serious philosophical issues at stake. See his introduction, 15–23, and his conclusion, 303–21.

38 See Moreau's excellent article in Nadler, ed. (2000) 87–111.

39 The Jansenists would therefore accept the common definition of liberty as absence of external constraint. In this sense, both the sinner and the saint act freely (they get what they want), but their very different desires are equally caused by factors outside their control. What the Jansenists would deny is that we can have freedom in the sense of having any power at all to shape our own ends.

40 See Gouhier (1948) 125.

41 Fénélon (260) accuses Malebranche of denying that God can create merit in the soul of a man. But to moral intuition this seems exactly right.

42 Gouhier (1948) 154.

43 Letter to de Mairan (quoted from *OCM* XVI v–vii).

44 Letter to André of June 8, 1714 (*OCM* XIX 880–1).

45 See Frankfurt.

46 See also Kremer in Nadler, ed. (2000) 214. This chapter was written before the appearance in 2000 of the *Cambridge Companion to Malebranche*. Although my account is independent of Kremer's, I am pleased to note that he has arrived at very similar conclusions.

10 The downfall of Malebranchism

1 See Israel, especially 485–94

2 See Moreau 129, 307.

3 Bayle, article *Manichaeans*, 144–53. Whether Bayle's retreat into sceptical fideism was sincere, or whether he actually wanted his arguments to be used for the anti-religious purposes, continues to divide historians.

4 See Bossuet's letter to D'Allemans, May 21, 1687 (quoted from *OCM* XVIII 445).

5 See the Preface to the *Recherche* (*OCM* I 23, LO xli). Malebranche reminds his readers again and again that one man is not the teacher and instructor of another.

6 See Pierre Costabel, 'Malebranche et la Réforme Mathématique', in *OCM* XVII–2 i–vi. It was this Leibnizian version of the calculus – not the rival Newtonian theory of fluxions – that came to dominate mathematics in Continental Europe.

7 For a detailed study of Malebranche's conception of the science of metaphysics, see Bardout.

8 See also *Recherche*, Book 4, Chapter 2 (*OCM* II 27–8, LO 276), where Malebranche again cites this as if it were self-evident, which on occasionalist principles it is not.

9 This provides Malebranche with a further argument against animal souls and in favour of the *bête-machine* of Descartes. If animals had souls, those souls would only serve the needs of their bodies, but this would be in violation of Order.

10 Real existence, says Bardout (302) remains like an additional extra in Malebranche's thought, a residue that forever resists metaphysical analysis and explanation.

11 See Gueroult, vol. 1, 242, and Rome 170–1.

12 For Leibniz's objections to Malebranche's suggestion that the laws of collision are arbitrary, see *OCM* XIX 669–70. I grant, says Leibniz, that God could have established other laws, but it would have been 'far from the rules of His wisdom' to do so.

13 Alquié 165.

14 See Bréhier, Kemp Smith, Gueroult, vol. 2, 66, Alquié 180–1.

15 For brief initial discussions of the moon illusion in the *Recherche* see *OCM* I 99, 116–17, 158, LO 35–6, 44–5, 68–9. For a more detailed defense of his account against the objections of Régis, see *OCM* XVII–1 263–78.

16 Robinet (1965) 308, Rodis-Lewis 46–7.

17 Hume, *Treatise* Book 1, Part 4, Section 1, 183.

18 Robinet (1965) 362.

19 For criticism of Nadler, see David Scott (1996).

20 Locke, *Examination* 221, 254.

21 See Brown (in Nadler, ed., 2000) 276. For Berkeley's debt to Malebranche, see the works of Luce (1934) and McCracken.

22 See Robinet (1965) 28.

23 Gueroult, vol. 2, 239–44. The crucial difference between Leibniz and Malebranche, says Gueroult, is that for Leibniz the laws of action of creatures are intrinsic, whereas for Malebranche they are extrinsic. The regularity of God's actions, Leibniz argues, makes no difference. If a power is not grounded in the nature of a creature, it is

miraculous. Cf. his objections to the Newtonian theory of gravity in Alexander, ed., 30, 43, 91–2. For further commentary, see Robinet (1955) and Costabel.

24 Gueroult, vol. 2, 38.

25 See André's comments on the circumstances of publication of Malebranche's *Traité de l'Amour de Dieu* (*OCM* XIV xiii–xxxiii).

26 See also *Recherche* Book 4, Chapter 5 (*OCM* II 45–9, LO 287–9).

27 Gueroult, vol. 3, 277; Alquié 344–5.

28 Rodis-Lewis 302.

29 Gueroult, vol. 2, 38; Alquié 487–90. The logic of Malebranche's position, according to these commentators, leads inevitably to the denial of a personal God.

30 See also Bayle's *Dictionary*, article *Rorarius*, p 219.

31 Alquié 55. The argument is not of course conclusive. One could always deny premise 2, and adopt the Pythagorean opinion that the sufferings of animals are punishments for sins committed in previous lives.

32 Quoted from *OCM* XI xvi. My translation.

33 Fénélon 100–5.

34 Fénélon 126.

35 For a similar line of criticism, see Gueroult, vol. 3, 348–51.

36 Voltaire, *Letters from England*, 28.

37 Fénélon 142–3.

38 See the comments of his biographer André on this phase of Malebranche's life (*OCM* XIX 702–5).

39 See Walton, appendix, 160–70.

40 McCracken, Chapter Five, 'English Malebranchians', 156–204.

41 Luce (1938).

42 For Malebranche's influence, see Stuart Brown, 'The Critical Reception of Malebranche', in Nadler, ed., 2000, 262–87.

43 Israel 485–94.

44 McCracken 119–21.

45 Locke, *Examination*, 210–11.

46 Luce (1934).

47 McCracken, Chapter Six, 205–53.

48 Berkeley, *Second Dialogue*, 177.

49 Hume, *Enquiry*, Section 7, Part 1, 72.

50 Bayle, *Dictionary*, article 'Paulicans', 1822–3.

51 Bayle, *Dictionary*, article 'Manicheans' (144–53) and Second Clarification (409–20).

52 Condillac, *Traité des Systèmes*, *Oeuvres*, vol. 2, 98–9.

53 Quoted from Rodis-Lewis 328.

54 Voltaire, *Siècle de Louis XIV*, vol. 2, 252–3.

55 Nadler, ed., 2000.

BIBLIOGRAPHY

Works and editions of pre-twentieth-century philosophers cited in the text and notes

Alexander, H.G., ed., *The Leibniz–Clarke Correspondence* (Manchester, University of Manchester Press, 1956).

André, Yves Marie, *La vie du R.P. Malebranche prêtre de l'oratoire avec l'histoire de ses ouvrages* (*c*.1720). First published 1886 (Paris), reprinted 1970 (Geneva, Slatkine Reprints).

Arnauld, Antoine, *La logique, ou l'art de penser*, co-authored with Pierre Nicole (Paris, Ch. Savreux, 1662), reprinted Paris, Delalain et Fils, 1874.

—— *Des vraies et des fausses Idées, contre ce qu'enseigne l'auteur de la Recherche de la Vérité* (1683) in the *Oeuvres de M. Antoine Arnauld*, vol. 38. Reprinted Fayard, 1986. English translation, *On True and False Ideas*, ed. and tr. Elmar J. Kremer (Lewiston/Queenston/Lampeter, Edwin Mellen Press, 1990).

—— *Défense de M. Arnauld, contre la réponse au livre des vraies et des fausses idées* (1684) in *Oeuvres complètes de M. Antoine Arnauld*, vol. 38.

—— *Reflexions philosophiques et théologiques sur le nouveau système de la nature et de la grâce* (1685–86) in *Oeuvres complètes de M. Antoine Arnauld*, vol. 39.

Augustine, *The Confessions*, tr. Edward Bouverie Pusey (New York, Quality Paperback Book Club, 1991).

—— *Anti-Pelagian Writings*, ed. Philip Schaff (Grand Rapids, MI, Eerdmans, 1971).

Bayle, Pierre, *Historical and Critical Dictionary, Selections*, ed. and tr. Richard Popkin (Indianapolis, Bobbs-Merrill, 1965).

Berkeley, George, *The Works of George Berkeley, Bishop of Cloyne*, 9 vols, eds, A.A. Luce and T.E. Jessop (London, Nelson, 1948–57).

Bonnot de Condillac, Etienne, *Traité des systèmes* (1749), in vol. II of his *Oeuvres complètes*, 16 vols (Geneva, Slatkine Reprints, 1970).

Boursier, Laurent, *De l'action de Dieu sur ses créatures* (Paris, Babuty, 1713).

Bovier de Fontenelle, Bernard le, *Doutes sur le système physique des causes occasionelles* (Rotterdam, 1686). *Oeuvres de Fontenelle*, 4 vols (Paris, 1818), vol. 1, 615–38.

Boyle, Robert, *Works*, ed. Thomas Birch, 6 vols (London, 1772).

Cordemoy, Géraud de, *Oeuvres philosophiques*, eds P. Clair and F. Girbal (Paris, Presses Universitaires de France, 1968).

Fénélon, François de, *Réfutation du système du Père Malebranche sur la nature et la grâce*, in *Oeuvres de Fénélon*, vol. 3 (Versailles, Lebel, 1820).

Forge, Louis de la, *Treatise on the Human Mind* (1644), translated with an introduction and notes by Desmond M. Clarke (Dordrecht, Kluwer, 1997).

Foucher, Simon, *Critique de la Recherche de la Vérité ou l'on examine en même-temps une partie des principes de M. Descartes* (Paris, Martin Courstelier, 1675). Reprinted with a new introduction by Richard A. Watson (New York, Johnson Reprint, 1969).

Gassendi, Pierre, *Selected Works*, ed. C.B. Brush (New York, Johnson Reprint Corporation, 1972).

Hume, David, *A Treatise of Human Nature*, ed. L.A. Selby-Bigge, 2nd edn, P.H. Nidditch (Oxford, Clarendon, 1978).

—— *Enquiry Concerning Human Understanding*, ed. L.A. Selby-Bigge, 3rd edn, P.H. Nidditch (Oxford, Clarendon, 1975).

Lamy, François, *De la connaissance de soi-même*, 4 vols (Paris, 1694–8).

Leibniz, Gottfried Wilhelm, *Philosophical Papers and Letters*, 2nd edn, ed. L.E. Loemker (Dordrecht, Reidel, 1969).

—— *Philosophical Essays*, eds and trs R. Ariew and D. Garber (Indianapolis, Hackett, 1989).

Locke, John, *An Essay Concerning Human Understanding*, 2 vols, ed. with an introduction by John Yolton (London, Everyman, 1972).

—— *An Examination of P. Malebranche's Opinion of Seeing All Things in God* (1693), published in Peter King, ed., *Posthumous Works of Mr John Locke* (London, A. and J. Churchill, 1706).

Martin, André (pseudonym Ambrosius Victor), *Philosophia Christiana*, 5 vols (Paris, P. Prome, 1667).

Moreau de Maupertuis, Pierre Louis, *Oeuvres*, 4 vols (Hildesheim, Olms, 1965).

Régis, Pierre-Sylvain, *Système de philosophie, contenant la logique, la métaphysique, la physique et la morale*, 3 vols (Lyon, Thierry, 1690).

Rohault, Jacques, *Traité de physique*, 2 vols (Paris, Jure, 1671).

de Spinoza, Benedict, *The Ethics Demonstrated in Geometric Order*, in *A Spinoza Reader*, ed. and tr. by Edwin Curley (Princeton University Press, 1994).

de la Ville, Louis, *Sentiments de M. Descartes touchant l'essence et la propriété des corps opposés à ceux de l'Église* (Paris, Michallet, 1680).

Voltaire, *Lettres philosophiques*, English translation *Letters on England*, Leonard Tancock (London, Penguin, 1980).

—— *Siècle de Louis XIV*, 2 vols (Paris, Garnier-Flammarion, 1966).

—— *Philosophical Dictionary*, ed. and tr. Theodore Besterman (London, Penguin, 1971).

Twentieth-century books

Alquié, Ferdinand, *Le cartésianisme de Malebranche* (Paris, Vrin, 1974).

Bardout, Jean-Christophe, *Malebranche et la Métaphysique* (Paris, Presses Universitaires de France, 1999).

Bastide, G., ed., *Malebranche: l'homme et l'oeuvre 1638–1715*, Centre Internationale de Synthèse (Paris, Vrin, 1967).

Brown, Peter, *Augustine of Hippo, A Biography*, a new edition with an epilogue (London, Faber and Faber, 2000).

Brown, Stuart, ed., *Nicolas Malebranche: His Philosophical Critics and Successors* (Assen/ Maastricht, Van Gorcum, 1991).

Brunet, Pierre, *L'introduction des théories de Newton en France au XVIIIe siècle*, vol. 1, avant 1738 (Paris, Libraire Scientifique Albert Blanchard, 1931).

Church, Ralph W., *A Study in the Philosophy of Malebranche* (London, George Allen and Unwin, 1931).

Clarke, Desmond, *Descartes' Philosophy of Science* (Manchester, Manchester University Press, 1982).

—— *Occult Powers and Hypotheses: Cartesian Natural Philosophy under Louis XIV* (Clarendon, Oxford, 1989).

Clatterbaugh, Kenneth, *The Causation Debate in Modern Philosophy, 1637–1739* (London, Routledge, 1999).

Connell, Desmond, *The Vision in God: Malebranche's Scholastic Sources* (Paris and Louvain, Nauwelaerts, 1967).

Copleston, Frederick, *A History of Philosophy, vol. IV, Descartes to Leibniz* (London, Burns Oats and Washburn, 1958).

Costabel, Pierre, *Leibniz and Dynamics*, tr. R.E.W. Maddison (Paris, Hermann, 1973).

Craig, Edward, *The Mind of God and the Works of Man* (Clarendon, Oxford, 1987).

Dijksterhuis, E., ed., *Descartes et le Cartésianisme Hollandais* (Paris, Presses Universitaires de France, 1950).

Dobell, Clifford, ed., *Antony van Leeuwenhoek and his 'Little Animals'* (New York, Dover, 1960).

Dreyfus, Ginette, *La volonté selon Malebranche* (Paris, J. Vrin, 1958).

Farley, J., *The Spontaneous Generation Controversy from Descartes to Oparin* (Baltimore and London, Johns Hopkins University Press, 1974).

Frege, Gottlob, *Philosophical Writings*, 3rd edn, eds P. Geach and M. Black (Oxford, Blackwell, 1980).

Garber, Daniel, *Descartes' Metaphysical Physics* (Chicago, University of Chicago Press, 1992).

Gaukroger, Stephen, ed., *Descartes* (Sussex, Harvester, 1980).

Gaukroger, Stephen, Schuster, John and Sutton, John, eds, *Descartes' Natural Philosophy* (London, Routledge, 2000).

Gilson, Étienne, *The Christian Philosophy of Saint Augustine*, tr. L.E.M. Lynch (London, Gollancz, 1961).

Gouhier, Henri, *La philosophie de Malebranche et son expérience religieuse*, 2nd edn (Paris, Vrin, 1948).

—— *Cartesianisme et Augustinianisme au XVIIe siècle* (Paris, Vrin, 1978).

Gueroult, Martial, *Malebranche, vol. 1, La Vision en Dieu* (Paris, Aubier, 1955).

— *Malebranche, vol. 2, Les cinq abîmes de la providence: l'ordre et l'occasionalisme* (Paris, Aubier, 1959).

—— *Malebranche, vol. 3, Les cinq abîmes de la providence: la nature et la grâce* (Paris, Aubier, 1959).

Gunther, R.T., ed., *Early Science at Oxford* 15 vols (Oxford, Oxford University Press, 1923–67).

Hall, T., ed., *A Source Book in Animal Biology* (Cambridge, MA, Harvard University Press, 1951).

Hazard, Paul, *The European Mind, 1680–1715*, English tr. J. Lewis May (London, Penguin, 1964).

Israel, Jonathan, *Radical Enlightenment: Philosophy and the Making of Modernity 1650–1750* (Oxford, Oxford University Press, 2001).

Jolley, Nicholas, *The Light of the Soul: Theories of Ideas in Leibniz, Malebranche, and Descartes* (Oxford, Clarendon, 1990).

Kirwan, Christopher, *Augustine* (London, Routledge, 1989).

Koyré, Alexandre, *Galileo Studies*, tr. J. Mepham (Sussex, Harvester, 1976).

Kubrin, D.C., *Providence and the Mechanical Philosophy* (Ann Arbor, MI, University Microfilms, 1971).

Loeb, Louis, *From Descartes to Hume* (Ithaca, Cornell University Press, 1981).

Lindeboom, G.A., ed., *The Letters of Jan Swammerdam to Melchisedek Thévenot* (Amsterdam, Swets & Zeitlinger, 1975).

Luce, A.A., *Berkeley and Malebranche. A Study in the Origin of Berkeley's Thought* (London, Oxford University Press, 1934).

McCracken, Charles J., *Malebranche and British Philosophy* (Oxford, Clarendon, 1983).

Moreau, Denis, *Deux Cartésiens: La polémique Arnauld–Malebranche* (Paris, Vrin, 1999).

Mouy, Paul, *Les loix du choc d'après Malebranche* (Paris, Vrin, 1927).

—— *Le développement de la physique Cartésienne: 1646–1712* (Paris, Vrin, 1934).

Nadler, Steven, *Arnauld and the Cartesian Philosophy of Ideas* (Manchester, Manchester University Press, 1989).

—— *Malebranche and Ideas* (Oxford and New York, Oxford University Press, 1992).

—— ed., *Causation in Early Modern Philosophy: Cartesianism, Occasionalism, and Pre-Established Harmony* (University Park, Pennsylvania State University Press, 1993).

—— ed., *The Cambridge Companion to Malebranche* (Cambridge, Cambridge University Press, 2000).

Nagel, Thomas, *Mortal Questions* (Cambridge, Cambridge University Press, 1979).

Osler, Margaret J., *Divine Will and the Mechanical Philosophy* (Cambridge, Cambridge University Press, 1994).

Popkin, Richard H., *The History of Skepticism from Erasmus to Spinoza* (Berkeley, University of California Press, 1979).

Pyle, Andrew, ed., *The Boyle Lectures*, 4 vols (Bristol, Thoemmes, 2000).

Radner, Daisie, *Malebranche: A Study of a Cartesian System* (Assen, Van Gorcum, 1978).

Riley, Patrick, *The General Will before Rousseau: The Transformation of the Divine into the Civic* (Princeton, NJ, Princeton University Press, 1986).

Robinet, André, ed., *Malebranche et Leibniz: rélations personelles* (Paris, Vrin, 1955).

—— *Système et existence dans l'oeuvre de Malebranche* (Paris, Vrin, 1965).

Rodis-Lewis, Genevieve, *Nicolas Malebranche* (Paris, Presses Universitaires de France, 1963).

Rome, Beatrice, *The Philosophy of Malebranche* (Chicago, Henry Regnery, 1963).

Roger, Jacques, *Les sciences de la vie dans la pensée Française du XVIIIe siècle* (Paris, Armand Colin, 1971).

Rosenfield, L.C., *From Beast-Machine to Man-Machine: Animal Soul in French Letters from Descartes to La Mettrie*, 2nd edn (New York, Octagon, 1968).

Schierbeck, A., *Jan Swammerdam, 1637–1689: His Life and Works* (Amsterdam, Swets & Zeitlinger, 1967).

Schmaltz, Tad, *Malebranche's Theory of the Soul: A Cartesian Interpretation* (Oxford, Oxford University Press, 1996).

Scott, W.L., *The Conflict Between Atomism and Conservation Theory, 1644–1860* (London, Macdonald, 1970).

Stump, Eleonore and Kretzmann, Norman, eds, *The Cambridge Companion to Augustine* (Cambridge, Cambridge University Press, 2001).

Vartanian, Aram, *Diderot and Descartes: A Study of Scientific Naturalism in the Enlightenment* (Princeton, NJ, Princeton University Press, 1953).

Watson, Richard, *The Downfall of Cartesianism* (The Hague, Martinus Nijhoff, 1966).

—— *The Breakdown of Cartesian Metaphysics* (Atlantic Highlands, Humanities Press, 1987).

Westfall, Richard S., *Force in Newton's Physics* (London, Macdonald, 1971).

Yolton, John, *Perceptual Acquaintance from Descartes to Reid* (Minneapolis, University of Minnesota Press, 1984).

Twentieth-century articles

Acworth, Richard, 'Malebranche and his heirs', *Journal of the History of Ideas* 38 (1977), 673–6.

—— 'La disparition de la matière chez les malebranchistes anglais J. Norris et A. Collier', in Jean-Luc Marion, ed., *La passion de la raison. Hommage a Ferdinand Alquié* (Paris, Presses Universitaires de France, 1983).

Balz, G.A., 'Gerauld de Cordemoy', *Philosophical Review* 40 (1931), 221–45.

Bell, Martin, 'Hume and causal power: the influences of Malebranche and Newton', *British Journal for the History of Philosophy* 5 (1997), 67–86.

Bergman, Gustav, 'Some remarks on the philosophy of Malebranche', *The Review of Metaphysics* 10 (1956), 207–26.

Black, Andrew G., 'Malebranche's theodicy', *Journal of the History of Philosophy* 35 (1997), 27–44.

Blondel, Charles, 'La psychologie de Malebranche', *Revue internationale de Philosophie*, 1 (1938), 59–76.

Bowler, P.J., 'Preformation and pre-existence in the seventeenth century – a brief analysis', *Journal of the History of Biology* 4 (1971), 221–44.

Bracken, Harry, 'Berkeley and Malebranche on ideas', *Modern Schoolman* 41 (1963), 1–15.

Bréhier, Émile, 'Les jugements naturels chez Malebranche', *Revue philosophique de la France et de l'étranger* 125 (1938), 142–50.

Brykman, Genevieve, 'Berkeley: sa lecture de Malebranche à travers du Dictionnaire de Bayle', *Revue internationale de philosophie* 114 (1975), 496–514.

Chappell, Vere, 'The theory of ideas', in A.O. Rorty, ed., *Essays on Descartes' Meditations* (Berkeley and Los Angeles, University of California Press, 1986), 177–98.

Church, R.W., 'Malebranche and Hume', *Revue Internationale de Philosophie* 1 (1938), 143–61.

Clair, Pierre, 'Louis la Forge et les origines de l'occasionalisme', *Recherches sur le XVIIe siècle* 1 (1976), 63–72.

Clarke, Desmond, 'Malebranche and occasionalism: a reply to Steven Nadler', *Journal of the History of Philosophy* 33 (1995), 499–504.

—— 'Causal powers and occasionalism from Descartes to Malebranche', in Gaukroger, Schuster and Sutton, eds, *Descartes' Natural Philosophy* (London, Routledge, 2000), 131–48.

Connell, Desmond, 'La passivité de l'entendement selon Malebranche', *Revue philosophique de Louvain* 53 (1955), 542–65.

Cook, Monte, 'Arnauld's alleged representationalism', *Journal of the History of Philosophy* 12 (1972), 53–62.

—— 'Descartes' alleged representationalism', *History of Philosophy Quarterly* 4 (1987), 179–95.

—— 'Malebranche versus Arnauld', *Journal of the History of Philosophy* 29 (1991), 183–99.

—— 'The ontological status of Malebranchian ideas', *Journal of the History of Philosophy* 36 (1998), 535–44.

Costa, Michael J., 'What Cartesian ideas are not', *Journal of the History of Philosophy* 21 (1983), 537–49.

Cottingham, John, 'Cartesian trialism', *Mind* 94 (1985), 218–30.

Frankfurt, Harry, 'Freedom of the will and the concept of a person', *Journal of Philosophy* 68 (1971), 5–20.

Gabbey, Alan, 'Force and inertia in seventeenth century dynamics', *Studies in the History and Philosophy of Science* 2 (1971), 1–67.

—— 'Force and inertia in the seventeenth century: Descartes and Newton', in Stephen Gaukroger, ed. (1980), 230–320.

Garber, Daniel, 'Mind, body, and the laws of nature in Descartes and Leibniz', *Midwest Studies in Philosophy* 8 (1983), 105–33.

—— 'How God causes motion: Descartes, divine sustenance, and occasionalism', *Journal of Philosophy* 84 (1987), 567–80.

Getchev, George S., 'Some of Malebranche's reactions to Spinoza revealed in his correspondence with Dortous de Mairan', *Philosophical Review* 41 (1932) 385–94.

Glauser, Richard, 'Arnauld critique de Malebranche: le statut des idées', *Revue de théologie et de philosophie* 120 (1988), 390–410.

Gouhier, Henri, 'La première polémique de Malebranche', *Revue d'histoire de la philosophie et d'histoire générale de la civilisation* 1 (1927), 23–48, 68–191.

—— 'Philosophie chrétienne et théologie: à propos de la seconde polémique de Malebranche', *Revue philosophique de la France et de l'étranger* 125 (1938), 151–93.

Hankins, Thomas, 'The influence of Malebranche on the science of mechanics during the eighteenth century', *Journal of the History of Ideas* 28 (1967), 193–210.

Hatfield, Gary, 'Force (God) in Descartes' physics', *Studies in the History and Philosophy of Science* 10 (1979), 113–40.

Hutchison, Keith R., 'Supernaturalism and the mechanical philosophy', *History of Science* 21 (1983), 297–333.

Johnston, Charlotte, 'Locke's examination of Malebranche and John Norris', *Journal of the History of Ideas* 19 (1958), 553–4.

Jolley, Nicholas, 'Leibniz and Malebranche on innate ideas', *Philosophical Review* 97 (1988), 71–91.
—— 'Intellect and illumination in Malebranche', *Journal of the History of Philosophy* 32 (1994), 209–224.
—— 'Berkeley, Malebranche, and the Vision in God', *Journal of the History of Philosophy* 34 (1996), 535–48.
Smith, Norman (Kemp), 'Malebranche's theory of the perception of distance and magnitude', *British Journal of Psychology* 1 (1905), 191–204.
Laporte, Jean, 'L'étendue intelligible selon Malebranche', *Revue internationale de Philosophie* 1 (1938), 7–58.
Lennon, Thomas M., 'Occasionalism and the Cartesian metaphysic of motion', *Canadian Journal of Philosophy*, supplementary volume no. 1 (1974), 29–40.
—— 'Representationalism, judgment and perception of distance: further to Yolton and McCrae', *Dialogue* 19 (1980), 151–62.
Lewis, Genevieve, 'L'intervention de Nicole dans la polémique entre Arnauld et Malebranche d'après des lettres inédités', *Revue philosophique de la France et de l'étranger* 75 (1950), 483–506.
Lovejoy, A.C., '"Representative ideas" in Malebranche and Arnauld', *Mind* 32 (1923), 449–61.
—— 'Malebranche et le Trinity College de Dublin', *Revue philosophique de la France et de l'étranger* 128 (1938), 275–309.
Matthews, H.E., 'Locke, Malebranche, and the representative theory', *Locke Newsletter* (1971), 12–21, reprinted in Ian Tipton, ed., *Locke on Human Understanding* (Oxford, Oxford University Press, 1977), 55–61.
McGinn, Colin, 'Can we solve the mind–body problem?', *Mind* 98 (1989), 349–66.
McRae, Robert, '"Idea" as a philosophical term in the 17th Century', *Journal of the History of Ideas* 26 (1965), 175–84.
Nadler, Steven, 'Cartesianism and Port Royal', *The Monist* 71 (1988), 229–46.
—— 'Occasionalism and the general will in Malebranche', *Journal of the History of Philosophy* 31 (1993), 31–47.
—— 'Descartes and occasional causation', *British Journal for the History of Philosophy* 2 (1994), 35–54.
—— 'Malebranche's occasionalism: a reply to Clarke', *Journal of the History of Philosophy* 33 (1995), 505–8.
—— 'Occasionalism and the mind–body problem', in M.A. Stewart, ed., *Studies in Seventeenth Century European Philosophy* (Oxford, Clarendon Press, 1997).
—— 'Louis de la Forge and the development of occasionalism', *Journal of the History of Philosophy* 36 (1998), 215–31.
—— 'Knowledge, volitional agency and causation in Malebranche and Guelincx', *British Journal for the History of Philosophy* 7 (1999), 263–74.
—— 'Connaissance et causalité chez Malebranche et Guelincx', *XVIIième siècle* 203 (1999), 335–45.
Pessin, Andrew, 'Malebranche's doctrine of freedom/consent and the incompleteness of God's volitions', *British Journal for the History of Philosophy* 8 (2000), 21–53.
Pessin, Andrew, 'Malebranche's distinction between general and particular volitions', *Journal of the History of Philosophy* 39 (2001), 77–99.
Pyle, Andrew, 'Animal generation and the mechanical philosophy', *History and Philosophy of the Life Sciences* 9 (1987), 225–54.
Radner, Daisie, 'Descartes' notion of the union of mind and body', *Journal of the History of Philosophy* 9 (1971), 159–70.
—— 'Representationalism in Arnauld's act theory of perception', *Journal of the History of Philosophy* 14 (1976), 96–8.
—— 'Is there a problem of Cartesian interaction?' *Journal of the History of Philosophy* 23 (1985), 35–49.
Richardson, R.C., 'The 'scandal' of Cartesian interactionism', *Mind* 91 (1982), 20–37.
Robinet, André, 'Dom Robert Desgabets. Le conflit avec Malebranche et l'oeuvre de la science', *Revue de synthèse* 95 (1974), 65–83.

—— 'La philosophie de P. Bayle devant les philosophies de Malebranche et de Leibniz', in Paul Dibon, ed., *Pierre Bayle, le philosophe de Rotterdam* (Institut Français d'Amsterdam, Maison Descartes, 1959), 48–65.

Schmaltz, Tad, 'Descartes and Malebranche on mind and mind–body union', *Philosophical Review* 101 (1992), 281–325.

—— 'Malebranche on Descartes on mind–body distinctness', *Journal of the History of Philosophy* 32 (1994), 49–79.

—— 'Human freedom and divine creation in Malebranche, Descartes, and the Cartesians', *British Journal for the History of Philosophy* 2 (1994), 3–50.

—— 'Malebranche's Cartesianism and Lockean colors', *History of Philosophy Quarterly* 12 (1995), 387–403.

Schrecker, Paul, 'Malebranche et le préformisme biologique', *Revue internationale de Philosophie* 1 (1938), 77–97.

Scott, David, 'Malebranche's indirect realism: a reply to Steven Nadler', *British Journal for the History of Philosophy* 4 (1996), 53–78.

—— 'Occasionalism and occasional causation in Descartes' philosophy', *Journal of the History of Philosophy* 38 (2000), 503–28.

Sleigh, Robert, 'Leibniz and Malebranche on causality', in Jan Cover and Mark Kulstad, eds, *Central Themes in Early Modern Philosophy* (Indianapolis, Hackett, 1990), 161–93.

Theau, Jean, 'Le critique de la causalité chez Malebranche et chez Hume' *Dialogue* 15 (1976), 549–64.

Wahl, Russell, 'The Arnauld–Malebranche controversy and Descartes' ideas', *Monist* 71 (1988), 560–72.

Walton, Craig, 'Malebranche's ontology', *Journal of the History of Philosophy* 7 (1969), 143–61.

Watson, Richard, 'The breakdown of Cartesian metaphysics', *Journal of the History of Philosophy* 1 (1964), 177–97.

Yolton, John, 'Ideas and knowledge in seventeenth century philosophy', *Journal of the History of Philosophy* 13 (1975), 145–66.

—— 'Representation and realism: some reflections on the way of ideas', *Mind* 96 (1987), 318–30.

INDEXES

Index of names

Index of subjects